The Underground
Economy in the
United States
and Abroad

The Underground Economy in the United States and Abroad

Edited by
Vito Tanzi
International Monetary Fund

LexingtonBooks
D.C. Heath and Company
Lexington, Massachusetts
Toronto

Library of Congress Cataloging in Publication Data

Main entry under title:
The Underground economy in the United States and abroad.

1. Informal sector (Economics) 2. Informal sector (Economics)—United
States. I. Tanzi, Vito.

HD2341.U48	336.24′16	80-8887
ISBN 0-669-04400-8		AACR2

Second printing, July 1983

Published simultaneously in Canada

Printed in the United States of America

International Standard Book Number: 0-669-04400-8

Library of Congress Catalog Card Number: 80-8887

To
Vito L.
Alexandre B.
Giancarlo O.

Contents

Chapter 10   **What Do We Know about the Black Economy in the United Kingdom?** *Andrew Dilnot* and *C.N. Morris*   163

Chapter 11   **Recent Empirical Surveys and Theoretical Interpretations of the Parallel Economy in Italy** *Daniela Del Boca* and *Francesco Forte*   181

Chapter 12   **The Second Economy of Italy** *Bruno Contini*   199

Chapter 13   **The Hidden Economy in Norway** *Arne Jon Isachsen, Jan Tore Klovland*, and *Steinar Strøm*   209

Chapter 14   **The Underground Economy in a High Tax Country: The Case of Sweden** *Ingemar Hansson*   233

Chapter 15   **The Second Economy of the USSR** *Gregory Grossman*   245

Part IV   *The Underground Economy in Selected Other Countries*   271

Chapter 16   **Canada's Irregular Economy** *Rolf Mirus* and *Roger S. Smith*   273

Chapter 17   **Illegal Trade Transactions and the Underground Economy of Colombia** *Roberto Junguito* and *Carlos Caballero*   285

Chapter 18   **The Underground Economy in Australia** *Mark Tucker*   315

Chapter 19   **Estimate of Tax Evasion in Israel**   323

                 Index   333

                 List of Contributors   339

                 About the Editor   341

Preface

"You've no right to grow here," said the Dormouse.
"Don't talk nonsense," said Alice more boldly: "You know you're growing too."
"Yes, but I grow at a reasonable pace," said the Dormouse: "Not in that ridiculous fashion."

—Alice in Wonderland

The phenomenon that goes under the name of underground economy, or under a host of alternative names, has in recent years been attracting increasing attention on the part of journalists, policymakers, economists, and other social scientists. As is often the case with new phenomena, there is still relatively little agreement about exactly what is meant by underground economy and, more importantly, about its size. For some experts, underground economy represents almost exclusively the income that is not reported to the tax authorities, regardless of whether such an income is, or is not, measured by the national accounts. For others, it is the relationship between the measured size of the economy (as estimated by the national accounts) and the actual size that is important, as the difference between total economic activity of a country and the measured part may influence economic policy in a variety of ways. This definitional question is discussed in several of the chapters in this book. Most of these chapters also attempt to measure the importance of this phenomenon in various countries. However, there is still considerable disagreement among experts about just how extensive this phenomenon is. It is my hope that this volume will stimulate more scholarly research on this phenomenon so that, perhaps, in the future the difference in estimations can be narrowed and more attention can then be paid to the implications of an underground economy of a certain size. These chapters show also that the basic causes for the existence of this phenomenon vary from country to country. One should expect that the reasons for this kind of activity in a country such as the USSR are likely to be quite different from those in the United States. The differences exist also between, for example, the United Kingdom and Italy.

This book is organized into four parts. Part I includes two general surveys of the field. The first describes the various methods scholars use in trying to assess the size of the underground economy and the second approaches the phenomenon from the point of view of its implications for employment. Part II includes six chapters, all dealing with the United States. The first is an overall survey of the literature on the underground economy in the United States; the next two deal with two attempts at measuring the underground economy in the United States; and the following three chapters deal with other issues, such as the extent to which the American national accounts are accurate measurements of economic activity or the significance of the increasing use of American currency by foreigners. Peter Gutmann's and Edgar Feige's work should, perhaps, have been included in this section, but the contributions of these scholars are discussed in such detail in other chapters that I felt it would have been redundant to include their work. Part III presents studies on the United Kingdom, Italy, Norway, Sweden, and the USSR. These chapters are very different in many ways, not only because the countries analyzed are different, but because of the particular interests of the writers. I would have liked to have included additional studies on European countries but, unfortunately, at the time this book was being planned I could not find any additional papers that I felt could have been included. One of the merits of several of the chapters in Part III is that they use survey techniques for estimating the size of the underground economy. This approach has still not been tried in the United States. Finally, Part IV presents studies on the underground economy dealing with Canada, Colombia, Australia, and Israel. The chapter on Colombia emphasizes the drug traffic as a source of underground income.

This book indicates that economists have risen to the challenge of trying to measure something that up to now was considered relatively unmeasurable. How successful they have been remains, of course, up to the reader to judge. One conclusion that seems to follow from most of these chapters is that the underground economy, while very important, is perhaps less important than one would have believed from some of the journalistic accounts of this activity. Also, it is not quite clear that this activity has been increasing at a fast pace in recent years, although some evidence of growth is presented.

Finally, I would like to thank the many people who have assisted me in various ways, from contacting potential authors to calling my attention to particular papers. It would be too lengthy to mention all of them. However, I feel that I would be doing an injustice if I did not single out Mrs. Anne Salda of the Joint Library of the International Monetary Fund, who brought many important papers to my attention. I would also like to thank Mrs. Chris Wu for statistical assistance, and Mrs. Sonia Piccinini and Ms. Luzmaria Valencia for assistance with the typing of the manuscript.

Part I
General Aspects

1

Measuring the Hidden Economy: Though This Be Madness, There Is Method in It

Bruno S. Frey and
Werner W. Pommerehne

Introduction

Few would deny that there is a hidden economy, and many can bring forward amusing examples of how the underground economy works. However, an equally overwhelming majority of people would state that the hidden economy is impossible to measure just because it *is* hidden. If one makes the effort of searching in the gray literature of yet unpublished papers one quickly finds out that this is not the case—there already exist a great many estimates of the size of the hidden economy (though not all researchers seem to be fully aware of this).

The underground economy is a very complex phenomenon comprising a lot of different but interrelated aspects. It is indeed not possible to measure its size directly, but the *traces* it leaves in other spheres of the economy can be analyzed and to some extent measured. Since the hidden economy leaves many different traces, many approaches have been suggested by researchers to capture the size of this sector. Thus, the estimates existing are based on a multitude of methods.

Aspects of Determining the Hidden Economy's Size

From Speculations to Estimates

The size of the hidden economy is quantified in three different ways:

1. Figures advanced on the basis of pure *speculation*, the rationale being that the public, politicians, and academics should be made aware that the phenomenon exists and that it can no longer be disregarded. Examples are the figures provided by DeGrazia (1980) for West Germany based on calculations of the Zentralverband des Deutschen Hand-

We are grateful for helpful comments by Friedrich Schneider, Gebhar Kirchgaessner, and Hannelore Weck.

werks according to which Germany's hidden economy comprises 2 percent of gross national product (GNP), or Intersocial (1980) that in the case of Japan it is 1 percent of GNP, or the Wirtschaftswoche (1980) that Italy's hidden economy amounts to 30 to 40 percent of GNP.

2. *Educated guesses,* based on some more or less coherent reasoning. The best known and widely quoted example is Sir William Pile's (then chairman of the United Kindgom Inland Revenue Service Board) figure that the British submerged economy plausibly amounts to 7.5 percent of GNP.[1] For the Soviet Union and other communist countries, educated guesses are often the only means of quantifying the size of the private— and in countries based on socialized production, usually the unofficial—economy. Kaiser (1976, p. 370) advances the figure of 20 percent of the official economy for unofficial legal and illegal activities in the USSR in 1970, while Katz (1973, p. 90) reports 10 to 15 percent for the 1960s. Grossmann (1977, p. 35) suggests that in the same country the size of the legal private economy has been falling from 22 percent (1950) to 10 percent (1968) and less than 10 percent of GNP in 1977, and Schroeder and Greenslade (1979, p. 4) report a figure of 8 percent of GNP for 1970.

3. Estimates based on *well-defined methods.* The present study will be restricted to this type of measurement.

With all three types of quantifying the hidden economy, *what* is being measured often remains unclear. Some authors take turnover (for example, in the case of illegal underworld activities, such as dealing in drugs, the total expenditures for such goods are counted) while other authors consider limited aspects of the hidden economy only (for example, tax evasion). There is a growing consensus, however, that the definition of the hidden economy involves two aspects:[2]

1. The hidden economy is the one that "escapes the purview of our current societal measurement apparatus" (Feige 1980b, p. 3);
2. The activities taking place in the underground economy should be measured in terms of GNP.

Such a definition allows a comparison of the size of the hidden economy with (officially measured) gross national product. What is to be included within national income, is, of course, a matter of accounting convention. We follow the standard national income accounting framework here, and thus exclude activities such as work in one's own private household (like cooking and child rearing) or the work performed in the voluntary or "third" sector. It suffices to point out here that this informal sector is being studied (see, for example, Weisbrod 1977, Gershuny 1978, 1979, and Badelt 1980) and that there are successful attempts to quantify "total incomes" including such things as household services and do-it-yourself.[3] What is neither included in the official national income accounts but what we *do* consider here are those income-producing activities which are either illegal or incorrectly reported, including in some cases in-kind and barter activities.

From Residuals to Identifying Determinants

The most straightforward approach to measuring the hidden economy is to attribute it to the *residual* which is left over after all other (known) influences are accounted for.[4] This procedure is, for example, followed if one attributes the difference between the income and the expenditure sides of GNP, or the change in currency compared to demand deposits to the underground economy.

It is more sophisticated to identify the factors which *cause* the rise and existence of the hidden economy. Almost without exception, authors stress *taxation* as the crucial factor which induces people to become economically active in the underground. Some studies (Tanzi 1980b, Klovland 1980) therefore explicitly estimate the influence of taxation on the rise of the hidden economy.

Taxation is not the only factor that causes the rise of an underground sector. Some studies (Feige 1980b, Frey and Weck 1981b) make an effort to identify further causes, such as regulation and tax morality.

The Many Methods of Estimation

In view of the extraordinary problem of estimating such a complex phenomenon as the unobserved economy where the participants make a strong effort to conceal their income-producing activity, one would not be surprised if a science confronted with this problem would just give up. It is a tribute to economics as a science that this has not been the case, but that ingenious methods have nevertheless been developed to measure the hidden economy.

The many methods can be classified in different ways, such as distinguishing between micro and macro, or accounting and econometric approaches. In order to prepare for an approach more deeply rooted in economic theory, we will classify according to the behavior of the various decision makers who generate the traces on the basis of which the hidden economy's size is estimated. Four general approaches are distinguished:

1. Traces in the form of *discrepancies between income and expenditures,* both at the macro and micro level;
2. Traces revealed by *tax auditing* and other *compliance methods;*
3. Traces appearing in the *labor market;*
4. Traces visible in *monetary aggregates.*

It is not surprising that these traces generated by the various kinds of behavior do not necessarily take into account the *same* aspect of submerged activities.

Traces in the Form of Discrepancies
between Income and Expenditure

While some income earned by an individual may go unreported or under-reported as such, much of it will later show up as expenditure. If this is true, then the discrepancy between income and expenditure gives a clue to the size of the hidden economy. Moreover, looking at year-to-year changes in the relative size of these discrepancies, it may be argued that this is an indication of the trend of the hidden economy. The first approach considered deals with such a comparison between income and expenditure at the macro (national income) level. The second approach deals with the micro level and looks at the income-expenditure discrepancy of particular individuals or groups.

Comparisons of Various Ways of Estimating Income. National income is assessed by statistical offices in two ways, the measurement of aggregate expenditure and of income. The first method of tracking the size of the hidden economy is to compare national accounts estimates of income with income estimates built up from tax returns. The difference should represent an estimate of the income not reported to the tax authority.

Such comparisons have been undertaken for various countries.[5] The most comprehensive study has been undertaken for the United States (Park 1979). It attempts to measure the "unexplained difference" or "residual error" between the estimate of personal income by the Bureau of Economic Analysis (BEA) and that of adjusted gross income on the basis of a sample of tax returns by the Internal Revenue Service (IRS). Due to the differences in the statistical coverage of national accounts data and tax data (for example, for some types of households and some minimal income no reporting to tax authorities is needed) as well as in the underlying income concepts, appropriate adjustments are required to make the estimates compatible. For 1977 the compatible estimate of adjusted gross income by BEA exceeds the IRS estimate by more than 82 billion (current) dollars or 4 percent in terms of measured GNP. For earlier years, however, Park finds a significantly higher fraction of GNP, namely 5.5 percent for 1968 and 9.4 percent for 1948. If this discrepancy is taken to be a reflection of the size of the hidden economy, it seems to have *fallen* since World War II.

O'Higgins (1980) finds for the United Kingdom and the 1970s an opposite development of the discrepancy between the aggregate amount of income in the national accounts and the aggregate income estimates based on (adjusted) tax returns. While officially measured national income increased threefold between 1970 and 1978, the unexplained difference increased ninefold. However, in absolute size the submerged economy is estimated to amount to only 2.5 to 3.0 percent of GNP in 1978 (Macafee 1980). Sweden's Statistika Centralbyrån estimates for the same year a residual error of 4.7 percent of officially measured GNP (Hansson 1980, p. 597 ff.), and the Danish Council of Economic Experts (Økonomiske Råd 1977, p. 118) estimates it to be 6 percent in 1974/1975. There are also estimates for other continental countries. Albers (1974) arrives at a discrepancy of 8.9 percent of GNP for the Federal Republic of Germany for 1968, while Frank (1972, 1976) arrives at somewhat less than 20 percent of GNP for Belgium in the years 1965, 1966, and 1970. Roze (1971) calculates an even larger size for France: The estimate of missing factor incomes is computed at roughly 23 percent of GNP for 1965.[6]

It may be noted that the estimates for the Central European countries are much larger and have a greater variance than those of Anglo-Saxon countries. They reflect at the same time the considerable differences according to which the tax authorities lay hands on individual incomes. The Anglo-Saxon countries and Germany aim at the most comprehensive grip of incomes as possible, while Latin countries rely more on the taxation of goods and services.

Survey and Sampling Methods. An "unexplained difference" also appears when expenditures and incomes of private households are considered. If the sample is representative, the survey results can be extrapolated to give an estimate of the hidden sector of the economy as a whole.

We are not aware of any study in which a comprehensive consumer survey has been used to extrapolate although research is underway in this direction in the United States. There have, however, been attempts to calculate expenditure-income discrepancies for specific types of households, occupational groups, and income classes and to compare them with the suitably disaggregated unexplained residuals on the macro level.[7] Undertaking such a comparison, O'Higgins (1980) concludes for the United Kindgom and 1978 that private households headed by self-employed persons have not reported £2.10 billion in their answers to the consumer survey. This corresponds to some 2 percent of national income. For the same group of households the British Central Statistical Office (CSO) by disaggregating its macro estimates comes to an unexplained residual of £2.15 billion, thus coming close to the extrapolation of the expenditure-income discrepancy based on micro survey results. The two methods of estimation differ, however, in another respect: according to CSO the share of unreported income of the self-employed tripled in the 1970s, but the consumer survey study does not report any such trend.

A more direct approach to estimating the hidden economy is to compare income and expenditures of private households relating to the underground economy. A survey of more than a thousand Jewish émigré families into Israel coming from cities of the European part of the Soviet Union indicates that between 10 and 12 percent of their total income came from private sources and some 18 percent of all consumption expenditures were made to private recipients. Taking into account various adjustments, the whole unofficial economy amounts to between 6 and 7 percent of GNP in 1973 (Ofer and Vinokur 1980, p. 51).

Shortcoming of the Discrepancy Approach. The two methods of estimation here discussed have various shortcomings. There are three major weaknesses of the comparison between incomes at the national accounting level (see for instance, Macafee 1980): (a) There are errors in *both* estimates of aggregate income; (b) there are errors due to differences in the statistical coverage; (c) the national income estimates are not always completely independent of the tax data based income estimates, that is, income not captured by tax authorities may also not appear in the national income data. This is, for example, the case in the United Kingdom which relies more strongly on tax statistics for estimating the national income compared to the United States and Germany which rely more on estimates on the output side. The small estimated size reported for the United Kingdom thus becomes well explicable.

According to many authors the discrepancies among the various income estimates must be regarded as the *lower* boundary for unreported income.[8] Only that part of income is counted which is in principle detectable by the tax authorities. It must be presumed that there are many sorts of income-creating activities which escape this measurement, such as income from bartering, an activity which seems to be important in some European countries, especially in the Latin countries, but also in Sweden recently (Rydenfelt 1980).[9]

The main problem with the micro studies lies in the insufficient quality of the income data, especially with respect to the self-employed.

Evaluation. Table 1-1 shows the estimates in terms of national income for the size of the underground economy based on the traces left in the form of "unexplained residuals" for a number of countries.

Table 1-1
Unexplained Differences in National Income Measures, Various Countries and Years
(percentage of GNP)

Country	Year	Estimate of Size (percent)	Author
United States	1948	9.4	Park (1979)
	1958	6.8	
	1968	5.5	
	1977	4.0	
United Kingdom	1970	1.0	O'Higgins (1980)
	1972	1.1	
	1975	1.8-2.4	
	1978	2.5-2.9	
Denmark	1964/65	12.4	Økonomiske Råd (1967, 1977)
	1970/71	10.0	
	1974/75	6.0	
Sweden	1978	4.6	Hansson (1980)
Federal Republic of Germany	1968	8.9	Albers (1974)
Belgium	1965	18.6	Frank (1972, 1976)
	1966	19.6	
	1970	18.9	
France	1965	23.2	Roze (1971)

As may be seen from table 1-1 there are sizable differences between the countries (for the late 1960s): in Anglo-Saxon and Scandinavian countries the discrepancy is relatively small (up to 10 percent of GNP). In Latin countries there are much larger discrepancies (around 20 percent of GNP and more). A very small "unexplained residual" such as that for the United Kingdom is dubious, however; it is partly due to the fact that national income is calculated to a large extent using tax statistics based data. Accordingly, O'Higgins (1980, p. 36) concludes that 5 percent of GNP is a lower boundary for the hidden sector of the United Kingdom in 1978.

For the United States the figures reported in table 1-1 suggest that the underground economy is of declining size in the postwar period. The same seems to be true for Denmark for the period 1965 to 1975. There is no trend visible for Belgium in the short period 1965 to 1970, while for the United Kingdom a slight increase for the 1970s is reported. All these estimates are based on the state of knowledge at a particular time. Over time this knowledge changes, resulting in the same phenomenon—the hidden economy—being accounted for with different intensity and scope.[10] Thus, the implied declining trend of the hidden economy is put into doubt. Moreover, many surveys indicate that more and more people consider tax fraud to be only a minor offense,[11] which must be expected to be accompanied by increased tax cheating and a growing underground economy.

Traces Revealed by Tax Auditing
and Other Compliance Methods

Approach and Some Results. This method considers information on the hidden economy based on active efforts of the tax authorities to detect concealed income, contrary to the voluntary responses in sample surveys. The main advantage of this approach is that detailed information is gained as to how far particular occupations and income groups underreport or do not report income. The extent to which tax auditing is used differs considerably among countries (OECD 1978a). In some countries, France in particular, various programs have been devised (such as randomly selected taxpayers in various departments, a national sample of taxpayer households) in order to gain detailed information on the size and distribution of income underreporting.[12] Moreover, discriminant analysis is used to develop an algorithm which helps to select those taxpayers who are expected to be the most worthwhile to audit.

As far as we know, only for Sweden and the United States are there attempts to extrapolate the tax audit results to the whole taxable population. The Swedish Riksskatteverk has estimated for 1978 that between 8 and 15 percent of declared income has been concealed (Hansson 1980, p. 598), using not only tax compliance data for detection but also additional information collected in various data banks.

A general problem with the normal tax compliance programs is that people not reporting at all very often are left out of account. For the United States the General Accounting Office (GAO 1979) has undertaken the interesting attempt to estimate the number of nonfilers of Federal income tax. Using a representative sample of 50,000 households it estimates that among the 65 million households required to file in 1972, between 4.1 and 5.3 million (6 to 7.8 percent) actually did not file. In comparison IRS found only 0.6 million nonfilers for the same year. Based on the GAO estimate IRS (1979a) has calculated unreported income for 1976, including both legal- and parts of illegal-source income. It was found that unreported income amounts to between 5.9 and 7.9 percent of official (legal) GNP. Even taking unreported legal-source income alone (4.4 to 5.9 percent of GNP) the estimated size is larger than the figure reached using the discrepancy approach (3.8 percent of GNP).

Evaluation. Tax auditing, however, does not allow estimation of the full size of unreported income for particular sectors, branches, and groups in which a high degree of tax fraud takes place. The extrapolations based on the results of compliance programs seem to be more reliable than those based on voluntary responses in the context of direct interviews and surveys due to the threat of legal sanctions for misreporting.[13] It is therefore plausible that the estimates of the hidden economy in Sweden and the United States using tax auditing results are higher than the corresponding estimates based on the "unexplained discrepancies."

Nor does tax auditing allow estimation of the full size of unreported income—but only that amount that could be detected if the same intensive audit techniques were applied to the tax population as a whole.[14] It is thus doubtful whether this approach is able to give much information about the level and trend of the hidden economy. The estimates are easily affected by changes in detection methods, tax structure, and tax legislation.

Traces Appearing in the Labor Market

The underground economy may reveal itself in the form of a low official labor force participation rate compared to periods and countries in which the hidden economy is of less importance. The difference between the official and "actual" participation rates allows an estimate of the size of the irregular labor force, and therefore of the hidden sector. The irregular labor force can also be captured by subtle interviews asking about one's participation as a buyer or seller in the market for irregular labor services.

Comparison of Participation Rates. This approach has mainly been used for Italy. According to OECD statistics the official participation rate in 1975 was only 35.5 percent, whereas in France it was 42.3 percent, in Germany 42.7 percent, in the United States 44.4 percent, in the United Kingdom 46.4 percent, and in Japan 48.0 percent (Fuà 1976, p. 29 ff, 1977). Moreover, the official participation rate in Italy has been falling since the late 1950s: in 1959 it was 44 percent, in 1971 36.2 percent, and in 1977 only 33.7 percent (Contini 1981b, p. 6).

It is possible to take the participation rate of other countries or of the beginning of the period considered as an estimate of the actual participation rate. This allows one to derive an estimate of the *relative* size of the irregular work force compared to other countries and periods. In order to get a figure for the (relative) size of the underground economy in terms of GNP an assumption is needed about the labor productivities in the official and unofficial sectors.

More relevant are attempts to capture the size of the underground economy in absolute terms by evaluating the actual participation rate with the help of well-designed interview methods, in particular follow-up questioning and time-use surveys.[15] The institute DOXA-ISFOL, for example, has estimated that the actual participation rate in Italy in 1975 amounted to 39.5 percent (see CENSIS 1976) which is 4 percentage points above the official rate of 35.5 percent.[16] Somewhat more than 10 percent of the total working population is thus attributed to the underground economy. For 1977 the Italian Istituto Centrale di Statistica (ISTAT) comes to 13 percent, and Contini (1981a, 1981b) to somewhat more than 17 percent, and if (part of) double job holders are included, 20 percent, and yet another institute (CERES, see Frey 1978) even to 25 percent of the total working population, including all multiple-job holders. If the more conservative of these estimates is taken, the size of the hidden economy is derived to be between 14 percent and 20 percent of officially measured GNP (Contini 1981c, p. 15). Using the higher CERES estimate for the actual participation rate, the underground economy amounts to between 25 percent and 33 percent (Martino 1980, p. 18).

Buyers and Sellers in the Market for Irregular Labor Services. A representative sample of the population is interviewed, asking whether they have actively participated in the hidden economy in their capacity as buyers or sellers of unregistered services.

A careful study, using a combined interview and postal-survey technique for a representative sample of about 900 persons was undertaken for Norway in 1980 (Isachsen, Klovland, and Strøm 1981). Not surprisingly, people were more willing to admit having bought irregular labor services (29 percent of persons interviewed) than having worked in that sector themselves (20 percent). Of the people interviewed, 9 percent were active in both capacities, so the overall participation can be calculated at 40 percent (29 percent + 20 percent − 9 percent) of the whole population. As it was also asked how many hours were worked in the past year, and what the hourly wage rate was, it was possible to compute the size of the hidden economy to be 0.9 percent of GNP (supply side). Using the expenditure on irregular labor services, the size rises to 1.5 percent of GNP (demand side). Taking the (higher) wage rates obtaining in the official economy the supply-side estimate rises to 2.3 percent of GNP.

Evaluation. Concentrating on the traces left by the hidden economy in the labor market has the advantage that both monetary and bartering income-creating activities are captured.[17] As buying irregular labor services is less risky and the possible punishment is lower as compared to offering to work in the underground economy, one can expect a relatively less biased answer from those buying as compared to those selling labor in the hidden economy (see also Miller 1979). A major problem with the buying side lies in deducting the value-added figures from the turnover (expenditures) reported.

The comparison of participation rates is obviously quite a crude method. The estimate of the size of the hidden economy in terms of GNP is crucially dependent on the assumptions made concerning the labor productivities in the regular and irregular sectors. Both methods consider work-source income only, disregarding irregular income from capital.

Traces in the Monetary Sphere

People working in the hidden economy have an incentive to change their behavior when dealing with money in order to conceal their activity. The existence of the hidden economy thus leaves traces in the monetary sphere. Two approaches assume that currency transactions are less visible than transactions involving banks (for example, checks or credit cards) and thus look at the changes taking place with respect to currency. A third monetary method is quite different, assuming that there is a fixed relationship between total money and total income-creating activity.

Denomination of Currency. When the size of the underground economy increases and thus also the need for currency, the number of high denomination notes in circulation must be expected to rise in order to facilitate payment.

In the United States, between the end of 1966 and mid-1978, the value of $100 bills in circulation rose by more than 250 percent while the total value of currency rose only by 125 percent (Ross 1978, p. 93). In the United Kingdom the ratio value of £10 and £20 bills to all other notes in circulation rose from 7 percent in 1967 to 47.6 percent in 1979 (Macafee 1980, p. 87; see also Freud 1979), an increase in £10 and £20 bills of 2,100 percent compared to 310 percent in other currency value.[18]

There is no need to go further into this particular measurement approach with its rather obvious shortcomings; indeed none of the authors mentioned derive therefrom an estimate of the numerical level or change of the hidden economy.

Currency/Demand Deposit Ratio. This method of measurement assumes that the size of the underground economy is reflected in an increase in the ratio of currency relative to demand deposits held with banking institutions. This approach was first used by Cagan (1956) but was made popular by Gutmann (1977). The relative increase in currency observed is transformed into a GNP estimate of the hidden economy by assuming that the velocity of currency circulation is the same in the hidden and in the official economy.

Gutmann takes 1937-1941 as the base period in which the currency-demand deposit ratio was "normal" and in which there existed no underground economy, an assumption that contradicts Cagan's findings and also commonsense knowledge that in war times (with controlled prices, other restrictions and high taxes) there always exists a sizable black market. Gutmann (1977, 1979a) reaches the widely publicized result that the hidden economy comprised at least 10 percent of officially measured GNP in the United States in the years 1976 and 1979. A "more realistic" figure would be 13 percent to 14 percent of GNP (Gutmann 1979b).

The method was exactly replicated for Australia (Commercial Bank of Australia 1980), except that it was simply assumed that in the base period the normal ratio of currency to current deposits in checking accounts was 30 percent (in Gutmann's estimate for the United States it was 21.7 percent in 1937-1941). The ratio fluctuated around this level from the late 1950s to the late 1960s, and increased only at the beginning of the 1970s (it actually decreased from 1962 to 1966). It is therefore estimated that in 1978/79 the underground economy in Australia amounted to 10 percent of GNP.

Feige (1980b) uses the method for the United States but makes four changes compared to Gutmann: the base year is shifted to 1964, the hidden economy is taken to comprise 5 percent of GNP in that year, only two-thirds of observed monetary activities use currency as the medium of exchange whereas the remaining third is paid through demand deposits, and that income generated per dollar in the hidden economy is 10 percent higher than income generated in the observed sector. Feige reaches an estimate for the underground economy of 28 percent for 1979.

The currency-demand deposit ratio is very sensitive to the choice of the base period and the assumption made with regard to the currency velocity in the shadow and the official sectors. Most authors (such as Gutmann, Tanzi 1980b, Commercial Bank of Australia 1980) take the velocity to be the same—probably on the basis of the principle of insufficient reason. Klovland (1980, table 9) makes an effort to test the sensitivity of this method to varying assumptions: For Norway and the year 1978, the estimated share of the hidden economy rises from 6.4 percent to 16 percent of GNP when the velocity of currency V is increased from 4.7 to 11.7; the corresponding estimate for Sweden is 6.9 percent (for $V = 4.7$) and 17.2 percent of GNP (for $V = 11.7$).

Calculations for the United Kingdom reveal that the choice of the base year crucially determines the size of the hidden economy. The currency ratio declined in the late 1960s and 1970s and was by 1974 only about two-thirds as great as it was in 1963, suggesting a falling hidden economy. If 1963 instead of 1974 is taken as a base year this would mean a *negative* hidden economy for 1974 (O'Higgins 1980, table 3).

Transactions Approach. The third method of deriving estimates of the size of the hidden economy from traces left in the monetary sphere starts from the proposition that all GNP—whether official or underground—must be transacted by money and that the relationship is constant. As the size of the total stock of money M (both currency and demand deposits) is easily observable it is possible to deduce the size of *total* GNP. Deducting from total

GNP the official estimate of GNP gives the size of the underground economy as a residual in terms of GNP. The method is based on the quantity equation $MV = PT$ (where V = velocity of money, P = price level, and T = volume of transactions). An assumption is needed concerning the relation of the value of transaction PT and nominal GNP, as well as about the velocity of money V.

This approach is due to Feige (1979) who takes 1939 as the base year for the United States in which there was no underground economy and in which the ratio of PT to nominal GNP was "normal" (it equals 10.3). He therefore derives an estimate for the hidden economy of 22 percent of official GNP for 1976, and of 33 percent for 1979. Over these two years the resulting increase of the underground economy amounts to 91 percent compared to a nominal growth rate of the official economy of only 23 percent.

The author himself notes (Feige 1980a, 1980b) that the results are not reasonable on various grounds. The transactions method as applied gives a *negative* hidden economy for the whole period from 1939 to 1968, and the unobserved sector seems to decline during World War II. He therefore modifies the transactions approach in various ways, in particular providing new estimates for the velocity of money based on an analysis of the life of paper currency. The modified estimate shows a dramatic growth in the hidden economy during World War II, followed by an absolute decline until 1968. Thereafter it shows a very rapidly increasing trend (Feige 1980b, figure 4). By 1979, its size is estimated to amount to 27 percent of official GNP.

Overcoming the Residual Approach. All three methods discussed that seek to estimate the size of the hidden economy from traces in the monetary sphere have one basic shortcoming: *all* changes in the ratio held to be crucial are attributed to changes in the underground economy.[19] Such a residual approach is reasonable only if there are no other factors influencing the ratio. It is well known from economic theory, however, that the monetary ratios used to estimate the hidden economy are subject to a great many factors. These are:

1. the relative price effects brought about by changes in the cost of holding currency and money, that is, changes in interest rates, in the rate of inflation, and in the risk involved in holding currency. When, for example, crime rates are high people will carry less cash, and in smaller deonominations;
2. income effects;
3. change in institutional arrangements, in particular the increased use of checks and credit cards;
4. change in tastes concerning the use of currency and money.

The need to control for these influences has been recognized by some authors. They make an effort to evaluate the influence of these factors on the ratio in order to ascertain that the residual changes in the ratio are really due to the working of the hidden economy.

In two important papers, Tanzi (1980b) and Klovland (1980) have modified the currency demand method by estimating a demand function for currency.[20] The two authors use similar variables to explain currency demand such as real income, the interest rate on bank deposits and—most important in our context—the tax rate. Tanzi (1980b, table 2) estimates the equation over the period 1929 to 1976 for the United States and finds that the tax variable has a highly significant positive effect on currency holdings (relative to $M2$). Using the actual figures for the explanatory variables, currency demand is predicted with the help of the equation estimated. The predictions underestimate actual currency holdings, indicating that the difference may be due to the illegal money fueling the hidden economy. Assuming that the volocity of money in the underground economy is the same as that of $M1$ in the legal economy, Tanzi reaches estimates of the U.S. hidden economy for 1976 of between 3.4 and 5.1 percent of GNP if the *increase* of taxes over the period is considered, and of between 8.1 and 11.7 percent of GNP if the *level* of taxes existing in 1976 is compared to no taxes at all.

Klovland's approach is very similar to Tanzi's, but he estimates a currency/demand deposit ratio equation. The results are, however, most puzzling because in the period 1952 to 1978 for Norway, taxes have a highly significant *positive* effect on this ratio, and only for Sweden is the effect significantly negative as theoretically expected. Only when currency demand is estimated directly (and not its ratio to demand deposits), is there a significantly positive effect of taxes on currency holdings for both Norway and Sweden. As in Tanzi's case, the estimated equation consistently underpredicts currency demand, and the difference between actual and predicted currency holdings are attributed to the hidden economy. Assuming equal velocity of currency in the official and underground economy, the hidden economy amounts in 1978 to 9.2 percent of GDP in Norway and to 13.2 percent of GDP in Sweden. This estimate is extremely sensitive to the velocity of currency assumed in the hidden economy.

Evaluation. The estimates of the underground economy based on the traces left in the monetary sphere are of a wide range, not only between countries but also for the *same* country and using the *same* variant of monetary approach, and being undertaken by the *same* author.

As can be seen from table 1-2, the estimates for the United States range from 3.5 percent (increase) or 8 percent (level) to around 30 percent, for Sweden between 7 and 17 percent, and for Norway between 6.5 and 16 percent. On the basis of these estimates it is not possible to say much about the

Table 1-2
Estimates of the Size of the Hidden Economy Using the Monetary
Approach, Various Countries and Years
(percentage of GNP)

Country	Year	Estimate of Size (percent)	Method Used	Author
United States	1976	13-14	currency/demand deposit ratio	Gutmann (1977, 1979b)
	1976	22	transaction	Feige (1979)
	1976	3.4-5.1 (increase) 8.1-11.7 (level)	modified currency/demand deposit ratio	Tanzi (1980b)
	1979	28	modified currency/demand deposit ratio	Feige (1980b)
	1979	33	transaction	Feige (1979)
	1979	27	modified transaction	Feige (1980b)
Sweden[a]	1978	6.9-17.2	modified currency-demand deposit ratio	Klovland (1980)
Norway[a]	1978	6.4-16		
Australia	1978/79	10	currency/demand deposit ratio	Commercial Bank of Australia (1980)

[a]Size measured as percentage of GDP.

development of the hidden economy over time, about the relative size of these sectors among countries, not to speak of the absolute size (in proportion to GNP) at a particular date. What table 1-2 *does* suggest is that the underground economy is of a noticeable size. It should be remembered, however, that the monetary method can yield estimates of a declining and negative hidden economy when the base year is changed.

Overall Evaluation of Approaches and Results

Four different approaches for estimating the unobserved sector have been discussed. *All* of these methods use the same methodological procedure. The hidden economy is taken to be a *residual,* but it is observed in different spheres:

1. as the difference between various income measures;
2. as the difference between declared income and what tax authorities find out to be income after auditing;
3. as the difference between the officially measured participation rate and the one deemed to be normal.
4. as the difference between currency normally needed and actually observed, or the difference between total and officially measured national income, given money supply.

The fact that the residual is observed in different spheres leads to a wide range of estimates even for the same country and the same year (and author). The discrepancy method (1) as well as the tax auditing method (2) will certainly estimate the *minimum size* of the hidden economy because concealed income either from legitimate or illegal activities and income from barter and in-kind activities are not fully counted. The participation rate approach (3) should be expected to be larger than approaches (1) and (2) because in principle it includes work bartering as well as concealed work income. However, it does not include concealed income and bartering from nonwork sources, and underestimates the size of the hidden economy, provided that work effort (productivity per man-hour) is larger in the submerged economy—which is likely to be the case. The monetary approach (4) is likely to lead to the relatively largest estimates, because in principle they include all money transactions in the hidden sector. The currency/demand deposit approach restricts itself to activities involving currency, and must therefore be expected to lead to smaller estimates than Feige's money transactions approach, which covers *all* monetary transactions. A comparison of the results given earlier in this chapter shows indeed that in general these expectations are borne out. To use the case of the United States, the only country to which three of the four approaches have been applied, the estimates for 1976 lie in the following range: The "unexplained income differences" approach yield an estimate of about 4 percent of GNP; the tax-auditing approach gives an estimate of between 6 and 8 percent of GNP; the currency/ demand deposit ratio method leads to an estimate of between 8 and 14 percent of GNP; and the transactions method leads to an estimate of 22 percent of GNP.

As the hidden economy is not directly measurable, the residual approach is eminently reasonable. However, the quality of the estimates of the hidden economy depends on whether the difference can be attributed solely (or at least overwhelmingly) to the working of the hidden sector. If there are other important factors to which the residual can be attributed, the resulting estimate of the hidden economy is dubious. The most advanced studies (Tanzi 1980b, Klovland 1980) make an effort to control for other influences. They attribute the whole residual to the increase in tax burden. This step forward has encountered difficulties, however. Klovland (1980) finds no consistent negative relationship between the tax rate and the currency/demand deposit ratio, while Feige (1980b) finds a positive relationship between his estimates of the size of the underground economy and the rate of taxation. A cross-section analysis (Frey and Weck 1981b) for seventeen OECD countries shows that it is quite implausible that the tax rate is the *only* determinant of the size of the hidden economy. If the relative size of the shadow economy depends on the burden of taxation (including social security), Sweden, Norway, the Netherlands, and Denmark would have the largest hidden sector, while Canada, Italy, the United States, and Spain would be among those countries with the smallest. This suggests that other crucial factors need to be taken into account.[21] One such factor is identified by one of the present approaches, namely the labor market. It seems to be evident that in countries with low participation, low working hours, and high unemployment, people have particularly good opportunities to become active in the submerged economy. Psychological preparedness is certainly important; thus, tax morality and attitudes toward the public sector should also be considered.[22]

Conclusion

Though many would feel that "this be Madness" to try to estimate the size of the underground economy, our survey has at least shown that "there is Method in it." It might even be argued that there are *too* many methods leading to incompatible estimates. We think such a line of reasoning is mistaken. Every method emphasizes a different aspect of the hidden economy, and thus has its strengths and weaknesses.

One aspect is, however, seriously deficient in all approaches existing so far: there is no theory behind the measurements which would explain the behavior of individuals acting in the regular and in the underground economy. Individuals choose rationally whether to work in the official or unofficial economy, comparing implicitly or explicitly the various benefits and costs associated with the particular choice of activity. Indeed, it is not sufficient to consider the private (official or unofficial) sector, but the public sector must be considered as well. One of the main reasons that seems to be causing people to switch to the underground economy is the burden of taxation, which in turn is determined by political decisions. A theoretical model explaining the size and development of the underground economy, thus, requires the analysis of the interdependencies among at least three sectors: the private official economy, the public sector, and the underground economy. (An initial attempt is made in Frey and Weck 1981a). From this point of view the estimation of the hidden economy is certainly not Madness but rather a fascinating research endeavor.

Notes

1. This figure is quoted by, among others, *Economist* (1979a, 1979b), Tanzi (1980a, (chapter 4, this volume), O'Higgins (1980), De Grazia (chapter 2, this volume), *OECD* (1980b), Macafee (1980), *Intersocial* (1980), Thurn (1980).

2. See Isachsen, Klovland, and Strøm, (chapter 13, this volume), Tanzi (chapter 4 this volume), Macafee (1980).

3. See for example, Hawrylyshyn (1976), Eisner (1978), Adler and Hawrylyshyn (1978), Hill (1979), Kendrick (1979).

4. There is an interesting analogy here to the early attempts in capturing the influence of technical progress—the "third factor" within growth theory, as first undertaken by Solow (1957).

5. For current attempts with yet unknown results see OECD (1978a).

6. Albers (1974, p. 89 ff.) suspects an even larger size of the discrepancy for Italy for the same year; this view is supported by a study by Campa and Visco (1972).

7. There are also some direct comparisons between the income reported in consumer surveys and income declared by the same persons to the tax authorities; for example see Mork (1975).

8. See for example, Albers (1974), Feige (1980a, 1980b), O'Higgins (1980).

9. In equilibrium, given the (differing) cost functions involved, the amount of bartering and the extent of evasion of taxes on goods and services will be positively related. For Italy Rey (1965) estimates that in the late 1950s the government was defrauded of at least 30 percent of the potential yield of the turnover tax; for Belgium the estimate for the mid-1960s was only slightly smaller (Frank, Delcourt, and Rosselle 1973, p. 236 ff.).

10. Before World War II, when national income was mainly or even exclusively calculated by extrapolating tax statistics, it was common practice to take into account that part of the income which is presumably concealed. See Jostock (1943, especially p. 43 ff.) for many examples.

11. For instance, a recent IRS (1979b) survey shows that between 1966 and 1979 the proportion of taxpayers who consider cheating a "very serious crime" has decreased. Similar observations have been made for other countries, such as the Federal Republic of Germany (Daeke 1978).

12. See OECD (1978a, 1980a) and the various "Rapports du Conseil des Impôts au Président de la République Française" (Conseil des Impôts 1972 to 1977).

13. This is also suggested by a recent taxpayer opinion survey on income tax evasion by the IRS (1979b) which uses both direct questions under assurance of anonymity, and a more subtle, randomized response technique. The latter yielded considerably higher figures for unreported income.

14. Tax experts from various industrialized countries (OECD 1978a, p. 5) agree "that the audit approach tends to be more successful in identifying overestimation of deductible expenses than the underreporting of income and particularly the nonreporting from certain sources."

15. A short presentation in English of these interview techniques is given in OECD (1978b, 1979, 1980b).

16. Regional studies for northern Italy even arrive at differences of 15 to 20 percentage points between the official and the estimated actual par-

ticipation rates (Canullo and Montanari 1980, Coen 1980, p. 62 ff.). Other regional studies report that irregular work comprises up to 30 percent of total work *time*; in agricultural areas this rises to over 50 percent (Camera di Commercio, Industria, Artigianato di Torino 1978, Zanoni 1980).

17. The discussion has so far assumed the conditions holding for an industrialized country. The most natural way to approach the measurement of the underground economy of developing countries would seem to be the labor market. For evidence as to the role of the "informal sector" within the labor market in some developing countries in Latin America see, for example, Prealc (1978). Another promising approach is based on data on tax evasion, see, for example, Herschel (1978).

18. For similar computations see Veckans Affaerer (1978) and Klovland (1980) for Sweden and Norway, and Commercial Bank of Australia (chapter 18, this volume).

19. For a more extensive criticism of the large denomination bill method see Macafee (1980), O'Higgins (1980), and Klovland (1980); for criticism of the currency/demand deposit ratio method see, for example, Feige (1979), Garcia (1978), Laurent (1979), Bowsher (1980); for criticism of the transactions method see, for example, Tanzi (1980a).

20. See also Isachsen, Klovland, and Strøm, chapter 13, this volume.

21. A broad view of the hidden sector as part of the whole economy is presented also by studies arguing qualitatively, such as Charreyron (1979), Chassaing (1979), Capodaglio (1979), Kaltzmann (1979), Heertje and Cohen (1980), and Bulletin de la Bank de Paris et des Pays-Bas (1980).

22. See, for example, Schmoelders (1970), Vogel (1974), Song and Yarbrough (1978), Lewis (1979), Van Veldhoven and Groenland (1980), and Waerneryd (1980).

References

Adler, Hans J. and Hawrylyshyn, Oli (1978). "Estimates of the Value of Household Work: Canada, 1961 and 1971." *Review of Income & Wealth* 24 (Dec. 1978):333-355.

Albers, Willi (1974). "Umverteilungswirkungen der Einkommensteuer." In *Oeffentliche Finanzwritschaft und Verteilung II,* edited by Willi Albers. Berlin: Duncker & Humblot, 1974, 69-144.

Badelt, Christoph (1980). *Sozioekonomie der Selbstorganisation.* Frankfurt: Campus, 1980.

Bowsher, Norman N. (1980). "The Demand for Currency: Is the Underground Economy Undermining Monetary Economy?" *Federal Reserve Bank of St. Louis Review* 62 (Jan. 1980):11-17.

Bulletin de la Banque de Paris et des Pays-Bas (1980). "Economies parallèles." *Conjoncture Parisbas* (Dec. 1980):167-174.

Business Week (1978). "The Fast Growth of the Underground Economy." *Business Week* (March 13, 1978):73-77.

Cagan, Phillip (1958). "The Demand for Currency Relative to Total Money Supply." National Bureau of Economic Research, Occasional Paper 62. New York, 1958.

Camera di Commercio, Industria, Artigianato di Torino (1978). "L'occupazione irregolare in Piemonte." Collona Ricerche e Documentazione No. 9, Camera di Commercio, Torino, 1978.

Campa, Giuseppe and Visco, Vincenzo (1972). "Una stima del gettito teoretico per classe di reddito familiare dell'imposta di richezza mobile sui reditti da lavoro dipendente nel 1968." *Tributi* 75 (March 1972): 127-143.

Cannullo, Giuseppe and Montanari, Maria Grazia (1978). "Lavoro regolare e lavoro nero in alcuni comuni delle Marche." In *Lavoro regolare e lavoro nero,* edited by Pietro Alessandrini. Bologna: Il Mulino, 1978, 147-182.

Cantelli, Paolo (1980). *L'economia sommersa.* Rome: Editori Riuniti, 1980.

Capodaglio, Giulio (1979). "Lavoro nero o anacoretismo economico?" *Rivista Internazionale di Scienze Economiche e Commerciali* 26 (July 1979):629-633.

Censis (1976). *L'occupazione occulta—Caratteristiche della partecipazione al lavoro in Italia* Rome: Fondazione Censis, 1976.

Charreyron, Anne (1979). "L'économie souterraine se développe à l'est comme à l'ouest." *Futuribles* 29 (Dec. 1979):101-106.

Chassaing, Phillipe (1979). "L'économie souterraine," *L'économie* 1369 (March 12, 1979):17-23.

Coen, Anna (1980). *I dati reperibili sulla opportunità e propensione al lavoro in rapporto alla occupazione ed alla educazione delle forze di lavoro marginale* Rome: Istituto di Studi per la Programmazione Economica, 1980.

Commercial Bank of Australia (1980). "The Underground Economy in Australia." *Commercial Bank of Australia Economic Review* (Sept. 1980):8-12, chapter 18, this volume.

Conseil des Impôts, Rapport du Conseil des Impôts au President de la République, *Journal Officiel de la République Française,* various years.

Contini, Bruno (1979). *Lo sviluppo di un'economia parallela: La segmentazione del mercato del lavoro in Italia e la crescita del settore irregolare* Milan: Edizioni di Comunitá, 1979.

Contini, Bruno (1981a). "Labor Market Segmentation and the Development of the Parallel Economy—The Italian Experience." *Oxford Economic Papers* 2 (1981), forthcoming.

Contini, Bruno (1981b). "The Second Economy of Italy." *Taxing and Spending* 4 (1981), forthcoming.

Contini, Bruno (1981c). "The Anatomy of the Irregular Economy." Mimeographed. Berkeley: University of Torino and University of California, 1981.

Daeke, Karl-Heinz (1978). "Steuermentalität der bundesdeutschen Steuerzahler." Mimeographed. Duesseldorf: Bund der Steuerzahler, 1978.

De Grazia, Raffaele (1980). "Clandestine Employment: A Problem of Our Time." *International Labour Review* 119 (Sept./Oct. 1980):549-563.

Economist (1979a). "Make the Best of the Black Economy." *Economist* (June 30-July 6, 1979):73-74.

Economist (1979b). "Exploring the Underground Economy." *Economist* (Sept. 15-22, 1979):106-107.

Eisner, Robert (1978). "Total Incomes in the United States, 1959 and 1969." *Review of Income & Wealth* 24 (March 1978):41-70.

Feige, Edgar L. (1979). "How Big Is the Irregular Economy?" *Challenge* 22 (Nov./Dec. 1979):5-13.

Feige, Edgar L. (1980a). "Den dolda sektorns tillvaxt—70-talets ekonomiska problem i nytt ljus." *Ekonomisk Debatt* 8 (1980):570-589.

Feige, Edgar L. (1980b). "A New Perspective on Macroeconomic Phenomena. The Theory and Measurement of the Unobserved Sector of the United States: Causes, Consequences, and Implications." Mimeographed. Wassenaar: Netherlands Institute for Advanced Study, August 1980.

Frank, Max (1972). "La sous-estimation et la fraude fiscale en Belgique: Ampleur et remèdes." *Cahiers Economiques de Bruxelles* 53, No. 1 (1972):5-46.

Frank, Max (1976). "Fraude des revenus soumis à l'impôt des personnes physiques et perte d'impòt qui en résulte pour le Trésor—Etude méthodologique." *Public Finance* 31, No. 1 (1976):1-30.

Frank, Max, Delcourt, E., and Rosselle, E. (1973). "Problèmes méthodologiques et statistiques relatifs à l'évaluation de la sous-estimation et de la fraude fiscale." In *L'exacte perception de l'impôt*. Brussels: Bruylant, 1973.

Freud, David (1979). "A Guide to Underground Economics." *Financial Times* (April 9, 1979).

Frey, Bruno S. and Weck, Hannelore (1981a). "Bureaucracy and the Shadow Economy: A Macro-Approach." In *Anatomy of Government Deficiency,* edited by Horst Hanusch. Detroit: Wayne State University Press, forthcoming.

Frey, Bruno S. and Weck, Hannelore (1981b). "Estimating the Shadow Economy: A Naive Approach." Institute of Empirical Research in Economics, University of Zurich, Mimeographed. March 1981.

Frey, Luigi (1978). *Il lavoro nero in Italia nel 1977: Tendenze dell'occupazione.* Torino: Fondazione Ceres, June 1978.

Fuà, Giorgio (1976). *Occupazione e capacità produttive: La realtà italiana.* Bologna: Il Mulino, 1976.

Fuà, Giorgio (1977). "Employment and Productive Capacity in Italy." *Banca Nazionale del Lavoro Quarterly Review* 122 (Sept. 1977):215-244.

Garcia, Gillian (1978). "The Currency Ratio and the Subterranean Economy." *Financial Analysts Journal* (Nov./Dec. 1978):64-66.

Gershuny, Jonathan I. (1978). *After Industrial Society? The Emerging Self-Service Economy.* London: Macmillan, 1978.

Gershuny, Jonathan I. (1979). "L'économie informelle." *Futuribles* 24 (June 1979):37-50.

Grossman, Gregory (1977). "The Second Economy of the USSR." *Problems of Communism* 26 (Sept./Oct. 1977):25-40, chapter 15, this volume.

Gutmann, Peter M. (1977). "The Subterranean Economy." *Financial Analysts Journal* (Nov./Dec. 1977):24-27, 34.

Gutmann, Peter M. (1978). "Off the Books." *Across the Board* (Aug. 1978): 8-14.

Gutmann, Peter M. (1979a). "Statistical Illusions, Mistaken Policies." *Challenge* 22 (Nov./Dec. 1979):14-17.

Gutmann, Peter M. (1979b). "Testimony before the Joint Economic Committee of the United States Congress on the Subterranean Economy." Mimeographed. Washington, D.C., Nov. 15, 1979.

Hansson, Ingemar (1980). "Sveriges svarta sektor." *Ekonomisk Debatt* 8 (1980):595-602.

Hawrylyshyn, Oli (1976). "The Value of Household Services: A Survey of Empirical Estimates." *Review of Income & Wealth* 22 (June 1976): 101-131.

Heertje, Arnold and Cohen, Harry (1980). *Het Officieuze Circuit* Utrecht and Antwerpen: Spectrum, 1980.

Herschel, Federico J., "Tax Evasion and its Measurement in Developing Countries," *Public Finance* 33, no. 31 (1978):232-268.

Hill, T.P. (1979). "Do-It-Yourself and GDP." *Review of Income & Wealth* 25 (March 1979):31-39.

Internal Revenue Service (1979a). *Estimates of Income Unreported on Individual Income Tax Returns.* Washington, D.C.: Government Printing Office, Sept. 1979.

Internal Revenue Service (1979b). "A General Taxpayer Opinion Survey." Mimeographed. Office of Planning and Research, Internal Revenue Service, Washington, D.C., Sept. 1979.

Intersocial (1980). "Le travail noir en Europe et aux U.S.A." *Intersocial* 61 (June 1980):3-16.

Isachsen, Arne J., Klovland, Jan T., and Strøm, Steinar (1981). "The Hidden Economy in Norway." chapter 13, this volume.

Jostock, Paul (1943). "Ueber den Umfang des der Besteuerung entgehenden Einkommens." *Weltwirtschaftliches Archiv* 57, No. 1 (1943):27-80.

Kaiser, Robert G. (1976). *Russia: The People and the Power.* New York: Pocket Books, 1976.

Katz, Zer (1973). "Insights from Emigrés and Sociological Studies on the Soviet Union." In *Soviet Economic Prospects for the Seventies.* Washington, D.C.: Joint Economic Committee, 1973, 87-94.

Kendrick, John W. (1979). "Expanding Imputed Values in the National Income and Product Accounts." *Review of Income & Wealth* 25 (Dec. 1979):349-363.

Klatzmann, Rosine (1979). "Le travail noir." *Futuribles* 26 (Sept. 1979):43-59

Klovland, Jan T. (1980). "In Search of the Hidden Economy: Tax Evasion and the Demand for Currency in Norway and Sweden." Discussion Paper 18/80, Norwegian School of Economics and Business Administration, Bergen, Dec. 1980.

Laurent, Robert D. (1979). "Currency and the Subterranean Economy." *Federal Reserve Bank of Chicago Economic Perspectives* (March/April 1979):3-6.

Lewis, Alan (1979). "An Empirical Assessment of Tax Mentality." *Public Finance* 34, No. 2 (1979):245-257.

Macafee, Kerrick (1980). "A Glimpse of the Hidden Economy in the National Accounts." *Economic Trends* (Feb. 1980):81-87, chapter 9, this volume.

Martino, Antonio (1980). "Another Italian Economic Miracle." Mont Pelerin Society, Stanford Conference, Mimeographed. Sept. 1980.

Miller, Robert (1979). "Evidence of Attitudes to Evasion from a Sample Survey." In *Tax Avoison.* London: Institute of Economic Affairs, 1979, 115-125.

Mork, Knut A. (1975). "Income Tax Evasion: Some Empirical Evidence." *Public Finance* 30, No. 1 (1975):70-76.

OECD (1978a). "Methods Used to Estimate the Extent of Tax Evasion." OECD, Mimeographed. CFA (78)6, Paris, Nov. 17, 1978.

OECD (1978b). "Unrecorded Unemployment: The Experience of the Italian 'Istituto Centrale di Statistica' in Investigating 'Non-Institutional Work'." Mimeographed. MAS/WP 7 (78)1, Paris, Dec. 29, 1978.

OECD (1979). "Unrecorded Employment," Mimeographed. MAS/WP 7 (79)6, Paris, Feb. 16, 1979.

OECD (1980a). "Une étude sur l'exactitude des déclarations de revenus en France." Mimeographed. DAF/CFA/WP 8/80.4, Paris, Jan. 23, 1980.

OECD (1980b). "Measuring the Volume of Unrecorded Employment." Mimeographed. MAS/WP 7 (80)3, Paris, March 28, 1980.

Ofer, Gur and Vinokur, Aaron (1980). "Private Sources of Income of the Soviet Urban Household." Rand Corp., R-2359-NA, Santa Monica, Aug. 1980.

O'Higgins, Michael (1980). "Measuring the Hidden Economy: A Review of Evidence and Methodologies." Mimeographed. Outer Circle Policy Unit, London, July 1980.

Økonomiske Råd (1967). *Den personlige indkomstfordeling og indkomstudjaevningen over de offentlige finanser.* Kopenhagen: Statens Trykningskontor, 1967.

Økonomiske Råd (1977). *Dansk økonomi.* Kopenhagen: Statens Trykningskontor, 1977.

Park, Thae (1979). "Reconciliation between Personal Income and Taxable Income, 1947-1977." Mimeographed. Washington, D.C.: Bureau of Economic Analysis, May 1979.

Prealc (1978). *Sector Informal: Funcionamento y Politicas.* Programa Regional del Empleo para América Latina y el Caribe (Prealc), Officina Internacional del Trabajo, Santiago, 1978.

Rey, Mario (1965). "Estimating Tax Evasions: The Example of the Italian General Sales Tax." *Public Finance* 20, No. 3/4 (1965):366-392.

Roze, Helêne (1971). "Prestations sociales, impôt direct et cellule de revenus." *Economie et Statistique* 20 (Feb. 1971):3-14.

Ross, Irwin (1978). "Why the Underground Economy is Booming." *Fortune* (Oct. 9, 1978):92-98.

Rydenfelt, Sven (1980). "The Limits of Taxation: Lessons from the Swedish Welfare State." Mont Pelerin Society, Stanford Conference, Sept. 1980.

Schmoelders, Guenter (1970). *Das Irrationale in der Finanzwirtschaft.* Hamburg: Rowohlt, 1970.

Schroeder, Gertrude E. and Greenslade, Rush V. (1979). "On the Measurement of the Second Economy in the USSR." *Association for Comparative Economic Studies Bulletin* 21 (Spring 1979), 3-22.

Solow, Robert M. (1956). "Technical Change and the Aggregate Production Function." *Review of Economics and Statistics* 39 (Aug. 1957), 312-320.

Song, Young-dahl, and Yarbrough, Tinsley E. (1978). "Tax Ethics and Taxpayers Attitudes: A Survey." *Public Administration Review* 38 (Sept./Oct. 1978), 442-452.

Tanzi, Vito (1980a). "Underground Economy Built on Illicit Pursuits is Growing Concern of Economic Policymakers." *IMF Survey* (Feb. 4, 1980), 34-37.

Tanzi, Vito (1980b). "The Underground Economy in the United States: Estimates and Implications." *Banca Nazionale del Lavoro Quarterly Review* 135 (Dec. 1980), 427-453, chapter 4, this volume.

Thurn, Max Graf (1980). "The Underground Economy." Mont Pelerin Society, Stanford Conference, Mimeographed, Sept. 1980.

U.S. General Accounting Office (1979). *Who's Not Filing Income Tax Reurns?* Report to the Congress of the United States by the Comptroller General, U.S. General Accounting Bureau, Washington, D.C., July 11, 1979.

Van Veldhoven, G.M., and Groenland, E.A.G. (1980). "Psychological Aspects of Taxation." Mimeographed. Tilburg University, 1980.

Veckans Affaerer (1978). "Nytt saett at maeta dolda ekonomin: naera 10 procent av BNP aer svart." *Veckans Affaerer* 22 (June 1, 1978), 11-13.

Vogel, Joachim (1974). "Taxation and Public Opinion in Sweden: An Interpretation of Recent Survey Data." *National Tax Journal* 27, No. 4 (1974), 499-513.

Waerneryd, Karl-Erik (1980). "Psychological Reactions to the Tax System." Mimeographed. Stockholm Schools of Economics, 1980.

Weisbrod, Burton A., ed. (1977). *The Voluntary Non-Profit Sector, An Economic Analysis.* Lexington and Toronto: D.C. Heath, 1977.

Wirtschaftswoche (1980). "Brutto gleich Netto: Schattenwirtschaft." *Wirtschaftswoche* 32 (Aug. 8, 1980), 22-23.

Zanoni, Magda (1980). "Indagine sul doppio lavoro e il lavoro irregolare in una comunità del Friuli et indicazioni per una stima nazionale dei dati sull'economia sommersa." Mimeographed. Laboratorio di Economia Politica, Università degli Studi di Torino, Sept. 1980.

2 Clandestine Employment: A Problem of Our Times

Raffaele De Grazia

Introduction

A complex phenomemon known variously as the parallel, twilight, underground, or black economy has become increasingly common in many countries during the last few years. The backbone of this economy, whose existence goes unrecognized in national accounts statistics, is work performed clandestinely and illegally—and therefore unregulated in any way by the authorities.

Clandestine employment is not a topic that lends itself easily to analysis. The conclusions of the few studies and surveys made of the subject hitherto vary widely because of differences of definition or approach, or because certain aspects were neglected. Instances are often reported in the press, but the information available, in particular the figures, must be treated with great caution; by definition, clandestine work tends to defy direct scientific investigation since the various parties concerned are obviously disinclined to provide information on the subject. For the purposes of this chapter, which is basically concerned with the situation in industrialized market economy countries,[1] clandestine employment can be defined as having a sole or secondary gainful, noncasual occupation that is carried out on or beyond the fringes of the law or the terms of regulations and agreements.

Types of Clandestine Employment

The last few years have seen radical changes in both the organization and practice of clandestine employment. Where it used to be primarily individual in character and limited to only a few categories of worker, there are now whole undertakings, workshops and networks operating clandestinely in many countries and embracing a growing number of occupations. A wealth of information corroborating this is to be found in the press.

Reprinted from *International Labor Review* 119, 5 (September-October 1980).

In France, for example, clandestine groups have built holiday homes in Brittany, a six-story building with three basement levels in Paris, a four-story house in Nice. In one district of Paris a police crack-down uncovered 217 clandestine tailoring workshops exploiting foreign workers without work permits. It was noted also that one beauty products factory employed some 2,000 female "counsellors" as sales staff: they had no employment contracts and their salaries were not declared in tax returns.

In Italy the phenomenon is even more blatant, if not universal. Entire neighborhoods of Naples have been transformed into secret workshops—specializing particularly in shoe- and garment-making—which move on quickly or disappear the moment a visit by the labor inspectors seems likely. In Milan there are only 5,000 homeworkers listed on the city's commercial register, while fewer than 1,000 home work enterprises carrying on business in the surrounding province are registered; the true numbers are estimated at about 100,000 and 50,000, respectively. Finally, to show how institutionalized the underground economy has become, there have even been press reports of a strike by cigarette smugglers in the southern Italian city of Bari!

In Japan managerial staff lacking adequate job satisfaction have established clandestine firms that do business only on Saturdays and Sundays. These specialize in assisting medium-sized enterprises with the streamlining of production or the manufacture and marketing of new products.

In the last few years cases of organized smuggling of foreign clandestine workers with a view to their illegal employment have been uncovered in many European countries (Switzerland, France, Italy, Federal Republic of Germany, Belgium, and so on). This type of trafficking is also booming on the United States-Mexican frontier as well as in many other parts of the world.

Certain changes in the remuneration of clandestine workers have been taking place as well. Whereas in the past they were nearly always very badly paid, nowadays they sometimes earn more than the take-home pay they would receive for identical work done legally. To quote the head of one French firm: "If I were to declare the work of a translator it would cost me 5,000 francs and she would get only 3,500 francs net. I'd rather give nothing to the taxman and pay her about 4,200 francs."[2]

The Scale and Economic Significance
of Clandestine Employment

Although it is impossible to measure the numerical and economic importance of the phenomenon with any certainty, some tentative estimates can nevertheless be based on certain studies and surveys conducted during the past decade.

The Numbers Involved

Broadly speaking, two major categories of clandestine workers can be distinguished: those carrying on clandestine work as their sole occupation; and those who, in addition to their regular jobs, also have one or more paid jobs performed illegally and going undeclared—this is called "double- (or multiple-) jobbing," or "moonlighting."

In the Federal Republic of Germany, where there are more than 700,000 people looking for jobs, 8 percent of workers are estimated to have paid but undeclared employment in addition to their normal jobs, making a total of 2 million moonlighters. One writer estimates that in the United States and Canada at least a quarter of the labor force are multiple-job holders.[3] In France the numbers regularly engaging in clandestine employment have been growing steadily: estimates place the present figure somewhere between 800,000 and 1,500,000. In Sweden a recent poll indicated that 750,000 of the 4,500,000 persons aged between 18 and 70 have jobs in the underground sector. The number of clandestine workers in Belgium is reckoned to be about 300,000 at present.

In Italy the number of female workers alone engaged in clandestine work was thought to be 1,887,000 in 1971, of whom 187,000 were aged under 14.[4] In 1975 a study on "noninstitutional work"[5] carried out by the Centre for Social Investment Studies (CENSIS) under the auspices of the Italian Ministry of Labor estimated the numbers working clandestinely at a minimum of 2,213,000; of this total, 1,068,000, or about 5 percent of the labor force, were moonlighters. Another estimate gave the number of clandestine workers in Italy as 4 million in 1977.[6]

The vast majority of those engaging in clandestine employment as their sole occupation consist of the unemployed, immigrant workers who entered the country clandestinely or whose status is illegal for some other reason, pensioners, self-employed workers not listed in the registers of their trade or occupation, housewives, undeclared temporary staff, students, and children. Some information is available on certain of these categories.

With regard to the unemployed, a Spanish government investigation showed that half of those receiving unemployment benefits in the Seville region had jobs. In France the employers' organizations in the Bouches-du-Rhone département estimated in 1976 that 80 percent of the unemployed were working clandestinely.

As for clandestine immigrant workers, in 1975 their numbers in the EEC countries were estimated at between 500,000 and 600,000,[7] and the number of "illegal" immigrant workers in the Federal Republic of Germany alone is thought to fluctuate between 200,000 and 300,000. The size of the clandestine immigrant labor force in the United States is particularly striking; the Immigration and Naturalization Service of the Department of

Justice put the figure at between 4 and 6 million in 1976 on the basis of estimates by its regional directors.

In some countries homeworkers form a particularly large proportion of those engaged in clandestine employment. In Italy, for example, where there are thought to be more than 1 million homeworkers, fewer than 10 percent are legally registered.

With regard to child labor, a recent ILO study points out that in most countries and in most cases the 52 million children throughout the world who work (an estimate perhaps on the low side) do so clandestinely.[8]

For other categories, the above-mentioned CENSIS study revealed that in Italy 11.5 percent of old-age pensioners, 9.9 percent of housewives, 9.6 percent of those on disability pensions, and 2.0 percent of students were working in the black sector of the economy in 1974.

The extent of clandestine employment is undoubtedly still greater if one is to believe some of the studies conducted in different municipalities, regions or sectors. In France the National Building Federation estimated at 500,000 the number of clandestine workers in this branch alone. In Italy several surveys carried out in different regions by university research institutes[9] showed that multiple-jobbing rates varied between 15 and 40 percent.

Its Economic Significance

The economic significance of clandestine employment is also considerable.

In the Federal Republic of Germany the Chamber of Commerce has estimated income from the underground economy at 2 percent of the gross national product (GNP). The same figure was mentioned by a leading personality in the iron and steel industry who believed the underground economy's turnover to lie between 25,000 and 30,000 million marks.[10] In France the Office of the Secretary of State for Manual Labor has reckoned that 50 percent of cement output is produced outside the official building sector. For its part, the French National Building Federation has calculated that clandestine work accounts for between 2 and 3 percent of the industry's turnover. In the United Kingdom the annual income of the underground economy has been estimated at some £10,000 million, or 7.5 percent of the country's GNP.[11] One economist has calculated the undeclared employment income in Japan as totaling $29,000 million. In Italy the available estimates suggest that real GNP would be 10 to 25 percent higher than the figure given in official statistics if the latter were to take into account output from the underground economy. In the United States the turnover of this sector was estimated at $195,000 million in 1977, or nearly 10 percent of GNP,[12] while another estimate put it as high as $542,000 million in 1978, or 27 percent of GNP.[13]

Characteristics of Clandestine Workers and Their Jobs

Research studies show that there are far more male than female moon-lighters, although participation by the latter is tending to increase both pro-portionately and in absolute numbers. The largest concentration of moon-lighters can generally be found among workers aged between 25 and 50 (50 to 70 percent) and among married persons (60 to 75 percent), which is in no way surprising since these are the groups that shoulder the heaviest financial responsibilities.

The vast majority of moonlighters have their primary occupation in the nonagricultural sectors. Sample surveys conducted by the Commission of the European Communities in the period 1969-1973[14] show that the propor-tion of moonlighters whose principal occupation was in industry was 51, 55, and 60 percent for Italy, the Federal Republic of Germany, and Luxem-bourg, respectively, while the percentage having their main activity in the service sector was 63 in the Netherlands, 64 in the United Kingdom, and 65 in Belgium.

The distribution of secondary occupations by sector varies widely, as can be seen from table 2-1 for the year 1973, which is based on Commission of the European Communities surveys.

Clandestine immigrant workers appear to be engaged primarily in agri-culture (United States, Italy, Federal Republic of Germany), hotel and res-taurant trades (Italy, Switzerland, France), garment-making (France, United States) and, generally speaking, in the construction industry and other sectors suffering from a labor shortage or where the work is unskilled or unpleasant.

With regard to the occupational status of moonlighters, in their main occupation they are as a rule much more likely to be wage earners than self-employed even though, proportionately, the latter more often have recourse to clandestine work than the former. Self-employment is common in the secondary occupation.

Table 2-1
Distribution of Secondary Occupations, by Sector, Various Countries, 1973

Country	Agriculture	Industry	Services
Federal Republic of Germany	71	5	24
Italy	38	27	35
Netherlands	13	11	76
Belgium	14	8	78
Luxembourg	20	20	60
United Kingdom	5	9	86

Source: Commission of the European Communities.

In most industrialized market economy countries, moonlighting has always been very widespread in some occupations (policemen, watchmen, firemen, teachers, civil servants). In Italy, for example, it is estimated that between 30 and 65 percent of state employees and 65 percent of university teachers have a second job.

Available information shows that the proportion of those working full time in both jobs is minimal and the percentage of those engaged part time in both jobs is relatively low, but much higher among women than among men. Most moonlighters (between 70 and 80 percent) work full time in their main job and part time in their secondary occupation, with the average number of hours devoted to the latter ranging between 9 and 18 per week (except for Italy where the CENSIS study gives 21 hours). Finally, more than half of all moonlighters of both sexes usually work a total of more than 50 hours per week in the two jobs.

Information on the characteristics of workers exclusively engaged in clandestine employment is almost nonexistent, but it can be assumed that they are generally not very different from those of the moonlighters.

A special category is composed of what one journalist has called "workers without chains," that is, individuals who have opted for a different life-style and prefer working irregularly and very often illegally. "They are young and they want to be free, not tied down. They prefer insecurity to dependence, risk to routine, the unexpected to the rut. For that reason they choose to work as and when they consider it compatible with their idea of happiness."[15] These "drop-outs," who are to be found in the countryside as well as in the towns, already run into hundreds of thousands and, given present-day attitudes of young people to work, their numbers could increase significantly in the years to come.

Motives and Causes

An analysis of clandestine employment would be incomplete without some consideration of the *motives* driving people to engage in it, in other words the subjective reasons why firms and private individuals make such employment available and why workers seek it, as well as of its *causes*, that is, the objective reasons explaining why the practice exists and is growing. Studies of motivation are rare and generally speaking confined to moonlighters. Analyses of the causes are commoner but often reflect the prejudices of their authors and are therefore singularly lacking in the requisite objectivity.

According to the Commission of the European Communities,[16] the causes of clandestine employment are to be found first of all in the taxation and social security system applying to small undertakings, and second, in the inadequate organization of the labor market, especially the failure of employment agencies to penetrate the market. I feel this list is too restrictive: the factors governing the existence and spread of clandestine employment are much more numerous and complex, and in any case they vary according to the economic and social situation of each country. To be persuaded of this one has only to look at some of the explanations advanced by workers' and employers' organizations.

The trade unions generally give the prime causes as being inadequate wages and retirement pensions, unemployment, steeply progressive income tax, boring and repetitive work, and insufficient controls on the growth of certain types of employment (temporary work, home work, subcontracting and part-time work).

Among workers themselves the motives seem to be mainly but not entirely economic or financial in origin. By way of illustration we may cite a survey carried out by the University of Turin in 1978[17] among workers in a small Piedmontese municipality that was considered to be representative of municipalities close to Italy's three major industrial cities. This showed that the workers' principal reasons for moonlighting were, first and foremost, the need for extra income; second, the desire for work allowing fuller use or improvement of their professional qualifications; finally, the desire for a modicum of independence in their work. It would not be rash to say the pecuniary motives have still greater weight for those whose sole occupation is clandestine than for moonlighters.

The reasons most frequently cited by employers' groups are the excessive social costs of "normal" employment, the insufficient room for maneuver left to firms in managing their labor force, the reduction of working hours and the heavy taxation burden on firms. So far as Italy is concerned, the Director for Trade Union Relations of the General Confederation of Italian Industry has identified a number of other reasons why employers recruit clandestine workers: these include the severe restrictions on overtime imposed by collective bargaining; excessive recruitment constraints on firms; over-generous unemployment benefits; the absence of a welfare infrastructure catering to female workers, leading them to prefer work at home; the introduction of equal pay for men and women; and the high number of persons on disability pensions.[18]

Financial concerns are of prime importance for small employers too: they can cut costs by contracting out minor jobs that can be done more cheaply in the underground economy.

One French author writes that "the main reason for clandestine employment is economic: one of the parties increases his income, the other reduces his costs. Two economic causes play a dominant role: inadequate remuneration and the burden of taxation and social security costs."[19] According to the same source the employer offers clandestine employment because of problems in finding people to do the work openly, and the worker accepts it because it gives him a satisfaction he does not get through legal work: in-dependence, a feeling of self-fulfillment; the chance to deal with the employer on an equal footing, to plan his working time, to improve his skills or change his trade; a way of escaping from the family in the evenings and at weekends, of fighting boredom, and so on.

It seems likely that the various arrangements designed to make working hours more flexible (continuous working day, compressed working week, flexitime, shift work, and so on) will also encourage the spread of clandes-tine employment, but this is a field in which there has hardly been any research so far.

The Effects of Clandestine Employment

The consequences of clandestine employment for individuals, enterprises and the community as a whole are manifold. Normally attention is focused on its harmful features, but there is increasing recognition that it also has important positive aspects.

Positive Aspects

On the positive side, the direct financial and economic disadvantages accru-ing to workers are usually invoked to explain or even to excuse their re-course to clandestine employment. Their income from clandestine work helps to provide them and their families with the basic necessities and to maintain or improve their living standards. In addition, as we have seen, clandestine employment sometimes gives them other, nonpecuniary satis-factions, for example when it offers scope for exercising initiative and greater responsibility.

Advocates of the system argue that, where small jobs are concerned, the practice also fulfills a useful function for the wider society in that it makes it possible to resolve certain everyday problems in a way that legitimate employment—in present circumstances—would find it difficult to match, either because of the excessive overheads involved or because of insufficient skilled labor. It is even claimed that in some sectors clandestine work helps to maintain the competitiveness and flexibility of production.

Finally, in the present climate of crisis and unemployment, the fact that workers have the possibility of working in the underground economy can act as a safety valve for discontent and social tensions.

Negative Aspects

The adverse consequences of clandestine employment have received more attention from observers, who lay particular emphasis on the financial losses incurred by the State and the social security institutions. The income lost to the social security system in France in 1978 has been estimated at 18,000 million francs (which may be compared with the forecast deficit for the same year of 17,000 million francs) and the loss to value added tax at 6,000 million. In the Federal Republic of Germany the annual loss to the state budget and social security institutions is thought to total 10,000 million marks. In Sweden 2,000 million kronor are lost in taxes each year in this way.

To justify the adoption of repressive measures, it is often argued that clandestine employment constitutes unfair competition for workers and firms not resorting to it—competition that is felt not only at the national level but also internationally. Thus, in explanation of the administrative action taken in France in 1979 to stem the inflow of clothing of various kinds from Italy, the authorities claimed that the massive scale of these imports was due to the fact that Italian textile firms were employing large numbers of clandestine workers.

One important question that is often asked, particularly since unemployment has been high, is whether clandestine work has much effect on employment levels. Although the available information is insufficient to allow of any categorical or definitive reply, a distinction ought perhaps to be made between moonlighters and those engaged exclusively in clandestine employment on a full-time, regular basis.

It is generally agreed that moonlighters rarely take away jobs from the unemployed because they devote only a limited number of hours to their secondary occupation, which in any case often requires professional qualifications, particular aptitudes and sometimes starting capital that the unemployed do not ordinarily possess. Moreover, many employers who have work available only intermittently would probably be unwilling to employ regular staff if the possibility of using clandestine workers did not exist. On the other hand, when clandestine employment is very widespread and engaged in as a sole, regular and full-time or almost full-time occupation, it is not hard to imagine that it may become an obstacle to efforts to expand official employment. In any event, since unemployment can be both the cause and the effect of clandestine work, the link between the latter and employment remains an ambiguous one.

Less frequently mentioned are the repercussions that clandestine employment can have on the health and safety of the workers concerned. The article on "double-jobbing" in the ILO *Encyclopaedia of Occupational Health and Safety* points to the fatigue resulting from the long hours of work involved and observes that "fatigue leads to insomnia which in turn leads to further fatigue so creating a vicious circle, perhaps rendering the individual more accident-prone." In addition, workers in the underground economy normally have no protection as regards working conditions and are not covered by social security.

Attitudes to Clandestine Employment

While generally condemned in public, clandestine employment is in practice rarely tackled with anything like the fervor displayed in official pronouncements on the subject.

Government Officials and Politicians

Recently the authorities in the countries most affected have been taking a number of general and specific steps to eliminate or reduce the recourse to this type of employment or to combat certain of its forms. Yet it should be noted that the clamp-down, whether in the shape of legislation or regulations, stems from pressure exerted by the social and economic groups who are particularly hard hit by the practice, that it is normally enforced only during periods of economic or social crisis, and that the results are generally considered disappointing by the very people who called for it in the first place.

Moreover, the publicly expressed views of politicians or government officials on the question vary from one country to another, and often within one and the same country. Thus in France the government has frequently stressed its determination to use diverse means of combating clandestine employment, saying it is not to be tolerated "because in the first place it is flagrantly unjust, a way of working at the expense of those who pay taxes and social security contributions. And secondly because it is tantamount to misappropriating jobs and this, in a period of unemployment, is inadmissible."[20]

On the other hand, a former Italian minister, speaking of the underground economy and clandestine employment, has stated:

> It is a sad thing to say, but these "deviations" are a positive thing, at least as far as employment is concerned. If the taxman were to intervene in this underground economy he would be acting in accordance with the principles of distributive justice but would be ruining not only a host of small businessmen and their workers but perhaps the country's economy and social peace as well.

For another political figure, on the other hand, the belief that Italy's economy is on the road to recovery is due precisely to the growth of clandestine employment, and "that is nothing to be overjoyed about."[21]

The Social Partners

The position of the employers' organizations, while theoretically hostile to clandestine work, actually reveals some important nuances. Organizations representing large-scale manufacturing generally assert that the practice does not exist in their branch or, if it does, that it is the fault of the trade unions and the government for raising wages and taxes to unrealistic levels. For example, the General Confederation of Italian Industry condemns clandestine employment which, in its view, disrupts the operation of the labor market, distorts the conditions for fair competition between firms and reduces the number of job opportunities for the unemployed;[22] yet its president told a press conference that the present level of wages was incompatible with full employment and warned that it would be utopian to imagine that clandestine work could be eliminated overnight.[23]

Employers' organizations representing particular business interests (builders' federations, chambers of commerce, craft associations, and so on) seem to be far more sensitive to the effects of a growing underground economy. It is mainly due to the pressure exerted by these groups that the governments of France, Belgium, and Luxembourg have recently been persuaded to introduce various measures designed to clamp down more effectively on this type of work in specific branches. Incidentally, these organizations have also carried out a number of studies and surveys, generally on a sectoral or local basis, that help to throw valuable light on the causes, characteristics, scale, and consequences of the phenomenon.

The attitudes of workers' organizations do not seem to be completely unambiguous either. Officially, they too condemn clandestine employment but their behavior can in some ways be surprising. In the first place there is hardly ever any mention of the matter in their official policy statements. And second, although most of them recognize that clandestine work exacerbates the economic crisis and the unemployment problem, they generally regard action to eradicate it as a double-edged weapon and are very often reluctant to lend it their full support.

Nevertheless the situation is gradually evolving. In Italy, for instance, the three main trade union confederations pledged themselves in 1978 to combat clandestine work and double-jobbing. In Belgium the General Federation of Labor has spoken out at its last two congresses for more energetic efforts to keep down overtime working, clandestine employment and moonlighting. In its 1978 action program the European Trade Union Confederation noted that if the grave unemployment problem was to be solved it was necessary, inter alia, to close down private employment agencies, since they encouraged moonlighting and other forms of clandestine work, and to extend the network of public employment services. It went on to reaffirm the need to take stern measures at both the Community and the national level against those trafficking in and employing clandestine immigrants.

Other Views

Divergent views on the matter are also to be observed in other circles, particularly among academics, where judgments on clandestine employment have of late been more qualified or even favorable in some cases. Thus Milton Friedman was recently reported by a French journalist to have argued that the clandestine economy, by enabling individuals to circumvent government restrictions on personal initiative, provided an important bulwark against state interference. He did not think clandestine employment was a good thing in itself. In a free enterprise society there should be no need for it, but in societies subjected to all manner of government constraints it was beneficial and should be encouraged. Support for this view came from a French sociologist asserting that:

> The intolerance shown towards clandestine employment is stupid. In France everyone is trying to restrict access to jobs or even to make it impossible. The underground economy is the only safety-valve for this situation. Thank heavens for it! It provides an outlet for the spirit of initiative, it's a nursery for future firms.[24]

Another commentator considered that the growth of "nonformal" employment provides "real and practical solutions to the integration problems of those who are not economically active (young people, women, the elderly) by affording them an opportunity to prove their importance to the economic life of the community."[25] An Italian professor of sociology noted that in his country it was thanks to clandestine employment that, despite being in the depths of a crisis, everyone could continue to eat well, drive a car, and even take decent holidays. He called this Italy's "second economic miracle" and considered that the Italian economy had been saved by clandestine workers; the system worked, and it should not be judged from a moral standpoint.[26]

Conversely, although recognizing that clandestine employment has positive economic and social effects in the short term, some observers consider that in the long term it is likely to have very serious social and economic repercussions. Thus, again in relation to Italy, one economist believes that everything possible should be done to combat clandestine employment, calling it an evil acting as a brake on the reconversion of industry that is indispensable if Italy is to have more in common with Europe than with Southeast Asia; if this type of employment continues to spread, he warned, the gulf between wages, working conditions, and workers' bargaining power in Italy and those in the rest of Europe will inevitably widen still further.[27]

Public Opinion

The same ambiguity of attitude can be seen in public opinion. In France, for example, a survey conducted by a leading research organization in 1979 revealed that as a rule such terms as "illegal work" and "undeclared work" did not have any pejorative connotations for the public. Clandestine employment is perceived and judged for the most part on the basis of its most benign forms (minor manual jobs, repairs, decorating, and household cleaning) and is looked upon as a widespread, recognized, and even worthwhile practice, which "suits everyone." The general public nonetheless takes a far less charitable view of clandestine employment in structural building work. Finally, whereas the employment of undeclared staff by private citizens usually meets with nothing more than indifference, if the same thing is done by undertakings, particularly where foreign workers are involved, it normally arouses strong condemnation.

International Organizations

The unchecked spread of clandestine employment in recent years has also caused serious concern in various regional and international organizations such as the European Communities,[28] the OECD,[29] and the ILO.[30]

Measures to Combat Clandestine Employment

As was mentioned above, several European countries have added new muscle to their legislation for the suppression of such employment or have adopted other measures for preventing or controlling it. Their efforts, which cannot be analyzed in detail here, have consisted in increasing the penalties against clandestine workers and those employing them, in strengthening the labor inspectorates and other forms of supervision, in making public opinion aware of the scale of the problem and the need to reduce it, and in extending the scope of the laws and regulations proscribing this form of employment.

There is little information enabling us to establish whether the measures taken have proved useful and the goals sought have been reached. However, the almost universal admission that clandestine employment is still on the increase suggests that they have been insufficient, if not totally ineffective. Consideration is therefore now being given to other approaches such as: the reduction or at least the stabilization of taxation and social security charges; changes in the application or content of certain labor legislation; and stricter enforcement of existing regulations (or the adoption of new ones) on home work, temporary work, and subcontracting work.

Concluding Remarks

Although this overview of the subject does not provide an answer to the fundamental question debated by many commentators—whether or not clandestine employment is an economic and social evil—it does allow certain conclusions to be drawn.

Clandestine employment is clearly a multifaceted and complex phenomenon whose scale, causes, characteristics, and consequences are still insufficiently understood. In addition to the objective difficulties of quantification that they have run into, the various surveys and studies conducted hitherto have produced rather mixed and not entirely convincing results, partly because of the disparate range of methods used. At the same time, one of their major findings in incontrovertible: clandestine employment is growing rapidly and continuously in most of the industrialized market economy countries (the number of workers engaged in it being sometimes higher than that of registered jobseekers) and will continue to do so in the years to come unless an attempt is made to eliminate or mitigate its real causes.

The basic problem is rooted in the fact that at the national level there is nothing like unanimity regarding the causes and effects of clandestine employment, nor on the necessity and most suitable ways of combating it. No end is in sight to the polemics between the opponents of such employment and those who stress the positive contribution it can make; its hard forms are generally condemned but over its softer forms opinion remains divided. The fact is that in a good many countries clandestine employment is reaching the point where the issue must be fully investigated and discussed because, in the final analysis, it is one that will inevitably affect the sort of society we live in.

Notes

1. It should nonetheless be noted that outside Europe the only available information of any substance is on North America and Japan. The information relating to Italy, on the other hand, is particularly extensive: probably because clandestine employment exists there on such a large scale, it has been the subject of numerous discussions, surveys, and studies.

2. L. Gazzo, *"Travail noir: les chômeurs voient rouge,"* in *Vision*, April 1977, p. 36.

3. R.L. Crawford, "Moonlighting: new look for an old practice," in *Supervisory Management,* August 1978, p. 4.

4. R. Padoa-Schioppa, *La forza lavoro femminile* (Bologna: Il Mulino, 1977), p. 110.

5. *L'occupazione occulta: caratteristiche della partecipazione al lavoro in Italia* (Rome, CENSIS, 1976). This study was conducted by direct interviews with a sample of 28,789 persons belonging to 8,148 families who were statistically representative of some 16,400,000 workers in employment.

6. Bruno Contini, *Lo sviluppo di un'economia parallela* (Milan: Edizioni di Comunitá, 1979).

7. Commission of the European Communities, *Clandestine Immigration* (Brussels, 1975), doc. SEC(75) 1705, p. 1.

8. E. Mendelievich (ed.), *Children at Work* (Geneva: ILO, 1979), p. 28.

9. See M. Brutti, *"Aspetti quantitativi e qualitativi del doppio lavoro,"* in *Industria e Sindacato,* October 12, 1979, pp. 12-13.

10. Dieter Spetmann, a director of Thyssen AG. See H. Baumann, *"L'irrésistible montée du chomage et les balbutiements de ses guérisseurs,"* in *Le Monde,* January 9, 1979.

11. Estimate by Sir William Pile, Chairman of the United Kindgom Board of Inland Revenue.

12. Estimate by P.M. Gutmann. See P. Chassaing, *"L'économie souterraine,"* in *L'économie,* March 12, 1979, p. 17.

13. Estimate by E.L. Feige, University of Wisconsin. See "The Underground Economy," in *U.S. News and World Report,* October 22, 1979, p. 51.

14. The results of these surveys were analyzed by M. Maraffi, Institute of Sociology, Milan, in *Politica dell'occupazione e seconda professione* (Milan, 1976), mimeographed, pp. 46-54.

15. D. Desanti, *"Des travailleurs sans chaînes,"* in *Le Nouvel Observateur,* October 1, 1979, p. 68.

16. See *Official Journal of the European Communities* (Luxembourg), vol. 20, no. C246 (October 13, 1977) (reply of the Commission to a written question dated June 29, 1977, by M. Durieux, a French deputy and member of the European Parliament, on the subject of clandestine work).

17. See M. Carcano, *"Doppio lavoro: come e perché,"* in *Conquiste del lavoro* (Rome: CISL, December 18-25, 1978.

18. See D. Mirone, "Profili e dinamica del mercato speciale e atipico del lavoro," in *Rivista di Politica Economica,* Rome, August-September 1978, pp. 1141-42.

19. R. Kaltzmann, *"Le travail noir,"* in *Futuribles 2000,* September 1979.

20. Statement by L. Stoleru, Secretary of State for Manual Workers and Immigrants, published in *Le Point,* April 25, 1977, p. 76.

21. C. Merzagora and U. La Malfa, reported in *24 Heures,* Lausanne, February 20, 1979.

22. Confederazione generale dell'industria italiana, *Una politica per l'occupazione* Rome, 1978, p. 23.

23. See J. Ferrier, *"Paradoxe italien: la lire résiste bien à la crise gouvernementale,"* in *Tribune de Genève,* February 23, 1978, p. 29.

24. Quoted by M. Roy, *"Le travail noir,"* in *Le Point,* November 12, 1979, pp. 77 and 79.

25. T. Picault, *"L'emploi informel, ou le bon usage de la crise,"* in *Le Monde Dimanche,* February 3, 1980, p. xiii.

26. F. Ferrarotti, Professor of Sociology, University of Rome, cited in *Newsweek,* May 15, 1978, and *Tribune de Genève,* October 27, 1977.

27. N. Cacace, *"Ma attenti a non finire nel Terzo mondo,"* in *L'Espresso,* July 29, 1979, p. 95.

28. The Commission of the European Communities has commissioned a study on marginal employment in Italy, is presently conducting a comparative study on clandestine work in Italy and the United Kingdom, and is planning to carry out a survey of such work in the manufacturing industries of its member states. It has also submitted to the Council of Ministers a proposal for a Council directive concerning the harmonization of the legislation of member states in order to combat illegal migration and illegal employment (Brussels, 1978), doc. COM(78) 86 final.

29. The Organization for Economic Cooperation and Development has published a report on illegal and undeclared employment in Italy by Professor P. Pettinati (Paris, 1979), doc. MAS/WP7 (79) 6.

30. The Third European Regional Conference of the ILO (Geneva, October 1979) adopted a resolution concerning the improvement of working conditions and the working environment in Europe, which, inter alia, recommended (paragraph 12) that "measures should be considered with a view to . . . eliminating moonlighting" (see *Provisional Record* No. 14, p. 20). In addition, a recent technical meeting for the leather and footwear industry adopted a resolution calling for a study of the various forms of clandestine labor by a meeting of experts drawn from government, employer, and worker circles; the same resolution also called on the ILO to prepare, on the basis of that study, a report on the relevant law and practice in member countries with a view to placing the question on the agenda of a future session of the International Labor Conference. See ILO: *Note on the Proceedings,* Second Tripartite Technical Meeting for the Leather and Footwear Industry, Geneva, December 1979 (Geneva, 1980), doc. LFI/2/1979/17, p. 62.

**Part II
The Underground Economy in
the United States**

3 America's Underground Economy

Barry Molefsky

A Perspective on the Underground Economy

For a variety of reasons the U.S. government collects information on the economy and requires the reporting of certain data. There are, however, a number of activities that occur outside the government's purview. The income generated by these activities is generally not reported for tax purposes or for the determination of public assistance, social insurance, or other income security benefits. In addition, these activities may be only partially reflected in official economic data. Such activities have been described as constituting an underground economy.[1]

Underground economic activity is not confined to the United States but is apparently a world-wide phenomenon. Reportedly, in Hungary "two out of three workers supplement their income" in a "flourishing" unofficial second economy.[2] French authorities have been driven to launch an advertising campaign to discourage participation in what is dubbed *le travail noir*—moonlighting.[3]

Most Americans participate, knowingly or unknowingly, as either buyers or sellers, in the underground economy. Anyone who has bought or sold anything at a garage sale, hired a teenager to shovel snow, mow the lawn, or babysit, is undoubtedly part of the underground economy. Instances of underground activity are constantly turning up. Recently, the *Wall Street Journal* reported that a black market in computer time had developed at the University of Chicago business school.[4] Press reports also indicate that some owners of single-family homes have illegally converted spare rooms into rental units.[5]

This is not a new phenomenon; sociologists have been aware of it for years. Undoubtedly, throughout history individuals have attempted to avoid paying taxes and to circumvent government regulations or statutes. During the twentieth century there have been at least two periods in the United States when underground activity was seemingly pervasive: Prohibition and World War II.

Reliable information on Prohibition is scarce. An analysis of its economic effects prepared in 1932 indicates that expenditures for alcoholic beverages was about $5 billion in 1929 and approximately $4 billion in 1930. This, it was estimated, was about equal to what spending would have been in the absence of prohibition—roughly 5 percent of the U.S. gross national product.[6]

Much more information is available on the World War II period.[7] After the United States entered the war the federal government imposed an extensive system of price controls and rationing. Ceilings were established for nearly all commodity prices and rents. Over six hundred price and rent regulations covering more than eight million items and controlling the distribution of essential products were issued by the Office of Price Administration (OPA). The reasons for introducing price controls and rationing were to ensure that adequate supplies were available for the war effort and that there was an equitable distribution of goods and services among the civilian population.

Reportedly, violations of the controls began to occur almost immediately. Between 1942 and 1947 the OPA conducted over a million investigations of violations. These infractions were apparently widespread and evident among all segments of society. Violations ranged from theft and counterfeiting of ration coupons to short-weighing, tie-in sales, and falsifying records. In 1943 the Department of Agriculture estimated that 20 percent of the U.S. meat supply was being sold on the black market. It was also estimated that roughly 5 percent of all gasoline was being sold illegally. Extensive violations of price control and rationing regulations were accompanied by widespread tax evasion. Taxes owed the federal government, but evaded, amounted to several billion dollars by the end of the war.

Facilitating the large-scale price control violations was the increased use of cash. During World War II there was an unprecedented rise in the amount of currency in circulation. Between 1941 and 1945 currency held by the public rose from $8.4 billion to $25.3 billion. The ratio of currency to the gross national product increased from 6.7 percent to 11.9 percent. A disproportionate amount of that growth was in large-denomination bills. In 1945 $50 and $100 bills accounted for 23 percent of outstanding currency compared with 18 percent before the war. The proportion of $10 and $20 bills also increased while that of $1, $2, and $5 bills and coins decreased.[8]

Some portion of the increase in outstanding cash can be attributed to higher prices, higher wages, and savings from legal income. With interest rates pegged at artificially low levels there was little financial penalty in holding savings in the form of currency rather than investing in financial instruments or time deposits. But these factors cannot account for all of the growth in currency.

In 1958 Phillip Cagan estimated that, at the end of World War II, currency outstanding in excess of normal, legitimate needs was nearly $13 billion, an amount associated with unreported income of $21 billion to $25 billion, or 12.4 percent to 14.7 percent of reported personal income.[9]

How Large is the Underground Economy Today?

Because participants in the underground economy make an effort to hide their actions the underground economy cannot be directly measured. Evidence of

the existence, size, and growth of underground activity is primarily cir-
cumstantial and anecdotal.

Nevertheless, a variety of estimates of the magnitude of underground
economic activity today have been made. These estimates range from
several billion dollars to several hundred billion. This variation is due to differing definitions—there is no generally accepted definition of what constitutes the underground economy—and vastly different procedures for
measuring such activity.

Activities associated with the underground economy can be grouped
into three categories:

1. Traditional criminal enterprises such as narcotics, loan-sharking,
    bookmaking, and prostitution. No attempt is made to explicitly include
    the value of such activity in official economic statistics;
2. Legally earned income which is not reported to the tax authorities, such
    as off-the-books employment and skimming. Such income should be
    included in economic data;
3. Organized noncash transactions, such as bartering through exchanges,
    which should probably be included in economic statistics.

There are two methods which can be used to measure the underground
economy. The first involves estimating the amount of each type of activity and
aggregating those estimates to arrive at an overall total. This requires that all
types of underground activity be accurately identified and measured. Failure
to include a particular activity or measuring an activity inaccurately will produce an erroneous total. The alternative method is to estimate the overall size
of the underground economy without attempting to measure individual
underground activities. An estimate can be derived by looking for discrepancies and discontinuities in published data on macroeconomic activity. Most
estimates of the underground economy use the latter approach.

There is a strong possibility that some underground activity is unknowingly included in the National Income and Product Accounts (NIPA),
which provides basic information on the country's economic performance
and includes indicators such as gross national product (GNP) and personal
income. If goods produced in the regular or official economy are consumed
as part of an underground transaction, the value of those goods will
undoubtedly be in the GNP; the value added that results from the
underground activity will most likely be omitted. For example, if a
homeowner contracts to have his house painted outside the regular
economy, the paint and other materials purchased will be in the GNP; the
value of the labor will not.

Inclusion of goods produced in the regular economy but consumed as
part of an underground transaction results from the Bureau of Economic

Analysis (BEA) "commodity-flow" technique. Under this procedure BEA estimates final demand for a manufactured good by adding transportation, wholesale, and retail markups to the value of the good reported by the producer.

One method of determining the extent of underground activity which may be included in the NIPA is to examine the statistics on personal income. For the most part, personal income is estimated by the BEA independently from the income statistics tabulated by the Internal Revenue Service (IRS) from individual income tax returns. Thus, the BEA's statistics can be used as a check on the IRS statistics of individual income. The two agencies, however, use substantially different definitions of income.[10]

BEA has prepared studies adjusting its personal income data to the IRS definition of adjusted gross income (AGI). These reconciliations show the BEA income series to be significantly higher than the IRS figures (table 3-1). This discrepancy can be considered income earned but not reported for tax purposes and therefore a measure of underground economic activity.

It is estimated that in 1978, the latest year for which data are available, unreported income totaling about $100 billion had been earned (table 3-1).[11] This represented nearly 8 percent of AGI reported by IRS and equal to about 5 percent of personal income. Since 1947, estimated unreported income has increased at an annual rate of 4.9 percent compared with a growth rate of 7.2 percent for AGI and 7.4 percent for personal income. Thus, unreported income has been declining as a proportion of both the AGI and personal income.[12]

BEA's estimate of unreported income is substantially greater than the amounts uncovered by IRS audits. For example, in tax year 1973 (returns filed in 1974) the IRS Taxpayer Compliance Measurement Program (TCMP) found that underreported income totaled $28.4 billion, compared with BEA's figure of $73.9 billion. The IRS figure does not include income earned by individuals required to file income tax returns but who failed to do so. In a recent report, the General Accounting Office (GAO) estimated that nonfiler taxable income in tax year 1972 totaled between $26 billion and $35 billion.[13]

If the data compiled by BEA represented the entire underground economy, this activity would constitute a considerable tax enforcement problem, but it would not seriously affect economic policymaking. However, it clearly does not represent the entire underground economy. This can be seen from the method used by BEA to estimate private nonfarm wages and salaries, a major component of personal income. This estimate is based on information supplied by state employment agencies, which adminster the unemployment insurance program, and the Social Security Administration. Thus, BEA relies upon what employers report to the government, not on what employees report. If, however, an employer does

Table 3-1
Adjusted Gross Income
(billions of dollars)

	Estimated by the Bureau of Economic Analysis (BEA)	Reported to the Internal Revenue Service (IRS)	Difference between BEA and IRS
1947	172.7	149.7	23.0
1948	186.7	163.5	23.1
1949	184.0	160.6	23.4
1950	202.7	179.1	23.6
1951	229.2	202.3	26.9
1952	241.9	215.3	26.6
1953	256.7	228.7	28.0
1954	254.9	229.2	25.7
1955	275.0	248.5	26.5
1956	295.5	267.7	27.7
1957	308.1	280.3	27.7
1958	312.8	281.2	31.6
1959	336.2	305.1	31.0
1960	348.1	315.5	32.7
1961	360.6	329.9	30.8
1962	380.7	348.7	32.0
1963	400.8	368.8	32.0
1964	434.0	396.7	37.3
1965	467.3	429.2	38.1
1966	512.9	468.5	44.4
1967	546.2	504.8	41.4
1968	599.9	554.4	45.5
1969	652.7	603.5	49.2
1970	686.0	631.7	54.3
1971	730.3	673.6	56.7
1972	804.8	746.0	58.8
1973	901.0	827.1	73.9
1974	978.4	905.5	72.9
1975	1,019.4	947.8	71.7
1976	1,132.0	1,053.9	78.1
1977	1,249.9	1,158.5	91.0
1978	1,404.6	1,304.2	100.4

Source: U.S. Department of Commerce, Bureau of Economic Analysis.

not report wage and salary payments, this income will not be measured by BEA. Income of workers who are completely off the books will most likely be omitted from the official statistics. This type of activity probably represents a substantial portion of the underground economy.

There is said to be some sentiment at the BEA that unreported income is somewhat higher than estimated.[14] Unofficial estimates of the underground economy have tended to be higher than the BEA's unreported income figure.

Probably the most widely quoted estimate of the size of the underground economy is that prepared by Peter Gutmann. In late 1977 he made the startling assertion that the underground economy amounted to $176 billion, equal to about 10 percent of the nation's reported GNP.[15] This level of activity exceeded the value of merchandise exported by the United States in 1976.

Gutmann's estimate is based upon the relationship between currency in circulation (cash) and demand deposits (checking accounts). Since 1961, currency in circulation has been rising more rapidly than demand deposits, reversing a long-term trend. The only other interruptions in that trend occurred during financial panics and wars, most notably during World War II. Considering the movement towards a "cashless" or "credit" society, this reversal is somewhat surprising. Gutmann attributes the rising use of cash to the requirements of the underground economy which uses currency to escape detection.

To calculate the size of underground activity, Gutmann made several assumptions regarding the use of cash. First, it was assumed that no underground activity existed during the 1937-1941 period. It was during those years that the ratio of cash to checking accounts was lowest. Second, the amount of cash needed for legal transactions today is assumed to be the same proportion of checking accounts as in 1937-1941. Cash in excess of this amount is considered to be used for underground activity. A third assumption is that the volume of GNP supported by currency and checking accounts is the same for both reported and underground activities.

It should be recognized that to a certain extent Gutmann's first assumption introduces a downward bias into his estimate. If there was underground activity during the 1937-1941 period then this estimate of such activity today is too low. One way of looking at Gutmann's estimate is to conclude that underground activity in 1976 was $176 billion higher than it would have been if the relation of money to GNP had been the same as it was during the prewar years.

Several criticisms have been made of Gutmann's approach. It has been noted that the ratio of cash to time deposits (savings accounts) has declined steadily. It has therefore been suggested that checking accounts have been growing too slowly rather than cash too rapidly.[16] Attempts to explain this shortfall in demand deposit growth have been unsuccessful.[17] It has also been suggested that if cash and checking accounts are adjusted for changes in the number of times they are used, the ratio of cash to demand deposits has not increased but has in fact declined.[18] Moreover, one paper has demonstrated that the rise in currency can be explained by changes in income, consumption, and interest rates.[19] It can also be argued that estimates of unreported income and imputed income should be excluded from the GNP before computing the underground economy.[20]

A potentially serious source of error in Gutmann's method concerns U.S. currency outside the country. An unknown quantity of dollars is in the hands of foreigners and not readily available for domestic use (see chapter 6, this volume). Therefore, the ratio of currency in circulation to demand deposits may actually be lower than indicated by the published data. As a consequence, the calculated size of the underground economy may be too high.

Furthermore, a recent Federal Reserve Board staff paper discussing the definitions used in tabulating monetary statistics indicated that innovations such as automatic transfers from checking to savings accounts and NOW accounts raise questions about the validity of comparisons over time of calculations such as the ratio of demand deposits to GNP.[21]

One advantage of Gutmann's method is that it does permit calculation of a time series of underground economic activity. Table 3-2 shows underground gross national product (UGNP) calculated on the basis of Gutmann's methodology, along with reported gross national product (GNP) for the 1948-1980 period. Over this thirty-two-year period the underground economy derived from Gutmann's formula has risen at a 10.0 percent annual rate compared with a 7.5 percent growth rate for reported GNP. Since 1972 growth of Gutmann's UGNP has been extremely rapid, advancing by about 23 percent a year as opposed to the 10 percent annual growth in GNP. During the 1948-1972 period the official economy grew at a slightly more rapid pace than did the underground economy. As a result, UGNP from Gutmann's formula has increased from about 6 percent of GNP to over 14 percent. Figure 3-1 presents underground GNP as a proportion of reported GNP for the past twenty years.

It should be noted that although the rate of growth in Gutmann's UGNP has been much faster than reported activity since 1972, in absolute dollar terms GNP has increased much more. Between 1975 and 1980 UGNP calculated from Gutmann's formula increased by $220 billion; this was about equal to the increase in GNP between 1978 and 1980.

One curious aspect of the behavior of this computation of UGNP is that before the 1970s a slowdown in the reported GNP was accompanied by a slowing of underground activity as well. For example, in 1958, a recession year, when the GNP growth rate slowed to 1.3 percent from over 5 percent the preceding year, Gutmann's UGNP declined by 20.6 percent. It might be expected that during periods of economic contraction, such as 1958, individuals would attempt to alleviate hardship by seeking income outside the regular economy, that is, by going underground. This can be seen in the BEA's data on unreported income. The BEA reports that in 1958 unreported income totaled $31.6 billion, up 14 percent from the 1957 level of $27.7 billion.

A basic premise of much of the work done on estimating the underground economy is that it primarily involves cash transactions. This is challenged by Edgar Feige.[22] He has prepared an estimate of the underground economy using a method somewhat similar to that developed by Gutmann. Like Gutmann's estimate, Feige's calculations are affected by

Table 3-2
Gross National Product
(billions of dollars)

	Official	*Underground*[a]
1948	259.5	17.6
1949	258.3	16.0
1950	286.5	13.4
1951	330.8	14.9
1952	348.0	15.3
1953	366.8	17.3
1954	366.8	13.2
1955	400.0	13.8
1956	421.7	14.7
1957	444.0	17.0
1958	449.7	13.5
1959	487.9	16.0
1960	506.5	16.2
1961	524.6	15.0
1962	565.0	18.3
1963	596.7	23.0
1964	637.7	26.4
1965	691.1	31.0
1966	756.0	40.1
1967	799.6	39.8
1968	873.4	43.2
1969	944.0	54.0
1970	992.7	61.1
1971	1,077.6	67.7
1972	1,185.9	71.1
1973	1,326.4	90.3
1974	1,434.2	123.5
1975	1,549.2	154.8
1976	1,718.0	188.7
1977	1,918.1	224.8
1978	2,156.1	267.5
1979	2,413.9	315.2
1980	2,626.1	374.8

Source: Reported GNP is from the U.S. Department of Commerce, Bureau of Economic Analysis. Underground GNP is calculated from data published by the U.S. Department of Commerce, Bureau of Economic Analysis and Board of Governors of the Federal Reserve System.

[a]Computed by the Congressional Research Service using methodology developed by Peter Gutmann. Gutmann's methodology can be expressed by the formula:

$$UGNP_t = \frac{GNP_t}{DD_t * 1.217} (M_t - DD_t * 1.217)$$

where:
GNP_t = reported gross national product
DD_t = demand deposits
M_t = narrowly defined money supply
$UGNP_t$ = underground gross national product

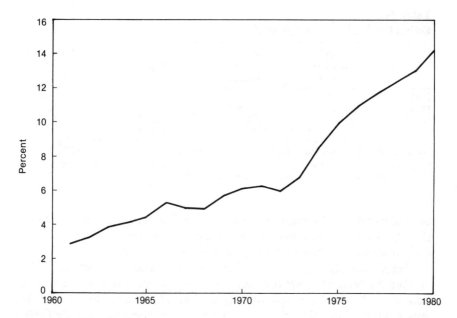

Source: U.S. Department of Commerce, Bureau of Economic Analysis; Board of Governors, Federal Reserve System.

Figure 3-1. Underground GNP as a Percentage of Reported GNP

changes in the relationship between GNP and monetary data, and currency held outside the United States.

Feige measures the underground economy by calculating the ratio of total transactions in the economy to GNP for 1939, 1976, and 1978. Total transactions is defined as the volume of checking transactions (demand deposits times the average turnover of those deposits)[23] plus the volume of currency transactions (currency in circulation times the average turnover of currency).[24] Feige finds that over time that ratio has been rising. In 1939 total transactions were 10.30 times reported GNP, by 1976 this had risen to 11.66 times, and rose to 12.95 times in 1978. Feige assumes there was no underground activity in 1939 and reasons that the volume of transactions in the economy today should bear the same relationship to GNP as in 1939; he attributes increases in that ratio to underground activity. Feige obtains an estimate of the underground economy in 1976 and 1978 by dividing the volume of transactions in these years by the 1939 ratio of transactions to GNP and subtracting reported GNP from that product.

These calculations, presented in table 3-3, indicate that in 1978 underground economic activity totaled $542 billion, or roughly 27 percent of reported GNP. In 1976 underground GNP is calculated by Feige at $226

Table 3-3
Estimated Underground Activity

	Total Transactions ($ billion)	Reported GNP ($ billion)	Transactions to GNP Ratio	Underground GNP[a] ($ billion)
1939	943.9	90.8	10.30	—
1976	19,899.4	1,706.5	11.66	225.5
1978	27,277.9	2,106.6	12.95	541.7

Source: Feige, Edgar L. *The Irregular Economy: Its Size and Macroeconomic Implications.* Social Systems Research Institute, University of Wisconsin at Madison, May 1979, p. 13.
[a]Computed by dividing total transactions (column 1) by the Transactions to GNP Ratio for 1939 (10.30) and subtracting reported GNP (column 2).

billion, equal to 19 percent of reported GNP.[25] Feige's calculations suggest that the underground economy has grown at an extraordinarily rapid rate. Cash transactions, however, play a minor role in this growth.

Feige suggests that only $21.7 trillion in transactions were needed to achieve the level of GNP officially recorded in 1978. But actual transactions according to his calculations totaled $27.3 trillion. Thus, there were excess transactions of $5.6 trillion. All currency transactions using Feige's method would have totaled roughly $2.0 trillion. Even if it is assumed that all currency usage was for underground activity, cash would account for only 37 percent of the excess transactions. Demand deposit transactions of $3.5 trillion, representing 14 percent of all demand deposit transactions, would have to account for the remainder of the excess transactions. While it is possible that some portion of underground activity is conducted using checks, it is questionable whether such a large proportion of demand deposit transactions is related to the underground economy.

A more serious objection to Feige's method is contained in a February 1981 research report prepared by Wertheim and Co., Inc., a New York-based securities firm. Using Feige's method, Wertheim calculated the size of the underground economy for every year since 1939. These computations show that before 1969 the size of the underground economy was negative.[26]

Another estimate of underground activity has recently been prepared by Vito Tanzi.[27] Tanzi first develops a model to explain the behavior of the ratio of currency to money supply ($M2$). This model explicitly includes a measure of tax rates. The model was tested using data for the 1929-1976 period and was found to have a high degree of explanatory power.

Tanzi reasons that if underground economic activity is entirely conducted in cash and is due to tax evasion then changing the tax rate variable in the model should provide an estimate of the amount of currency associated with underground activity. This currency figure can then be used to determine underground GNP, assuming that the ratio of excess currency to underground GNP is the same as the ratio of legally used money to reported GNP.

Two different estimates of the underground economy in 1976 were produced. The first estimate shows the size of underground GNP resulting from the increase in tax rates during the past fifty years. This implies that there has always been underground activity which has been aggravated by steadily rising tax rates. The second estimate measures total underground activity associated with 1976 tax rates.

The model found that the rise in tax rates between 1929 and 1976 resulted in an increase in the underground GNP of between $58 billion and $86 billion, or between 3.4 percent and 5.1 percent of reported GNP. Total underground GNP in 1976 was found to be between $138 billion and $199 billion, or 8.1 percent and 11.7 percent of reported GNP.

Several other estimates of underground activity have been made; the most notable of these was that prepared by IRS. In 1979, IRS published a study indicating that in 1976 between $75 billion and $100 billion in legally earned income and $25 billion to $35 billion in illegal-source income had not been reported for tax purposes.[28] A breakdown of unreported income, by type of income, is presented in table 3-4. These figures are not, however, comparable to the measures of underground transactions discussed earlier. IRS is measuring unreported income which includes income, such as capital gains, omitted from the GNP accounts. In addition, for certain types of income, particularly interest and dividends, the IRS estimate is based on the BEA reconciliation of personal income discussed above. Thus, a considerable proportion of the unreported taxable income is in the reported GNP. Other sources used by IRS were the TCMP, the Exact Match File, and the Consumer Expenditure Survey (CES).

Use of the CES is perhaps the most interesting aspect of the IRS report. The CES is a comprehensive study of household purchasing patterns, last conducted in 1972-73, which is used to construct the consumer price index. IRS examined a large number of expenditure items and estimated the proportion of spending channeled to informal, or underground, suppliers. For example, it estimated that 25 percent of consumer spending for private lessons was "paid in informal arrangements." Using this method IRS determined that, depending on its size, in 1976 the average family paid informal suppliers between $242 and $637, for an aggregate amount of roughly $33 billion.[29]

The Underground Labor Force

While considerable attention has been focused on the dollar volume of the underground economy, such activity may have serious implications for what is perhaps the most politically sensitive economic indicator; the unemployment rate.

Table 3-4
Internal Revenue Service Estimates of Unreported Income
(billions of dollars)

Type of Income	Lower Estimate	Higher Estimate
Legal Source Income:		
Self-employment	33.0	39.5
Wages and salaries	21.3	26.8
Interest	5.4	9.4
Dividend	2.1	4.7
Rents and royalties	3.2	5.9
Pensions, annuities, estates, and trusts	3.6	5.4
Capital gains	3.9	5.1
Other[a]	2.3	2.9
Subtotal	74.9	99.7
Illegal Source Income:		
Illegal drugs	16.2	23.6
Bookmaking	4.0	5.0
Numbers	2.4	3.0
Other gambling	1.6	2.0
Prostitution	1.1	1.6
Subtotal	25.3	35.2
Total	100.2	134.9

Source: Internal Revenue Service, *Estimates of Income Unreported on Individual Income Tax Returns*, Publication 1104 (Washington, D.C.: Government Printing Office, September 1979), pp. 7 and 17.

Data on the size and composition of the labor force are obtained through surveys of households. Since 1940 the Bureau of the Census has conducted a monthly survey of households called the Current Population Survey (CPS). Interviews are conducted at 56,000 households to determine the employment activity of household members.

Individuals are counted as being employed if, during the week the CPS is taken, they did any work as either a paid employee, or in their own business, profession, or farm, or worked fifteen or more hours as an unpaid worker in a family-operated business. Persons are also considered employed if they had a job but were temporarily absent due to illness, vacation, or a labor-management dispute. Individuals are considered to be unemployed if they have been actively seeking paid employment. The labor force represents the sum of employed and unemployed individuals.

In responding to inquiries from census enumerators would participants in the underground economy acknowledge their work activity?

If underground workers do not report that they are employed, there could be significant errors in the labor force data, particularly the unemployment rate, which could result in inappropriate policy decisions on the part of Congress and the executive branch. Whether or not underground workers are counted as employed may depend on a number of factors. An individual working in the regular, official economy with a second underground job need only acknowledge his regular employment to be counted as employed. Workers with two jobs in the regular economy are only counted once in the employment data. Individuals whose only employment is in the underground economy might say that they are employed or self-employed since no questions are asked regarding place or nature of employment. For example, a study by the Internal Revenue Service found that 47 percent of the workers classified as independent contractors did not report any of their earnings for income tax purposes. Twenty-two percent of those independent contractors considered professional workers failed to report any of their compensation.[30] These individuals are obviously part of the underground economy. But many of them are also established businessmen and if asked about their employment status would probably say that they were self-employed. Those who are collecting benefits under various government programs and who have underground jobs might be reluctant to admit their employment. It should be noted that less than half the unemployed collect unemployment benefits.

In a 1978 paper Louise Berndt argued that because of the way labor force data are collected, figures on employment probably include workers engaged in underground or irregular activities.

> Theoretically the CPS estimates of employment should classify irregular workers as employed. No questions are asked regarding unemployment insurance payment, AFDC, social security, disability or any income received other than through the job. Unless we assume a substantially greater degree of caution with respect to reporting irregular work than our own research leads us to expect, we can assume that many, if not most, irregular workers *are* counted as employed by the CPS.[31]

Berndt's thesis may be supported by the sharp rise in the number of self-employed workers. In 1980 6.85 million individuals were classified as self-employed, 3.0 percent higher than in the previous year. Total employment rose by only 0.3 percent in 1980. Since 1970 the number of self-employed persons has expanded by over 31 percent, compared with a 24 percent rise in total employment. Moreover, there has been a substantial increase in the number of persons holding a nonagricultural wage or salary job who moonlight in their own business. Since 1970 the number of such multiple-job holders has increased by more than 45 percent. Presumably, the self-employed have greater opportunities to hide income and participate in the underground economy than do other workers.

According to Berndt, "it is quite possible for a person to be 'officially' unemployed, and collecting unemployment insurance on the insured unemployment series and employed working 40 hours a week on the CPS."

Peter Gutmann takes a different view. In discussing the reliance on the CPS to measure employment he observes:

> The government naively takes for granted that the questions are answered with the gospel truth. But there is a great deal of incentive to do otherwise. Put bluntly, plenty of respondents lie; they lie consistently, and they lie with good reason. Will someone collecting unemployment insurance—but also working "off the books," paid in cash in the subterranean economy—tell the Census interviewer that he is, in fact employed? Of course not. He knows that what he is doing is illegal. Will someone collecting welfare benefits, who has been required to register for employment as a condition for receiving such benefits, tell the Census interviewer that he is, in fact, not looking for work? Of course not. He knows that he is supposed to be tossed out of the program if he fails to look for work.[32]

In another paper Gutmann attempts to quantify the underground labor force. He notes that between 1951 and 1976 the male labor force participation rate declined from 86.5 to 77.5 percent and that participation rates among the prime working age groups declined over the 1961-1977 period. The participation rate of men 25-34 years of age dropped to 95.4 from 97.5 percent and in the 35-44 age group the rate fell from 97.6 to 95.7 percent. "Where did all these men go? . . . A large percentage of those who left the labor force did not just disappear: They went 'off the books,' being paid in cash without intercession of the tax collector . . . they constitute the permanent core of the subterranean economy."[33]

The cause of the decline in male labor force participation rates is a mystery. An article by a Bureau of Labor Statistics analyst attributes the falloff to illness or disability. About 45 percent of men in the 25-54 age group who were not in the labor force in 1976 reportedly left their last job because of illness. In addition, it was suggested that the increase in the number of working wives permits men to drop out of the labor force. But these explanations are not considered conclusive.[34]

To estimate the number of persons outside the labor force who participate in the underground economy, Gutmann applies the 2 percent decline in the participation rate of men in the prime age groups to the total reported labor force of 98.87 million in April 1978. This calculation produces a figure of 1.98 million persons who, according to Gutmann, "work on a full or part-time basis exclusively in the subterranean sector, while they are officially not in the labor force at all." These individuals, however, according to Gutmann, account for only 85 percent of the underground labor force. The remaining 15 percent, Gutmann claims, are those classified as unemployed who are actually working. This assumption means that the underground labor force totaled 2.35 million in April 1978.[35]

This method, however, is unsatisfactory. Gutmann offers no justification for his assumption that the 2 percent decline in labor force participation by prime working age males is representative of all demographic groups. He is implying that the reported participation of all age groups, of both sexes, is 2 percent too low. This also implies that the underground labor force has the same demographic characteristics as the reported labor force.

Moreover, if Gutmann's estimate of the underground labor force is correct, his estimate of underground GNP cannot be accurate. Gutmann estimates that in 1978 underground GNP was well over $200 billion. The underground labor force of just over 2 million workers was, therefore, extremely productive: each worker produced goods and services valued at more than $100,000. By comparison, official data show output per worker at about $22,000.

Gutmann's method also suggests that the underground economy has a permanent work force. This notion is contradicted, to some extent, by a study of irregular economic activity in Detroit. Case histories presented in that study suggest that in many instances work in the underground economy is temporary, and only intended to supplement regular income during periods of hardship, not to substitute for regular employment.[36]

It is apparent from the preceding discussion that there is no firm evidence as to whether the official labor force data includes individuals participating in the underground economy. Some portion of the underground labor force is undoubtedly counted; how large a proportion is an open question.

Why Is There an Underground Economy Today?

Three reasons are generally cited as explanations for participation in the underground economy: to evade taxes; to avoid losing government benefits; and to circumvent regulations and licensing requirements.

1. The interaction between inflation and the progressive federal income tax system is frequently blamed for spurring underground activity. As nominal incomes rise with inflation, taxpayers are pushed into higher marginal tax brackets. According to Treasury Department figures, illustrated in the bottom panel of figure 3-2, for a family of four earning the median family income, the marginal tax rate has increased from 17 percent in 1965 to 24 percent in 1980 and could rise to 28 percent in 1981.[37] Thus, effective tax rates rise even though there may have been no gain in real gross income, and real after-tax income is squeezed. For some taxpayers, cheating the taxman by hiding income or engaging in barter may become necessary to avoid a decline in living standards.

This does not necessarily mean that a reduction in tax rates will eradicate the underground economy. Participants in the underground economy enjoy an effective marginal tax rate of zero percent. Lowering statutory rates by a few percentage points is unlikely to provide much of an incentive for these people to report their incomes. At best, a tax cut would reduce the incentive for new people to join the underground labor force.

It should also be recognized that not all participants in the underground economy owe taxes. According to a report by the General Accounting Office, many people who do not file income tax returns have incomes so low that they do not have any federal income tax liability.[38] In fact, the government probably owes them money because of the earned income credit.

Some have argued that the onerous burden of income and payroll taxes, which gives rise to underground activity, can be relieved by reducing those levies and imposing a value-added tax (VAT).[39] European experience with the VAT does not, however, support this view. Large and thriving underground economies exist in all of the West European countries where the VAT is imposed. Moreover, a March 1981 study by the General Accounting Office warns, "The ordinary VAT is about as vulnerable to evasion and avoidance as most other taxes." Evasion can be abetted by means such as collusion between buyers and sellers and false invoicing. The combination of an income tax and a VAT "offers evaders increased rewards for their evasion." For small businessmen who routinely fail to report, or underreport, their income, "registering for a VAT would reveal their income tax evasion. Failure to register could enable them to collect the VAT and keep it for themselves or to increase their business by giving their customers a discount equal to the VAT."[40]

2. Eligibility and benefit levels for many government income security programs are based on a means test. If incomes exceed a specific level then individuals may no longer receive all or part of their benefits. For example, social security recipients between 65 and 72 years of age lose 50 cents in benefits for every dollar in earned income over $5,500. This amounts to an extremely harsh tax or penalty on beneficiaries and encourages underground activity. In 1977, the latest year for which statistics are available, 1.2 million social security beneficiaries, or 12 percent of those affected by the earnings test lost all or part of their benefits.[41] This is probably the tip of the iceberg. As Peter Drucker has observed, "A large number of those officially 'retired' do work, only they know better than to tell Uncle Sam about it, lest they lose many of their Social Security benefits."[42]

3. In many jurisdictions the practice of certain occupations requires licenses or other types of permits. These requirements, however, may tend to artificially reduce the supply of some goods and services. Unlicensed individuals may try to fill any gaps. In New York City, for example, a shortage of medallioned taxis in slum areas produced a large fleet of so-called gypsy

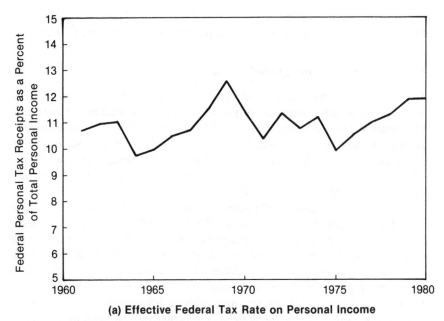

(a) Effective Federal Tax Rate on Personal Income

Source: U.S. Department of Commerce

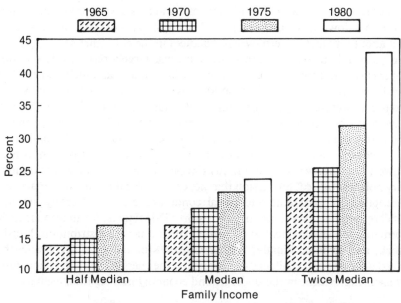

(b) Marginal Income Tax Rates for Four-Person Families

Source: U.S. Department of the Treasury

Figure 3-2. Personal Tax Burden

cabs to provide service in the affected communities. Operators of such unlicensed businesses undoubtedly have the opportunity to conceal earnings.

Congress and the Underground Economy

Congressional interest in the underground economy has tended to wax and wane in recent years. Between July and November 1979 three committees—the House Ways and Means Subcommittee on Oversight, the House Government Operations Subcommittee on Commerce, Consumer, and Monetary Affairs, and the Joint Economic Committee—held hearings on the subject. These hearings tended to focus on IRS tax enforcement procedures. No hearings have been held since late 1979.

Numerous bills that would affect the underground economy have been introduced in the current Congress. These include measures prohibiting firms from hiring illegal aliens, changing the minimum wage, removing the social security earnings test, and withdrawing $100 notes from circulation.

Congress has not, however, addressed the broader questions raised by a large and growing underground economy. An active, expanding underground economy can present serious problems for economic policymakers. Data purporting to show the state of the economy will actually provide a misleading picture of existing conditions. An example of this may have occurred in 1978 and 1979. At that time many analysts were predicting that an economic downturn was imminent. They also expected such a recession to last about a year. Concern over imbalances in the consumer sector, particularly a sizable increase in consumer debt, was largely responsible for those forecasts. The recession occurred much later and was much shorter than predicted. Because of underground activity consumer incomes may have been considerably higher than reported, thus consumer ability to take on new debt obligations may have been greater than believed, accounting for the actual course of events and misleading forecasters and policymakers.

Underground activity can have a serious impact on areas such as manpower, housing, welfare, and industrial policies as well as fiscal and monetary policies. Indeed, any action that depends on reliable statistics or accurate perceptions of economic and social conditions can be adversely affected. Underground activity does not just distort GNP figures; it can also affect information on employment and unemployment, income distribution, housing stock, and savings. Finally, neither Congress or the executive branch has faced up to the real challenge of channeling the energies, initiative, and entrepreneurship evident in the underground economy into legitimate enterprises.

Notes

1. A great many terms have been used to describe the underground economy, including hidden, black, irregular, informal, and subterranean.

2. *Wall Street Journal*, June 6, 1979, p. 1.

3. *Economist*, May 5, 1979, p. 95.

4. John Curley, "MBA Students Learn the Cost of Education," *Wall Street Journal*, May 18, 1981, p. 36.

5. For example, see Nancy Zeldis, "City Has Hidden Rental Market," *Alexandria Journal*, May 22, 1981, p. 1. Also see "Economic Diary," *Business Week*, April 20, 1981, p. 16.

6. Clark Warburton, *The Economic Results of Prohibition* (New York: Columbia University Press, 1932).

7. The discussion of World War II presented here is primarily based on Marshall Clinard, *The Black Market: A Study of White Collar Crime* (Montclair, N.J.: Patterson Smith, 1969).

8. "Changes in Currency Circulation," *Monthly Review*, Federal Reserve Bank of New York, March 1948, pp. 27-28.

9. Phillip Cagan, "The Demand for Currency Relative to Total Money Supply," National Bureau of Economic Research Occasional Paper 62, 1958, p. 12.

10. BEA defines personal income as the income received by all persons from all sources. It is the sum of wage and salary disbursements, other labor income (such as employer contributions to private pension, health, and welfare funds), proprietors' income, rental income, dividends, interest income, and transfer payments less personal contributions for social insurance. IRS defines adjusted gross income (AGI) as gross income from all sources subject to tax less certain deductions. Gross income subject to tax includes specified items of money income: net business and farm income; net capital gains income; and other items. Deductions allowed in the calculation of AGI include various expenses considered necessary in earning income, certain allowances for capital gains and losses, contributions to retirement funds by the self-emloyed, a portion of sick pay and other items. See Stephen C. Lehman, "Relationship Between Personal Income and Taxable Income, 1947-74." *Survey of Current Business*, Dec. 1979, p. 17.

11. This includes some income not reported to IRS because it is earned by individuals whose income is below the filing requirement level.

12. Lehman, "Personal Income and Taxable Income," p. 18, and unpublished data from the Bureau of Economic Analysis.

13. U.S. General Accounting Office, "Who's Not Filing Income Tax Returns?" Report to the Congress of the United States by the Comptroller General, July 11, 1979, p. 5.

14. "The Fast Growth of the Underground Economy," *Business Week*, March 13, 1978, p. 74.

15. Peter M. Gutmann, "The Subterranean Economy," *Financial Analysts Journal*, November/December 1977, pp. 26-27, 34.

16. Gillian Garcia, "The Currency Ratio and the Subterranean Economy," *Financial Analysts Journal*, November/December 1978, pp. 64-66,

69. Also see Richard D. Porter, and Stephen S. Thurman, "The Currency, Ratio and the Subterranean Economy: Additional Comments," Board of Governors of the Federal Reserve System, January 26, 1979.

17. Stephen M. Goldfeld, "The Case of the Missing Money," *Brookings Papers on Economic Activity*, no. 3, 1976, pp. 683-739.

18. Robert D. Laurent, "Currency and the Subterranean Economy," Federal Reserve Bank of Chicago, *Economic Perspectives*, March/April 1979, pp. 3-6.

19. Porter and Thurman, "The Currency Ratio," pp. 4-8.

20. The GNP includes estimates of imputed income; that is, income which does not take measurable monetary form, for example, food produced and consumed on farms. In 1978 imputed income totaled over $148 billion, and has been increasing more rapidly than total GNP.

21. "A Proposal for Redefining the Monetary Aggregates," *Federal Reserve Bulletin*, January 1979, p. 24.

22. Edgar L. Feige, "The Irregular Economy: Its Size and Macroeconomic Implications," Social Systems Research Institute, University of Wisconsin at Madison, May 1979.

23. Feige adjusts the demand deposit turnover data to exclude banks in financial centers as a means of eliminating purely financial transactions. It should be noted that there have been several major revisions of the demand deposit turnover data during the past forty years. Thus, the published statistics for 1976 and 1978 are not strictly comparable with those for 1939. It is not clear how Feige coped with this problem.

24. There are no official data on currency turnover. Feige estimates currency turnover by dividing an estimate of the number of lifetime transactions performed by a unit of currency by the estimated average life of a unit of currency. The number of lifetime transactions is taken from a doctoral dissertation by Robert Laurent. Laurent estimated that a unit of currency could perform about 125 physical transfers before it was retired. The average life of a unit of currency is calculated by Feige by dividing currency in circulation by the volume of currency redeemed by the U.S. Treasury each year. See Feige, "The Irregular Economy," pp. 11-12.

25. Feige also presents an alternative calculation of the underground economy. This calculation is based on the Bureau of Engraving's claim that the paper used for currency has been strengthened. Consequently, Feige reasons, a unit of currency can perform a greater number of transactions over its lifetime. He arbitrarily increases the number of lifetime currency transfers to 225 from 125 and calculates underground activity of $369 billion in 1976 and $704 billion in 1978.

26. Richard X. Bove and Thomas D. Klingenstein, "The Underground Economy: How Is It Measured?," New York, Wertheim & Co., Inc., February 23, 1981, p. 14.

27. Vito Tanzi, "The Underground Economy in the United States: Estimates and Implications," *Banca Nazionale del Lavoro Quarterly Review* 32 (December 1980):427-453.

28. Internal Revenue Service, *Estimates of Income Unreported on Individual Income Tax Returns*, Publication 1104 (Washington, D.C.: Government Printing Office, September 1979), pp. 11 and 17.

29. Ibid., pp. 122 and 124.

30. U.S. Congress, Joint Committee on Taxation, "Description of Proposals Relating to Independent Contractors Scheduled for a Hearing Before the Subcommittee on Select Revenue Measures of the Committee on Ways and Means on July 16 and 17, 1979." (Committee Print) July 13, 1979, p. 20.

31. Louise E. Berndt, "Effects of the Irregular Economy on the Reliability of Estimates of Labor Force Utilization." (Paper presented at the annual meeting of the American Sociological Association, San Francisco, September 1978), p. 4.

32. Peter M. Gutmann, "The Grand Unemployment Illusion," *Journal of the Institute for Socioeconomic Studies*, Summer 1979, pp. 25-26.

33. Peter M. Gutmann, "Are the Unemployed Unemployed?" *Financial Analysts Journal*, September/October 1978, p. 27.

34. William V. Deuterman, "Another Look at Working-Age Men Who Are Not in the Labor Force," *Monthly Labor Review*, June 1977, pp. 9-14.

35. Gutmann, "Are the Unemployed Unemployed?" pp. 27-28.

36. Louis A. Ferman, Louise Berndt, and Elaine Selo, "Analysis of the Irregular Economy: Cash Flow in the Informal Sector" (Unpublished report to the Bureau of Employment and Training, Michigan Department of Labor, March 1978), pp. 2.1-3.36.

37. Donald T. Regan, Statement before the Senate Committee on Finance, March 13, 1981. Exhibit I.

38. U.S. General Accounting Office, "Who's Not Filing Income Tax Returns?"

39. See, for example, Al Ullman, "Statement of the Honorable Al Ullman upon the Introduction of H.R. 7015, the Tax Restructuring Act of 1980," Congressional Record [daily edition] v. 126, April 2, 1980: H2481.

40. U.S. General Accounting Office, "The Value-Added Tax—What Else Should We Know About It?" PAD-81-60, Washington, D.C.: March 3, 1981, pp. 33-34.

41. Barbara A. Lingg, "Beneficiaries Affected by the Annual Earnings Test in 1977," *Social Security Bulletin*, December 1980, p. 4.

42. Peter F. Drucker, "Working Women: Unmaking the 19th Century," *Wall Street Journal*, July 6, 1981, p. 12.

Underground Economy and Tax Evasion in the United States: Estimates and Implications

Vito Tanzi

Definition and Causes

After being ignored for many years, the underground economy has finally worked its way to the center stage of American public and official attention. The discovery of the underground (or subterranean) economy in the United States is attested by recent editorials and articles in leading newspapers and magazines, hearings by four congressional committees, reports by official agencies (Internal Revenue Service and General Accounting Office), coverage in popular television programs, and professional articles. In this discovery the United States has followed other countries in which the underground economy has been the subject of official and unofficial attention and studies for some time.

The 1977 Report of the *Deutsche Bundesbank* reported (p. 23) that "[in Germany] cash payment is unquestionably gaining ground again in some fields, notably in the "grey areas" of business activity where services are rendered without taxes . . . and [are] settled in cash." Sir William Pile, then chairman of the board of Britain's Inland Revenue Service, was quoted in 1979 to the effect that "unrecorded income" may be as high as 7.5 percent of that country's gross national product (GNP). That figure was recently revised downward to 3.5 percent by the Central Statistical Office. In recognition of unrecorded activities of different origin, Italy's Istituto Centrale di Statistica in 1978 made upward revisions, of the order of 10 percent, to the 1975-1978 national accounts series. This substantial adjustment was still considered inadequate by some observers. The Economic Council of Denmark estimated the underground economy of that country at 10 percent in 1970 and 6 percent in 1974/75. Upward revisions of the national accounts data have also been made in recent years by France, Germany, Japan, Sweden, and several other countries. Furthermore, discussions of international tax evasion and avoidance connected with unreported offshore activities have been placed on the agenda of various international official meetings. Thus, like the wind, the underground economy may still be hidden to the eye, but its presence is now very much felt.

Reprinted with permission from Banca Nazionale del Lavoro, *Quarterly Review*, December 1980.

To make sure that the concept of underground economy means the same thing to different observers, it must be defined; an explicit and satisfactory definition is not readily available. Some observers seem to think in terms of a gross concept, that is, one based on the *total* expenditure on illegal and/or unreported activities, while others have in mind a concept related to the net use of resources. Thus, some observers would include all expenditure on illegal drugs and gambling; others would include only the incomes that originate from these activities. Often the definitions given do not specify whether the observers are using gross or net concepts. A simple and convenient definition of the underground economy is the following: it is gross national product that, because of unreporting and/or underreporting, is not measured by official statistics. This is the definition followed here. Of course to the extent that this would be taxable income, it is associated with a loss in tax revenue.

The two main groups of factors that create an underground economy are taxes and restrictions. Both can bring about an underground economy.

Taxes

Even if there were no restrictions on activities, taxes alone would force some activities underground so that they would go unrecorded and would thus escape the payment of taxes. All taxes would do this but, in a given country at a given time, certain taxes are likely to be more important than others. In the United States the discussion has almost exclusively centered on income taxes. In Europe, on the other hand, social security taxes and value-added taxes have also been prominently mentioned. If one extends the coverage to developing countries, foreign trade taxes would have to be added to the list. The role of taxation in bringing about underground activities will be discussed in greater detail below

Restrictions

If there were no taxes, there would still be an underground economy because of various governmental restrictions on the activities of economic agents. The restrictions are imposed either because the activities themselves are inherently criminal or illegal or for other socioeconomic reasons. The restrictions, especially when accompanied by high penalties and/or efficient controls, may at times prevent these activities from coming into existence. More often, however, they will force those activities underground. As these activities still use resources and generate incomes, they inevitably bring into existence an underground economy. Furthermore, to the extent that these incomes are not reported to the tax authorities—while they use resources that might have gone into the generation of legal, and thus taxable, incomes—the incidence and possibly the level of total tax revenues are also affected.

Restrictions on legal activities are, for example, those that prevent individuals from receiving social security benefits (for retirement or disability), or welfare payments, from earning incomes that exceed statutory limits; or those that prevent aliens without valid work permits to hold jobs; or those that prevent employers from paying wages below the legal minimum. Often, the recipients of these incomes will not report them to the tax authorities. And the payors are not likely to comply with reporting requirements for fear of being fined. Often the related payments are made in currency rather than with checks.

Many activities are inherently illegal and, therefore, forbidden. These include narcotics trafficking, illegal gambling, loansharking, prostitution, bribing of officials, fencing of stolen goods, and the like. These activities are conducted almost exclusively through the use of currency, in order to remain anonymous, and contribute to an increase in currency requirements in the economy. They are not tax-induced as they would exist even in the absence of taxation. And they are rarely, if ever, recorded. If the resources that go into these activities would have gone into legal (and thus measurable) activities, rather than remaining unemployed, the net result of the growth of these illegal activities will be a fall in legal GNP in relation to total GNP which would include the legal economy plus the underground economy. As tax revenues are collected from the legal economy and not from the underground, they are inevitably affected.

Review of Available Estimates

Until recently there were no estimates of the size of the underground economy in the United States. Recently, however, three different estimates have become available in published papers reflecting three different approaches. Of these, one, by the Internal Revenue Service, reflects an attempt to measure directly the underground economy by relying on various bits of information, some far less reliable than others.[1] The other two, by Gutmann and Feige, reflect indirect approaches using monetary data. Space limitation precludes a full discussion of these approaches so that only the most salient features will be presented.

Internal Revenue Service

The Internal Revenue Service study analyzes separately unreported legal-source income and unreported illegal-source income. Unreported *legal-*

source income was estimated on the basis of information from the IRS Tax-payer Compliance Measurement Program (TCMP) covering the tax year 1973. This program subjects a probability sample of about 50,000 individual income tax returns to a thorough audit examination. Through a weighting procedure the results from this examination were adjusted to provide national figures for 1973. The national 1973 results were then inflated to provide data for 1976. The 1976 estimates obtained by use of the TCMP were once again adjusted upward by recourse to information available in the Exact Match File—which matched for 50,000 households information provided by a 1973 household survey, by the records of the Social Security Administration, and by the IRS Individual Master File—and in the Bureau of Economic Analysis of the Department of Commerce. Unreported *illegal-source* income was obtained from a collage of estimates, guesstimates, and just plain hunches by various sources. For the various categories of unreported income, the IRS study provided lower and higher estimates. These are shown in table 4-1.

Thus, according to the IRS study, the underground economy in 1976, as measured by unreported income, ranged from about $100 billion to about $135 billion. In relation to (legal) GNP it ranged from 5.9 percent to 7.9 percent.

Table 4-1
U.S. Estimates of Unreported Income for 1976
(billions of dollars)

Type of Income	Lower Estimate	Higher Estimate
Legal-source incomes:	74.9	99.7
Self-employment	33.0	39.5
Wages and salaries	21.3	26.8
Interest	5.4	9.4
Dividends	2.1	4.7
Rents and royalties	3.2	5.9
Pensions, annuities, estates, and trusts	3.6	5.4
Capital gains	3.9	5.1
Other	2.3	2.9
Illegal-source incomes:	25.3	35.2
Illegal drugs	16.2	23.6
Bookmaking	4.0	5.0
Numbers	2.4	3.0
Other gambling	1.6	2.0
Prostitution	1.1	1.6
Overall total	100.2	134.9

Source: Internal Revenue Service, *Estimates of Income Unreported on Individual Income Tax Returns* (Washington, D.C.: Government Printing Office, September 1979).

Gutmann's Estimate

Peter Gutmann was the first to use monetary statistics as an indirect measure of the underground economy in an article published in 1977.[2] His method was applied to 1976 and gave an estimate of an underground economy equal to $176 billion. He has recently reestimated his results for 1979 and has concluded that, in this more recent year, the underground economy could be conservatively estimated at $250 billion. For both years the estimates are a little over 10 percent of (legal) GNP. Gutmann's method is simple and is based on a few key assumptions. First, he assumes that all underground activities avoid the use of checks and rely on currency for making payments. Second, these activities are the net result of high taxes and government-imposed restrictions. Third, and most important, the ratio of currency (C) to demand deposits (D) is influenced only by changes in taxes and other government rules and restrictions introduced since 1937-1941 and by nothing else. Fourth, the C/D ratio that prevailed in 1937-1941 is considered normal, implying that there was no underground economy in that period. Therefore this ratio would have prevailed in 1976 (or 1979) had it not been for the change in the level of taxation and in the rules and restrictions. As it was, the C/D ratio in 1976 was much higher than in 1937-1941. Assuming that the level of demand deposits in 1976 was normal, he calculates the extra currency attributable to the existence of the underground economy. This extra currency is then multiplied by the ratio of (legal) GNP to legal (that is, excluding the extra currency) money. The result is assumed to reflect income rather than gross expenditure and is thus taken as an estimate of the underground economy.

Feige's Estimate

In a recent article Edgar Feige has presented yet another, and somewhat more extraordinary, estimate of the underground or, as he calls it, the irregular economy.[3] Feige's method is derived from Irving Fisher's quantity theory of money. That theory can be written as $MV = PT$ where M is money (both checks and currency), V is the transaction (and not income) velocity of money, P is an average price level for *all* goods exchanged (not just newly created ones), and T is an index of the physical volume of all transactions. Thus if M (checks plus currency) and V (the transaction velocity of currency and checks) are known, MV, and consequently PT, can be calculated. If the ratio of PT (total dollar transactions) to nominal GNP is known and is assumed constant, nominal GNP can be estimated for any year, once PT is known. In the absence of an underground economy, the nominal GNP so derived should, ceteris paribus, be equal to the GNP that is measured in the national accounts. Feige assumes that in 1939 there was no underground economy so that the ratio of total dollar transactions to nominal GNP that he derives for that year (10.3) was normal. He then calculates PT for 1976 and 1978. Dividing the results by the 1939 ratio, he derives estimates of nominal GNP for 1976 and 1978. The difference between these indirectly obtained GNPs and the official ones in the national accounts are assumed to measure the underground economy. The underground economy is estimated to be between $225.5 billion and $369.1 billion in 1976 and between $541.7 billion and $704.4 billion in 1978. In relation to GNP these estimates range from 13.2 percent to 21.7 percent in 1976 and from 25.5 percent to 33.1 percent in 1978.

A New Approach

As indicated above, Peter Gutmann was the first to attempt to measure the underground economy through the use of currency statistics. Unfortunately, he relied on an assumption that surely cannot be accepted, namely that the ratio of currency to demand deposits is influenced only by changes in taxes and government restrictions and by nothing else. In this section an attempt is made to derive a more firmly based estimate of the underground economy by making the demand for currency explicitly a function of several variables, including the level of taxes. By measuring the sensitivity of currency demand to taxes, an estimate of currency held for illegal purposes is derived. From this illegal currency, estimates of the underground economy and of income tax evasion are also derived. Therefore, the method proposed depends basically on the derivation of a good demand-for-currency equation.

While much effort has gone into the analysis of the factors that determine the demand for money ($M1$ and/or $M2$), the literature dealing with the demand for currency is meager. Of the few studies that deal with the demand for currency, Phillip Cagan's remains, after two decades, the most comprehensive.[4] He carefully identified various factors that might affect the ratio of currency to money, the latter defined as incorporating time deposits ($M2$). His comprehensive list included: (a) the opportunity cost of holding currency; (b) expected real income per capita; (c) volume of retail trade; (d) volume of travel per capita; (e) degree of urbanization; and, finally, (f) the level of income taxation. He proceeded then to a statistical, time-series analysis covering the period 1919-1955. In that analysis, the ratio of currency to $M2$ was made to depend on: (a) interest paid on time, and until the Depression years (1929-1933), on demand deposits; (b) "expected," or "permanent," per capita real income; and (c) the ratio of personal income taxes to personal income. He eliminated retail trade, travel, and degree of urbanization from his independent variables either because of lack of data, or, more important, because of expected multicollinearity with income.[5]

This chapter proposes a somewhat modified version of Cagan's original model, but I analyze the relation between tax evasion and currency use much more closely than Cagan did. The statistical analysis covers the period 1929-1976, the longest for which the needed data are available for the United States at this time.[6]

The dependent variable can be taken to be either the ratio of currency to demand deposits or the ratio of currency to $M2$. There are reasons for preferring either one of these two ratios. For much of the period covered by the statistical analysis—1929-1976—commercial banks did not pay interest on demand deposits; therefore, the C/D ratio allows the elimination of the rate of interest from the explanatory variables.[7] As it is difficult to generate a good series on a rate of interest that is relevant to the choice between currency and $M2$ (the latter being made up of currency, demand deposits, and time deposits), this is an important advantage. On the other hand to the extent that, during the period, checking deposits may have been replaced by time deposits, one could get a fall in the C/D ratio caused by a decline in D rather than by an increase in C. Several writers have made this assertion. For this reason, and also because of a better statistical fit, the $C/M2$ currency ratio has been preferred.[8]

It is assumed that this currency ratio is affected by what could be called legal as well as illegal factors. The legal factors are distinguished between those of a long-run, or structural, nature and those of a short-run, and/or cyclical, nature.[9] The illegal factors are distinguished between those that are tax-related and those that are not.

Legal Factors

Among the long-run, or structural, legal factors that might affect the currency ratio, one must include: (a) the introduction and increasing use of credit cards; (b) volume of travel per capita; (c) degree of urbanization; and (d) the spreading of branches of commercial banks throughout the country. As it would be difficult or impossible to obtain time series for specific variables that could measure each of these structural factors, I shall use, as did Cagan, per capita income (in both its measured and its permanent version) as a proxy for these developments. It is hypothesized that increases in real per capita income would bring about decreases in the currency ratio.

Among the short-run, and/or cyclical, legal factors, there are (a) the composition of income and (b) the relative cost of holding currency vis-à-vis demand deposits.

Composition of Income. Casual observation indicates that in the United States, while interest, dividends, and rents are almost always received in the form of checks, wages and salaries are paid partly by check and partly by currency. Therefore, changes in the composition of income received could induce changes in the currency ratio. More specifically, while *salaried* employees are overwhelmingly paid by check, nonsalaried workers are often paid in currency, especially in such industries as construction, agriculture, and mining. If the total compensation of employees could be broken down between wages and salaries, one could use, as one of the explanatory variables in the statistical analysis, the share of wages (that is, excluding salaries) in personal income. Unfortunately, such a breakdown is not available. Thus, the ratio of total wages and salaries in personal income is used. It is hypothesized that as this ratio increases, so will the currency ratio.

Relative Costs. The ratio of currency to $M2$ can be expected to be influenced by relative cost considerations. For much of the period analyzed, there have been some explicit costs in the form of service charges associated with the holding of demand deposits. Dividing these charges by total deposits provides an estimate of this relative cost. Unfortunately, this series suffers from shortcomings so serious as to make it worthless. First, the service charges are available only for member banks of the Federal Reserve System and, thus, are not representative of the whole commercial banking system. Second, as mentioned earlier, up to the depression years, demand deposits received significant interest payments that exceeded the service charges. Third, the series would ignore costs associated with losses of deposits that were due to failures of commercial banks. Finally, an ideal series should account not only for costs related to holding of deposits but also for costs related to the holding of currency owing to losses—fires, burglaries, robberies. To the extent that these costs have changed over time, they could also affect the currency ratio. For these reasons, I shall not be able to account for these relative costs in the statistical analysis, although I do recognize that they may play a significant role.[10]

As the dependent variable is the ratio of currency to $M2$, it is necessary to add to the independent variables the rate of interest, as suggested by Cagan, as a measure of the opportunity cost of holding currency. The rate on time deposits is the one used.

Illegal Factors

Even if taxes did not exist, the currency ratio would be affected by illegal or criminal activities. For example, activities related to gambling (both legal and illegal), smuggling, narcotics distribution, moonshining, and the like, are almost always carried out through the use of currency, so that an increase in these activities would increase the currency ratio. Because of a lack of suitable data, I shall not be able to take into account the effects of these activities. I shall, therefore, concentrate on the effect of tax evasion on the currency ratio. But, of course, to the extent that the incomes associated with these activities are not reported to the tax authorities they also contribute to tax evasion.

There is now an extensive literature that deals with the factors that determine tax evasion, and particularly income tax evasion.[11] These factors include, among others: (1) the perceived fairness of the tax laws; (2) the attitude of taxpayers vis-à-vis their government; (3) their basic religious and cultural characteristics; (4) the severity of the penalties imposed on the tax evaders that are apprehended; (5) the facility with which taxes can be evaded; and, finally, (6) the monetary rewards to the taxpayers associated with *not* paying taxes.

The first four of these factors either are not measurable or have only short-term measurements. Either for these reasons or because it is assumed that they have remained relatively unchanged over the period covered by this study, they are ignored. On the other hand, as is argued later, the last two of these factors could, in theory at least, be measured and are likely to have changed over the period. Suppose that there was a variable, T^*, that provided a perfect measurement, over the period, of the taxpayer's rewards for not paying taxes, and another variable, K^*, that provided an ideal measure of the facility of evading taxes. Then one could write

$$E = f(T^*, K^*, U) \tag{4.1}$$

where E is a macromeasure of tax evasion and U is a catchall variable for all the random and/or nonmeasurable factors. In this expression, one would expect that increases in T^* and K^* would lead to increases in E. If one assumed further that tax evasion leads directly to greater use of currency, then one could introduce T^* and K^* among the explanatory variables of the currency ratio. However, as is shown later, the relationship between E and the currency ratio is not as simple or straightforward as it is often assumed to be, so that this relationship needs to be analyzed carefully.

Tax Evasion and the Demand for Currency. In the United States, payors of wages and salaries, interests, and dividends have a legal obligation to report to the authorities the making of those payments. Furthermore, employers must also withhold estimated income taxes for wages and salaries and must transfer them to the tax authorities. For these particular incomes, although collusion between payors and payees aimed at reducing tax liability is of course possible,[12] tax evasion, to the extent that it exists, is generally an activity that concerns mainly the payee and does not involve the payor.[13] The payee simply underreports this income. This is mainly true for interests and dividends as, as already said, the pay-as-you-earn (PAYE) system prevents this from happening for wages and salaries. Thus, tax evasion neither necessarily leads to greater currency use nor, incidentally, does it bias the national accounts data, as these are based largely on the reporting by the payors.[14]

For types of income other than those just mentioned, there is no reporting obligation on the part of the payors. Furthermore, for independent contractors engaged in professional and business activities, incomes often are not received from others but are directly created, as differences between gross receipts and allowable expenses, in the process of rendering services or selling goods. Especially for these activities, collusion between the providers and receivers of services, aimed at evading the payment of taxes, is not only possible but, often, because of the nature of the transaction, easy.[15] Such a collusion benefits both parties: it benefits the purchaser through a reduction in the cost of the service; it benefits the provider through a reduction in the income that he declares. The service is rendered for a lower price, provided that the payment is received in currency and is thus difficult to trace. The purchasers of these services will face two alternative supply curves: a lower one if the payment is in currency, and a higher one if the payment is made by check. Thus, high income taxes are likely to bring about a black market for services in the same way that price controls and rationing bring about a black market for goods.[16]

This black market will be associated with a greater use of currency, and will distort the national accounts data as, for certain types of income, these will be based on the (understated) incomes reported to the tax authorities. This means that one must be very cautious in using national accounts data to measure tax evasion.[17] For this reason, one cannot take as a measure of K^* in equation 4.1—that is, as a measure of the facility of evading taxes— the ratio of presumably more easily evadable incomes, such as rents and proprietors incomes, to national income, as the numerator of that ratio (and, to a lesser extent, the denominator) has been distorted by tax evasion. In conclusion, although it is recognized that the facility with which taxes can be evaded is likely to affect the evasion rate, it is not clear how this necessarily leads to greater use of currency; furthermore, the data that conceivably could be used to introduce this variable would be distorted by evasion itself. For this reason, in these statistical tests I ignore this variable and concentrate instead on the variable that would measure the rewards of taxpayers associated with *not* paying taxes.

One objective measure of the benefit, or reward, of not paying income taxes is provided by the level of the legal tax liability. When that liability is low, the reward from tax evasion is also low. In such cases, the cost of being an honest taxpayer is not high. However, as the legal effective tax rates rise, so do the benefits from tax evasion. Honesty becomes a more expensive virtue. One would thus expect that, ceteris paribus, the temptation to evade taxes would rise with the rise in the tax level. But how does one measure such a level?

One possibility, used by Cagan and Macesich, is to take the ratio of total income tax revenue to personal income. The variable thus obtained suffers from three shortcomings: first, the numerator of the ratio uses actual tax revenue rather than potential (without evasion) revenue. In other words, the ratio may be reduced by the existence of evasion. Second, the denominator itself may have been affected by underreporting of some incomes. Third, the ratio may remain unchanged even when the rate structure is changing.[18] This last shortcoming is possibly the most serious, as it is the marginal tax rate on a taxpayer's income—rather than the average rate—that is more likely to determine whether he evades the tax on the marginal dollar. If the average tax rate is also high, there could be an income effect that might reinforce the taxpayer's propensity to evade the tax. A variable of this type will be used as one of three alternative ways of measuring the monetary rewards from income tax evasion. However, as transfer payments, which are largely nontaxable, have increased tremendously over the period 1929-1976, personal income net of transfer payments is taken as the denominator. This variable is referred to as $T1$.

A second possibility is to use the top-bracket statutory tax rate for each year as a proxy for the effective marginal rates that affect taxpayers. The major shortcoming of this variable is obvious: a relatively small and changing proportion of all taxpayers is subject to this rate. However, to the extent that often, although not always, the whole rate structure moves together in the same direction, the top-bracket rate will have informational value for the whole rate structure and can thus serve as a proxy for the entire structure. This variable is referred to as $T2$.

A third possibility is presented by the availability of an effective weighted average tax rate on interest incomes that was constructed for other purposes.[19] This series is likely to provide yearly rates that may be closer to some modal average taxpayers' tax rates than would be the previous two alternatives. Therefore, in spite of its limited nature, this series is likely better to capture changes in the level of income taxes over the period. It is indicated by $T3$.

Summarizing, let

$C/M2$ = ratio of currency holdings to money defined as $M2$.

$T1$ = ratio of personal income taxes to personal income net of transfers.

$T2$ = top-bracket statutory tax rate.

$T3$ = weighted-average tax rate on interest income.

W = share of wages and salaries in personal income.

R = interest rate on time deposits.

Y^m = real per capita income from national accounts (that is, "measured" income).

Y^p = real per capita income as estimated by Friedman and Schwartz (that is, "permanent" income).

The truncated version of the model that is subjected to empirical tests can be written

$$(C/M2)_t = \alpha_0 + \alpha_1 T_t + \alpha_2 W_t + \alpha_3 Y_t + \alpha_4 R_t + u_t \qquad (4.2)$$

where t refers to the specific year, *u* is an error term, and *T* and *Y* can take, respectively, the values of *T1*, *T2*, and *T3*, and *Y^m* and *Y^p*. From the previous discussion, one would expect a negative sign for the *Y* and *R* variables and positive signs for the *T* and *W* variables. This model is tested for the 1929-1976 period. Assuming some inertia in the adjustment of the currency ratio to changes in the independent variables, equation 4.2 is also tested with the addition of the lagged dependent variable. The tests are conducted in log form.

Empirical Results

The regression equations for equation 4.2 are shown in table 4-2. The results, which are remarkably good, can be summarized briefly. The adjusted R^2 are very high, exceeding 0.94 for all equations and reaching, for some, 0.97. This indicates that the model is capable of explaining most of the variance in the dependent variable over the period. In most cases, the value of the Durbin-Watson statistics and, for the equation with the lagged variable, the H statistics, are at satisfactory levels.[20] However, the equations that use *T2*—that is, the top-bracket statutory tax rates—are definitely the worst. This is not surprising, as the top bracket rates were often left unchanged for several years. The tax variable is highly significant in all cases, but especially when *T3* is used. Furthermore, it has the right (positive) sign, indicating that an increase in the tax rate, presumably through an evasion effect, brings about a greater relative use of currency. The variable indicating the composition of income, *W*, is also highly significant in all cases and again has the expected (positive) sign, indicating that a larger share of wages and salaries in national income brings about a greater relative use of currency.[21] The rate of interest variable is also highly significant and has the expected (that is, negative) sign.

On the other hand, the per capita income variable, regardless of whether "measured" or "permanent" income is used, is in many cases not significant, casting doubts, at least for the United States, on the hypothesis that economic development reduces the currency ratio.[22] However, since by 1929 the United States was already a highly developed country, this particular result might simply indicate that all the development-induced shift between C and $M2$ had already occurred before 1929, so that no further change should have been expected from this factor.

The table also shows the equations obtained when a stock-adjustment process is assumed. In fact, it is possible that, when the independent variables change, the dependent one does not adjust instantly but does so with some lag. Or, putting it differently, it takes some time for individuals to adjust their currency ratios to their optimal level. The addition of the lagged dependent variable among the exploratory variables has only a marginal effect on the value of the coefficients. As the analysis refers to annual data, this result is also not unexpected, as a year is a long enough period in which to make adjustments.

Estimates of the Underground Economy and Tax Evasion

The previous analysis has established that most of the variance in the currency ratio can be explained statistically through the use of a few variables. It has also established a connection between changes in the level of income taxes and changes in the $C/M2$ ratio. This connection can be attributed to the existence of a tax-induced underground or subterranean economy in which transactions are carried out mainly through the use of currency; the incomes thus generated are not reported and escape taxation.

The previous analysis can be used to attempt an estimation of tax-induced currency holdings and, subsequently, of the total values of tax-evading transactions and tax evasion. Figure 4-1 outlines graphically the methodology that will be followed and the key assumptions on which the estimations will be based. The total rectangle BCDA includes the whole economy, whether measured or not. This economy is assumed to be made up of two parts—a legal part (BEFA) equal to the measured or official GNP, and an unmeasured or underground part (ECDF) connected with tax-evading activities. The area BCIG measures total money in circulation needed for the functioning of the whole economy. As this money is needed for transactions purposes, it is identified with total currency plus demand deposits in circulation. BEHG measures the money needed for transactions in the legal economy, while ECIH measures the money needed for tax-evading transactions (the underground economy). BEHG is referred to as legal money, and ECIH as illegal money. The bottom rectangle (JLDA)

Table 4-2
Regression Equations for Equation 4.2
(Log-linear formulation)

Equations	Constant	T1	T2	T3	R	W	Y1	Y2	(C/M2) − 1	$\bar{R}^2$	D-W or H Statistic
(a)	−5.3938 (3.86)**	+0.1977 (6.11)**			−0.2434 (6.41)**	+1.9687 (6.03)**	−0.3121 (2.75)**			0.955	1.819[b]
(b)	−5.6312 (3.60)**		+0.2819 (4.44)**		−0.2731 (6.09)**	+1.6685 (4.38)**	+0.1786 (2.24)**			0.942	1.432[b]
(c)	−5.3751 (4.54)**			+0.3395 (8.31)**	−0.2181 (6.98)**	+1.7059 (6.01)**	−0.0849 (1.31)			0.968	1.793[b]
(d)	−5.3073 (4.72)**	+0.1339 (3.90)**			−0.1999 (5.34)**	+1.8102 (6.06)**	−0.2205 (2.11)*		+0.2103 (2.40)*	0.956	0.791[a]
(e)	−5.4539 (4.35)**		+0.2164 (3.91)**		−0.1758 (3.99)**	+1.5135 (4.87)**	+0.0786 (1.01)		+0.3176 (3.83)**	0.955	1.689[a]
(f)	−5.2163 (5.13)**			+0.2618 (6.62)**	−0.1715 (5.39)**	+1.5989 (6.53)**	−0.0955 (1.64)		+0.2042 (2.98)**	0.971	0.932[a]
(g)	−6.1362 (4.51)**	+0.1812 (5.95)**			−0.2470 (6.11)**	+2.1441 (6.70)**		−0.3278 (2.38)*		0.952	1.857[b]
(h)	−5.3963 (3.55)**		+0.2873 (4.52)**		−0.2835 (6.20)**	+1.6013 (4.33)**		+0.2370 (2.35)*		0.941	1.392[b]
(i)	−5.4079 (4.78)**			+0.3466 (8.51)**	−0.2082 (6.29)**	+1.7141 (6.35)**		−0.1280 (1.55)		0.968	1.822[b]
(j)	−5.9482 (4.81)**	+0.1121 (3.27)**			−0.2114 (5.41)**	+1.9452 (6.50)**		−0.1779 (1.37)	+0.2237 (2.45)*	0.952	0.666[a]
(k)	−5.5183 (4.58)**		+0.2176 (3.92)**		−0.1878 (4.15)**	+1.5129 (5.05)**		+0.1396 (1.40)	+0.3229 (3.90)**	0.954	1.620[a]
(l)	−5.4231 (5.50)**			+0.2626 (6.36)**	−0.1708 (5.10)**	+1.6517 (6.98)**		−0.1142 (1.50)	+0.1987 (2.85)*	0.970	0.916[a]

Notes: a = *H* statistic; b = Durbin-Watson. Regression equations have been corrected for serial correlation using a first-order Cochrane-Orcutt correction factor. Numbers in parentheses are *t* statistics.

* significant at .05.
** significant at .01.

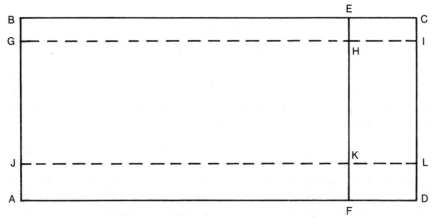

BCDA = Total gross national product (GNP)
BEFA = Measured (or legal) GNP
ECDF = Nonmeasured (or underground) GNP
JKFA = Taxes paid (on measured GNP)
KLDF = Taxes evaded
BCIG = Total money in circulation
BEHG = Legal money used
ECIH = Money used for tax-evading activities

Figure 4-1. Schematic Presentation of Measured and Nonmeasured
Economy

measures total income taxes that would be paid if the whole economy were legal and thus taxable. JKFA measures the taxes actually paid, while KLDF measures the taxes evaded.

If one could estimate the amount of money presumed to be used for illegal activities (ECIH), that amount could be multiplied by the ratio of measured GNP to legal money to approximate the underground economy. This would imply that the income velocity of money in the underground economy is assumed to be the same as in the legal economy. Once the underground economy has been measured, one could then estimate tax evasion by multiplying the underground economy by the ratio of taxes actually paid to measured (or legal) GNP.[23]

For 1976 actual measurements are available for currency, demand deposits, and $M2$; therefore $C/M2$ can be calculated. From the regression equations in table 4-2, one can calculate the predicted level of the currency ratio $\left(\frac{C}{M2}\right)$ and, therefore, the predicted level of currency holdings $\hat{C}$, given the actual 1976 figure for $M2$. The procedure used to obtain $\hat{C}$ from the equations in table 4-2 is outlined below.

Let the dependent variable in the regression equations of table 4-2 be represented by Z. Therefore:

$$Z_t = \ln\left(\tfrac{C}{M2}\right)_t = \ln C_t - \ln M2_t \qquad (4.3)$$

Rewriting this equation in terms of $\ln C_t$, we get:

$$\ln \hat{C}_t = Z_t + \ln M2_t \qquad (4.4)$$

where the hat on the C indicates that this is the value predicted from the regression equation. Solving this equation, we get:

$$\hat{C}_t = \exp\left(Z_t + \ln M2_t\right) \qquad (4.5)$$

This is the value of currency at time t predicted by the regression equations in table 4-2. The values of C obtained from equations c and f in table 4-2 are shown in table 4-3, column 3. These two equations were chosen because, statistically, they were the best. Column 6 in table 4-3 shows the differences between the actual value for currency in 1976 and the predicted values. These differences are quite small reflecting the equations' substantial explanatory power.

With the aid of table 4-3 we can now proceed to the estimation of the underground economy. We can follow two alternative and conceptually different ways depending on what we want to measure. First, we might want to measure the size of the underground economy brought about by the *increase* in taxes over the 1929-1976 period. In other words, we might wish to answer the question: what underground activities were induced by the increase in taxes between 1929 and 1976? The second alternative does not concentrate on changes over time but attempts a measure of the total underground economy associated with the 1976 level of taxation. This alternative approach obviously gives a somewhat larger estimate.

I prefer the first approach because it recognizes that as long as there are taxes (and other restrictions) there will be some underground activity. As it is unrealistic to conceive of an economy without taxes (and restrictions), it does not seem very productive to attempt to measure all the underground activities but it seems preferable to concentrate on changes over relevant periods. Nevertheless, I shall provide estimates for both alternatives.

To obtain the predicted values of currency for 1976 shown in column 3 of table 4-3, the regression equations estimated in table 4-2 were solved for the 1976 values of the independent variables. These equations can alternatively be solved in the same way except that for the first alternative mentioned above, we assume that the tax variable, instead of having the 1976 value, has the lowest value over the period; and for the second alternative we assume that the value of the tax variable falls to zero. In both cases it is assumed that the coefficient of the other variables does not change. For the first alternative we refer to the new predicted value of currency holdings as $\hat{\hat{C}}$, while for the second alternative we refer to it as $\overset{\approx}{C}$.

Table 4-3

Actual and Predicted Values of Currency Holdings in the United States in 1976

Equation Used (1)	Actual 1976 C (2)	Currency Predicted with 1976 Tax Level $\hat{C}$ (3)	Currency Predicted with Lowest Taxes over Period $\hat{\hat{C}}$ (4)	Predicted with Zero Taxes $\hat{\hat{\hat{C}}}$ (5)	Differences $C - \hat{C}$ (6)	$\hat{C} - \hat{\hat{C}}$ (7)	$\hat{C} - \hat{\hat{\hat{C}}}$ (8)
(c)	77.8	78.3	63.8	46.8	−0.5	14.5	31.5
(f)	77.8	78.0	68.1	55.5	−0.2	9.9	22.5

Source: Table 4-2 and text.

More specifically, let Z^* indicate the value of the dependent variable in the regression equations obtained when, ceteris paribus, the tax variable is assumed to be at its lowest level over the period. Then C is:

$$\hat{\hat{C}}_t = \exp(Z^*_t + \ln M2_t) \tag{4.6}$$

The predicted values for $\hat{\hat{C}}$ are shown in table 4-3, column 4; the differences between $\hat{C}$ and $\hat{\hat{C}}$ are shown in the same table in column 7.

There is a technical difficulty in trying to derive an estimate of $\hat{\hat{\hat{C}}}$ simply by setting the tax variable equal to zero and solving the equation as it was done for $\hat{\hat{C}}$ above: the double-log formulation that proved best in the specification of the regression equations, does not allow the setting of taxes equal to zero, as the logarithm of zero is minus infinity. This problem can be solved by replacing, in the estimation of the regression equations, the tax variable T by a variable $(T + K)$, where K is a constant calculated through a search procedure. Therefore a new set of regression equations was estimated.[24] From these new equations $\hat{\hat{\hat{C}}}$ was estimated using the same procedure as for $\hat{\hat{C}}$. The results are shown in column 5 of table 4-3. The differences between $\hat{C}$ and $\hat{\hat{\hat{C}}}$ are shown in column 8.[25]

Table 4-3 (column 7) indicates that between $10 billion and $14 billion of currency holdings can be attributed to the *change* in the tax factor between its lowest level in the 1929-1976 period and that reached in 1976. It also indicates (column 8) that between $22 billion and $31 billion could possibly be attributed to the *existence* of taxes although, as argued above, the basis for this further assertion is somewhat weaker. In any case these are our estimates of the illegal money that can be assumed to be fueling the underground economy. If taxes had remained at their lowest level, or if there had been no taxes at all, currency holdings would be correspondingly lower.

If it is assumed that the relationship between tax-induced currency holdings (illegal money) and the underground economy is the same as that between legal money holdings used for transactions (including currency and demand deposits) and legal or measured GNP, one can then multiply illegal money by the income velocity of legal money[26] to obtain an estimate of the underground economy.[27] Once the underground economy has been estimated, one can proceed to estimate tax evasion.

Table 4-4 provides the estimates for the underground economy and income tax evasion. Columns 1 and 2 allocate total money for 1976, equal to $304.3 billion, between legal and illegal money. Column 3 calculates the income velocity of legal money—equal to GNP divided by legal money. Column 4 calculates the underground economy by multiplying illegal money by the income velocity of legal money. A key assumption here is that the velocity of money for currency in the underground economy is the same as that for $M1$ in the legal economy. This is clearly a debatable assumption. Column 5 shows the underground economy as a proportion of GNP while column 6 shows the estimates for tax evasion. Tax evasion is calculated by assuming that the average tax liability for underground incomes would be the same as for legal incomes. This is also a key assumption.

The estimates indicate that the increase in taxes over the period brought about an underground economy of between 3.4 and 5.1 percent of GNP and a tax evasion of $4.5 to $6.7 billion. On the basis of a somewhat more debatable procedure, the table indicates also that the existence of taxes (as distinguished from their increase) may have generated a total underground economy of between 8.1 and 11.7 percent of GNP and a tax evasion of between $10.6 and $15.4 billion.

Implications and Conclusions

The existence of a substantial underground economy would have important and, at time, disturbing implications for the measurement of macroeconomic variables, the pursuit of economic policy, and the efficient functioning of the economy.

Employment statistics are related to workers engaged in economic activities within the legal sector of the economy. To the extent that individuals are counted in the labor force but, being employed in underground activities, are not counted among the employed, the unemployment rate could be overstated. The degree of overstatement will, of course, depend on the size of the underground economy. Feige and Gutmann, in independent recent articles, have argued that this overestimation of the unemployment rate is substantial.

It has been argued by some observers (for example, Feige) that the inflation rate is also overstated as prices in the underground economy are likely

Table 4-4

Estimates of Underground Economy and Tax Evasion, 1976

Equation Used	Illegal Money ($ billion) (1)	Legal Money ($ billion) (2)	Income Velocity of Legal Money (3)	Underground Economy		Tax Evasion ($ billion) (6)
				($ billion) (4) = (1)·(3)	Percentage of GNP (5)	
			With lowest taxes			
(c)	14.5	289.8	5.94	86.1	5.1	6.7
(f)	9.9	294.4	5.85	57.9	3.4	4.5
			With zero taxes			
(c)	31.5	272.8	6.31	198.8	11.7	15.4
(f)	22.5	281.8	6.11	137.5	8.1	10.6

Source: See table 4-2 and text.

to be growing at a lower rate than in the legal economy. In fact part of the alleged shift from legal to underground activities, for those areas where the two economies are in competition, is attributed to this differential in price changes.

Besides the unemployment and the inflation rates, other macroeconomic variables will be distorted: the true rate of growth of the economy will be higher than the measured growth, if the underground economy is growing relatively to measured GNP; the measured size of the public sector, whether measured as a ratio of taxes or expenditure to GNP, will be magnified; statistic on income distribution as well as those on tax incidence will also be distorted.

As economic policy responds to the signals provided by these macroeconomic variables, the policies that may be pursued will be distorted so that at times they could do more harm than good. For example, to the extent that the unemployment rate is consistently (and, possibly, increasingly) biased upward, the policymakers will pursue policies that are too expansionary vis-à-vis actual needs and will thus promote inflation. If, as indicated above, the cost-of-living index is overstated, and if inflationary expectations as well as actual indexing clauses (for wages and salaries, pensions, and the like) are based on the distorted index, the inflationary effects will be compounded. And these effects could be magnified if the monetary authorities, in the pursuit of a monetary rule, based the expansion of the money supply on the rate of change of the consumer price index. In such case the monetary authorities might be induced to accommodate a higher rate of inflation by expanding the money supply at a faster pace than warranted by the true rate of inflation.

The underground economy will affect the functioning of the economy in different ways and will probably have negative effects on efficiency. For example, as the total economy (both legal and underground) expands, the need for public services will grow. However, taxes are collected only from its legal part so that the tax level on legal activities will increase. This increase will force more activities underground as the benefits from tax evasion will grow. Untaxed underground activities will compete with taxed, legal ones and will succeed in attracting resources even though these activities may be less productive in a social (rather than a private) sense. This flow of resources from legal, and taxed, activities toward underground, and untaxed, ones can be expected to continue as long as ceteris paribus, the net-of-tax rate of return, adjusted for the risk of being caught and having to pay penalties, is higher in the underground economy. There will of course be significant welfare losses associated with this transer. The resulting equilibrium, if reached, will imply an allocation of resources different from the optimum. An application to this process of the methodology used by Harberger in connection with his model of the shifting of the corporate income tax should prove productive.

For all of these reasons, it is important that we improve our knowledge of the underground economy. Unfortunately, the results available so far are widely different, as can be seen with the aid of table 4-5. The range between the lowest and highest estimates in that table is uncomfortably high. Furthermore, it is not clear whether these four estimates are actually measuring the same thing.

Feige and Gutmann both measure changes in the underground economy since the late thirties—since 1937-1941 for Gutmann and since 1939 for Feige.[28] Only if in 1937-1941 or in 1939, there was no underground economy, as Feige and Gutmann assume, can their results be assumed to measure the *level* of, rather than the *change* in, the underground economy. But as long as the underground economy results from criminal as well as tax-evading activities surely it must have existed in the thirties. After all, the era of Prohibition extended into that decade and the New Deal had already sharply increased income taxes. What this means is that, if Feige's and Gut-

Table 4-5
Underground Economy in the United States: Comparison of Estimates
(percentage of GNP)

| | Feige | | Gutmann | Internal Revenue | | Tanzi | |
	Low	High		Low	High	Low	High
1976	13.2	21.7	10	5.9	7.9	{3.4[a] 8.1[b]	{5.1[a] 11.7[b]
1978	25.5	33.1	10				

[a]associated with tax increase
[b]associated with tax level

mann's methods were right, the present level of the underground economy in the United States would be sharply higher than their already extraordinary estimates. To this observer that requires a total suspension of disbelief.

Postscript

One of the important issues related to the underground economy is whether it has been growing in recent years. To approach this question, I have applied the method presented in this chapter to each of the years between 1970 and 1978 and have, in this way, reestimated the size of the underground economy for each year. The results are shown in table 4-6, which provides

Table 4-6
Estimates of Underground Economy and Tax Evasion, 1970-1978
(With lowest tax, in billions of dollars)

Equation	Illegal Money	Legal Money	Income Velocity of Legal Money	Underground Economy Dollars	Underground Economy Percentage of GNP	Tax Evasion (dollars)
1978						
(c)	14.1	338.7	6.37	89.82	4.17	7.54
(f)	10.0	342.8	6.29	62.90	2.92	5.28
1977						
(c)	13.2	312.8	6.13	80.92	4.22	6.65
(f)	9.3	316.7	6.06	56.36	2.94	4.63
1976						
(c)	13.1	291.2	5.90	77.29	4.50	5.92
(f)	9.2	295.1	5.82	53.54	3.12	4.1
1975						
(c)	11.4	278.0	5.57	63.50	4.10	5.02
(f)	8.0	281.4	5.51	44.08	2.85	3.48
1974						
(c)	10.8	266.9	5.37	58.00	4.04	4.81
(f)	7.6	270.1	5.31	40.36	2.81	3.35
1973						
(c)	9.3	254.7	5.21	48.45	3.65	3.77
(f)	6.6	257.4	5.15	33.99	2.56	2.64
1972						
(c)	9.0	234.2	5.0	45.00	3.84	3.64
(f)	6.3	236.9	4.9	30.87	2.64	2.50
1971						
(c)	8.5	221.3	4.81	40.89	3.85	3.32
(f)	6.0	223.8	4.75	28.50	2.68	2.31
1970						
(c)	7.6	206.1	4.77	36.25	3.69	3.34
(f)	5.3	208.4	4.71	24.96	2.54	2.30

Source: See tables 4-2 and text.

the same information as that given in table 4-4 but is limited to the assumption of lowest taxes. It should be noted that, in view of recent revisions to various data used (money supply, GNP, and the like), the results shown in table 4-6 for 1976 are a bit different from those in table 4-4. The table is largely self-explanatory. The basic conclusion is that over the 1970-1978 period there was some increase in the relative size of the underground economy; however, that increase was relatively small. As mentioned in chapter 6, there is some indirect evidence to indicate that after 1978 the size of the underground economy might have grown more rapidly due to the sharp increase in marginal tax rates.

Notes

1. See Internal Revenue Service, *Estimates of Income Unreported on Individual Income Tax Returns* (Washington, D.C.: Government Printing Office, September 1979).

2. Peter M. Gutmann, "The Subterranean Economy," *Financial Analysts Journal,* November-December 1977, pp. 26-27 and 34.

3. Edgar L. Feige, "How Big Is the Irregular Economy?" *Challenge,* November-December 1979, pp. 5-13.

4. Phillip Cagan, *The Demand for Currency Relative to Total Money Supply,* National Bureau of Economic Research, Inc., Occasional Paper 62 (New York, 1958). Published also in the *Journal of Political Economy,* August 1958.

5. A similar analysis using the same variables was carried out for Canada by George Macesich, "Demand for Currency and Taxation in Canada," *The Southern Economic Journal* 29 (July 1962):33-38.

6. In a recently published paper dealing with the demand for currency for a more recent period, Gillian Garcia and Simon Pak follow a totally different approach, which gives no role to the tax factor. See "The Ratio of Currency to Demand Deposits in the United States," *Journal of Finance* 34 (June 1979):703-15. In spite of its title, this article deals separately with the demand for currency and that for deposits.

7. Demand deposits received significant interest payments up to the depression years. After 1933 these payments were reduced to insignificant levels.

8. In an earlier version of this study the C/D ratio was taken as the dependent variable.

9. As this study concentrates on annual variations, seasonal factors that affect the demand for money within the year, such as Christmas shopping, are not considered.

10. The series obtained by dividing the service charges by total demand deposits   for member banks was tried in the initial statistical analysis. Because of its poor performance and its shortcomings, it was subsequently dropped.

11. Serge-Christophe Kolm, "A Note on Optimum Tax Evasion," *Journal of Public Economics* (July 1973):265-270; Michael G. Allingham and Agnar Sandmo, "Income Tax Evasion: A Theoretical Analysis," *Journal of Public Economics* 1 (November 1972):323-338; Richard D. Schwartz and Sonya Orleans, "On Legal Sanctions," *University of Chicago Law Review* 34 (1967):274-300; Internal Revenue Service, "Factors Affecting Taxpayer Compliance with Federal Tax Laws" (mimeographed, January 1970).

12. In such a case, payors may underreport actual payments to the authorities.

13. This discussion is relevant to the United States. For some other countries it has been reported that attempts to evade high social security taxes, which fall on both employers and employees, have actually resulted in collusion between them. Equally important, where lending activities do not involve the banking system but are outside organized money markets, collusion between lenders and borrowers aimed at evading taxes may lead to greater currency use and thus may bias the national accounts data.

14. From this it should not be concluded that there is no evasion vis-à-vis these incomes—only that this evasion is not necessarily associated with the use of currency. For 1976, the latest year for which this information is available, the U.S. Department of Commerce (Bureau of Economic Analysis) estimates of adjusted monetary personal interest income and of adjusted personal income dividends were, respectively, $70.8 billion and $30.2 billion. By contrast, Internal Revenue Service returns showed $48.4 billion and $24.5 billion, respectively. These large "unexplained differences" are, of course, not necessarily due to tax evasion.

15. Unpublished estimates by the Internal Revenue Service indicate that *at most* only 74 percent of the total income received by independent contractors is reported. For additional evidence on tax evasion by occupation, see Comptroller General of the United States, *Who Is Not Filing Income Tax Returns?* Report to the Congress of the United States (Washington, General Accounting Office July 11, 1979) Appendix III, pp. 103-112.

16. Of course, high consumption taxes (including those on imports) may also stimulate a black market for goods. In some cases, collusion is not explicit in the sense that both parties know why the payment is made in currency but neither has specifically asked that it be made in this form.

17. As was done, for example, in Vito Tanzi, "Income Tax Treatment of Different Kinds of Income," ch. 5 in *The Individual Income Tax and Economic Growth: An International Comparison—France, Germany, Italy, Japan, United Kingdom, United States* (Baltimore: The Johns Hopkins Press, 1969), pp. 50-76.

18. This, for example, may happen when exemptions and rates are increased at the same time.

19. For the period up to 1958, this series was prepared by Colin Wright for his study, "Saving and the Rate of Interest," in *The Taxation of Income from Capital,* ed. Arnold C. Harberger and Martin J. Bailey (The Brookings Institution, 1969), pp. 275-300. This series was extended, by Tanzi, to 1976.

20. The equations in table 4-2 have been adjusted for serial correlation.

21. No significant change is observed when national income is replaced by personal income.

22. The equations using permanent income cover the years 1929-1975, rather than 1929-1976.

23. This assumes that the effective average tax rate is the same in the legal and in the underground economy.

24. These equations have not been included to economize on space. They are practically identical to those in table 4-2.

25. Another difficulty with this second alternative is that it requires solving the estimated regression equations for a value of the tax variable outside the range used for the estimation.

26. The income velocity of legal money is obtained by dividing GNP by legal money.

27. The assumption that the income velocity of money is the same in the underground and in the legal economy is clearly a crucial one. It is the result of agnosticism. The author is unable to take a position between those who would argue that the velocity of money in the underground economy must be lower than in the legal economy, and those who would argue the contrary. The first alternative was backed by Nancy H. Teeters in a recent statement before a congressional committee. See *Federal Reserve Bulletin* (September 1979), pp. 742-743. The second alternative is backed by Edgar Feige in "How Big Is the Irregular Economy?" *Challenge,* November-December 1979, pp. 5-13.

28. Therefore, methodologically they are measuring the same phenomenon as in our estimates associated with tax increases rather than that measured by the Internal Revenue or our estimates associated with tax level.

5

The Direct Approach to Measuring the Underground Economy in the United States: IRS Estimates of Unreported Income

Berdj Kenadjian

Introduction to the Estimates

The notion that individuals are hiding their taxable income from the tax authorities at increasing rates has been a subject of considerable interest and publicity over the past three years. In particular, a large number of commentators have been painting a disturbing picture of millions of people working off the books and skimming off the top in a so-called underground economy. To try to separate fact from fancy, and to have a realistic assessment of the problem, in the spring of 1978, the Commissioner of the Internal Revenue Service, Jerome Kurtz, designated a study team to evaluate the unreported individual income problem in the United States. The findings of this study team, of which I was a member, were released on August 31, 1979, in a report called *Estimates of Income Unreported on Individual Income Tax Returns.*[1] The object of the study was to review all available data relevant to the unreported income problem and to develop the best possible estimates of its size and associated tax gaps.

The study team considered both the direct and indirect (essentially monetary) approaches to measuring unreported income. The direct estimation methods, in general, made it possible to derive separate estimates of underreported and unreported incomes of tax return filers and nonfilers. When such gaps are derived by type of income—distinguishing the gaps, say, in reporting wages and salaries from the gaps associated with interest, dividends or other incomes—specific rates of noncompliance can be calculated for each income source. These rates can be explicitly evaluated one by one to see whether they appear to be plausible in the light of institutional experience and legal requirements. For example, when the law requires withholding of tax on some incomes at the source, or filing of information returns by third parties to inform the tax authorities, one would not expect large reporting gaps for these components of taxpayer income.

Paper presented at the 1980 meeting of the American Economic Association (Denver, Colorado). The views expressed are those of the author, not necessarily those of the Internal Revenue Service.

93

The indirect, currency-related approaches, based on the notion that unusually large and growing volumes of currency are indicative of large amounts of untaxed illegal-source incomes or other forms of tax evasion do not yield estimates which lend themselves to an item by item review of the implied compliance rates. Thus, because the implications of such total gap estimates in terms of specific noncompliance rates for specific sources of income cannot be determined, it becomes virtually impossible to say whether the total gap estimates calculated by such methods are realistic. The study team, however, had a more fundamental reason for choosing not to work with an indirect, currency-related approach. As explained in great detail in appendix B to the main text of its report, the study team did not feel that simple ratios of currency to demand deposits or other financial relationships provide a reliable basis for estimating the size of the total individual income reporting gap. In an economy as dynamic as that of the United States, such relationships cannot be expected to remain sufficiently constant to throw any light on what may be happening to compliance with the tax laws. Consequently, although the estimation effort benefited from a study of both the direct and indirect methods, the IRS estimates of the income reporting gaps were based on a direct estimation method.

The Findings

I shall now present briefly the basic findings of the IRS study team. Based on available data, it was estimated that, in 1976, individuals failed to report about $13 to $17 billion of income tax due on about $75 to $100 billion of unreported income from legal sources. In the same year, individuals reported income taxes totaling $142 billion on $1,073 billion of income. Thus about 6.5 to 8.5 percent of income from legal sources and about 8.3 to 10.8 percent of the tax due on these incomes were not reported to the IRS.

The study team also estimated that, in 1976, an additional $6 to $9 billion in taxes was not paid on $25 to $35 billion of unreported individual income from illegal activities in narcotics, gambling, and prostitution. These were the only three areas generating illegal-source income on which reasonably adequate sources of information could be found in the time available. Because of the lack of data on illegal-source incomes, generally, the unreported income estimates for the legal sector are more reliable than the corresponding estimates for the illegal sector. Moreover, the latter are not comprehensive and are not likely to be so in the future since it is improbable that data will be found on which to base reliable estimates of unreported income from many illegal activities such as extortion, loansharking, or bribery.

Table 5-1 summarizes the study team's estimates of the amount of unreported income from legal sources in 1976, broken down by type of

Table 5-1

Estimates of Unreported Income for 1976, by Type of Income
($ billion)

| Type of Income | Lower Estimates | | | | Higher Estimates |
| | Underreporting Based on: | | | | |
	TCMP[a]	Other Sources	Nonfiling	Total	
Legal-sector incomes:					
Self-employment[b]	19.8	3.5	9.7	33.0	39.5
Wages and Salaries	3.5	5.0	12.8	21.3	26.8
Interest	1.4	1.8	2.2	5.4	9.4
Dividends	1.4	—	0.7	2.1	4.7
Rents and royalties	2.6	—	0.6	3.2	5.9
Pensions, annuities, estates and trusts	2.1	—	1.5	3.6	5.4
Capital gains[c]	2.9	1.0	—	3.9	5.1
Other[d]	1.7	0.6	—	2.3	2.9
Total	35.4	12.0	27.5	74.9	99.7

Note: Sum of components may not add to totals due to rounding.

[a]Stands for Taxpayer Compliance Measurement Program, the principal means IRS uses to measure unreported income amenable to detection through very thorough audits of tax returns filed.

[b]Self-employment income covers net earnings of farm and nonfarm proprietorships and partnerships (at times referred to as unincorporated business income) as well as net earnings of self-employed individuals working outside the context of regularly established businesses in the legal sector.

[c]Excluded from the National Income and Product Accounts (NIPA) income concept which defines income as earnings arising from the current production of goods and services.

[d]Includes alimony, lottery winnings, prizes and awards and other types of income. Most of the incomes included here are excluded from NIPA since they represent transfer payments.

income. Table 5-2 relates the table 5-1 estimates of unreported income to total amounts of income which should have been reported on tax returns. Note that compliance for different types of income ranges from extremely high for wages and salaries which are subject to withholding to relatively low for self-employment and rental incomes. The pattern identified is seen to be strongly influenced by whether or not the specific type of income is, first, subject to withholding—as in the case of wages and salaries—and second, subject to information document coverage—for example, dividends and most interest payments. Where there is no income tax withholding at the source and very limited information document coverage—for self-employment and rental incomes, for example—voluntary compliance is low.

Table 5-3 presents the tax losses associated with unreported income from legal activities by type of delinquency. Note that estimated tax losses due to failure to file are fairly small in relation to volumes of unreported

Table 5-2
Estimated Amount of Unreported Income for 1976 as Percentage of Reportable Amount, by Type of Income

Type of Income	Amount of Income Reportable on Tax Returns ($ billion)	Amount Reported on Tax Returns	
		Total[a] ($ billion)	As Percentage of Amount Reportable
Legal-source incomes:			
Self-employment	93-99	60	60-64%
Wages and salaries	902-908	881	97-98
Interest	54-58	49	84-90
Dividends	27-30	25	84-92
Rents and royalties	9-12	6	50-65
Pensions, annuities, estates and trusts	31-33	27	84-88
Capital gains	22-24	19	78-83
Other	9-10	7	70-75
Total	1148-1172	1073	92-94

Note: Sum of components may not add to totals due to rounding. Percents of amounts reportable were computed from unrounded figures.

[a]Includes a small amount of illegal-source income. This does not significantly affect the percentages.

income. This disproportion is, in part, attributable to the preponderance of relatively modest incomes in nonfiler segments of the estimates—covering, for example, household workers, migrant laborers, and small entrepreneurs operating cottage industries. A more important reason for the disproportion between unreported income and associated tax loss due to nonfilers is the fact that the tax involved is an average tax on average income and not a marginal tax on marginal income. In other words,if a nonfiler were to file a tax return, he or she would be entitled to claim exemptions for dependents and itemized or standard deductions from the income reported for selected

Table 5-3
Estimates of Unreported Income and Associated Tax Loss for 1976
($ billion)

	Unreported Income	Tax Loss
Total	74.9-99.7	12.8-17.1
Filers	47.4-64.1	10.6-14.3
TCMP-based	35.4-36.5	7.8- 8.0
Other	12.0-27.6	2.8- 6.3
Nonfilers	27.5-35.6	2.2- 2.8

expenditures and taxes. In the case of an underreporter of income who files a tax return, presumably exemptions and deductions have already been subtracted from the taxable income reported. Consequently, the tax loss to the government is a marginal tax on a marginal (underreported) income.

The Methodology

In selecting an appropriate methodology the study team considered the wide variety of situations in which reported incomes may be earned. It was clear that tax evasion is not confined to receipts in the form of currency. For example, an investor may earn interest on money market instruments, not subject to information document coverage, and not report all or part of this even though the interest is paid by check.

Income has many distinct meanings in different contexts. After considering a number of possibilities, the study team decided to ground its estimates in a broader concept than the one used for the National Income and Product Accounts (NIPA), by including generally all incomes required to be reported to the Internal Revenue Service on individual income tax returns. Thus, the unreported earnings in tables 5-1 and 5-2 include all unreported incomes both from regularly established enterprises or occupations and from legal activities that are sometimes called irregular because they take place in informal settings. The latter includes cash wages of moonlighters or completely off-the-books workers. While there are differences of opinion, I believe that the statistical sources used for the NIPA are not sufficiently inclusive to cover all such cash wages or self-employment incomes.

As may be seen from table 5-1, separate estimates were prepared for underreporting by taxpayers who do file returns and the unreported incomes of nonfilers, with the latter adjusted downward to allow for withholding of taxes on incomes from wages. Underreported incomes are broken down into Taxpayer Compliance Measurement Program (TCMP) and non-TCMP components. TCMP is the principal IRS program for obtaining systematic data on the nature and extent of compliance with the internal revenue laws. Although procedures vary somewhat across different types of returns, the basic approach starts with selecting for examination a probability sample of returns filed (about 50,000 in the case of individual tax returns). These are examined by a thorough and controlled procedure on which detailed reports are kept. TCMP provides not only a basis for discriminant formula (DIF) development to select returns having a high probability of tax error potential for the regular examination programs of the IRS, but also provides reliable measures of income and tax gaps for types of earnings which are amenable to detection through quality audit procedures.

Thus, the TCMP-based estimates of underreported income measure the total amount of additional income which would be identified if all individual returns filed were examined on a quality basis by well-qualified auditors as in the returns included in the TCMP surveys. The IRS recognizes that not all unreported incomes can be detected through examinations of tax returns. For example, incomes from illegal activities or such incomes as payments to irregular suppliers operating off the books, household workers, agricultural laborers, or interest receipts of individual holders of bearer securities—not subject to information reporting—are particularly difficult to discover on audit. The study team, therefore, had to use information from a number of special studies and roundabout procedures to arrive at the estimates presented in the second column of table 5-1.

Last year, the General Accounting Office (GAO) estimated nonfiler incomes. Although the methods used by GAO differ in some respects from the one preferred by IRS, both agencies based their estimates of unreported nonfiler income on the Exact Match File. The starting point for this file was a household survey conducted in early 1972, involving a sample of 50,000 households containing approximately 100,000 persons 14 years or older. These interview data were merged outside IRS with data available through the records of the Social Security Administration and the IRS Individual Master File. The Exact Match File was created several years ago as a public use data base for general statistical research. Data from the IRS Information Returns Program, which is a document matching program, were also examined to assess the significance of nonfiler incomes.

A further source of data for estimating nonfiler wage incomes was a perfected file of employee compensation reported to IRS by employers on Forms 941 and 941E. A comparison of estimates from this source with estimates of W-2 wages reported by taxpayers in 1976 established a useful second estimate of delinquent nonfiler wage income gap.

A final major source of macroeconomic data related to unreported income came from the Bureau of Economic Analysis (BEA) of the Department of Commerce. BEA furnishes annual comparisons between estimates of total income received by individuals and total incomes reported on tax returns. The shortfalls these reconciliations show, labeled by BEA as "unexplained differences," however, do not necessarily measure noncompliance in reporting taxable income. For one thing, some of the unexplained differences are due to incomes received by individuals who are legitimate nonfilers, having incomes which fall below filing thresholds. Therefore, elaborate further analysis was required to convert BEA's unexplained differences into reporting gaps which were even then regarded as higher estimates only.

Limitations of time do not permit further descriptions of methods used. Suffice it to say that, because of the inherent limitation of all the approaches used, the study team designed some cross-check methods, explained in the report, to validate the estimates of legal-source unreported incomes that were prepared. These cross-checks were in the main satisfactory, keeping in mind that precision is bound to prove illusory in tracking tax evasion or other forms of unreported income.

On the other hand, the measures of illegal-source income gaps leave much to be desired. As mentioned earlier, they are not comprehensive. Moreover, the estimates that were prepared should at best be regarded as soft. The components measured may be seen in table 5-4. The illegal drug estimates were based on volumes of the illegal drug traffic in 1977 prepared for the National Narcotics Intelligence Consumers Committee composed of members from the various federal law enforcement agencies. Going beyond the drug traffic to other illegal activities, namely, unauthorized gambling and prostitution, it was necessary to collate data from a variety of other sources, primarily outside IRS, including FBI, the Policy Sciences Center in New York and state and local police departments.

Comparative Size of the IRS Estimates

I shall now briefly comment on whether the IRS estimates of unreported income confirm the popular notions about a large and flourishing "subterranean economy." These ideas were triggered mainly by the works of Peter Gutmann[2] who based his conclusions about a rapidly expanding underground economy on increasing ratios of currency to demand deposits over a historical period of rising tax rates. As is well known, currency is a preferred medium of exchange when tax evasion is intended.

Table 5-4
Selected Estimates of Illegal-Source Unreported Income for 1976, by Type of Income
($ billion)

Type of Income	Amount of Unreported Income
Illegal drugs	16.2-23.6
Bookmaking	4.0- 5.0
Numbers	2.4- 3.0
Other gambling	1.6- 2.0
Prostitution	1.1- 1.6
Total Income	25.3-35.2
Addendum	
Estimated tax revenue loss	6.3- 8.8

The IRS study team found no reliable evidence for disproportionate growth in the unreported portion of total individual incomes in the United States. Comparing the IRS estimates with those of Gutmann's in a single year (1976), presents difficulties especially since neither inquiry started with a precise definition of exactly what is being estimated. Reflection on the implications of Gutmann's estimation procedures will show that his estimates are grounded in payments made in currency. From the standpoint of the IRS, this concept is too narrow since there is no reason to believe that significant amounts of rents, royalties, alimony, and interest, not to mention dividends or estate and trust income are paid in currency. Checks may also be used in generating wage or self-employment income, part of which may not be reported. On the other hand, the IRS estimates of illegal-source incomes are not comprehensive. Because of such differences, opinions may differ on the degree to which the IRS estimates deviate from those of Gutmann's. As one economist who has considered and reconsidered this issue many times over the past two years, it is my judgment that the midpoint of the range bracketing the IRS estimates, after adjustment for the relevant conceptual differences, would fall far short of Gutmann's $176 billion estimate for 1976. Moreover, further research now in progress at the IRS seems to indicate that, if anything, the midpoint of the IRS range may be too high an estimate of the size of the so-called subterranean economy.

Conclusions

The IRS study of income reporting gaps represents an important first step in going to the limits imposed by available data to assess the dimensions of the so-called underground economy of unreported individual incomes. The methods used leave considerable room for improvement, of course. Recognizing this situation, the IRS is conducting further research aimed at the further refining and updating of its unreported income estimates. The figures relating to the completely off-the-books and other informal suppliers in particular need firming up through empirical studies. Fortunately, properly designed household sample surveys can be used to collect from buyers of informally supplied goods and services the data needed to estimate unreported incomes earned in the informal cash economy. Balanced and comprehensive research efforts, however, should go beyond the individual cash economy to the underground economy of unreported corporate, trust and other incomes as well.

The researchers at IRS are open to constructive new ideas. In fact, we would encourage further economic research in all areas of tax evasion and tax avoidance in order to strengthen the U.S. voluntary compliance system which is fundamental to the American concept of self-government.

Notes

1. Internal Revenue Service, *Estimates of Income Unreported on Individual Income Tax Returns* (Washington, D.C.: Government Printing Office, September 1979).

2. See, in particular, Peter M. Gutmann, "The Subterranean Economy," *Financial Analysts Journal*, November/December 1977, pp. 26-27.

6

A Second (and More Skeptical) Look at the Underground Economy in the United States

Vito Tanzi

Defining the Underground Economy

In all branches of human activities fashions come and go. What is highly fashionable today is forgotten tomorrow. Economics is not immune from these cycles. Problems that we did not even know existed are all at once discovered, move to the center of our attention, and eventually fade away. At times the problems fade because they are solved; more often they fade just from our consciousness and from the front page of newspapers because we lose interest in them. One common mistake we make is to assume that just because an issue or a problem becomes newsworthy it is necessarily a new one. Pollution, for example, was there long before it became fashionable to talk about it. And it is still there, even if we do not talk much about it anymore.

What we call the underground economy is now holding center stage; in fact, writing on it is becoming a growth industry. But just what is the underground economy? Is it a new phenomenon? How large is it and how fast is it growing? The definitional question is particularly significant—in the scientific, or at least the professional, world definitions are necessary preconditions for measurement, and we cannot be relaxed about them. Unless we can define precisely what we are measuring, the measure itself will have only a limited and subjective value.

Underground economics has meant different things to different people. For example, to Edgar Feige and Peter Gutmann it has meant unmeasured GNP, or better, gross national product which, given current conventions, should be measured but is not. On the other hand, to the Internal Revenue Service and, to some extent, to me, it has meant income that is not reported to the tax authorities and that may or may not have been included in the estimations of national income. Both of these definitions are important and both are useful but one must not lose sight of the fact that they relate to different things. Therefore, when, for example, Gutmann compares his own estimate of the underground economy to that of the Internal Revenue Service, he is really comparing two different animals having only vague similarities.

Paper presented at Wertheim's Conference on the Underground Economy, held in New York City, June 24, 1981.

From a macroeconomic point of view, perhaps the more important of the two definitions is the one that defines underground economy as unmeasured gross national product. The reason is that much of our economic policy is based on variables derived from the national accounts. Should the national accounts give erroneous information, the policies based on them would be erroneous too. This is an aspect that has been very much emphasized by both Gutmann and Feige. They have gone so far as to argue that the economic malaise of recent years—as measured by inflation, unemployment, and the like—may be only a statistical illusion. From this point of view, the underground economy is a subject of interest to my institution, as the International Monetary Fund deals essentially with macroeconomic policies.

Gutmann and Feige must be complimented for having introduced a degree of skepticism vis-à-vis the statistics in the national accounts. This skepticism was long overdue. Those statistics are estimates at best. At worst, they are, as a Latin American cynic put it, "cuentos nacionales" or "national tales." We have placed too much confidence in small changes in some of these variables and, perhaps because of this, we have pursued policies of fine-tuning to an excessive degree. But once this is recognized, does it mean that national accounts are useless? They would be if they were as wrong as implied by some of the current literature on the underground economy. This, of course, raises the issue of the extent to which these accounts are underestimated because of the existence of an underground economy.

Measuring the Underground Economy

Let us ask the question: just what do we know about the underground economy? We all have been exposed to anecdotal information and to some direct evidence about its existence through stories in newspapers and magazines. Some of us have also been part of this underground economy, sometimes knowingly, sometimes unknowingly. Perhaps we made cash payments to the baby-sitter or the piano teacher or the repairman; they did not report this income to the tax authorities and thus these payments were not picked up in the national accounts. We may have heard of doctors and lawyers bartering services. Furthermore, we are painfully aware that there are many illegal transactions taking place in the economy which are not recorded and measured.

Now two questions must be raised: first, are these activities new? Second, how important are they? It seems to me that it is very difficult to make a case that the phenomenon which goes under the name of underground economy is something new in the United States. As Barry

Molefsky states, (chapter 3, this volume), there is ample evidence that in past decades, and especially during the period of Prohibition and World War II, underground economic activities flourished.

What do some of the figures recently mentioned in discussions imply for an average family? Take for example a family of four with an income equal to the nation's average. This family would have to spend close to $5,000 a year on underground goods and services, if the underground economy were 10 percent of the GNP. It would have to spend $15,000 if the underground economy were as high as Feige estimates. Even an underground economy of 5 percent implies an expenditure of $2,500 a year on the part of a family with four members. Ask yourself whether you are spending this much (or proportionately more if your income is above average) for underground economic activities. Or are we facing here the kind of phenomenon described in the statement: "Don't look at him, don't look at me, look at the fellow behind the tree"? There is an aura of unreality vis-à-vis some discussions of the underground economy; it is supposed to be so huge that everybody should be in it up to his neck, or at least up to his waist; on the other hand, when you begin to ask yourself the question about who the participants are, you often come to the conclusion that it must be the fellow behind the tree.

If the existence of a *large* underground economy is not obvious from our immediate environment, where does the evidence often cited in support of this contention come from? A close analysis reveals that essentially it comes from the use of selective monetary ratios. This approach has always made me think of the person who wanted to measure a girl's height by the length of her skirt.

There is a basic difference between the approaches followed by Gutmann and by Feige. This difference is not so much in the methods as in one basic assumption; namely, for Gutmann the underground economy is being fueled by transactions *in currency*. On the other hand, Feige tells us to forget about currency and concentrate on checks presumably made out to cash. I shall come back to this distinction but I must declare my sympathy for Gutmann, having myself made the same assumption. But I want to call attention at this point to some salient aspect of these two approaches. Gutmann tells us to look first at what is happening to the level of currency in the United States. In 1980 it had reached the astronomical figure of $616 per capita, or $2,464 for a family of four (see table 6-1 and figure 6-1). Clearly, nobody in his right mind would argue that a family of four needs to hold so much cash. Second, Gutmann tells us to look at the ratio of currency to demand deposits. This ratio has grown from around 20 percent, just before the war, to around 40 percent at the present time. A modern economy is supposed to move out of currency, not into it. Third, he tells us to look at the composition of the currency. The proportion of large bills ($100 denomination and over) has risen from 18 percent in 1933 to 36 percent in

Table 6-1
Currency in Circulation, 1930-1980
(dollars per capita)

Year	Total Currency in Circulation	< $100	= $100	> $100
1930	37.3620			
1931	43.1910			
1932	43.1385			
1933	43.8864	35.9095	4.9087	3.0183
1934	43.7628	36.5138	4.5613	2.6877
1935	46.1695	38.2339	4.9215	3.0141
1936	51.0374	42.2075	5.5148	3.8151
1937	50.7752	41.8217	5.5039	3.4496
1938	52.7385	42.6923	5.9231	4.1231
1939	58.0443	45.9206	7.0206	5.1031
1940	66.1014	51.3248	8.4179	6.3588
1941	83.6582	66.2669	10.7421	6.6492
1942	114.2328	93.3506	14.1586	6.7235
1943	149.5903	119.6050	21.3021	8.6832
1944	182.8540	141.4379	30.0072	11.4090
1945	203.8242	164.4675	30.1644	9.1923
1946	204.7525	162.1358	33.7412	8.8755
1947	200.3331	156.5996	35.1889	8.5496
1948	192.5239	150.2115	34.6112	7.7012
1949	184.9866	148.8204	33.8874	7.2788
1950	182.1471	142.6527	33.1123	6.3821
1951	188.5474	148.9477	33.6152	5.9845
1952	193.1028	153.0266	34.5622	5.5140
1953	192.1411	152.0974	34.8377	5.2060
1954	187.1718	147.8160	34.4294	4.9264
1955	187.8119	149.2285	34.0024	4.5811
1956	188.2179	150.2072	33.7715	4.2392
1957	185.0814	147.6860	33.4419	3.9535
1958	184.0652	146.6381	33.6535	3.7736
1959	183.3015	146.6142	33.2565	3.4308
1960	181.8982	145.7499	32.9496	3.1987
1961	184.6380	148.3778	33.2390	3.0212
1962	189.4799	151.9786	34.5737	2.9276
1963	199.2178	158.7104	37.5793	2.9281
1964	206.4565	164.0542	39.5518	2.8504
1965	216.4488	171.8013	41.8682	2.7792
1966	227.1770	180.0305	44.4303	2.7162
1967	237.6749	188.1379	46.8596	2.6774
1968	253.9163	201.0463	50.1644	2.7055
1969	266.1569	209.2551	54.3463	2.5555
1970	278.6384	217.3499	58.9751	2.3133
1971	294.8720	227.9479	64.7706	2.1535
1972	318.5632	244.1284	72.4042	2.0307
1973	344.5675	260.4658	82.1673	1.9344
1974	376.3237	278.6739	95.7905	1.8594
1975	405.1826	295.0515	108.3287	1.8024
1976	435.4879	309.8095	123.9219	1.7565
1977	478.6123	334.8133	142.0839	1.7151
1978	524.2112	356.5249	166.0082	1.6781
1979	569.3563	377.5113	190.2085	1.6364
1980	615.9964	393.2765	221.1131	1.6068

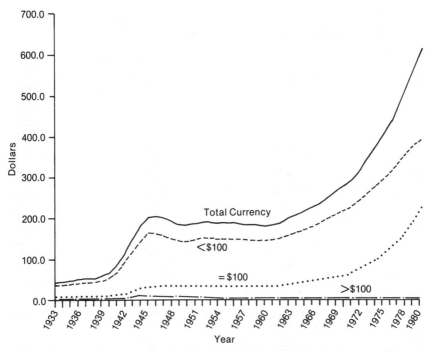

Figure 6-1. U.S. Currency in Circulation, Per Capita in Current Prices

1980 (see table 6-2 and figure 6-2). Interestingly, much of the increase occurred during the 1970s. Gutmann has made a strong case but, as often happens, there is another side to the story. His case begins to look somewhat less convincing when we consider the following factors:

1. Although the amount of currency per capita has been growing at a very fast pace in *nominal* terms, its increase looks much more moderate when we take account of price changes. For example it must surely come as a surprise to many to find out that in *constant* dollars, currency holdings per capita were 55 percent greater in 1945 than in 1980 (see table 6-3 and figure 6-3). In other words, once we adjust for price changes, per capita currency holdings have decreased rather substantially since the war. Even in the large bills category, per capita holdings were in 1980 the same as in 1944. Since real per capita income has doubled during this period, the behavior of currency appears less unusual than one has been led to believe.

2. Several writers have shown that the increase in the currency/demand deposit ratio is probably due more to a fall in demand deposits than to an increase in currency. If, in the denominator, demand deposits are replaced by total deposits, the currency/deposit ratio *falls* significantly. For example, it was 0.16 in 1959 and fell to 0.12-0.13 in the most recent years. Given the ease with which deposits could be transferred between demand and

Table 6-2
Currency in Circulation, by Denomination
(Percentages)

Year	< $100	= $100	> $100
1933	81.9170	11.1977	6.8853
1934	83.4357	10.4227	6.1416
1935	82.8120	10.6596	6.5284
1936	82.6991	10.8054	6.4955
1937	82.3664	10.8397	6.7939
1938	80.9510	11.2310	7.8180
1939	79.1129	12.0953	8.7918
1940	77.6454	12.7348	9.6198
1941	79.2115	12.8405	7.9480
1942	81.7197	12.3945	5.8858
1943	79.9550	14.2403	5.8047
1944	77.3501	16.4105	6.2394
1945	80.6909	14.7992	4.5099
1946	79.1862	16.4790	4.3348
1947	78.1696	17.5627	4.2677
1948	78.0223	17.9776	4.0001
1949	77.7464	18.3188	3.9348
1950	78.3173	18.1789	3.5038
1951	78.9975	17.8285	3.1740
1952	79.2462	17.8983	2.8555
1953	79.1592	18.1313	2.7095
1954	78.9734	18.3946	2.6320
1955	79.4563	18.1045	2.4392
1956	79.8050	17.9427	2.2523
1957	79.7952	18.0687	2.1361
1958	79.6664	18.2835	2.0501
1959	79.9853	18.1430	1.8717
1960	80.1272	18.1143	1.7585
1961	80.3615	18.0022	1.6363
1962	80.2083	18.2466	1.5451
1963	79.6668	18.8634	1.4698
1964	79.4619	19.1575	1.3807
1965	79.3727	19.3433	1.2840
1966	79.2468	19.5576	1.1956
1967	79.1577	19.7158	1.1265
1968	79.1782	19.7563	1.0655
1969	78.6209	20.4189	0.9601
1970	78.0043	21.1655	0.8302
1971	77.3040	21.9657	0.7303
1972	76.6342	22.7284	0.6374
1973	75.5921	23.8465	0.5614
1974	74.0516	25.4543	0.4941
1975	72.8194	26.7358	0.4448
1976	71.1408	28.4559	0.4033
1977	69.9550	29.6866	0.3583
1978	68.0117	31.6682	0.3201
1979	66.3049	33.4076	0.2874
1980	63.8440	35.8952	0.2608

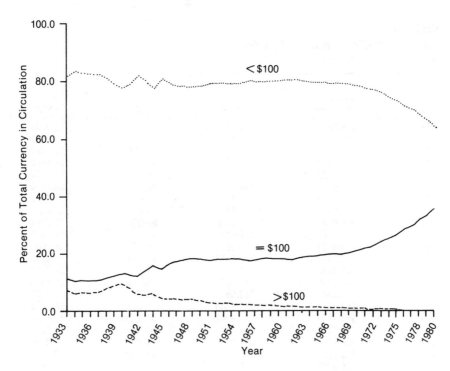

Figure 6-2. U.S. Currency in Circulation

time, it should be no surprise that many depositors have decreased their holdings in demand deposits and have increased them in time deposits which earn interest.

3. Even the increase in the proportion of large bills in total currency holdings might have some explanation unrelated to the underground economy. Consider the following. As the average price level increases, the price of most of the things we buy increases also; therefore large bills become more useful. This became obvious in some countries, such as France in the late 1950s, where monetary reforms simply eliminated the small bills. Similar proposals have been made for Italy. However, in my opinion, the more important explanation of this change in the composition of the currency in circulation and one that has a large bearing on the discussion of the measurement of the underground economy is to be found in the amount of dollar bills held outside of the United States. I've always wondered why I rarely see $100 bills here in the United States, while I seem to see them often when I am traveling abroad. In some countries I have

Table 6-3
Currency in Circulation, 1930-1980
(Per capita, in 1972 dollars)

Year	Total Currency in Circulation	< $100	= $100	> $100
1933	174.3690	142.8379	19.5253	12.0058
1934	160.4798	133.8974	16.7263	9.8561
1935	166.0775	137.5320	17.7033	10.8423
1936	182.6680	151.0647	19.7381	11.8652
1937	173.3533	142.7849	18.7910	11.7774
1938	184.4647	149.3260	20.7173	14.4214
1939	203.8073	161.2379	24.6511	17.9183
1940	226.9188	176.1921	28.8976	21.8291
1941	266.9374	211.4450	84.2761	21.2163
1942	332.1686	271.4470	41.1708	19.5507
1943	413.4614	330.5831	58.8782	24.0001
1944	493.7997	381.9548	81.0349	30.8100
1945	537.5110	433.7222	79.5475	24.2412
1946	465.8759	368.9096	76.7717	20.1946
1947	403.0847	315.0897	70.7926	17.2025
1948	362.3638	282.7244	65.1443	14.4951
1949	351.7524	273.4748	64.4370	13.8407
1950	339.5732	265.9446	61.7306	11.8981
1951	329.2255	260.0798	58.6961	10.4496
1952	332.9358	263.8391	59.5900	9.5068
1953	326.3266	258.3176	59.1673	8.8417
1954	313.5731	247.6394	57.6804	8.2533
1955	307.9894	244.7170	55.7599	7.5124
1956	299.2335	238.8032	53.6907	6.7396
1957	284.6530	227.1394	51.4332	6.0804
1958	278.6333	221.9771	50.9439	5.7124
1959	271.4773	217.1418	49.2542	5.0812
1960	264.8874	212.2468	47.9826	4.6580
1961	266.5098	214.1712	47.9777	4.3609
1962	268.5753	215.4196	49.0060	4.1497
1963	278.2760	221.6935	52.4924	4.0901
1964	283.9451	225.6281	54.3967	3.9203
1965	291.2390	231.1643	56.3351	3.7395
1966	295.9575	234.5369	57.8821	3.5385
1967	300.7781	238.0890	59.3009	8.3883
1968	307.5164	243.4859	60.7538	3.2767
1969	306.9152	241.2997	62.6687	2.9468
1970	304.9894	237.9049	64.5524	2.5321
1971	307.0944	237.3962	67.4554	2.2428
1972	318.5632	244.1284	72.4042	2.0307
1973	326.0171	246.4432	77.7437	1.8303
1974	327.4658	242.4938	83.3540	1.6180
1975	322.7004	234.9885	86.2764	1.4355
1976	329.6404	234.5087	93.8021	1.3296
1977	342.2815	239.4431	101.6119	1.2265
1978	349.3577	237.6041	110.6353	1.1184
1979	349.7919	231.9293	116.8572	1.0054
1980	347.1380	221.6266	124.6059	0.9055

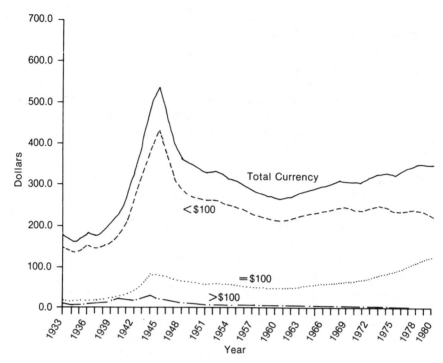

Figure 6-3. U.S. Currency in Circulation, Per Capita in 1972 Prices

literally witnessed old ladies standing in line in banks or in exchange houses to deposit or exchange stacks of $100 bills. Incidentally, many of the bills in American currency that one sees abroad *are* $100 bills which is exactly the category that has been growing fastest in the United States. What would explain this exodus of $100 bills from the United States?

First, we know that in some countries (Panama, Liberia, the Bahamas, Haiti, for example) American currency circulates as freely as the local currency. Second, foreign travel brings about an increase in the demand for larger-denomination bills and foreign travel has increased dramatically over the years. Third, newspaper articles have at times reported that some of the increased oil revenues flowing to the Middle East have taken the form of American currency. Fourth, several countries, where imports are restricted, such as Somalia, Pakistan, and Yemen, have in recent years introduced import systems whereby importers who have available foreign exchange, which often means dollars, can get import permits. Fifth, some countries, like Egypt and Korea, have introduced duty-free zones whereby goods are sold duty-free only if the payment is made in foreign exchange which, again, often means dollars. Sixth, large incomes derived from illegal activities, such as drugs, may often be converted to large bills which may be smuggled out of the country. Finally, and perhaps much more important, high rates of inflation in some countries (such as Argentina, Israel, and Brazil) have resulted in a phenomenon referred to as currency substitution; namely, dollars have often replaced part of the domestic currency. In some countries, the traffic in dollars is so common that quotations of the black market rate are regularly published. For example, in Brazil, the *Journal de Comercio* publishes weekly and monthly data for the black market premium for dollars. The world out there is very large and it would not take much for billions of dollars to find their way outside the United States. The titles of two recent unpublished papers, one coauthored by Rudiger Dornbush of MIT, the other written by Guillermo Ortiz of the Bank of Mexico, tell part of the story. The first is entitled "The Black Market for Dollars in Brazil," the second is entitled "Dollarization in Mexico: Causes and Consequences."

A few basic points need to be emphasized. The first is that there are many reasons to believe that many dollar bills are outside the United States. Unfortunately, there seems to be no way of making an assessment of just how many dollars are out there. Various inquiries on my part to the Federal Reserve, the Treasury, or even to officials from various countries have led nowhere; even guesses seem to be missing. This is clearly a research area that should attract more attention; the question is an important one. An informal inquiry to foreign exchange dealers indicated that (a) there are large net shipments abroad of U.S. currency; (b) these shipments are growing in size; (c) most of them are in large-denomination bills; (d) most demand comes from South America, the area where currency substitution is likely to be greatest, and to a lesser extent from the Far East and the Middle East; (e) there is a net inflow from Europe. This behavior is quite consistent with the hypothesis of currency substitution and the data shown in table 6-4.

Second, it makes a lot of sense to believe that this exodus of dollar bills consists mainly of $100 bills—these are relatively easy to carry and yet not so large as to be difficult to cash. Third, many of the arguments presented above would indicate that this exodus of dollars accelerated in recent years. In fact, if one had to make a guess, 1973 could have been a turning point; in that year the price of oil went up sharply and the rate of inflation accelerated, reinforcing the currency substitution effect mentioned above. By 1975, for example, a considerable proportion of the total demand for money in Argentina was probably being satisfied by the holding of American currency as the ratio of domestic money to GDP had been cut in half. Table 6-4 gives some indication of the differential rates of inflation between the United States and other key areas.

Table 6-4
Differentials between Inflation Outside of the United States and U.S.
Inflation, 1960-1980

Year	World	Industrial Countries	Oil Exporting Countries	Africa	Asia	Middle East	Western Hemisphere
1960	1.1	0.3	4.0	−0.1	1.7	−0.1	13.3
1961	1.5	0.6	−0.2	2.8	0.8	1.8	14.3
1962	2.5	1.4	0	0.5	1.5	0.1	21.2
1963	2.7	1.4	−0.8	1.7	2.2	1.5	27.3
1964	3.3	1.1	1.0	5.6	10.3	3.4	33.7
1965	3.1	1.4	0.2	2.9	6.1	7.9	25.7
1966	2.0	0.4	−0.4	2.0	6.4	5.0	20.9
1967	1.6	0.3	−2.5	2.6	8.7	−0.9	16.1
1968	0.2	−0.3	−3.3	1.9	−1.3	−3.8	10.1
1969	−0.2	−0.6	1.6	−1.0	−2.7	−3.1	6.9
1970	0.1	−0.3	−0.7	−1.6	−0.2	−1.0	7.4
1971	1.6	0.9	0.6	0.8	1.0	2.1	11.6
1972	2.5	1.4	0.9	2.5	3.9	2.7	18.7
1973	3.3	1.4	4.6	3.5	10.6	6.0	25.2
1974	4.4	2.4	5.2	5.0	16.5	12.4	20.0
1975	4.2	1.9	9.4	6.4	1.0	11.6	32.5
1976	5.4	2.5	10.1	9.8	−6.7	12.3	51.4
1977	4.9	1.9	8.7	13.4	1.5	14.3	41.8
1978	2.3	−0.3	3.1	8.2	−1.7	15.9	34.0
1979	0.9	−2.1	−0.9	6.1	−1.8	19.7	36.3
1980	2.0	−1.6	0.5	2.3	0.5	39.2	42.6

Source: International Monetary Fund, *International Financial Statistics.*

While it makes a lot of sense to assume that U.S. currency held abroad is mainly in the form of $100 bills, I am far less convinced that this denomination represents the major means of exchange in the underground economy within the United States. Clearly, large drug transactions and other activities by organized crime may be, at least in part, settled in $100 bills. However, many of the underground activities emphasized by some of the writers (payment of babysitters, wages of illegal aliens, and the like) surely are settled in currency of smaller denomination. Therefore, I find it hard to see a direct connection between the expansion in the circulation of $100 bills and the growth of the underground economy in the United States.

Let me turn now to Edgar Feige's analysis. His approach consists of relating the ratio of total transactions, in both currency and checks, to gross national product. Increases in that ratio are seen as indications of growth in underground economic activities. Quite apart from technical issues related to his analysis, issues that have been raised by various writers, and especially by Richard Porter of the Federal Reserve Board (see reference in chapter 3 of this volume), I have a hard time accepting the result that the underground economy in the United States is essentially a phenomenon associated with the use of *checks* rather than with the use of currency.

In table 6-5, I have combined Gutmann's and my own assumption about the predominant use of currency with Feige's transaction approach. The table covers the 1960-1980 period. Column 1 shows total currency in circulation while column 2 shows total currency redeemed in each year. Column 3, which is the ratio of columns 1 and 2, gives the average lifetime of the currency in circulation, that is, the average number of years it remains in circulation. Again, something interesting happens: while the average lifetime did not change very much up to the early 1970s, it started to increase rather fast after 1973. This last result fits quite well with our earlier discussion about the movement of currency abroad. An increase in the lifetime of the currency in circulation indicates that either it was being used more and more as a store of value, that is, it was being hoarded and therefore performed fewer transactions per year and/or it was being held outside of the United States. A key year in our analysis seems to be 1973; in that year inflation really took off in many parts of the world (table 6-4) and the adjustment in the price of oil took place. Therefore, the results in the table are consistent with the analysis that has preceded.

Combining the information in column 3 with the Laurent-Feige estimate of the total number of times a unit of currency can change hands before it becomes so dirty and old that it must be retired, we get transactions per year per currency unit. According to Laurent, the total transactions per unit is 125; therefore, dividing this transaction figure per unit by the average lifetime of the unit we get column 5. Multiplying total currency in circulation by the number of transactions per year, we get total currency transactions for each year. Finally, following in part Feige's method, we divide total transactions into GNP; this is column 7. These results are also shown graphically in figure 6-4. The remarkable thing about the graph is that it indicates that if Feige had tried to measure his underground economy by using currency transactions rather than checks, as, for example, Gutmann did, he would have found an underground economy that had been falling rather considerably over the past twenty years, especially up to 1978. Interestingly, the ratio increases after 1978 when, due to inflation, marginal tax rates rise dramatically. Incidentally, the trend would not be affected if the number reflecting transactions per unit of currency were changed from, say, 125 to 250. I know that Feige will reply that some underground activities are conducted by check. But I, for one, find it difficult to believe that in situations where the underground economy is growing at a pace as remarkable as he claims, people would be *reducing* transactions in currency to the extent shown in the figure while at the same time sharply increasing transactions in checks.

Table 6-5
Estimation of Total Currency Transactions, 1960-1980

Year	Total Currency in Circulation ($ million) (1)	Currency Redeemed ($ million) (2)	Average Lifetime (3) = (1)/(2)	Total Turnover per Unit (4)	Transactions per Year per Unit (5) = (4)/(3)	Total Transactions in Currency per Year ($ million) (6) = (1) × (5)	Ratio of Total Transactions to GNP (7)
1960	32869	7663.0	4.289	125	29.142	957875.0	1.891
1961	33918	7686.5	4.413	125	28.328	960812.5	1.832
1962	35338	7861.7	4.495	125	27.809	982712.5	1.739
1963	37692	8107.1	4.649	125	26.886	1013387.5	1.698
1964	39619	9443.5	4.195	125	29.795	1180437.5	1.851
1965	42056	9157.1	4.593	125	27.217	1144637.5	1.656
1966	44663	9482.2	4.710	125	26.538	1185275.0	1.568
1967	47226	10931.0	4.320	125	28.933	1366375.0	1.709
1968	50961	10776.0	4.729	125	26.432	1347000.0	1.542
1969	53950	11570.0	4.663	125	26.807	1446250.0	1.532
1970	57093	12280.0	4.649	125	26.886	1535000.0	1.546
1971	61068	12768.0	4.783	125	26.135	1596000.0	1.481
1972	66516	13499.0	4.927	125	25.368	1687375.0	1.423
1973	72497	14642.0	4.951	125	25.246	1830250.0	1.380
1974	79743	15154.0	5.262	125	23.754	1894250.0	1.321
1975	86547	15127.0	5.721	125	21.848	1890875.0	1.221
1976	93717	14913.0	6.284	125	19.891	1864125.0	1.085
1977	103811	15113.0	6.869	125	18.198	1889125.0	0.985
1978	114645	16229.6	7.064	125	17.695	2028700.0	0.941
1979	125600	19275.4	6.516	125	19.183	2409425.0	0.998
1980	137244	21320.2	6.437	125	19.418	2665025.0	1.015

Source: Currency redeemed for 1960-1977 comes from Richard D. Porter, "Some Notes on Estimating the Underground Economy," August 10, 1979; for 1978-1980 it comes from the *Annual Report of the Secretary of the Treasury*.

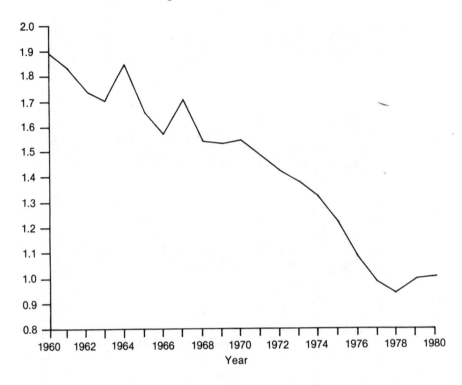

Figure 6-4. Ratio of Total Currency Transactions to GNP

Underground Economy and the National Accounts

I must conclude that the case for a very large and growing underground economy made by Gutmann and Feige is far from convincing. However, one must not jump to the conclusion that there is no underground economy in the United States; other evidence indicates that these activities can be substantial. However, it is far easier to prove that there is a substantial underground economy, when this is defined as total income not reported to the tax authorities, than when it is defined as income not measured by the national accounts authorities. Defined in terms of unreported incomes, the underground economy has been estimated by the Internal Revenue Service at somewhere between 6 and 8 percent of GNP for 1976. My own estimate for that same year would be in the same range of magnitude. Although some increase is likely to have occurred since that time, due to the growing marginal tax rates brought about by inflation—the behavior of the ratio in the last two years shown in figure 6-4 and in column 7 of table 6-5 supports this—I would be doubtful that the increase would account for more than one or two percentage points of GNP. But, of course, this is a hunch rather than an estimate.

Do these estimates indicate that measured GNP is equally underestimated? In my judgment, the answer to this question is, simply, not likely. There are various reasons for this. One is that much income reported by payers to the national accounts authorities is not reported by payees to the tax authorities. This is particularly true for interest income, dividends, and some wages. This differential, between income as reported to the tax authorities and income as reported to the national accounts authorities, is still considerable but has been falling over the years. For example, it was almost 11 percent in 1947 but has been only in the range of about 5-6 percent in more recent years. An interesting study by Susan B. Long for the U.S. Department of Justice has provided yearly estimates of these differences between 1947 and 1977. These estimates show clearly that the differential has been falling.

GNP is measured on the expenditure side as well as on the side of incomes received. Expenditure-based estimates are generally measured independently of income payments and, except for particular expenditures such as those for drugs and in a few other illegal activities, there is no reason these should be underestimated. Measurements of GNP from the income side would, of course, fall short of those made on the expenditure side if the national accounts authorities relied on the data provided by the tax authorities without an adjustment. In the United Kingdom there has been considerable discussion in the past year about the measurement of the underground economy made on the basis of the difference in GNP measured as a consumption concept and GNP measured as an income concept. In that country, that difference, that has been growing, is in the range of about 3 percent of GNP. In the United States, however, that difference, referred to as statistical discrepancy, is very low, as shown in table 6-6, and has been falling.

Of course, some activities may not be picked up either on the expenditure side or on the income side. This is particularly the case for illegal activities but may extend also to the activities of people who do not file an income tax return and who are mainly providing services. Also, to the extent that barter arrangements are accompanied by income creations the growth of barter can also bring about some underestimation of the GNP.

In conclusion I will make a few guesses about the underestimation of GNP in the United States because of the existence of underground economic activities. Up to about 4 percent I would consider it likely; from 4 to 6 percent I would consider it possible; from 6 to 8 percent I would consider it unlikely but still in the range of possibility; to accept an understatement exceeding 8 percent, I feel that one would need faith rather than reason.

Table 6-6
Statistical Discrepancy

Year	Gross National Expenditure ($ billion)	Gross National Income ($ billion)	Statistical Discrepancy ($ billion)	(Percent of GDP)
1971	1,077.6	1,073.5	4.1	0.38%
1972	1,185.9	1,182.6	3.3	0.28
1973	1,326.4	1,325.6	0.8	0.06
1974	1,434.2	1,430.5	3.7	0.26
1975	1,549.2	1,543.5	5.5	0.36
1976	1,718.0	1,712.9	5.1	0.30
1977	1,918.0	1,913.6	4.4	0.23
1978	2,156.1	2,149.7	6.4	0.30
1979	2,413.9	2,411.7	2.2	0.09
1980	2,627.4	2,625.7	1.7	0.06

Source: Economic Report of the President, 1981.

References

Feige, Edgar L. "How Big Is the Irregular Economy?" *Challenge*, November-December 1979.

Gutmann, Peter M. "The Subterranean Economy." *Financial Analysts Journal*, November-December 1977.

Internal Revenue Service. *Estimates of Income Unreported on Individual Income Tax Returns*. Washington, D.C.: Government Printing Office, September 1979.

Long, Susan B. *The Internal Revenue Service: Measuring Tax Offenses and Enforcement Response*. U.S. Department of Justice, National Institute of Justice, Washington, D.C. September 1980.

Molefsky, Barry. "America's Underground Economy." chapter 3, this volume.

Tanzi, Vito. "The Underground Economy in the United States: Estimates and Implications." *Banca Nazionale del Lavoro Quarterly Review*, no. 135, December 1980. Chapter 4 of this volume.

7 Statement of Robert Parker

Robert Parker and
John Gorman

I have been invited to appear before this committee to present comments by the Bureau of Economic Analysis on the Internal Revenue Service (IRS) Report: *Estimates of Income Unreported on Individual Income Tax Returns.*

Evidence from the national income and product accounts (NIPA), supports the $75 billion estimate of unreported income from legal sources on individual income tax returns presented by IRS.

The amount of income not reported to IRS does not represent a corresponding understatement in the national income product accounts, because of the limited use of tabulations of individual income tax returns in preparing the NIPA estimates. Only 6 percent of GNP in 1976 is estimated from IRS tabulations of individual income tax returns. This includes BEA's direct use of IRS tabulations and BEA's use of Census Bureau estimates which rely to some extent on information from IRS.

Where the unreported income is due to noncompliance on reported returns, BEA, in most cases, makes adjustments based on the taxpayer compliance measurement program. Where the unreported income is due to nonfilers, BEA does not have sufficient information to adjust the NIPA estimates.

We have constructed very rough estimates of how much GNP is understated for nonfiling for the single year 1976. The estimates indicate that from $6 to $10 billion—or about one-half of 1 percent of total GNP—is missing.

To summarize, we correct for noncompliance on reported returns; we estimate roughly a shortfall of $6 to $10 billion from nonfiling.

It is important to note that estimates of a large share of the NIPA components are based on the employer's quarterly federal tax returns; the universe of firms filing these returns provides the Census Bureau with the mailing list for many of the major statistical sources used to estimate the NIPAs.

There is no indication either in the IRS report or from other studies IRS has made on the compliance of these returns that there is any significant underreporting. Thus, tabulations of surveys based on this universe are assumed to be virtually complete.

Reprinted from U.S. Congress, House of Representatives, Committee on Ways and Means, Oversight Subcommittee, *Underground Economy*, Hearings July 16, September 10, October 9 and 11, 1979, Washington, U.S. Government Printing Office, 1980, pp. 199-205.

The development of a better estimate of the GNP shortfall depends on the availability of additional studies by IRS and BEA such as:

1: A compliance study of the employers' quarterly federal tax return.

2: The creation of an Exact Match File for additional years. However, before a file is created, it is first necessary to improve the reporting of income data in the Current Population Survey (CPS), to increase the sample size underlying the tabulations of the individual tax returns, and to provide statistical agencies access to the individual tax return records. The 1972 Exact Match File was developed by statistical agencies with access to individual tax returns. Such access may have been removed or limited by the Tax Reform Act of 1976.

3: A compliance study of the self-employed nonfilers.

BEA has no information on the extent of income generated from illegal activities and cannot comment on this aspect of the IRS report. Illegal transactions are omitted from the present measure of GNP, primarily because there is no feasible method of estimating the extent of such activities.

Mr. Chairman, I am prepared to answer any questions on this statement that you might have and to the extent necessary for providing details for the record.

Mr. Gibbons: On the bottom of page 2, what is the meaning of that last sentence in paragraph 2? It says: "The 1972 Exact Match File was developed by statistical agencies with access to individual tax returns."

Mr. Parker: Prior to the 1976 Tax Act there was an Executive Order 10911, and a Treasury Decision 6547, which allowed access by the Commerce Department to individual income tax records. As a result of the 1976 Tax Reform Act, such access was limited to selected returns of corporations only and our access to individual records or individual tax returns was removed.

It is not clear how this removal of access would affect other agencies who were involved in the creation of the 1976 exact match.

Mr. Gibbons: It is significant in obtaining proper statistics?

Mr. Parker: the exact match provides us with a means, and I think perhaps the best means, of quantifying some of the problems relating to the underground economy and the compliance on tax returns.

However, the basic part of the exact match is the Current Population Survey, a statistical report collected by a statistical agency, and the Internal Revenue Service does not have any access to that information. Therefore, it is imperative in our judgment that any type of exact match study be conducted by a statistical agency not associated with the IRS.

To do otherwise, would have IRS be more involved and that would be a breach of the confidentiality in which the Census Bureau operates and would create serious problems to them. That is the reason why in the statement we emphasize that particular problem or potential problem, I should say.

Mr. Gibbons: Have you just ignored the extent of the illegal activities in the United States or why haven't you done anything at all about that?

Mr. Parker: Basically, we have no means of collecting any information or we have no access to any reliable statistical sources which would permit us to make these estimates. It is very clear if we had that information and it was statistically reliable, we would attempt to include that. This treatment is a long-standing practice here and probably in other countries that keep national income accounts. The reason we have no comment is that we could not confirm or deny the validity of the information that the IRS has presented.

Mr. Gibbons: So really what you report is the legitimate economy that somehow ends up in the record, is that correct?

Mr. Parker: That is correct. The $6 to $10 billion shortfall that I mentioned refers to an estimate of what additional GNP there would be if we had reports from all of those people who did not file any reports. The information that we use now in the accounts are already adjusted for noncompliance by filers.

Mr. Gibbons: Where you have filers, you can make that adjustment because you have the information to correct for underreporting. But you estimate that nonfiling accounts for only one-half of 1 percent of GNP?

Mr. Parker: That is correct.

Mr. Gibbons: Have you ever been to a farmers' market on Saturday morning? I realize that is a small transaction, and I have no idea really how much it is.

Mr. Parker: Mr. Chairman, let me respond for just a moment. I know from taking my lunch-time strolls and observing street vendors—the situation you are concerned with. There are many of them who use charge accounts and are quite sophisticated. However, it is not clear to me that seeing more street vendors necessarily leads to an understatement. I have looked at the extent of reporting to IRS by small businesses, where small businesses are defined as those who have no employees at all and no paid employees. There are literally millions and millions of these small businesses who have filed reports with IRS. This, to me, is an indication that there is, perhaps not complete compliance, but a very heavy compliance by these very small businesses in our tax reporting system.

Mr. Gibbons: How about the extent that barter is used in this country? That is within that one-half of 1 percent of GNP?

Mr. Parker: There are two types of barter that would affect our accounts. One of them would have very little effect and that is a transaction between businesses where one business service is transacted or is bartered for another. In that case, since GNP does not include intermediate purchases, there would be no effect whatsoever. In the case of barter between individuals, here I believe we would be missing the profit someone would make on barter.

In GNP, used goods are not valued at the sale price. Only the margin that the seller earns goes into GNP. Mr. Gorman has been working with the barter economy more than I have and perhaps he would like to expand on that answer somewhat.

Mr. Gorman: Between businesses, presumably the selling business would buy what it acquires and value it at what it costs, and therefore, we need have no discrepancies in the accounts. Presumably at the end result of these transactions, it is going to be a cash deal, meaning to keep bargaining and bartering and turning over, and you never get something to eat unless you sell something.

So we feel that there is not a volume of consequence to the business economy, but there may be a problem in the transfer of used assets between people. That may be involved.

Mr. Gibbons: How does this one-half of 1 percent compare with other industrialized economies?

Mr. Parker: I am sorry, I do not know the answer to that.

Mr. Gibbons: I was thinking about the Swedes. Do we have any idea what they are finding in their economy? I was in Sweden a few years ago and the government officials over there were telling me that they were appalled at what had happened to their tax system because their tax rate was so high. They thought there was an awful lot of the economy that was outside of the system.

Mr. Parker: While I have no direct way of answering that, perhaps it would be helpful to explain in a different context why these transactions result in such a little impact on GNP. It deals with how we construct GNP, if I may digress for a moment.

If one utilizes a great deal of tax return information in assembling the estimates of gross national product, then one clearly has problems to the extent that there is noncompliance. We measure GNP as the sum of final product flows. That is we sum together personal consumption expenditures, private business investment, net exports and government purchases. All of the data that we use for that, with the exception of the 6 percent that I mentioned in my statement, comes from sources other than tax return records. So that in order to assess the impact of the underground economy, one must look at those other data sources to see where we have other potential shortfalls.

One of the areas mentioned most frequently as a problem area is retailing. The estimate of personal consumption expenditures for goods that we utilize does not depend on the level of retail sales. We use what we call the commodity-flow approach where we take the output of each particular good and add to that transportation margins, and wholesalers' margins, and retailers' margins, and taxes. And we arrive at a figure which becomes the purchaser price value of a particular good. Those goods are all summed up to give us personal consumption expenditures for goods.

The role of retail sales in that tabulation is very small. The major inputs into those calculations are the values of manufacturers' shipments of goods tabulated by the Bureau of Census. We do not believe that there are any serious or significant underground economic activities in the manufacturing area. At least we have not read reports of any, and that is why in the statement that I have read, I talked about the quarterly tax return because that is the basic source of the Census of Manufacturers mailing list.

To the extent that we have complete reporting in manufacturing, which we feel we do, then the problems of understating personal consumption expenditures for goods are not very serious.

In the area of the government, while we have the government records, various budget documents from both federal, state, and local, we do not feel we have a problem here. Export data are primarily based upon Customs documents and there may be some illegal smuggling but we do not believe there is any particular underaccounting of the value of exports and imports. We are not aware of any.

In business investment, here again we collect data from two sources. One is manufacturers' shipments of capital equipment and the other is the value of construction. Both of those come from the Census Bureau. The shipments data of manufactured goods, as I explained before, are complete so that I do not think there is a problem. The value of construction is also related to various government records, primarily building permits.

However, the Census Bureau, who collects this, makes an adjustment in those data for construction for which a building permit has not been obtained and should have been obtained. We already are adjusting our construction figures for noncompliance with various building permit requirements at the local level.

Again, we do not feel that we have a particular problem there. In major additions and alterations to residential construction, which is discussed as a potential problem area, we collect the data there by a household survey. That is, the Census Bureau goes to the households and asks how much they spent during this first quarter for various additions to your house. We have not been able to determine whether those people who pay the carpenter in cash, in effect, do not respond on this survey. We do believe they are responding properly, which would mean that although in measured income we may be missing the income of contractors who are moonlighting, we are not missing their contribution to gross national product measure of construction activity.

The one area that I have not touched on and it happens to be the one that we have the most problem with, is consumer purchases of services. There we do utilize the Internal Revenue Service and Census data for receipts of services from consumers. Most of the $6 billion to $10 billion estimate, or I think one-half of it, is coming from this area.

This long-winded explanation is related to other countries because understatement depends upon how these other countries measure GNP. To the extent they rely on tax return data they may be underestimating. Many countries, however, do not get their income data from income taxes. What they do, and this deals with how the national accounts are constructed, relates to the fact that there are several ways of measuring GNP. We measure gross national product in the way I just mentioned, which is the sum of purchases. We also measure it as the sum of various income items, wages and profits and proprietors' income and interest.

In this country, we have a direct estimate of each of these components. We prepare these estimates and obtain another measure of gross national product which we call "changes against gross national product." Statistically, that should be equal to gross national product. It differs slightly. In 1976, for example, the difference was $6 billion, which means that in this particular year when we added up our final product flows, we got $6 billion more than an independent estimate of GNP derived from income flows. This, by the way, is another check that we use to assure that our GNP figures are correct.

In many European countries, because of the problems with the tax data, they do not use the tax information to estimate income. What they do is to measure the gross national product in a similar manner to what we do. They estimate those components of income such as wages and salaries for which they have good information and simply subtract all of these items on the income side from the total GNP and obtain as a residual "business income" or "operating surplus." Thus, they do not have a problem in measuring income because they do not try to use it from the tax returns.

Mr. Gibbons: Was there anything in the recent IRS study released that surprised you about the size of the underground economy as they estimated?

Mr. Parker: I do not believe so. We have been tabulating and publishing for a number of years a reconciliation of our measure of personal income to the adjusted gross income which comes from the individual tax returns.

For 1976, that comparison, after adjustment for noncomparability as referred to in the IRS report, shows about a $65 billion difference. In other words, the personal income as measured in the national accounts is $65 billion higher than the comparable adjusted IRS gross income. Now, we have not been able to really do an in-depth analysis of the exact causes of that $65 billion but very clearly, some of it we have always assumed is due to some noncompliance in the reporting of tax returns. A good bit of the difference comes from the fact that the published IRS numbers are not adjusted for the taxpayers' compliance measurement program results and our numbers are.

So, we are not surprised at the relative size of the problem as identified by the IRS report.

8 The Irregular Economy and the Quality of Macroeconomic Statistics

Peter Reuter

Government agencies are understandably reluctant to admit the failings of their data on matters of policy significance. Academics, on the other hand, are all too willing to show the great deficiencies of published data and "the need for further research." The tension between the two is presumably a healthy one. The stubborn certainty of agencies forces academics to provide constructive means for obtaining better data. Indeed, this interaction has even been institutionalized, in the form of bodies such as the National Academy of Sciences.

When academics fail to press for better data, one has cause for alarm. Academics can become complaisant clients of agencies. Having used official data to explain and predict, one generation of researchers acquires a stake in defending those data against the attacks of the next generation. The data become, literally, "given."

This certainly is the case with national income data. Empirical macroeconomics is now a well-established profession. Respected academic economists are consulted by government and business for their views on macroeconomic policy, views which usually depend on analysis of official data. Journals are filled, and careers are made, by sophisticated manipulation of these same data. Theories of increasing complexity are tested using the data, and paradoxes of the data are explained by more refined theory. To suggest that the data are badly deteriorating does not provide comfort to academic macroeconomists.

Yet the sudden interest in the possible growth of tax evasion in the United States has suggested to some that perhaps many of the paradoxes of recent macroeconomic performance are not the failing of theory but of the data. GNP growth may be underestimated, inflation and unemployment overestimated. Observed paradoxes may be resolved at a stroke. Government agencies, under attack from elected politicians and besieged by media allegations based on anecdote, have started to present elaborate defenses of their data. On the one hand they have shown that what they *can* quantify

The work reported here has been supported by a grant from the Ford Foundation to the Center for Research on Institutions and Social Policy, New York. An earlier version of the paper was presented at the Second Annual Conference of the Association for Public Policy Analysis and Management in Boston, October 1980 concerning the alleged deficiencies of the data indicate that such deficiencies are trivial. On the other hand, they challenge the critics to produce meaningful evidence, beyond anecdote, about that which they *cannot* quantify. Alarmingly, almost no major academic macroeconomists have participated in the debate, at least so far. The commitment to the verities of past models and predictions appears to outweigh curiosity about possible new shortcomings in the data on which they are based.

This chapter is an early effort to justify alarm about economists' complaisance with respect to some fundamental data sources. I do not assert that the quality of National Income and Product Accounts (NIPA) estimates or other macroeconomic data has declined significantly. I do claim that it is a possibility and one that is well worth investigating, both for its policy significance and its intellectual interest. Many issues in current macroeconomics which are treated as issues for theoretical resolution may well be the consequence of changes in the quality of the underlying data. The data are not generated in some magical fashion, by omniscient agencies; they are the result of reporting and monitoring programs which are sensitive to changes in the structure of the economy. Only by understanding the sources of the reported data series and their sensitivity to recent changes in taxation and regulation can we test whether at least some of the apparent paradoxes are real or are the consequence of changes in the relationship of reported data to actual values.

At this stage I can present no definite quantitative results. Instead, I want to make two points through a small series of examples. First, if the irregular economy is growing, that growth may have far-reaching effects on the quality of macroeconomic data. Indeed, *insidious* is scarcely too strong a word for the potential effects. The section of this chapter on tax evasion illustrates this point. Second, there are some contemporary macroeconomic puzzles which might quite plausibly be explained by these effects. More precisely, changes in the quality of the underlying data may turn out to be at least partially responsible for some of the observations that current macroeconomic analysis has difficulty explaining.

I would also like to make two more polemical points. In reviewing the literature, in the part of this chapter entitled "Irregular Sector," I argue that there is a confusion about definition that goes to explain some of the differences in varying estimates of the size of the irregular economy. The problem is further compounded by the unhistorical view taken by most writers on the subject. The second polemical point concerns the complaisance of economists. I believe that there is ample evidence to justify the claim that economists have been insufficiently skeptical about their data; "The Faith of Economists," later in this chapter, provides some examples to justify this charge and even some casual sociology to explain it.

Irregular Sector: Definition and Estimation

Interest in the existence of a sector of unrecorded economic activity within the U.S. economy clearly began with a short article by Gutmann (1977), who coined the term "subterranean" economy. He defined that as comprising all "transactions that escape from taxation," (Gutmann 1979; p. 4). This is not a helpful definition, since a single transaction may be subject to numerous taxes, and Gutmann's estimate of the size of the subterranean economy is probably not equally sensitive to all forms of taxation. For example, efforts to escape sales tax obligations on a particular transaction may have less effect on the accuracy of GNP estimates than efforts to escape the income tax obligations of the seller arising from the same transaction. However it is noteworthy that the definition focuses on transactions, not individuals. It is likely that many persons function in each sector of the economy, often both as consumers and producers.

As always in the early stages of a debate, shifts in definition tend to pass unnoticed and have important implications. Macafee (1980) and Tanzi (1980), using different terms for the sector ("hidden" for Macafee and "underground" for Tanzi), provide similar definitions, which are distinct from that of Gutmann and have significantly different statistical consequences. "The hidden economy is defined for national accounts purposes as 'being the economic activity *generating factor incomes* which cannot be estimated from the regular statistical sources used to compile this income measure of gross domestic product'." (Macafee, p. 81, emphasis added) "The underground economy . . . is gross national product that, because of unreporting and underreporting, is not measured by official statistics." (Tanzi, p. 2) These definitions focus attention on the relationship between official statistics and reality generally, not simply on the failure to report income for tax purposes. The difference between them reflects the difference between the methods used for generating the expenditure side of the NIPA estimates in the United Kingdom (Macafee) and the United States (Tanzi). In the United Kingdom these expenditures, except for certain sensitive items (for instance, liquor) are estimated from expenditure surveys that show no obvious bias.[1] The excluded items, notably liquor and cigarettes, are subject to specific taxation which yields high-quality independent estimates for household expenditure.

It is interesting to note that Tanzi, though he states that the difference between his definition and that of Gutmann and Feige (1979) may have consequences for the estimates they each generate, identified only one such consequence. He notes that, in the bench-mark years (1937-1941 for Gutmann, 1939 for Feige), tax differences notwithstanding, at least one part of the underground economy still existed, namely illegal markets. But he assumes that the quality of statistical reporting, for purposes of GNP estimates, has not changed, an assumption which is, for various reasons, highly questionable. For example, before 1942 there was no tax-withholding program for wages and salaries and it is an axiom of tax administration in this country that withholding is the key to compliance (IRS 1979, p. 3). This issue is treated in more detail in the section on tax evasion.

Most attention has been paid to those transactions which result in income not reported to IRS. For political purposes this is undoubtedly the proper focus, namely, a set of transactions which could, through improved tax administration, produce additional revenues to the government. Here I shall refer to a broader concept, the "irregular economy," consisting of transactions which are not included in official reporting programs, although they fall within the intended scope of such programs.[2]

This is not the place in which to review the various estimates of the size of the irregular economy, these being dealt with in other chapters in this volume. For the United States the range is broad, as low as 5.9 percent of GNP (IRS 1979) to 33.1 percent of GNP (Feige 1980). Definitional differences are probably not critical here, given the rather crude macroeconomic approaches used for developing most estimates. The one study that does merit review here because its work touches directly on the data quality issues which are the substance of this paper is that of the Internal Revenue Service (1979).

In 1978, responding to pressures from Congress, the Commissioner of the IRS appointed a study team to prepare estimates of the extent and sources of unreported personal income. The study team filed its report (referred to hereafter as *Unreported Income*) in 1979; the report was immediately subject to intense congressional scrutiny (U.S. Congress 1980) that has already ensured preparation of yet more detailed studies in the near future.

IRS, after providing an intelligent critique of the aggregate approaches, presented an item-by-item analysis of possible underreporting. For legal-source income, IRS estimated that in 1976 the unreported figure was between $75 and $100 billion, compared to a reported total of $1,073 billion (all figures are for 1976). Illegal-source income (that is, income generated by activities that are themselves illegal) IRS estimated to lie between $25 and $35 billion. After adjustments for different income concepts, the total comes close to Gutmann's 10 percent estimate for the same year.

Unreported Income is an extremely sophisticated analysis of a variety of government data sources. It is not, ultimately, a very convincing one. Indeed, there are times when one is not certain that the study team itself is persuaded of the validity of the data.[3] Great reliance is placed on the efficacy of audits, in particular the intense and sophisticated program known as the Taxpayer Compliance Measurement Program (TCMP). Unfortunately, the study team had to make use of rather outdated TCMP measures of the extent of audit-detectable unreported income; it used data on income returns for the calendar year 1973. Since there is a widespread belief that compliance may have declined significantly since 1973, this already imparts a conservative bias to the estimates. The other critical data (Exact Match File), used mostly to estimate the number and characteristics of nonfilers, are also based on 1973, again probably imparting a conservative bias.

Estimates of illegal-source income are clearly less good than those for legal-source income. IRS had to depend on figures provided primarily by law enforcement agencies which have never acquired the technical skills necessary to collect and analyze the data for sound estimates (Reuter and Rubinstein 1978). Moreover, only a relatively small number of illegal activities were included in the data set for which estimates were presented. Though I am inclined to agree with the implicit IRS assumption that the other criminal activities produce a trivial amount of personal income, not making a systematic effort to study these other components is certainly a noticeable omission.

Moreover, the IRS estimates do not help answer what is generally perceived to be the important policy question and is certainly the question of interest here. Is the irregular economy growing relative to the rest of the economy? The study team tentatively concluded that there is no evidence that it is, but *Unreported Income* provides little guidance.

Tax Evasion and the Quality of Macroeconomic Data

While political and popular interest in the irregular sector has mostly focused on the possibility that significant tax revenues remain uncollected, academic interest has also been concerned with the possibility that macroeconomic data are deteriorating, as a result of the growth of the irregular sector (Feige 1980). In this section I argue that while indeed there may be a serious problem, it requires an understanding of the means by which macroeconomic statistics are generated. The simple inferences of Gutmann, in particular, but also those of Feige, may produce misleading results. In addition, I argue that there is evidence that the quality of macroeconomic data is probably higher now than it was in the early postwar era.

Let me begin by presenting a simple framework in which to discuss the accuracy of the basic data used for macroeconomics. There are three broad categories of data sources. The first consists of material generated in the course of complying with tax obligations. Income tax returns are the most obvious and important example, but the category is much broader. Social Security filings, which involves a tax obligation for the employer, with no corresponding return, is another important example. The second category consists of voluntary responses to surveys; the Current Population Survey (CPS) (unemployment rate) and the Consumer Price Index (CPI). Finally, there is a category of nonvoluntary materials which have to be provided by certain entities but which do not have immediate tax implications for the respondents. The Census of Manufacturers and the Census of Retailers, which provide data for generation of national income estimates, are examples.

It seems plausible to assume that the accuracy of all three categories is correlated. A self-employed businessman who underreports income, for income tax purposes, will probably provide materials reflecting this underreporting to other government authorities, to the extent that it is possible, and will either fail to provide income data in a survey or will underestimate. These are only guesses, but the extensive literature on self-reporting of deviant behavior (for example, Forrington 1973) makes this clear. Nonetheless, as tax rates increase we should expect, all things being equal, a deterioration in the quality of data from all three categories.

However, there are many factors other than tax rates which affect the accuracy of tax filings. Large enterprises, with more complex internal controls and more potential internal informants, are in less of a position to underreport income. They may use more sophisticated forms of tax avoidance, unavailable to most small enterprises, but underreporting of gross income, at least, is less likely. Thus the increasing percentage of GNP generated in large enterprises and the government sector is likely to be accompanied by a rise in the quality of reported data on economic activity in many dimensions.

On the other hand, compliance is also affected by monitoring. This in turn is determined not only by the severity of formal penalties for noncompliance but by the intensity and efficacy of auditing. IRS now audits a smaller percentage of personal income tax returns (2.1 percent in 1978) than it did in the early 1960s (5.6 percent in 1963). Predictably, the accuracy of filings has declined. TCMP audits found underreporting accounted for 6.7 percent of tax liability in 1973, compared to 4.8 percent in 1963 (Long 1980, p. 62).

Monitoring is also relevant to the third category of data, nontax mandatory filings. Here perhaps the most pertinent observation is the fractured and uncoordinated nature of the regulatory and tax system. Agencies at the same level of government exchange little information; much more so for those at different levels. Moreover, each agency has its own forms and filing requirements. It is possible for the one entity to provide inconsistent information to different agencies, without the inconsistencies being detected.[4]

If this is the case, then the accuracy of each source may indeed be uncorrelated. Retailers may underreport sales levels when filing sales tax reports, while correctly reporting wage data for social security purposes, because the probability of detection for sales tax evasion is much smaller. Indeed, the conclusions of a recent study of states sales tax administration (Due and Mikesell 1980) are worth noting. After reviewing the programs in thirteen states they concluded that "For most states the present (audit) coverage is even less adequate than it was a decade ago" (p. 43). Not only do most states audit an unacceptably small percentage of accounts but they seem to have little sense of strategy in carrying out their audits. This contrasts with the sophisticated audit selection program of the IRS, based on complex analysis of prior audit experience with various classes of returns. "Few of the states indicated any specific objective in audit coverage." (p. 39) Even with these low and ill-directed audit rates, audit recovery is a nontrivial percentage of sales tax receipts. The most aggressive of the states in the Due-Mikesell sample, Rhode Island, audited 4.4 percent of its accounts and recovered 5.5 percent of total receipts through audit. The possibility that sales are underreported by 20 percent, in less well administered states, cannot be dismissed.

This suggests that each macroeconomic series requires separate scrutiny. Broad references to increasing incentive for tax evasion cannot substitute for careful examination of the process generating the data on which each series is based. In what follows I shall illustrate this by considering a few series.

Let me begin with unemployment estimates. Feige and Gutmann both assert that there is now a substantial upward bias in measured unemployment which is dependent on the Current Population Survey (CPS). The CPS reports interview data from approximately 56,000 households. How do irregular sector workers reply to questions about their employment status?

I have been unable to find any literature specifically dealing with this issue. A review of the survey instrument itself suggests that the matter is a complex one. Respondents are not asked to label their employment as regular or reported.[5] Indeed, the questions probe very little into the nature of the employment setting. Nor are respondents ever asked whether they are unemployed; they are only asked if they are looking for work.

The first issue for the irregular sector worker, when approached by the CPS interviewer, is whether to become a respondent. It seems reasonable to assume that he is more likely to be a nonrespondent than he would be if he were not in the irregular sector. But the nonresponse rate for the CPS is surprisingly low; about 4 percent overall, with refusals amounting to 2.5 percent of the total. If irregular sector workers tend to be nonrespondents, the consequence for measured unemployment is minor.

Alternatively, and it is clear that this is what Feige and Gutmann assume, irregular sector workers may classify themselves as unemployed. Total labor force counts would be unaffected but measured unemployment would be raised. This possibility cannot be discounted but it is not obviously the dominant response pattern, among the three alternatives.

First, the respondent may also be employed in the regular sector. Given the conditions of social security, unemployment insurance, and medical insurance programs, the optimal situation may in fact be part-time employment in both sectors. In that situation the CPS, insofar as it is used simply to estimate the overall unemployment rate, will not be biased by irregular sector employment.

Second, if the irregular sector worker has no regular sector employment and is not looking for work, he may choose to provide a pattern of responses which leads to him being classified as "not in the labor force." This will lead to an underestimate of the labor force but have only a second-order effect on measured unemployment.

The third situation is the one that Gutmann and Feige probably refer to, an irregular sector worker who is receiving unemployment benefits. Presumably he responds to the questions solely in his capacity as registered unemployed, thus raising measured unemployment. However, in order to be eligible for unemployment benefits the worker must have held, within a relatively recent period, a job in the regular sector. While one cannot discount the possibility that a significant portion of the registered unemployed is able to move at will between regular and irregular employment, it does require implausibly high access to regular sector jobs.

Let me turn now to the NIPA figures. The generation of national income estimates is an impressively complex task. The 100-page description in the 1954 *National Income* provides only a bare outline. One suspects that, like the large macroeconomic models, detail may have overwhelmed design. I consider here only two data series, though I conjecture that the problems are generic.

Consider the value of new residential construction, a major component of fixed investment ($68.1 billion in 1976). When the chief of the National Income Division of the Department of Commerce testified before the House Ways and Means Committee (1979, p. 203) he stated that "The value of construction is . . . related to various Government records, primarily building permits. However, the Census Bureau, who collects this, makes an adjustment in those data for which building permits have not been obtained and should have been obtained. We already are adjusting our construction figures for noncompliance with various building permit requirements at the local level."

On the face of it this is a satisfying response; a responsible agency of the federal government is taking cognizance of noncompliance in developing estimates based on filings which have financial consequence for the filers. However, an effort to determine the nature of the adjustment procedures produced a far less reassuring picture.[6] The adjustments are based on extremely dated bench-marks, which are potentially biased downward.

The most important adjustment is that dealing with valuation of housing starts in permit-issuing areas (most major urban areas). For those houses for which permits are actually obtained, the value is raised by 17.5 percent from the value declared on the permit. That figure is based on a

1956 survey, which has never been replicated. The builder who files the permit pays a fee based on the value that he files; his incentive is to underreport. To compensate for this, apparently many permit-issuing officers use a standard square-footage value for particular areas of their jurisdiction.

The Census Bureau also adjusts for housing starts in permit areas for which permits are not obtained. A survey carried out in the early 1960s, apparently involving actual counts on individual blocks then checked against permit records, yielded a figure on the proportion of starts that should have been registered but were not. This ratio is then used to adjust upward the total value of housing starts in permit-issuing areas. It is apparently assumed that the mean value of an unregistered housing start is equal to that of a registered start.

Thus the adjustment procedures, so airily referred to by the National Income Division, reflect data on evasion collected approximately twenty years ago. There surely are numerous reasons as to why nonreporting of starts and undervaluation of reported starts *might* have become more significant. Permit rate charges may have risen, local governments may have cut back the size of inspectorates, the universe of construction companies may now include a higher proportion of companies which have an interest in reducing the extent of documentation of their level of business because they are not paying various taxes. I cannot assert that these changes have actually occurred, but they all seem quite plausible. The use of twenty-year-old bench-marks seems highly questionable, given all the potential changes in the meantime.

IRS source materials appear to play a relatively minor direct role in the generation of national income estimates. Indeed a claim to that effect lies at the heart of the Bureau of Economic Analysis's refusal to adjust national income estimates in light of the IRS findings concerning underreporting. In fact, IRS materials have a pervasive influence. For example, the Census of Manufacturers and the Census of Retailers, both of which are necessary for the determination of the expenditure side of NIPA, are rooted in IRS filings. It is worth describing the relationship.

The Census Bureau's universe of establishments for the Census of Retailers and other sectors come from IRS-SSA listings. The Bureau of Economic Analysis (1980) acknowledges only a more limited dependence, namely the use of IRS documents for the smallest establishments, for whom the census forms would be a substantial burden. But the dependence on tax and social security filings for identifying the universe of establishments is more significant. If there does exist a substantial irregular sector of informal enterprises, which provide no filings for their employees for social security or for the owners' tax obligations, then the basis for estimates of various expenditure and income items (those dependent on markup estimates) is biased. Moreover, to repeat the standard assertion, there is some reason to believe that the bias may be of increasing significance since the incentives for nonfiling have increased, and monitoring levels have not.

The Consumer Price Index, perhaps the most widely quoted inflation indicator, at least for short-term political purposes, also is subject to distortions from the same source. Indeed, in this case the Feige-Gutmann assertions may be valid in their new form.

The problem arises from the "point-of-purchase" sample used to determine the actual prices of the goods in the commodity basket. It appears that informal vendors are generally not included in the sampling, so that the lower-price irregular sector transactions are excluded, precisely as suggested by Feige and Gutmann. As far as I can determine, and written accounts are difficult to obtain, the survey aggregates expenditure categories in such a way as to make it difficult, if not impossible, to isolate the extent to which informal vendors play a role.

These examples could be multiplied. Indeed, I am in the process of doing just that. But I think that the pattern of vulnerability to growth in the irregular sector is clear. Bench-marks for critical adjustments of major series may be outdated. There is hidden circularity in the accounts which may mean that weaknesses in a small number of series will affect many others. The lack of comprehensive written descriptions of the generation of these series, which often require the cooperation of various agencies, creates inconsistencies and makes the process of revision particularly difficult. It is certainly plausible that the quality of macroeconomic data declined in recent years.

On the other hand, the long-run pattern of change in the quality of macroeconomic estimates is probably quite different. Whether or not Feige is correct that the 1960s was the Golden Age of government, it is certainly plausible to assume that the growth of government involvement in the economy, through taxation, regulation, and expenditure programs, greatly increased the scope and accuracy of its statistical programs compared with, say, the immediate pre-World War II era.

Kahn (1959) provides some interesting evidence concerning the change even before 1960. He estimates that only 38.2 percent of entrepreneurial income was reported on tax forms in 1939, compared to 72.3 percent in 1957. Much of the increase came from the decline in the importance of the farm sector. For 1939 he estimated that only about 5 percent of farm income (sole proprietorships and partnerships) was reported on tax returns. Changes in the tax schedule and farmers' incomes during World War II raised this figure, but only to about 45 percent.

The National Income Division (NID) was not unaware of the problem. In particular, it attempted to find independent sources of data for the incomes of independent professionals (doctors, lawyers, and others) and farmers. For the first of these the NID relied on sample surveys which yielded response rates of less than 25 percent. Though analysis of nonresponse patterns in dimensions such as age, region, and size of city yielded no obvious source of bias, without a model of the determinants of tax evasion it is hard to place much confidence in survey data with such a low response rate.

The problem is even more serious for the other components of entrepreneurial income. Here the national income estimates are based on audit-adjusted tax return data, with a further adjustment for unreported entrepreneurs on the basis of census data. As Kahn remarks, "These corrections, while, of course, in the right direction, are not entirely satisfactory for our purpose to the extent that they rely on audit data since the IRS audit control program of 1948-49 could not, and was indeed not designed to, uncover all errors in reporting." (p. 1446) I also suspect, on the basis of current census practice, that the census data had a circular relation to the IRS filings.

Paradox and Measurement

The possibility that the major paradoxes of U.S. macroeconomic performance in the last decade may be explained as essentially measurement error is both tempting and troubling. On the one hand it would be comforting to find out that real performance has been better than measured and also that theory has not failed. On the other hand, if we cannot trust the data that are available to us, what is left for the empirical macroeconomist to do?

We hope that we shall find that measurement error has not been drastic and that there are appropriate means of providing more accurate and reliable measures of the critical variables. In the meantime I would like to suggest some current paradoxes for which the growth of the irregular economy might provide a satisfactory explanation.

Feige (1980) has already made some progress in this respect. He finds that his measure of the relative size of the irregular sector does well in explaining some troublesome macroeconomic series. For example, he is able to explain 65 percent of the variation in Denison's (1979) productivity residual (what Denison was unable to explain using conventional factors) during the period 1970-1976 (p. 42). Since there are serious questions concerning the measure that Feige has developed for estimating the irregular sector, it seems useful to present a more general discussion of some macroeconomic problems for which growth in the irregular sector may be an important explanatory factor.

At this stage I focus on secular rather than cyclical changes. While it is only a minor challenge to the imagination to develop cyclical theories of the relative size of the irregular sector (Feige 1980, p. 42), the important effects are presumably those arising from its long-run growth, since it is long-run change in the structure of the economy that has generated the apparent growth.

Consider the responsiveness of wages to changes in the unemployment rate. It is commonly believed that this has decreased (Hall 1980), that is, that in the late 1970s a 1 percent increase in unemployment had a smaller impact on the rate of increase in monetary and real wages than it would have had (at the same rate of initial unemployment) in the 1950s. While Wachter (1976) has provided a sophisticated challenge to this assertion, I use this merely to illustrate the slightly sinister explanatory power of irregular sector growth.

Assume that over time there has been a gradual shift of labor input into the irregular sector. There is no need to assume that this distorts measured unemployment; for simplicity assume that all irregular sector workers answer CPS interviews as though they are not in the work force. But actual wages will bear a changing relationship to observed wages, since the former are a weighted average of wage rates in the two sectors. Assume that there is a simple Phillips curve relationship between actual wage changes and actual unemployment, but that efforts are made to fit an equation in which the dependent variable is change in observed wage rates.

If one then compares the impact of unemployment increases on observed wages, at widely separated points in time, the coefficient of unemployment will have a time element, even though the true coefficient may have stayed constant over time. We simply have a secularly increasing error of measurement in the dependent variable, assuming irregular wages will always be lower than reported wages because of reduced tax obligations. The result is an unemployment coefficient that declines over time.

Of course a simple mechanical view of the effect of irregular sector growth has even more power. If irregular sector workers show up as unemployed in the CPS, then one of the central failures of macroeconomic modeling in the 1970s is easily explained. The apparent rise in the "full employment" unemployment rate is simply a result of misclassification.

The apparent decline in productivity in the United States is another significant macroeconomic puzzle that has defied satisfactory explanation. The most authoritative study of the decline (Denison 1979) concluded, with reference to the post-1973 period: "What happened is, to be blunt, a mystery." (p. 4) While I would not be so rash as to suggest that all this is mere measurement error, I believe that a plausible case can be made for testing whether it does not contribute something to reducing the size of the residual.

Productivity, of course, involves measures from both sides of NIPA. I have already commented on some of the difficulties of labor measures created by irregular employment. Given the labor-intensive character of what is generally believed to be produced in the irregular economy, I do not think that it is likely to be a serious source of problems for measures of capital. Here I want to deal with output measures, in particular value added by sector.

The opportunities for understatement of value added, in order to evade tax or regulatory obligations, are not equal for different sectors. Roughly, it seems that opportunities for evasion depend on the size of the enterprise (declining with scale) and the extent to which sales are made to final consumers, for whom the expenditure has no tax implications. Mining firms and telephone companies represent one extreme, small, independent restaurants and retail stores the other. Skimming off a small percentage of total receipts can lead to a substantial understatement of value added; in the retail sector the gross markup may be only about 15 percent (for foodstuffs), so that skimming of 5 percent of gross receipts reduces value added by about one third.

Assume then that there has been an increase in the extent of such skimming in small enterprise, retail sectors, in response simply to increasing marginal personal tax rates. We should expect that value-added productivity measures for these sectors should be lower than for sectors in which skimming opportunities have remained minor, after the effects of measurable factors are taken into account. In other words, the residual for fitted productivity measures should be consistently negative for the retail and, less clearly, services sector.

Unfortunately neither Denison nor the other major recent study of productivity slowdown (Norsworthy et al. 1979) present figures on the residual by industrial sector. All I can point to at this stage is the rapid slowdown in the retail sector growth rate in output per manhour post-1973 (Denison 1979, table 9-1). I plan to calculate the residual by sector and test the hypothesis. If this is correct then it may go some way toward explaining Denison's residual.

The Faith of Economists

Economists are unique among social scientists in that they are trained only to analyze, not to collect, data. While psychologists are taught experimental techniques, sociologists learn of the vagaries of interviewing, and anthropologists devote much of their training to field work, economists are provided only with the tools for data analysis. One consequence is a lack of skepticism about the quality of data.

The problem pervades both academic and official sectors of the profession. Economics is better represented in the official sector than is any other social science; indeed President Carter's original, technocratic cabinet contained four members with Ph.D.'s in economics. People such as the head of the Bureau of Labor Statistics and the head of the Bureau of Economic

Analysis are often well-respected academics. There is a harmony between the official and academic sectors, certainly in terms of orientation, which is notably lacking in other spheres of social policy and reseasrch. This may have contributed, along with the lack of training in data collection itself, to the rather unquestioning attitude economists have taken to the data.

Perhaps the most telling evidence of this complaisance is the very absence of a current account of the data collection techniques underlying the National Income and Product Accounts. The most recent comprehensive statement of the sources of data is the 1954 edition of *National Income.* The Department of Commerce is currently working on a revision that should be published in 1982. In the meantime there have undoubtedly been some major revisions, which I cannot deal with because there is no published description of them. The fact is that economists, despite their heavy reliance on NIPA for macroeconomic analysis, have failed to concern themselves sufficiently with the underlying data to require that the highly professional National Income and Wealth Division provide a description of ongoing revisions of the data-collection techniques.

Yet Simon Kuznets, the creator of NIPA as we know it, had no illusions about the quality of the data. Dividing GNP into 520 cells, he and his colleagues who were involved in producing the original estimates, provided an expert judgment as to the probable error for each cell. In some cases they estimated the error to be as much as 60 percent. Overall they concluded that the error for the National Income estimate might be about 10 percent. (Kuznets 1942) As far as I know, no one since then has attempted the same exercise. No doubt there have been substantial refinements in procedures which ought to improve the quality of estimates. But there are numerous reasons, discussed earlier, for assuming that other things have changed, possibly in a direction adverse to the quality of the NIPA estimates. Anyway, without a comprehensive description of the sources and techniques used for NIPA, an evaluation is impossible.

Nor, despite public interest in possible growth of the irregular economy and its effects on basic economic statistics, has there been any interest in trying more direct examination of the problem. For example, the National Commission on Employment and Unemployment Statistics (1979) recently concluded its deliberations and issued a report, together with three volumes of technical papers. The commission's membership included three leading labor economists. Its staff was highly professional and recruited an impressive list of labor economists to write papers on all aspects of the problem of measurement of employment and unemployment.

Yet the commission did not even allude to the problems raised by irregular sector employment. Indeed, the chairman of the commission, when asked to testify at Congressional hearings on the issue, said precisely that. The report does include, as the chairman mentioned in his testimony, a brief reference to the problem of illegal aliens, a component of the irregular sector, but only to conclude that too little was known about the numbers to permit the commission to provide any helpful comments. The technical papers, as far as I can tell, include only one brief comment on the issue (Ferman 1980, p. 271).

It is also of interest to report here the results of an OECD survey of unemployment statistics (OECD 1979). The survey presented a set of questions to the governments of twenty-three member nations. One question concerned irregular sector activities. "Are people who work illegally (that is, do not declare themselves because of tax or social security evasion) likely to be a significant gap in statistics of employment?" (p. 17) Thirteen nations said that illegal employment did not constitute a significant problem for measures of employment; this group included Italy, for whom it has been alleged that irregular sector activity accounts for between one-third and one-fifth of total GNP. The remaining countries, including the United States, simply said that they did not know whether there was a problem. (p. 44)

Work on the distribution of income, a major area of empirical research for economists also reflects credulity. For example, Lydall (1968) tested a new theory of the distribution of income, using data from a number of economies over a long period of time. At no stage does he consider that variations in the tax and employment structures of these economies might have an important effect on the reported distribution figures, through their impact on the accuracy of the data. Similarly, Richard Goode (1976) in his well-known text on the individual income tax, presents data on income distribution in the United States for the period 1890-1970 with no comment on shifts in the efficacy of reporting programs arising from changes in economic structure. He reports that only 4 percent of households paid federal income tax in 1939, compared with 56 percent in 1950; at no stage does he consider the possibility that this was the result of increased effectiveness of the tax system as well as changes in the tax schedule. Yet it is hard to ignore the impact of mandatory withholding of taxes on wages and salaries which was put into effect (originally on an interim basis) during World War II.

Conclusions

The incentives to evade taxation and regulation have complex effects on the quality of macroeconomic data. Moreover, the extent of evasion is determined not only by incentives but by opportunities, which are themselves sensitive to policy changes. Only by understanding the ways in which data are collected and the nature of monitoring and audit systems can one determine whether macroeconomic statistics have in fact deteriorated and the likely pattern of such deterioration.

There is plenty of incentive for carrying out research on this topic. Measurement error may account for many of the macroeconomic phenomena that have puzzled economists throughout the 1970s. While I have presented examples only of long-term problems which may be resolved by analysis of the growth of the irregular sector, as we come to learn more about its structure it may also turn out that it shows short-run cyclical sensitivity which has even more explanatory power. The policy utility of an understanding of this sector is obvious and important.

The small literature on the irregular sector has focused on the public policy incentives for its growth: since taxation and regulation have become steadily more onerous over the last two decades it is assumed that this sector must have grown relative to the recorded economy. But consideration of the opportunity structure does not clearly support this. The growing use of non-cash means of payment, of third-party payments for medical services, more active auditing of government benefit programs, and decreases in independent professional practice, all mitigate against avoidance of reporting requirements (Reuter 1980). None of the aggregative approaches is sufficiently convincing for us to be sure that the sector actually has increased in relative size.

Identifying the possible sources of changing bias in a particular series is only the first step in testing whether puzzles can be eliminated by improved measures. The next, and more difficult, step is the estimation of the contribution from various sources of bias, created by growth in the irregular economy. Given the absence of hard data on most of the phenomena that I have discussed, simulations with "pseudodata" seem likely to be the most fruitful approach. This would at least suggest the sensitivity of the data to plausible assumptions about reporting errors arising from strategic considerations.

What I think will emerge from such work is an understanding of how easy it is to find sources of error that can affect both the income and expenditure sides of NIPA almost equally. The relatively small size of the statistical discrepancy has always been a source of comfort to both the generators and users of the accounts, since it is assumed that the two sides of the accounts are essentially independent (Morgenstern 1963, chapter 14). The thrust of my examples is that the links between the two sides are in fact numerous and important. The statistical discrepancy may be seen rather as the bottom line for the producers of NIPA. They have enough discretion in the estimation of various components that it requires no great skill to ensure that the discrepancy is kept modest.

Notes

1. Expenditure surveys, whether based on interviews or diaries, are generally subject to downward bias. The recent Consumer Expenditure

Survey of the Bureau of Labor Statistics (BLS) did include questions on tobacco and alcohol expenditures, though BLS noted the low level of response for those questions as a potential source of bias. This has important consequences for the Consumer Price Index since its commodity weighting is based on the Consumer Expenditure Survey.

2. I prefer the term "irregular" to "subterranean" since the latter is too close to "underworld," with its implications of criminality.

3. I think that the following statement could be considered to aim more at reassuring the writer than the reader. "While there is undoubtedly much more to be learned about the details and extent of off-the-books employment and moonlighting and the illegal alien problem, it was the judgement of the study team that the present estimates, and especially the grand totals, are reasonable in the light of all available data." (*Unreported Income*, p. 97).

4. This issue has recently arisen in the context of taxation of the tobacco industry, which is taxed at the federal, state, and (often) local levels. See the series of articles in the New York *Daily News* by Cosgrove and Browne, October 12, 1980 to October 17, 1980.

5. The sequencing is the key issue here. Question 19 in the Current Population Survey is "What was . . . doing most of last week"; the four noted responses are "Working, Keeping House, Going to School or Something Else." Only then does the survey move to job content. My conjecture is that irregular sector workers are likely to say they work rather than "something else"; it would be interesting to analyze some of the nonresponse patterns in the subsequent job content questions.

6. This description is based on a series of telephone calls to the Census Bureau. I was unable to locate a written reference for this procedure and was assured by one official that such a document did not exist.

References

Bureau of Economic Analysis. "The Understatement of GNP and of Charges Against GNP in 1976 Due to Legal-Source Income Not Reported on Individual Income Tax Returns." Unpublished memorandum, July 1980.

Due, John F. and John L. Mikesell. "State Sales Tax Structure and Operation in the Last Decade—A Sample Study." *National Tax Journal* 33 (March 1980).

Feige, Edgar. "How Big Is the Irregular Economy?" *Challenge*, November-December 1979.

Feige, Edgar. "A New Perspective on Macroeconomic Phenomena: The Theory and Measurement of the Unobserved Sector of the United States Economy." Paper read at the ninety-third annual meeting of the American Economic Association, Denver, September 1980.

Ferman, Louis A.; Berndt, Louise; and Elaine Selo. "Analysis of the Irregular Economy: Cash Flow in the Informal Sector." Unpublished paper, Institute of Labor and Industrial Relations, The University of Michigan—Wayne State University, 1978.

Ferman, Louis A. Discussion of Teresa Sullivan and Phillip Hauser. "The Labor Utilization Framework: Assumptions, Data and Policy Implications." In Appendix Vol. 1 to National Commission on Employment and Unemployment Statistics, *Counting the Labor Force*, 1980.

Forrington, D. "Self Reports of Deviant Behavior: Predictive and Stable." *Journal of Criminology and Criminal Law* 64 (1973).

Goode, Richard. *The Individual Income Tax*. Washington, D.C.: Brookings Institution, 1976.

Gutmann, Peter. "The Subterranean Economy." *Financial Analysts Journal*, November-December 1977.

Gutmann, Peter. "The Subterranean Economy." *Taxing and Spending*, April 1979.

Hall, Robert. "Employment Fluctuations and Wage Rigidity." *Brookings Papers on Economic Activity*, November 1, 1980.

Internal Revenue Service. *Estimates of Income Unreported on Individual Income Tax Returns*. Publication 1104, Washington, D.C.: Government Printing Office, September 1979.

Kahn, C. Harry. "Coverage of Entrepreneurial Income on Federal Tax Returns." *Tax Revision Compendium*, House Ways and Means Committee, November 16, 1959.

Kuznets, Simon. *National Income and Its Composition*. Princeton, N.J.: National Bureau of Economic Research, 1942.

Long, Susan B. *The Internal Revenue Service: Measuring Tax Offenses and Enforcement Response*. U.S. Department of Justice, National Institute of Justice, Washington, D.C.: 1980.

Lydall, Harold. *The Structure of Earnings*. Oxford: Oxford University Press, 1968.

Macafee, Kerrick. "A Glimpse of the Hidden Economy in the National Accounts." *Economic Trends*, no. 316, February 1980.

Morgenstern, Oskar. *On the Accuracy of Economic Observations*. Princeton, N.J.: Princeton University Press, 1963.

National Commission on Employment and Unemployment Statistics. *Counting the Labor Force*. Washington, D.C.: Government Printing Office, 1979.

Norsworthy, J.; Michael Harper; and Kent Kunze. "The Slowdown in Productivity Growth: Analysis of Some Contributing Factors." *Brookings Papers on Economic Activity*, no. 2, 1979.

Office of Business Economics. *National Income: 1954 Edition*; A Supplement to the Survey of Current Business. Washington, D.C.: Government Printing Office, 1954.

O'Higgins, Michael. *Measuring the Hidden Economy: A Review of Evidence and Methodologies.* A background paper for the Outer Circle Policy Unit seminar on Tax Evasion, Bath, England, March 1980.

Organization for Economic Cooperation and Development. *Measuring Employment and Unemployment.* Paris, 1979.

Reuter, Peter. "A Reading on the Irregular Economy." *Taxing and Spending*, vol. III, no. 2, 1980.

Reuter, Peter, and Rubinstein, Jonathan. "Fact, Fancy and Organized Crime." *The Public Interest*, no. 53, Fall 1978.

Tanzi, Vito. "The Underground Economy in the United States: Estimates and Implications." *Banca Nazionale del Lavoro Quarterly Review*, no. 135, December 1980, chapter 4, this volume.

U.S. Congress, House of Representatives, Committee on Ways and Means, Oversight Subcommittee *Underground Economy* Hearings July 16, September 10, October 9 and 11, 1979, Washington, D.C.: Government Printing Office, 1980.

Wachter, Michael. "The Changing Cyclical Responsiveness of Wage Inflation." *Brookings Papers on Economic Activity*, no. 1, 1976.

**Part III
The Underground Economy in
Some European Countries**

9

A Glimpse of the Hidden Economy in the National Accounts of the United Kingdom

Kerrick Macafee

Reports and anecdotal evidence from this country and others suggest that tax evasion and other fraudulent behavior have reached epidemic proportions. It is alleged that for some economies the size and growth of unreported economic activity have impaired the credibility of official statistics. How do we fare? Have statistics of economic activity been corrupted here? This chapter sets out to describe within the framework of the national accounts the activities that constitute the hidden economy and the difficulties surrounding the estimation of its size and reputed growth.

Description of the Hidden Economy

A number of terms have been employed to describe the sum total of hidden transactions: cash, black, hidden, unofficial, informal, dual, unrecorded, moonlight, twilight and underground. One frequently used term, cash, is particularly unsuitable as hidden transactions can be conducted without money changing hands or by the use of undisclosed bank accounts. Furthermore, since the range of transactions relevant to the national accounts covers legal untaxed transactions as well as tax evasion and other frauds, the term "hidden economy" is preferred in the present context. More precisely, the hidden economy is defined for national accounts purposes as being the "economic activity generating factor incomes which cannot be estimated from the regular statistical sources used to compile the income measure of gross domestic product."[1] Throughout this chapter these types of income are described as "concealed" incomes. The term in this context is different from the concept of concealed transactions as seen by the Inland Revenue whose main concern is tax revenue. A comparison with the black economy as defined by the Inland Revenue is provided at the end of the chapter.

The income and expenditure-based measures of gross domestic product (GDP) at current prices result from two almost wholly independent methods of estimation. The income measure of GDP is the sum total of factor incomes arising from United Kingdom productive activity, while the expenditure measure is the sum total of final expenditures on United Kingdom

Reprinted with permission from *Economic Trends* (London), no. 316 (February 1980), pp. 81-87.

147

production. For any given period, the two measures should, by definition, be equal to each other since the value of each final transaction can be measured either by the sum of money spent on the good or service by the final purchaser or by the identical sum of incomes generated in producing it. For example, production of apples grown in the United Kingdom can be measured either from sales by greengrocers and other retailers or by the income earned from those sales which accrue to the retailer, wholesaler, farmer, and others. Adjustments for exports and the import and tax content of sales are made in compiling the expenditure measure of GDP so that it represents expenditure on United Kingdom productive activity, which equals the income arising from that activity.

The Inland Revenue is the main source of data in the compilation of the income measure of GDP. Estimates of the largest component, the United Kingdom wages and salary bill, are primarily based on tax forms prepared by employers (except for the latest quarters when more timely indicators from the Department of Employment are used).[2] The estimates of the expenditure measure of GDP are derived mainly from a wide range of industrial and household surveys designed specifically for statistical purposes and from central government and local authority accounting data. The two estimates of GDP for any one year will inevitably contain some inaccuracies and are unlikely to be exactly equal in value. It is believed that estimates of items of final expenditure are unbiased since there is little reason for respondents to the Family Expenditure Survey (FES) or other inquiries to disguise or exaggerate expenditure, except in the case of sensitive items of household expenditure such as alcoholic drink. (Expenditure on tobacco and alcoholic drink is estimated from customs and excise data on duties paid rather than from replies to the Family Expenditure Survey.) Since it is not illegal for the receiver of the service to pay cash, for example to window cleaners and house repairers, whether or not there is an understanding that a higher price would be charged for payment by check, it is supposed that these types of payments would not normally be concealed from FES interviewers, especially since the sums involved may often be small. Thus, the expenditure estimate of GDP is regarded as an unbiased estimate of the value of all transactions apart from some illegal, immoral, or sensitive items wherever special steps are not taken to cover the expenditure. In contrast, the income measure is dependent to a large extent on income data supplied to the Inland Revenue and it is possible that the levels of reported income may fall short of true income levels especially for some of the self-employed who are themselves responsible for the "income from main job" part of tax returns which form the basis of the self-employment income estimates.[3] Estimates of factor incomes derived from sources other than tax data are not believed to be important sources of error, as was explained earlier.

If the main bias in the two estimates of GDP arises from the underreporting of incomes, a comparison of the two initial estimates should reveal that the sum of the recorded factor incomes is less than that for recorded final expenditures. This supposition is indeed correct and comparisons show that the initial estimates of the income measure consistently understate GDP as shown by the expenditure measure. This difference is termed here the "initial residual difference" (IRD) and for any one year will be affected by three types of error: underreporting of factor incomes; timing errors: transactions recorded in different time periods by the two parties to the transaction; other errors of estimation such as those arising from the use of samples.

Estimates of final expenditure are sometimes compared with data from alternative sources, and these tests, such as the regular comparison of FES data with data from other household surveys and retail enquiries, confirm that there is little ground for believing that the final estimation of these categories of expenditure is biased in any particular direction. The timing and other errors are assumed to be random in nature and thus the trend line of the initial residual difference is assumed to represent unreported income. Current national accounts estimates of tax-evaded income are mainly based on the average size of this gap.

There are, however, two further parts of the hidden economy that are not represented by the gap between the income and expenditure measures of GDP. These are concealed expenditure (and the income accruing from it) and concealed income-in-kind. Expenditure on illegal drugs and the income of drug sellers would be examples of the first category, while the unauthorized, though perhaps condoned, use of office telephones to make private calls would be of the second type.

Another type of concealed expenditure arises from the national accounts choice of data sources. A sample survey of household expenditure like the FES should in principle provide a full account of expenditure by households. For more accurate and timely figures though, inquiries to retailers and others are used for certain items. However, by switching the inquiry point to the vendor rather than the buyer, it is possible that the sale of goods by informal producers will be missed. Thus, the informal sale of fruit by the side of country roads will be identified, in principle, by the sample survey called the National Food Survey since this is the normal data source for this type of expenditure. In contrast, the informal sale of home-made wines to friends and neighbors will be missed since expenditure on alcohol is generally more reliably estimated by using customs and excise statistics on quantities on which duty has been paid. This type of expenditure, which is missing because of dependence on statistics from official sources and inquiries to established sellers, may be seen in the particular example of articles of clothing produced and sold informally by outworkers, a loss of data which may be exacerbated if the cloth itself is pilfered. In the long term some of this missing expenditure may be identified when estimates of expenditure obtained from official sources in past years are compared with sample survey statistics of expenditure.

Both concealed expenditure and concealed income-in-kind will not be identified by either the income or expenditure data sources. Figure 9-1 shows the relationship between the hidden economy and the published estimates of GDP(E) and GDP(I) and indicates why the definition of the hidden economy is phrased in terms of factor incomes.

Types of Hidden Transactions

Figure 9-2 further describes the range of productive activity not included in the preliminary estimates of GDP(I). If perfect information on these activities were available at a low cost they could all be included within a measure of national *economic* welfare. For national accounting purposes this is impracticable since the problems of assessing the values of nonmarket transactions, including those shown in category A, are large and the errors arising from any estimating process prevent meaningful analyses of short- and medium-term movements of economic activity.[4] With the main excep-

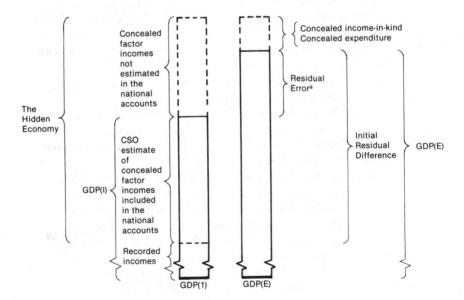

Note: Diagram not drawn to scale.
[a]The residual error can be negative or positive. Here it is shown as positive.

Figure 9-1. The Hidden Economy and the National Accounts

Type of personal gain:	Part of hidden economy?	Some examples (including some types that may belong to more than one category):
A Working for no remuneration, often thereby avoiding paying others to carry out the work concerned	No. This is outside the boundary of production. It is termed here the household economy.	Housework Do-it-yourself Gardening Voluntary charity work Car-pooling
B Working for money, fully declared as necessary to the Inland Revenue	No. This is termed here the formal economy.	Pay-as-you-earn, etc.
C Enjoying a personal benefit and possible tax advantage from "expense account living "	Yes	Enjoying first-class accommodation when conducting important business abroad on behalf of employer
D Receiving remuneration of goods or services greater than their valuation for tax purposes	Yes—to the extent undervalued	Fringe benefits
E Illegally submitting an incorrect or insufficient tax declaration	Yes	Undeclared income from second job. Self-employed undeclared gross income or overstated expenses. Undeclared earnings, for example, tips. Company tax evasion. Some undeclared barter transactions. Undeclared earnings gained when "unemployed" or "sick."
F Frauds connected with the production of goods and services in the formal economy (not exclusively related to tax fraud)	Yes	Office pilfering. Fiddling of customers or employers by employee. Employment of employees "off-the-books." Shoplifting.
G Undeclared criminal or immoral earnings	Yes, in principle	Drug-trafficking Prostitution

Figure 9-2. Summary Description of the Household, Formal, and Hidden Economies

tion of owner-occupied and rent-free accommodation for which a notional rent flowing from "occupier" to "owner" is imputed, all nongovernment transactions involving goods and services which are not customarily exchanged for money are excluded from the national accounts measures of economic activity.

At the other end of the scale, a judgment must be taken on the extent to which criminal and "immoral" activities should be included in the national accounts definition of the hidden economy. The difficulties of measurement, combined with the incongruity of relating an increase in crime with an increase in economic activity, suggest that the inclusion of crime within the national accounts definition of the hidden economy is problematical and that estimates of value added arising from crime should await better data.

The other types of activities (categories, D, E, and F) represent the core of the hidden economy, with tax-evaded income earned from legal activities probably accounting for the largest share of unrecorded income. Certainly the present estimates of unrecorded income in the national accounts are implicitly based on estimates of this type of concealed income. However, the other types of activities may also be important, especially since they represent concealed income-in-kind which is not fully allowed for in any of the measures of gross domestic product.[5]

An example of the relevance of all types of concealed factor incomes is provided by reference to the various types of expense fiddling. In common with the Inland Revenue, the national accounts need to take account of tax evasion arising from fictitious claims for tax relief on expenses (category E in figure 9-2). Less important, there is a national accounts interest in the extent to which taxpayers, especially the self-employed, take the opportunity to claim tax relief for genuine, though not always obviously justified, expenses incurred during the course of business. Anecdotal evidence suggests that the self-employed and others sometimes receive full or partial tax relief for expenses that others might have considered to be entirely consumer expenditure. In some cases also it simply may not be worth a tax inspector's time to argue about small amounts of tax. It is worth noting that an increasing awareness and taking-up of opportunities to reduce tax liability would, if unchecked, unduly depress the estimates of both GDP(I) and GDP(E) as items of consumer expenditure were increasingly treated as business expenditure.[6]

The amount that an employee pockets when he claims to travel first class and instead travels second class is clearly a missing factor income that is part of the hidden economy. Less tangibly, the hidden economy also includes any personal benefit that may arise out of business expenditure (category C in figure 9-2). Thus, if a company underwrites the expenses of an employee who considers some or all of the payment to be a perk of the job, or even a welcome or unexpected bonus, then this is a factor income of the employee. Its size is dependent on the employee's valuation of its worth.

There are a number of conceptual as well as technical difficulties associated with valuing the worth of some of the missing factor incomes described in the previous paragraph. For example, some salesmen may enjoy entertaining potential clients on a lavish scale others may not. It is assumed that this type of missing income-in-kind is not growing at such a rate that special steps must be taken to assess it for national accounts purposes.

As a footnote to this description of the hidden economy it should be noted that some concealed transactions are not treated as part of the hidden economy. Undeclared interest receipts arising from transfers between persons do not constitute missing *factor income*, whereas those received from the company sector are measured as part of company profits before distribution. Plain theft from individuals is also not part of the hidden economy since it is viewed as an involuntary transfer payment between persons. Some frauds, such as working in a legitimate job while drawing sickness benefit, are not part of the hidden economy since employment income will be recorded by the employer. On the other hand, as explained at the beginning of the chapter, those factor incomes which are not covered merely through lack of proper measurement (for example some earnings of juveniles) are not part of the hidden economy.

Present Method of Estimating Unrecorded Income

It has already been explained that the initial residual difference does not fully represent all concealed factor incomes. However it does provide some indication of the size of the hidden economy and its growth. Figure 9-3 shows the size of the initial residual difference expressed as a percentage of GDP from 1960 to 1978.

The figure shows that the gap between the unadjusted estimates of GDP(I) and GDP(E) widened considerably during the period 1973 to 1978. Although the national accounts adjustments for unrecorded income are largely based on the IRD, this abrupt widening has been discounted to some extent and thus there has been an unusually long sequence of positive residual errors in recent years. This cautious approach appears to have been justified by the provisional estimates for the first part of 1979 in which the quarterly figures all show substantial negative residual errors. A less pragmatic view of the relationship between the initial residual error and unrecorded income would imply that in 1979 the hidden economy contracted, but there is no obvious reason why this should have occurred.

Although the national accounts adjustments for unrecorded income are largely based on the general size of the initial residual difference, advice from other government departments, such as the Inland Revenue, and evidence from production accounts also contribute to the estimation of missing factor incomes. A large part of the estimate is attributed to self-employment income since the income of employees is largely based on returns by their employers under the pay-as-you-earn (PAYE) scheme.

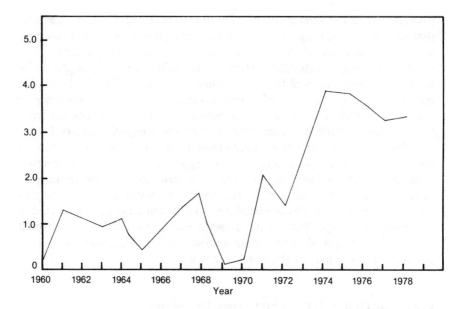

Figure 9-3. Initial Residual Difference

Self-employment income evasion includes that arising from work carried out by employees working on their own account in a second job. Company profit evasion, mainly in the form of undeclared payments to proprietors, is thought to be relatively small, but it is possible that the allowance at present included is too low. Table 9-1 shows the adjustments included in the 1979 Blue Book estimates.

Alternative Ways of Measurement

A number of methods for measuring the hidden economy have been proposed in recent months. One of the most enduring beliefs, especially in the United States, is that the large and increasing amount of cash held by persons indicates a flourishing economy dominated by cash transactions for work carried out off-the-books. In the United Kingdom, it has been estimated that the amount of notes in circulation was equivalent to about £200 per adult in 1979. Certainly the level of cash in circulation has fallen less than might have been expected given the steady increase in payments for goods and services by bank check and credit card transactions (see table 9-2). In recent years the number of higher denomination notes in circulation has risen more sharply than a simple comparison with inflation would suggest (£10 and £20 notes accounted for 24 percent of the value of notes in

Table 9-1

Adjustments Included in 1979 Blue Book Estimates of GDP

(£ million)

	1972	1975	1978
Self-employment income	410	1,720	2,760
Wages and salaries	100	320	850
Company profits	25	25	25
All evasion	540	2,070	3,640
GDP(I) at factor cost	54,950	192,610	140,930
As a percentage of published item			
Self-employment income	8%	19%	21%
Wages and salaries	0.3	0.5	1.0
Company profits	0.3	0.2	0.1
All income	1.0	2.2	2.6
Initial residual difference as percentage of GDP(E) at factor cost	1.4	3.6	3.3

Source: Central Statistical Office.

circulation in February 1976 and for 48 percent in February 1979) and this has been cited as evidence of a mushrooming hidden economy. Table 9-3 shows the changes in the notes in circulation and denomination of those notes in recent years.

The significance of changes in the circulation of cash is difficult to assess. The United Kingdom has had a history of paying employees in cash and many covert transactions can be conducted using open checks or even crossed checks, especially if second bank accounts are employed. The Bank of England considers that the recent increases in the circulation of higher denomination notes are consistent with the public's tendency to economize on the number of notes they carry. The number of notes in circulation varies inversely with the average denomination. Concrete instances of the increasing use of notes of higher denomination in quite open transactions are the agreements between employers and trade unions to include £10 notes in wage packets. Even so, the circulation of higher denomination notes would have needed to have risen faster than it did for the average denomination to have kept pace with inflation. The problems surrounding the interpretation of movements in the amount and type of cash in circulation suggest that this cannot be a reliable method of measuring the hidden economy.

If the hidden economy is growing, then it is reasonable to suppose that the numbers in groups who can more easily take advantage of its benefits, should they choose to do so, and those who can best avoid detection—self-employed persons, double-job-holders, and unregistered unemployed persons—should be increasing. Available data from the General Household Survey are shown in table 9-4.

Table 9-2
Notes and Coins as a Proportion of Money Stock and Gross Domestic Product
(percentage)

Year[a]	Cash M1	Cash M3	Cash GDP
1963	30.7	19.5	7.4
1964	32.4	20.2	7.4
1965	33.6	20.1	7.4
1966	34.4	19.9	7.1
1967	33.3	18.8	7.0
1968	32.5	17.8	6.6
1969	34.1	18.1	6.5
1970	34.5	18.3	6.5
1971	32.4	17.5	6.3
1972	32.2	15.5	6.4
1973	32.9	13.1	6.0
1974	34.5	13.5	6.2
1975	33.8	14.6	5.7
1976	34.5	14.9	5.4
1977	32.5	15.5	5.4
1978	32.3	15.6	5.5

Note: Cash comprises notes and coins in circulation with the public. M1 is cash plus sterling sight deposits with institutions included in the United Kingdom banking sector held by the private sector only. M3 is cash plus sterling and other currency deposits with institutions included in the United Kingdom banking sector held by United Kingdom residents in both public and private sectors.

GDP in this table is the current price estimate for the whole of the preceding year in terms of the expenditure measure of GDP at market prices.

[a]Year-end.

Although many people active in the hidden economy are unlikely to respond to government-sponsored surveys, the data shown in table 9-4 give no indication that more persons are becoming multiple-job holders, self-employed, or unemployed and unregistered. Other surveys, such as the Family Expenditure Survey, confirm these stable patterns.

The Family Expenditure Survey covering both the income and expenditure of households throughout Great Britain has been cited as a fruitful source of information on hidden transactions. It is certainly the only present source of expenditure data for goods and services, such as house repairs, which may be carried out to some extent by persons involved in the hidden economy. However, the *income* data in the FES, especially for the self-employed, are subject to respondent and nonresponse errors. As the income and expenditure data do not cover the same reference periods, comparisons of income and expenditure for various groups like the employed and self-employed tend to be somewhat misleading.

Table 9-3
The Value of Notes in Circulation

Year[a]	Value of Notes in Circulation excluding Notes Larger than £20[b] (£ million)	£10 and £20 Notes (£ million)	£10 and £20 Notes as Percentage of Total
1967	2,760	193	7.0
1968	2,900	243	8.4
1969	3,022	278	9.2
1970	3,103	315	10.1
1971	3,503	431	12.3
1972	3,559	531	14.9
1973	4,032	711	17.6
1974	4,400	968	22.0
1975	5,123	1,212	23.7
1976	5,762	1,657	28.8
1977	6,497	2,248	34.6
1978	7,462	3,024	40.5
1979	8,562	4,073	47.6

[a]End of February.

[b]At the time of writing (1979), notes larger than £20 were used for internal Bank of England purposes only: a £50 note is expected to be issued during 1980.

The Inland Revenue is charged with the duty to assess correctly the tax liability of persons and given the size of the problem and the resources available cannot be expected to provide each year evidence of income retained through tax avoidance. Other means must be sought. Estimation of the real value of company perquisites may be assisted by access to recent

Table 9-4
Self-Employed Persons, Double-Job Holders, and Unemployed as Percentage of All Working

	1972/73[a]	1974/76	1977/78
All working	100.0	100.0	100.0
Persons with more than one job	3.3	3.2	3.2
Persons self-employed in main job	7.9	8.0	7.7
All economically active	100.0	100.0	100.0
Persons unemployed and unregistered	1.0	1.2	1.3
Persons unemployed and registered[b]	2.3	2.7	3.7

Source: General Household Survey.

[a]Unlike later years, 1972 data include 15-year-olds and a small number of full-time students working in the reference week.

[b]This group of persons does not include those who are registered as unemployed yet describe themselves as economically inactive.

business surveys concerning this growing phenomenon. The data in published reports will be studied when making future estimates of this type of missing factor income.[7]

The criminal statistics published by the Home Office for theft and fraud offenses are dependent on victims' reports to the police and understate the level of crime. Estimation of this understatement by means of surveys to businesses and households is expensive and methodologically difficult, so it is unlikely that any valuation of the criminal economy can be included in the national accounts for the time being.

All the above-mentioned methods of evaluating the hidden economy are considered rather unpromising. There are three other areas of research that promise to be more rewarding. They are

1. A thorough study of the initial residual difference in order to confirm that the increase in its size in recent years has been primarily due to an increase in concealed income rather than for any other particular reason.

2. A specialized expenditure survey concentrating on transactions thought to be imprecisely recorded by the Family Expenditure Survey. This would include payments for house repairs and other jobs, with a special emphasis on work paid for in cash on the understanding that other forms of payment would entail a higher price.

3. A long-term, in-depth study of the incomes of persons likely to be concealing income. This type of survey will have to be carried out by experienced, nongovernment researchers who would need both patience and skill in order to gain the trust of their interviewees. There is no easy method of confirming anecdotal evidence that some types of workers conceal large parts of their income.

The two surveys just described would be costly and are viewed as long-term options. In the meanwhile evidence of the hidden economy will be sought by some of the less costly methods listed earlier.

The Size of the Hidden Economy

In 1978 the national accounts included an allowance of 2.5 percent for tax-evaded income and a further small allowance for concealed income-in-kind, reflecting, in part, the recent high values of the initial residual difference. Apart from the large increases between 1972 and 1975 increases in the adjustments have been modest over the last twenty years.

It has already been argued that factor incomes not declared for tax purposes are likely to form the largest part of the hidden economy and that this may be broadly evaluated by the size of the initial residual difference—3.5 percent. Even if out-and-out crime is ignored, it seems likely that the hidden economy as a whole is rather larger than this, but perhaps not substantially so. The long-term movements in the initial residual difference suggest that the hidden economy has grown over the last twenty years and especially since 1970, but the overall increase has been unspectacular.

The emphasis within the national accounts on missing factor income rather than lost tax revenue means that the above estimate of the size of the hidden economy cannot be directly compared with the recent comments about the size of the black economy by Sir William Pile, then Chairman of the Board of Inland Revenue. He said that it was not implausible that income not declared for tax purposes (including a small amount of income not liable to tax because of personal allowances, and so on) might amount to 7.5 percent of GDP. As has been shown, the national accounts take note of other types of missing income such as that retained through tax avoidance, as well as income associated with tax evasion. Also, concealed transfer payments that may be liable for tax do not affect the measurement of GDP. And finally, it should also be noted that nontaxable income unreported to the Inland Revenue, such as the small earnings of married women, are not considered hidden since they are not deliberately concealed and are, at least in principle, measurable by survey methods.

Future Adjustments

Before the publication of the 1980 Blue Book minor improvements to the national accounts estimates of some components of the hidden economy, especially concealed income-in-kind, will be attempted.

Notes

1. Factor incomes are defined as incomes, such as wages and salaries and gross trading profits, arising from the production of goods and services.

2. Estimates of the element of wages and salaries not entered in these forms such as the small earnings of married women below the tax threshold are derived from other sources, including the United Kingdom income and expenditure household survey known as the Family Expenditure Survey (FES). Self-employment income estimates are initially based on incomes reported to the Inland Revenue by the self-employed. Estimates of the gross trading profits of companies are also provided by the Inland Revenue from accounts submitted by companies operating in the United Kingdom. Other components of the income measure are either small (such as the imputed charge for consumption of nontrading capital), especially reliable (for example, employers' contributions and the gross trading surpluses of public

corporations) or exactly equal to an item in the expenditure measure of GDP (for example, the notional rent of owner-occupied dwellings).

3. An anomaly in the national accounts is that the estimates of incomes of farmers, their families, and agricultural workers are not estimated from Inland Revenue data but are taken from the production account for farming carried out each year by the Ministry of Agriculture, Fisheries, and Food (MAFF). It is worth noting that a comparison with Inland Revenue data shows that the reported income of self-employed farmers, and the (formally unpaid) members of their families is appreciably lower than the income calculated by MAFF. Part of this shortfall results from differences in definition and timing and, of course, not all farming income would in fact be charged to tax—for example, the small earnings of farmers wives. Unreported farmers' income has not been regarded in this study as part of the hidden economy as described above. However, it is arguable that it should be included in an overall assessment of the hidden economy.

4. Nevertheless, for long-term and international comparisons of economic well-being some assessment of these hidden transactions could prove helpful. For instance, in recent years the United Kingdom may have experienced a rapid uncharted increase in economic welfare from increased self-service through greater use of both consumer durables, such as cars and washing machines, and self-service facilities such as supermarkets.

5. The impact of any growth of the hidden economy on the output measure of gross domestic product is not discussed in the main text. There are two ways in which the measurement of output may be affected by a growing hidden economy. First, the output measure is, by and large, heavily dependent on formal, often large-scale, inquiries to producers and others and will miss many small businesses and informal producers. If insufficient allowance is made for concealed transactions in this part of the economy then the output measure will not fully reflect the growth of output in the whole economy. Concealed income-in-kind is part of net output, although as the expression suggests it is not easy to identify. Second, in some industries production is measured by deliveries with an adjustment for stock changes in work-in-progress and finished goods. If there is a growth in pilfering of the finished and partly finished goods in these industries over a period of time the output indicators for these industries and GDP(0), as a whole, will be depressed.

6. In the longer-term GDP(0) may also be affected. See note 5.

7. It may be noted, in passing, that in answer to a parliamentary question to the Chancellor of the Exchequer on 19 November 1979, it was estimated that the additional tax receipts associated with the figures for scales of car benefits quoted in the Inland Revenue's recent consultative paper on the subject could have amounted to over £300 million in the

1979-80 financial year. The income-in-kind associated with this tax could therefore reach over £1 billion at present prices. A large part of this income-in-kind is already included in GDP estimates.

10 What Do We Know about the Black Economy in the United Kingdom?

Andrew Dilnot and
C.N. Morris

Much interest has recently been expressed in the scope and growth of the black economy, and several estimates of its size have been presented, which invariably receive wide coverage in the press and elsewhere. Almost without exception, this discussion seeks to convey the impression that the black economy is large and growing, and that it raises major issues for tax policy and economic management.

The purpose of this chapter is to inject a note of skepticism into the argument. We review a number of widely cited studies and conclude that they contain virtually nothing of value. The only estimates of the size of the black economy that we believe deserve serious attention are those made for the United States by the Internal Revenue Service. We consider possible methods of obtaining evidence, and describe an exploration of our own with one of these—the identification of individuals whose reported expenditure could not be supported by their reported income. There are many reasons for adopting a cautious view of the reliability of this procedure. But the results are consistent with the position that although a substantial proportion of the population may participate in the black economy it accounts for no more than 2 to 3 percent of national income.

The smallness of this figure may come as a surprise to many people. Most discussion of the black economy quickly degenerates into the exchange of anecdotes, and there can be few who do not have some personal experience of "black" transactions. These interchanges indicate that the black economy exists, but that is all. It is important to stress that the black economy can be large enough to yield a rich vein of anecdotes without necessarily being a phenomenon of quantitative significance. Most black economy purchases are made by the household sector, and a black economy of even 3 percent of gross national product (GNP) would imply that the average household spent £300 per year on black economy goods. Britain has achieved degrees of industrial concentration unparalleled among other major countries in the western world, and a consequence is that the vast majority of transactions go through large organizations where no question of black activity arises.

Reprinted with permission from *Fiscal Studies*, The Journal of the Institute for Fiscal Studies, vol. 2, no. 1, March 1981.

It will never be possible to offer a firm estimate, or even an upper bound, for the size of the black economy. After all, there could be an island in the North Sea, full of economic activity, subject to United Kingdom (UK) tax jurisdiction, but still undiscovered by the Inland Revenue; and who could prove that such an island did not exist? But there must come a time when those who have failed to find evidence of its existence are entitled to ask those who assert that it is there to spell out the basis of their claims. We offer our estimate of the size of the black economy with little confidence. But we hope it will stimulate a more critical appraisal of those who make larger claims on the basis of less evidence.

Perhaps the most widely quoted estimate of the size of the black economy is that of Sir William Pile, the former chairman of the Board of Inland Revenue. He told the Expenditure Committee of the House of Commons that it was "not implausible" that in 1977 it amounted to some 7.5 percent of gross domestic product (GDP). No justification of this figure has been published, and subsequent Inland Revenue estimates have simply been scaled-up versions of the same figure. We can therefore make no comment on these official figures.

A rather better documented official guesstimate is that of the Central Statistical Office (CSO) Macafee, chapter 9, this volume. This is based on the residual error between the income estimate of GDP—based primarily on data derived from tax returns—and the expenditure estimates. The theory is that black economy activity will not be included in income but will be recorded in expenditure, and in recent years it has generally been the case that expenditure estimates of national income have exceeded income estimates—by as much as 4 percent in 1975.

To see both the problems and possibilities of this approach, consider how the national accounts might treat some typical black economy transactions.

1. *The publican pays the barmaid out of the till at closing time.*

Expenditure in pubs is estimated on the basis of customs and excise records of dutiable beer production multiplied by average retail prices. It should therefore, in principle, include the undeclared earnings of the barmaid.

2. *I tip a restaurant waiter who fails to enter it in full on his tax return.*

Expenditure is based on estimated movements in catering turnover. It would probably not include the tip if the waiter did report it.

3. *A shopkeeper removes goods from stock for his personal use.*

It depends what the goods are. Expenditure may be based on wholesale throughput (in which case these goods will be included, and at their full retail value); on retail sales (in which case the goods will not be included); or on the Family Expenditure Survey (in which case the goods should in principle be included but in practice probably are not). Exactly the same treatment would apply in each case if the goods were shoplifted.

4. *I employ a small builder who requests payment in cash.*

Expenditure on repairs and maintenance is based on the Family Expenditure Survey, and since there is nothing illegal about paying in cash I will probably record it. However since relatively few people incur large items of such expenditure in any fortnightly period, reports of it are poor and supplemented from other sources.

It is also worth noting how the following transactions might be treated.

5. *I engage in avoidance schemes to reduce the tax burden on my investment income.*

In these cases there will be only a remote correspondence between income and expenditure measures of the impact of this transaction, and the latter estimate is almost certainly higher.

6. *My employer buys petrol for my private motoring.*

This will be included in the expenditure measure at its cost and in the income measure at its taxable value (in this case zero).

7. *I rent out premises for use as a brothel.*

The rent will probably be included in the income estimate of GDP but there are no provisions for recording the corresponding expenditure.

8. *I engage in drug-trafficking.*

In principle, the difference between the import cost and street price is value added in the U.K. and should be included in both income and expenditure estimates of GDP. (We imagine most people would feel this treatment was incorrect.) Some income items will appear in GDP—such as purchases of goods and services of a kind which might be used by legitimate businesses—although profits and some earnings are presumably undeclared. Little or nothing will be registered on the expenditure side, and if the import is recorded—presumably under a false description—the impact on the expenditure measures of GDP will actually be negative.

In general, then, certain black economy transactions will have the effect that the expenditure measure of GDP exceeds the income measure, although others will often contribute to recorded income but not to recorded expenditure. This difference will also include elements—such as avoidance and fringe benefits—which although they contribute to erosion of the tax base are not part of the black economy in the common usage of the phrase.

But, as our examples 1-4 illustrate clearly, even if all transactions were entirely legitimate, errors in sampling and discrepancies in timing would lead to divergences between income and expenditure figures. Our suspicion is that apparent recent increases in the residual error owe more to the increased significance of timing differences when prices are rising rapidly than to the black economy. Our discussion suggests that there is scope for highly disaggregated analyses of national accounts data to yield indications of black economy activity. But the overall residual error is precisely that—a conflation of a whole series of statistical errors of which inaccurate reporting of taxable income is only one, rather minor, part. The smallness of the residual error is partly a tribute to the professionalism of the CSO, and is also an indicator that despite the difficulties, these national accounts figures do come close to recording what they are intended to record. This does suggest that the black economy may not be very large relative to the regular economy. We do not think that it is possible to draw any firmer conclusion at this aggregated level.

Some alternative approaches to the measurement of the black economy rely on the belief that the black economy operates mainly through currency while legitimate transactions often use the banking system. Some journalists (Ross, in *Fortune,* 9 October 1978; Freud, *Financial Times,* 9 April 1979) have noted that the use of large denomination notes has increased disproportionately. The observation is certainly correct; thus Freud noted that the aggregate value of £10 and £20 notes in circulation rose by 470 percent between 1972 and 1978 while the value of all notes rose by 110 percent. But it can be more simply explained. If the average amount of money I hold in my wallet rises from £20 and £40, the number of £10 and £20 notes I am likely to hold will much more than double. As O'Higgins (1980) explains, the substitution of large currency notes for small ones in legitimate transactions at higher prices is sufficient to account for observed behavior.

Two American studies, those of Feige (1979) and Gutmann (1977), have received wide attention. The basic principles applied are similar. Gutmann assumes that economic activity in the legitimate economy is financed partly from cash and partly from current bank accounts, in fixed proportions, while that in the black economy is financed wholly by cash. Hence movements in the ratio of black to legitimate activity can be inferred from movements in the ratio of currency to deposits in current accounts. If there were no American black economy in Gutmann's base period 1937-1941, this method suggests that it would now account for over 10 percent of GNP.

Feige supposes that the value of total transactions, based on multiplying currency and bank deposits by average velocity, bears a constant relation to national income. Again using 1939 as base, this reveals a black economy in 1978 of 33 percent of GNP (or 25 percent of total economic activity including black transactions—at this level the definition becomes important).

We report in table 10-1 the result of an analogous study of the U.K. Our basic assumption is essentially that of Gutmann; economic activity requires lubrication by the same volume of money in both black and legitimate sectors but in the black economy this entirely takes the form of cash. We use as

Table 10-1
The Size of the Black Economy

Year	GDP (£ billion)	Notes and Coin (£ billion)	Black Economy as Percent of GDP
1952	13.8	1.4	34.3
1957	19.4	1.9	31.3
1962	25.3	2.2	24.3
1967	34.9	2.8	19.9
1972	55.1	4.1	16.2
1977	125.2	7.5	7.5
1979	164.0	9.7	7.2

base 1977, and Sir William Pile's estimate of 7.5 percent, and deduce changes in the size of the black economy from changes in the ratio of currency to GDP. We observe a steady decline in the size of the black economy, from 34 percent of GDP in 1952 to 7 percent of GDP in 1979.

We should emphasize that these calculations are not intended seriously as estimates of the size of the black economy or of trends in its development. Their purpose is to illustrate two points. If changes in monetary behavior are really to be taken as indicators of changes in the size of the black economy then the prima facie case is that the black economy is in steady decline and only a somewhat strained approach can yield different results. But we do not believe for a moment these figures do in fact reflect a decline in the black economy; they reflect changes in the financial system which imply greater economy in the use of currency. It is possible to estimate the effect of these changes, but only roughly, and we doubt whether the small difference between two large and uncertain magnitudes could reasonably be attributed to the black economy. We think these results deserve as much—or preferably as little—attention as those of Gutmann and Feige.

An alternative line of enquiry was pursued by O'Higgins (1980), who noted that the Family Expenditure Survey reveals substantially higher levels of expenditure by the self-employed than by employees at similar income levels. This is suggestive; but while employee incomes are reported on a current basis the incomes of the self-employed relate to accounting periods some time in the past. A rough adjustment for this virtually eliminated the difference. Analysis of this kind is pursued more systematically later in this chapter.

The U.S. Internal Revenue Service (IRS 1979) has attempted to estimate the amount of unreported income in that country. The principal source used is the Taxpayer Compliance Measurement Program. The IRS uses information derived from detailed audits of selected taxpayers to analyze the characteristics of those who are likely to underreport income. The primary purpose is to facilitate computer selection of taxpayers for subsequent audit, but an incidental merit is the capacity to estimate the additional revenue which could be raised from all taxpayers if their affairs were subject to this degree of scrutiny. These calculations are supplemented by information derived from the Exact Match File, a compilation of several sources of government information on a group of 50,000 households, which allows estimates of income obtained by those who fail to make any return of incomes. The IRS conclusion is that between 91 and 94 percent of income from legal sources is reported to it.

The underrecording of 6 to 9 percent which this identifies has wider coverage in some respects than the black economy. For example, about one-third of additional income attributed to taxpayers relates to deductions (of which the U.S. tax code provides a wide range) that do not survive detailed scrutiny, and much of this does not reflect the black economy as ordinarily meant. On the other hand, this estimate does not include an additional 2 to 3 percent of income from illegal sources, the bulk of which relates to traffic in drugs.

Of legal but unreported income, somewhat less than half relates to self-employment, one quarter to investment income (for which withholding provisions are much more limited in the United States than in the U.K.) and the remainder to income from employment.

It is clear that the IRS study is more serious and substantial than the other studies we have discussed in this section by some orders of magnitude.

Three groups of approaches to the problem of measuring the black economy can be distinguished. One group examines the relationship between economic activity and monetary aggregates. We can see no purpose in pursuing this line of enquiry. Long-term movements of monetary aggregates are affected far more by changes in the organization of the financial system, and we cannot estimate a small number as a residual between larger numbers whose estimation is subject to enormous uncertainty.

A second approach is to undertake detailed scrutiny of the financial affairs of a sample of actual or potential taxpayers with a view to determining their true income. This is the basis of the American IRS estimates. Official agencies have obvious advantages in conducting such surveys. Quite apart from the resources and personnel available to them, they have investigative powers and legal authority to demand information. The tax recovered, and the exemplary effect on other taxpayers, will also help to defray the costs involved. Against this, government agencies can require compliance but cannot compel cooperation, and it is possible that a private survey which sought voluntary disclosure but could give credible assurances that no consequences would follow would secure a better response from those with something to conceal. We have no doubt that valuable information about the social effects of the black economy could be obtained from informal surveys by sympathetic interviewers, but are skeptical about whether sufficient firm data would result to form the basis of an economic assessment. We believe that a systematic approach to taxpayer compliance, such as that undertaken in the United States, would here as there yield useful information about the black economy and assist enforcement. We also believe both purposes would be helped if the Inland Revenue had more effective powers of investigation—the Keith Committee is currently considering this issue.

The third approach to measurement of the black economy compares reported income and expenditure at a disaggregated level. We have already expressed skepticism about this procedure at a highly aggregated level, but believe disaggregated analysis potentially more fruitful. Such disaggregation might be undertaken at the sectoral level—we might look for industries where reported net output exceeds reported income. At first sight, this appeared to us to be the most promising direction of approach, but examination showed that the difficulties of achieving disaggregated data of this kind which was at all comparable in coverage were immense. An alternative direction of disaggregation is to individuals—to examine the behavior and characteristics of individuals who report expenditures inconsistent with their incomes. Comparability is possible here because a single survey—the Family Expenditure Survey (FES)—attempts to record both for a sample of households each year. We know of no previous analysis of the black economy which has pursued this and it is therefore an exploration in this area which we report.

Our approach was essentially a pragmatic one. We began by examining the first 1,000 households in 1977 FES in considerable detail, beginning with very simple income/expenditure relationships and gradually drawing on more and more information to refine the isolation of households exhibiting apparent hidden economy activity. Once a robust identification technique had been developed for this group, it was applied to the whole sample (of some 7,200 households) and our final estimates are based on this information.

Household expenditure as recorded in FES is based mainly on diary record book entries and credit and hire purchase information collected over a two-week period. Expenditure may appear abnormally high if, for example, durables have been purchased in this period. At the Institute for Fiscal Studies (IFS) we are seeking to develop measures which compensate for this (see IFS Working Paper 14), but for the present study a rough adjustment was performed, setting the expenditure of households with very "lumpy" expenditure patterns to the average for their type and group. Thus inclusion in the estimated hidden economy because of recent purchase of, say, a refrigerator was prevented. Items such as clothing, durables, transport, and services were all adjusted in this manner.

Second, gross incomes were converted to net by the use of recorded tax and National Insurance contributions information. We checked that these were in fact the tax and NI amounts which the household type and income information would indicate, and found that they matched well. As well as enabling us to derive net income information easily this also indicated that the income reported to FES matches well that reported to Inland Revenue. Windfall gains from betting and gambling were also included as income.

In the case of self-employment income information, which may be several years out of date, base tape information does indicate the date to which this relates. We scaled self-employment income for each household individually using information supplied by CSO on the movement of self-employment income overall in the period 1974-1977.

Having corrected for the more obvious deficiencies of the data, we then isolated a sample of households whose expenditure exceeded first 1.5 and then smaller proportions, down to 1.15 of their reported income. These households were systematically examined using all the information available on FES (approximately 680 income and expenditure variables per household, as well as information on household characteristics).

The group isolated consisted of three main types of household; the self-employed, those with unoccupied heads and those where the head was in full- or part-time work. In some cases the discrepancy between adjusted income and expenditure could be explained by factors other than nonreporting of income; the expenditure pattern may indicate unusual purchases, the current level of income may be considerably below normal, people with capital (notably pensioners) may be running this down in order to sustain a level of expenditure, overseas students may be living off lump-sum scholarship income, benefit recipients may be running up debts or living off accumulated income while temporarily away from work. Where any of these reasons appeared a significant course of entry to the black economy population, we developed systematic traps to exclude such households, but when the trap might be too strong we included it in our lower-bound estimates but not in the upper-bound.

One specific trap was the removal of all pensioners from our sample for the lower-bound. Although we do not doubt that some black economy activity is carried out by pensioners, we found that in the majority of the cases isolated household expenditure could be explained by the hypothesis that they were running down previously accumulated wealth. In half of the cases the pensioners isolated were outright owners of their houses, in many of the others they did declare some investment income. Actual holdings and realization of wealth are inadequately recorded in FES for direct evidence on this. The majority of the pensioners excluded had low discrepancies between adjusted income and expenditure. Pensioners were included in the upper-bound sample.

A second exclusion from the lower-bound sample was those households where the head was temporarily away from work, where the household was sustaining a level of expenditure in excess of its income. This was either by running down assets or incurring debts. Again the total exclusion of such households may be too strong, and they were included in the upper-bound sample.

Another category of exclusions were students, and those for whom although the percentage excess of expenditure over income was high its absolute amount was low. We introduced an absolute minimum of £3 for the discrepancy. We chose a 20 percent cut-off as our principal criterion. This is a pragmatic decision; at higher levels we seemed to be excluding households which seemed on the basis of all other information potential black economy candidates while 10 to 15 percent brought in groups which obviously were not. Although the number of households in the sample is sensitive to this level, the amount of activity included is much less sensitive, because the marginal discrepancies are less than average.

Our approach, in principle, includes two types of black economy activity; tax evasion and social security fraud. These categories are not quite mutually exclusive or exhaustive but they are nearly so. We therefore identified separately those of our sample who were benefit recipients. About 2.5 percent of the 17.3 percent in the upper-bound sample fell into this category, very few of the lower-bound sample. Their inclusion would add around 0.4 percent to the upper-bound proportion of GDP. The figures reported in table 10-2 relate to potentially taxable income. Some support is provided for the suggestion that tax evasion is a substantially greater quantitative problem than benefit abuse.

We now turn to examining the characteristics of those households whose expenditure, after all the adjustments described in the previous section, was greater than their recorded income. For this purpose, we concentrate on the lower-bound sample.

A possible limitation to our analysis is that some households may be running down wealth. Although we have taken account of income from investments and savings, these are probably less well reported than other in-

Table 10-2
Lower and Upper Bounds for the Black Economy, 1977

	Lower Bound	Upper Bound
Proportion of Family Expenditure Survey sample	9.6%	14.8%
Average discrepancy between income and expenditure	£31 p.w.	£30 p.w.
Approximate grossed-up size of the black economy	£3,200 million	£4,200 million
Implied proportion of 1977 GNP	2.3%	3.0%

come and expenditure variables (for reasons other than the black economy). FES does not ask about either holdings of assets or the realization of these assets. So some of the discrepancy may be explained by this factor—although we have excluded pensioners and those whose income has fluctuated recently for this reason.

There is considerable evidence that savings follow a life-cycle pattern—that is, people borrow early in life, accumulate assets in the middle, and dissave at the end. If the realization (or accumulation) of assets was a serious cause of bias we would expect the black economy sample to contain proportionately more young, and (on the higher bound) old, than the overall sample.

We therefore examined the age profiles of both the upper- and lower-bound samples compared to the overall FES sample. The upper-bound sample does seem to contain proportionately more households in both the earlier age range (20-30) and in the over 65 group and less in the middle range, indicating that life-cycle saving may account for some of the isolated discrepancy. There was no clear pattern in the lower-bound sample, which of course excluded pensioners for precisely this reason.

Table 10-3 indicates the occupation and employee status breakdown of our lower-bound sample. The sample isolated does in fact consist mainly of households where the occupation of the head would indicate, a priori, that black economy activity is feasible; teachers, clerical staff, local and central government employees, and shop assistants hardly feature at all. About 20 percent of heads were self-employed, and over 70 percent full-time employees. Over half the self-employed branded themselves professional, technical, administrative or managerial, the remainder (mostly skilled)

Table 10-3
Occupation and Employee Status for Lower Bound Black Economy Sample
(percentage)

	Head of Household			
	Self-	*Full-Time*	*Part-Time*	
Occupation	*Employed*	*Employee*	*Employee*	*All*
Professional and technical	9	10	5	9
Administrative and managerial	33	12	5	16
Skilled manual	43	39	14	39
Semiskilled manual	11	21	42	20
Unskilled manual	1	4	9	4
Others[a]	3	14	25	12
All	100	100	100	100
All	22	71	6	100

[a]Teachers, clerical workers, shop assistants, members of armed forces, retired, unoccupied.

manual workers. Of the full-time workers, 60 percent were skilled or semiskilled manual workers.

A rather more interesting question than "what are the characteristics of the black economy population?" is "how likely are particular types of people to participate in black economy activity?" Overall, some 9.6 percent of the households in the FES sample were in the lower-bound black economy sample. If everybody were equally likely to participate, then 9.6 percent of each occupation, or employee status group would enter. However, we have seen that this is not the case. Tables 10-4, 10-5, and 10-6 present what we call "participation ratios" for the black economy. These are the ratios between the observed number of workers in any category and the expected number if participation were equally likely for all groups. Thus a ratio in excess of 100 percent indicates a set of characteristics which are positively associated with activity in the black economy.

Table 10-4 indicates that the self-employed of all types are the most likely to participate, and that others are more likely to if their work is part time.

Table 10-5 shows that although there is little variation by tenure type, there is some evidence that those in private unfurnished accommodation are most likely to participate, but that this varies between occupational groups.

The self-employed who participate are likely to be either owner-occupiers or council tenants, while part-time participants are somewhat more likely to be living in unfurnished rented accommodation.

The estimates we have presented are based on the sample of households who agree to participate in the Family Expenditure Survey. This is a demanding exercise, and only 70 percent of those asked do in fact respond.

A major concern in interpreting our results is the possibility that the 30 percent who do not participate engage more extensively in the black economy than those who agree to take part.

Respondents are given assurances of confidentiality, and these assurances are true; although we have attempted to isolate black economy households there is no means by which we, or the department sponsoring the survey, or the Inland Revenue, could determine which specific households these are. However we must expect that in spite of this, individuals with something to hide will be more reluctant to respond to an official survey of their income and expenditure, and therefore that the Family Expenditure Survey underrepresents the black economy. We imagine that reluctance to participate would be greater on the part of those engaged in major tax fraud than those with small amounts of moonlighting income who may not realize there is anything illegal and probably think there is nothing immoral in their failure actively to seek out a tax inspector to whom to report these earnings. It is this kind of activity, limited in scale and typically subsidiary to principal employments, which is the basis of much recent concern about the growth of black economy activity and which we believe our techniques are quite likely to identify.

Table 10-4
Participation Ratios, by Occupation and Employee Status

	Professional and Technical	Administrative and Managerial	Teachers	Other Nonmanual	Skilled	Manual Semiskilled	Unskilled	Overall
Self-employed	117.5	226.9	0	329.3	248.3	289.1	148.2	222.1
Full-time	79.6	86.7	65.2	100.8	99.6	98.2	92.0	94.0
Part-time	87.2	164.7	48.3	97.2	148.2	136.1	53.9	100.8
Other	0	46.3	0	0	4.1	13.6	0	7.2
Overall	82.5	119.4	53.3	98.0	106.8	100.5	70.2	100

Table 10-5
Participation Ratios, by Occupation and Tenure

	Professional and Technical	Administrative and Managerial	Teachers	Other Nonmanual	Skilled	Manual Semiskilled	Unskilled	Overall
Council rented	123.5	143.8	0	94.3	98.7	93.6	82.9	97.6
Rent unfurnished	85.5	148.2	67.4	123.5	124.4	136.1	95.6	123.8
Rent furnished	123.5	67.4	67.4	125.8	76.0	74.1	0	97.9
Mortgage	70.1	107.9	65.2	95.8	119.0	100.7	55.6	99.4
Owned	98.8	140.9	30.9	85.2	81.5	105.8	22.5	96.0
Overall	82.5	119.4	58.3	98.0	106.8	100.5	70.2	100

Table 10-6
Participation Ratios, by Employee Status

	Self-Employed	Full-Time	Part-Time	Other	Overall
Council rented	265.1	103.1	121.1	3.4	97.6
Rent unfurnished	246.7	101.2	162.4	0	123.8
Rent furnished	92.5	109.4	0	46.3	97.9
Mortgage	212.4	90.1	131.6	7.6	99.4
Owned	223.1	71.8	64.0	0	96.0
Overall	222.1	94.0	100.8	7.2	100.0

We can assess the problem of response bias by comparing the characteristics of FES respondents with those of the population as a whole. Workers in some industries, such as construction or vehicle repairing, are rather more likely to have participation opportunities. If it were the case that those who participate do not answer FES questionnaires, we would expect to find evidence that the FES was undersampled among such people.

However, the task of determining whether the FES sample is representative of the U.K. as a whole is a daunting one. Very little other information exists, and where it does it is rarely on a comparable basis. There are perhaps four possible sources of information with which to compare the FES sample.

The first of these is the census. The last census was carried out in 1971, and refers to households in Great Britain. Published FES for 1971 refers to households in the U.K., and few categories match well—with the result that little can be concluded from comparing published figures.

However, a study of differential response in the FES was carried out by directly comparing census returns with households in the 1971 FES sample (Kemsley 1975). Table 10-7 summarizes the relevant results.

In addition, the study provides evidence that response is higher in households with children and declines as age of head of household increases. The only clear message for our purpose is that this exercise found lower response among self-employed households in 1971.

Comparing published FES 1971 with the published census leads to a rather different conclusion, for the 1.43 million self-employed males 15 and over in the census compare with around 1.6 million from a grossed-up FES figure.

The second possible source of information is the General Household Survey (GHS), a survey which is carried out each year and which concentrates mainly on questions about housing and medical history, but also asks some (less detailed than FES) questions about income. Households who do not respond to FES interviewers may not respond to GHS either, but there is some possibility that because the main information requested is on, for

Table 10-7

Differential Responses to Family Expenditure Survey, by Characteristics of Respondents

		Response Rate (percent)
Overall response rate, 1971 Family Expenditure Survey		69.5
Employment status of head of household		
Self-employed:	with employees	56
	without employees	63
Employees:	managers	65
	foremen	74
	others	72
Tenure		
Owner occupied		68
Council rented		72
Rented unfurnished		69
Rented furnished		75

Source: W.F.F. Kemsley, "Family Expenditure Survey." A study of differential response based on a comparison of the 1971 sample with the Census. *Statistical News*, November 1975.

example, health and housing rather than income and expenditure, response might be better.

We have compared FES and GHS published information for 1977. Although there is some problem of different definitions of groups, the two samples look broadly similar. The distributions between tenure types is almost identical. It is impossible to match accurately GHS and FES occupational codes from published data. Although income questions are asked in the GHS questionnaire, little is included in the published figures.

A third, and possibly the richest, source of information is the New Earnings Survey (NES). This covers employees in Great Britain. However, comparison is again difficult because definitions vary between NES and FES. We have attempted to compare the occupational and industry breakdown of individuals in FES and NES. To do this, we have extracted from the FES 1977 tape all full-time male employees aged 21 and over and all full-time female employees aged 18 and over in Great Britain and allocated them to occupational and industry groupings. The industry groupings in NES match those in FES fairly well but the occupational groupings present a greater problem. The NES profile was derived by allocating all subcategories in tables 99 and 100 of NES to FES categories using information on the contents of these categories provided by the Department of Employment. In some cases, the allocation is ad hoc, particularly between skilled, semiskilled and unskilled manual workers.

This exercise provides some evidence that FES, far from being under-sampled in the areas of possible black economy activity, does seem to contain a slightly higher proportion of manual workers and workers in construction, vehicles, and miscellaneous services. In fact, the two distributions appear very similar, and provide no evidence of undersampling among the employee population. Comparison with NES clearly provides no information on the self-employed.

The final source of possible information is the National Income and Expenditure "Blue Book." Income information from FES can be "grossed up"[1] and compared with the national aggregate. Perhaps the most interesting for our purposes is to compare self-employment income recorded in FES with the CSO figure. FES gives an average figure for 1977 of £5.47 per household, which grosses up to £5,750 million. The corresponding Blue Book figure is £11,129 million. However, these two figures are not directly comparable.

The first reason is that self-employment income as recorded in FES can refer to a tax year several years ago. We have examined every self-employment entry in the 1977 FES tape and scaled those which are out of date by unpublished self-employment indexes supplied by CSO. This increases the self-employment total by 18 percent, bringing the FES figure to £6,785 million.

The Blue Book figure contains a CSO estimate of evasion, which is around £2,400 million,[2] which leaves an adjusted figure of £8,729 million. Up to another £1,000 million may be due to different treatment of depreciation, so the final discrepancy is nearer to £1,000 million. This source of comparison therefore provides additional evidence that self-employment income is underreported in FES.

So there is some evidence, both from the Kemsley article and from National Income statistics that there is low response in FES among the self-employed. If this is true, then our estimates of black economy activity will be low on this account.

On the implausible assumption that the self-employed who do not respond are participating to no greater extent than those who do, and using the Kemsley figures for underreporting, we estimate that this would increase the estimated proportion of GDP on our lower-bound sample from 2.3 to 2.4 percent.

Conclusion

If the black economy can be kept within very limited bounds, it is not obvious that it is something to be regretted. The existence of small amounts of economic activity on which the marginal rate of tax is zero, much of which would simply not be undertaken at all if it were confined to the formal economy, may reduce the disincentive effects of taxation and add to social relationships. When this achieves proportions that encourage wide-scale fraud or lead to a cumulative collapse of the moral force of the tax system, our reactions should be rather different; what is the honest taxpayer in Italy to do? But there is nothing more likely to encourage such fraud and such collapse than the wide circulation of exaggerated, and unfounded, reports of the extent of black activities. We hope that this chapter may contribute to a more careful assessment of these reports.

Notes

1. This is usually done, as here, by multiplying by the ratio of total U.K. population to the number of persons in the FES sample.
2. Interpolation from Macafee.

References

Feige, Edgar L. "How Big Is the Irregular Economy?" *Challenge*, November-December 1979.

Gutmann, Peter M. "The Subterranean Economy." *Financial Analysts Journal*, November-December 1977.

Kemsley, W.F.F. "Family Expenditure Survey." A study of differential response based on a comparison of the 1971 sample with the Census. *Statistical News*, November 1975.

Macafee, Kerrick. "A Glimpse of the Hidden Economy in the National Accounts," *Economic Trends* (February 1980). Reprinted as chapter 9, this volume.

O'Higgins, Michael. "Measuring the Hidden Economy: A Review of Evidence and Methodologies." Outer Circle Policy Unit, 1980.

Internal Revenue Service. *Estimates of Income Unreported on Individual Income Tax Returns* Washington, D.C.: Government Printing Office, September 1979.

11 Recent Empirical Surveys and Theoretical Interpretations of the Parallel Economy in Italy

Daniela Del Boca
and *Francesco Forte*

Definition of the Parallel Economy

The underground economy is a widely known yet imperfectly studied phenomenon. It is often held that the underground economy is pathological, deviant, or irrational when compared to the economic rationality of the surface economy. Therefore, when we find that a considerable portion of labor activities and output belongs to the underground economy, we are inclined to conclude that the stool of the economic system rests on a worm-eaten leg that cannot possibly last. There are also those who tend to consider it the result of a fiscal pathology, explaining the existence of a vast underground economy essentially as an attempt to escape taxes. And finally, some refer to the underground economy as a victory for the taxpayer in his revolt against excessive taxes: according to this interpretation, the underground economy is not a pathological fact, but rather a kind of "nature's revolt," a sort of healthy reaction to fiscal pathology.

We do not deny that these mutually conflicting factors can contribute to explaining the underground economy and judging its rationality and vitality. But they are not the only factors, nor even, in many cases, the principal ones.

In any case, we feel that an inquiry into the matter is hindered by considerable terminological confusion. The underground economy is very widespread, at least in Italy; and we can assume that it has become more, rather than less, important in the last few years, as the economic system has acquired more and more the characteristics of mature capitalism or, in certain areas, of postcapitalism.

We can define *underground economy* as those activities that are characterized by a lack of formal transactions. Certain transactions are absent due to the lack of exchange between labor and income, or they exist but in an informal fashion. The surface economy refers to the same phenomena when they are carried out by means of formal transactions. The definition of underground economy, as we can see, is in relation to that of surface economy: it is constructed in contrast to the former and to its normal degree of formalization. Therefore, we can call the underground economy a parallel economy. This economy, not completely formalized or not formalized at all, does not contravene, but is simply outside the scope of ordinary business laws. Surely the activities of this parallel economy are carried out in violation of the regulations specified in union agreements, but these cannot be considered as peremptory laws. Several economists, attempting to measure the importance of the underground economy, tend to quantify it in a figure that is logically identical to the undervaluation of the gross national product (GNP). But the value added which escapes the measurements of the GNP is not the same thing as the underground economy, according to our definition. In fact a part of the underground or parallel economy falls within the estimates of GNP. In the same way, the fact that many people carry on parallel agricultural activities, having a second job which does not appear in any contract, and which goes unnoticed in any ordinary employment or income survey, does not necessarily determine an undervaluation of the Italian agricultural product.

In fact, wheat production, for example, is estimated on the basis of crop volume, and this, in turn, is determined by sample surveys of annual crops and by apparent consumption, taken from data on family budgets, on foreign trade, and on estimates of the consumption of foreign tourists less those of Italian tourists abroad. On the other hand, a part of the added agricultural value goes unnoticed whether it is obtained through the activities of the parallel economy or not. For example, there are poultry and vegetable products, which, because of statistical errors, are not included in the Italian agricultural product, even though they belong to the surface economy and may even be sold through transactions subject to value-added tax.

Similar considerations can be made for many services, which are not included in the GNP, because of incomplete classification of the services of final nature, even when they are performed by firms belonging to the surface economy, and not by workers active in the parallel economy.

Industrial production in Italy has often been undervalued and it is likely that it is still undervalued, because of the use of statistical techniques whose imperfection has nothing to do with the existence of the underground economy: in compiling the physical index of production, the activities of firms assessed in the base year are considered, without taking into account new firms which may have sprung up in the meantime, and only the relevant products in that year are considered, ignoring those of new types which may have become widespread in the meanwhile.

Finally, in the case of incomes deriving from the construction industry, there is a tendency to consider, as added value, not that which would exist without rent controls, but the official "controlled" rent. This method also applies to the premises directly occupied by the owners. This undervaluation, which is enormous, does not necessarily have any relation to the underground economy; on the contrary, it concerns buildings which belong to the surface economy, and which often pay taxes correctly.

Demand and Supply of Labor
in the Parallel Economy

The term parallel (or underground) economy includes a range of different productive activities which have in common a need (a) to evade (or reduce) tax and social security burdens, (b) to achieve greater flexibility in the remuneration and employment of labor, and (c) to bypass trade union vigilance. Most studies on the parallel (or underground) economy have examined the problem mainly from the point of view of firms and their motives.

However, the proliferation of this kind of activity cannot simply be explained in terms of the cheapness of the labor force. In the last few years, this phenomenon also expresses the family's need to reallocate its time. It is useful to attempt to measure the parallel economy in order to obtain a more accurate estimate of GNP, but it is even more important to try to understand its dynamics and analyze its social and economic causes. An analytical study of this trend is of considerable importance in planning fiscal, economic, and labor policies.

One of the most distinctive features of Italian economic development, which has become even more widespread since the middle 1970s, is the persistence and increasing vitality of a wide sector of small industries and artisan workshops. In fact, the Italian economic development may be distinguished from that of other industrialized nations (except Japan) by the prevalence of small- and medium-sized industries. While in the past, this feature was considered solely as the symptom of a backward economy, today, in view of more recent studies, it appears to be a more complex and contradictory phenomenon.

Most studies have pointed out the connection between the Italian economy's need for flexibility and an international division of labor which places it in a subordinate role in the advanced technology sector; it is specialized in labor-intensive industries, which are particularly subject to demand volatility. The structure of the small firm is most suitable because it ensures the necessary flexibility and makes it possible to keep down labor costs by relying heavily on apprenticeship, work done at home, and second jobs. The use of an irregular labor force thus represents a way of reducing labor costs, just as the employment of second-job workers permits business concerns to avoid paying social security (and to do so without arousing any particular social tension) since these are already borne by the second-job workers' official employers.

It has been pointed out that the increase in these activities should not be interpreted solely as a sympton of economic backwardness, or an adjustment to an inferior position imposed by the international division of labor, but as a particular mode of "functional" development which meets the specific requirements of the Italian economy. (Contini 1979, Paci 1980) In fact, these business enterprises cannot be considered of marginal importance (except for a few), but rather should be viewed as economically competitive units of production, both as autonomous industries and as complementary ones (that is, operating within integrated productive cycles). Actually the persistent vitality of parallel activities can be considered a reemergence of the traditional pattern of Italian economic development based on labor-intensive "mature" products, in which, however, the surplus labor supply is no longer as openly manifest as it was at the beginning of the Italian "economic miracle," but is, on the contrary, "hidden." (Contini and Del Boca 1978)

There have been fewer studies on the fundamental reasons for the supply of parallel labor. The first studies which have shifted the focus of attention to the features which encouraged the supply of this type of labor, concentrated on those socioeconomic areas where the existence of an artisan tradition formed the necessary basis for the emergence of a particular type of industrialization characterized by the prevalence of small business concerns. (Paci 1980)

In these regions, the industries' advantage in greater flexibility of productive factors very often coincides with a similar advantage for the families themselves. The extended family (especially that of sharecropping origin), which is still tied to agriculture, appears to be an ideal structure, perfectly capable of meeting intermittent labor demands (as needed by small industries). In this type of family structure the whole labor capacity of the various members of the family is put to use, including part-time capacity, and the family's total income results from the sum of the various components deriving from both its agricultural and industrial activities. Consequently the family is a highly functional unit, not only insofar as it can keep down the social cost of reproducing the labor force, but also as a means of fostering the flexibility of labor supply on the market. (Paci 1980)

This type of family's ties to agriculture seems to create a basic structure possessing features of security and continuity such as those ensured by the secondary and tertiary sectors.

Within the family, some of its members, such as women, adolescents, and senior members, alternately (According to the family's specific needs) engaging in various market and nonmarket activities, possess the highest degree of time flexibility, seasonal intermittence, as well as availability for marginal work; such characteristics are needed for the type of flexibility required by this kind of industrial structure. (Becattini 1978) In fact, the basic agricultural activity with its typical seasonal and occasional nature, employs its labor force discontinuously and consequently leaves room for other activities, provided they also display a similar flexibility in the use of labor time. In these family structures we can find the other types of economies.

As several hypotheses based on the theory of human capital suggest, the family is an economic association wherein the transaction and communication costs are relatively lower (due to the proximity of its members) and there are greater incentives for sharing the knowledge and work capability of each individual member; this fact distinguishes it from other types of associations. (Benham 1974)

Moreover, it can be maintained that self-employment produced within these structures, by allowing one to use his own human capital (rather than leasing it to others) can justify investments in training and apprenticeship which are more rational and consistent with the activity that is actually carried out. Since the individual himself is the one who determines, and in a more autonomous way, the type of service to be rendered, it is possible to evaluate with greater accuracy the costs and benefits (both monetary and nonmonetary) associated with the various training alternatives.

In urban areas and in areas where the productive structure is heavily industrialized, the relationship between the demand and supply of underground activities is quite different. In these areas, the vast reservoir of labor coming from agricultural areas has, for a number of years, been exhausted. Labor in urban areas displays higher expectations and a higher degree of rigidity. Here we are dealing with a more educated labor force, better adjusted to its urban social environment, protected by a decade on welfare policies, and no longer willing to accept work under any conditions. At the same time, however, this type of labor is more constrained in the distribution of its worktime. The development of the urbanization and industrialization processes has created an increase both in job opportunities and in the range of consumer choices; however, it has also produced environmental diseconomies, due to the increasing difficulty of reaching the goods and labor market (also because of the growing costs of communication and information).

More specific and at the same time more sophisticated demands (due to higher income and educational levels) for goods and services of better quality (better educated youth, more "personalized" services, a job better suited to one's specific needs) are faced with the rigidity and the inefficiencies of the urban social context.

The difficulty of obtaining them (in terms of costs) and the inadequacy (in terms of quality) of the services available induce people to rely increasingly on the family organization as a unit for the production of goods and services. In the same way, because of the inefficient and often biased nature of employment and information agencies, those seeking a job must rely on their family connections to gain access to the labor market.

Even when it is not producing for the market, the family is, nonetheless, a unit of production, since it is producing those goods and services necessary to its welfare. (Schultz 1974)

While, at first sight, it seems reasonable to assume that, in more advanced social contexts, because of the introduction of home "labor-saving" appliances, family production would require a decreasing time input, thus leaving more time available for market work, on closer analysis, the situation appears to be more complex. In fact, the higher expectations and the disamenities of the urban environmental context impose more complex and time-consuming tasks on family activities.[1]

In family production, investment activities (in human capital), that is, those aimed at increasing individual and family production (such as training, job seeking, and scanning the goods and services markets) become more important than mere maintenance (of human capital stock) activities. The complexity of such activities (which, unlike mere preservation activities, cannot easily be delegated outside the family), increases the marginal value of extramarket time for the individuals involved in them, while reducing their availability for market work.[2] In fact, we can assume that the higher the value of extramarket time (VMT), and consequently, the demand for time which must be devoted to these activities, the lower is the supply of time for the labor market (L).

The differentiation of the labor supply can be explained by the division of roles within the family in relation to the way in which the family itself carries out its structural functions. Women, engaged in family production (especially in the most intensive stages of the family life cycle) present a higher marginal value of time than that of other members of the family. The same holds for young people, who as students, are engaged in producing human capital stock. On the other hand, we can assume that the marginal value of the extramarket time of adult males and heads of families is nil, and in some cases, negative.[3] This explains why many families still consider a second job for the head of the family as one of the simplest ways of increasing their disposable income, since the head of the family, already possessing a secure position on the official labor market, is consequently more favored on the parallel labor market.

Both irregular labor and second jobs are ways of bypassing existing restrictions on production. The opportunities for making use of time are not sufficiently flexible, nor are individuals confronted with a range of alternatives wide enough to allow them to achieve the best possible distribution of their time between market work and other activities. In fact, unlike other industrialized countries, part-time work is very limited in Italy, and similarly, ways of making work schedules more flexible have, so far, been relatively unexplored.

Therefore, the demand for flexible labor, arising mainly from certain members of the family, must necessarily turn to activities which run parallel to official ones.

Methodological Studies of the Parallel Economy

Several recent studies have tried to estimate the size of this phenomenon as expressed by the ratio between the underground or parallel economy and the official or surface economy.

Patterns of growth in the consumption of electricity for productive use have been compared to those relating to industrial production. The gap between variations in growth of electricity consumption and variations in industrial production is noticeably greater, especially in typically decentralized industrial sectors (such as the textile and garment industries). This can be construed as proof that the actual rate of growth in these sectors has been higher than that expressed by the index of industrial production, and this gap is due to the underground part of the economy. (Lizzeri 1979)

Other estimates have made use of monetary statistics as a means of indirectly measuring the underground economy. (Gutmann 1977; Feige 1979; Tanzi 1980) Some of these estimates are based on the hypothesis that underground activities avoid the use of checks, resorting to cash instead, and therefore, that the ratio between currency and current demand deposits varies only as a result of growth in the underground economy. It is further assumed that the amount of income generated by one lira produced in the underground economy is equal to the amount of income generated by one lira produced in the surface economy. Recently this method of estimation has been tried in Italy. (Saba 1980) From this estimate, GNP shows an average annual rate of growth, in nominal terms, of 16.7 percent in the period from 1968 to 1978, while the nonofficial sector has grown an average of 30.8 percent. As a percentage of GNP, the underground economy would have exceeded 30 percent in 1978, while it was less than 10 percent in 1968.

Another type of estimate of the submerged economy is based on data relating to regular and irregular employment. These data clearly reveal the anticyclical nature of this phenomenon, and indeed, the increase in the number of marginal workers, since 1973/74 has coincided with a marked decrease in stable and regular employment (especially in large industrial firms).

However, it is also very important to identify the complex strategies which form the underlying basis of this phenomenon; hence the importance of surveys covering certain well-defined geographical areas of the country, which can provide us with very valuable information (even though obviously limited in scope by the fact that they cannot give us a picture of the Italian situation as a whole).

From a comparative study of the results of several representative sample surveys, we can extract a number of data that enable us to quantify the phenomenon, to analyze its main features, to determine in which sectors it is most widespread, and see what type of labor force it employs.

The CENSIS survey, which was the first nationwide study of unofficial employment, estimates that irregular labor and second jobs amount to about 5.6 percent of official activities (3 million additional jobs). (CENSIS 1976). If we compare these results with those obtained from other surveys covering only certain parts of the country, townships in Piedmont (Deaglio 1974) and in Friuli we find even higher percentages (table 11-1).

A survey made by the Turin Chamber of Commerce shows that, in one of the two communes studied in a semirural area, 53.7 percent of the work (in terms of hours) was done by unofficial workers. In another area, near large factories, the percentage of unofficial working hours was 19.2 percent. Professor Deaglio, in a pioneer study of a commune in the province of Cuneo made in 1974, noticed that unofficial workers accounted for 51 percent of the hours. Finally, a survey of an industrial area and an agricultural area in Friuli showed that unofficial workers did 34 percent of the working hours in the agricultural and 24.5 percent of the hours in the industrial area.[4]

A comparative study of these three surveys provides us with data which enable us to classify this phenomenon. In the agricultural sector, we find a higher percentage of irregular labor, while in the industrial and tertiary sectors, the percentages of second jobs are higher (as is confirmed by the CENSIS estimates, based on Istituto Centrale di Statistica (ISTAT) data).[5] Moreover, the percentage of self-employment has noticeably risen since 1975 both in the industrial and tertiary sectors, especially in traditional fields, such as textile and trade, where it is more frequent to find the family acting as the center of a micro-business enterprise (in the labor market). And it is precisely in these traditional industrial sectors, where decentralization and more flexible employment of the labor force are easier and more widespread, that we find a considerable rise in labor productivity in the last few years.

The outcome of the surveys on unofficial work also provide us with useful information on the type of labor force involved in underground ac-

Table 11-1
Proportion of Total Working Hours Done by Unofficial Workers
(percent)

Survey	Agricultural Area	Industrial Area	Total
Turin Chamber of Commerce (1976)	53.7	19.2	29.6
Prof. Deaglio (1974)	51.7	—	—
Communes in Friuli (1979)	34.5	24.5	28.5

tivities. We find that irregular work employs mostly women of all ages, very young or elderly males. Therefore, irregular work seems to require less-skilled manpower—adolescents, who have not yet completed their training, and consequently cannot yet qualify as skilled manpower, elderly men, who are no longer qualified, and women, whose human capital has deteriorated as a result of their limited or discontinuous participation in the labor market. (Mincer and Polachek 1974). Second jobs, on the contrary, seem to attract mostly male workers in the prime age groups, traditionally the most stable and best-qualified manpower on the market.[6]

Another kind of survey taken in an urban area (in the North) has provided information not only on the actual behavior of individuals and families in the labor market, but also on their preferences for certain work schedules, thus providing several useful suggestions. (Colombino, Del Boca, and Negri 1980) Besides the need to reduce the total amount of worktime, and to distribute it in a different and more balanced way (during the day, the week, the year), we also find the desire for autonomy, creating a strong tendency towards self-employment. An individual's need to reallocate time varies according to his particular role in the family organization.

Many young people would like part-time work, probably in order to finance their own training, or, at any rate, to give them a period of time in which to scan the labor market and seek a job they consider more acceptable and more consistent with their own qualifications. Most nonworking (married) women would also be willing to work but only at special schedules and not far from home (60 percent would accept jobs part-time and near home). Among those who are employed, we find more women who would prefer fewer working hours, while male heads of families seem to prefer longer working hours.

The outcome of these surveys provides us with a general picture of the underground labor market (both actual and potential) that reproduces, on the one hand, the division of labor (by sex and age) that we find in the surface labor market, while reflecting, on the other hand, the traditional division of roles in family organization.

The data resulting from these studies enable us to identify several factors which seem to form the basis of the processes that determine the "sinking down" of productive activities. The factors differ according to geographical area, each of which presents a different social and productive context, as well as a differently structured family organization.

In areas of "peripheral" economy, the supply of parallel activities seems to be "pulled" by a relatively flexible demand for agricultural and industrial labor, variously backed by the persistence of economic ties within the extended family structure (figure 11-1).

Furthermore, we can assume that high transportation costs in these areas also partially explain the importance of parallel activities. Rising trans-

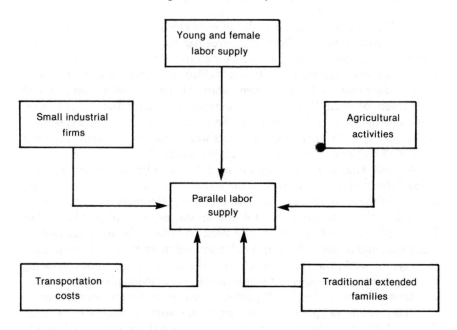

Figure 11-1. The Supply of Parallel Labor in Italy

portation costs may make it less convenient for people to accept jobs for which commuting is necessary.

In this case we are dealing with an adjustment to a demand for labor arising from a particular type of productive arrangement, characterized by the coexistence of an agricultural sector which is still considerably important, with industrial and tertiary activities. The labor supply's gain from flexibility is explained by its gain from pooling incomes flowing from various sources.

In urban industrial contexts, on the other hand, the supply of parallel activities seems to depend on the rigidity due to the type of productive structures, to the characteristics of the service system, and to the family structure itself. The gain from flexibility reflects the need to reallocate time by those having to cope with the growing complexity of extramarket activities which make it more difficult for people to organize their work on the basis of prevailing schedules (figure 11-2).

We can assume that in these areas, characterized by heavy rush-hour traffic, coinciding with the time at which regular workers come and go, the disproportionate length of time needed for transportation induces more and more people to turn to parallel activities, which allow more flexible schedules, and even, at times, the possibility of working (at least in part) at home.

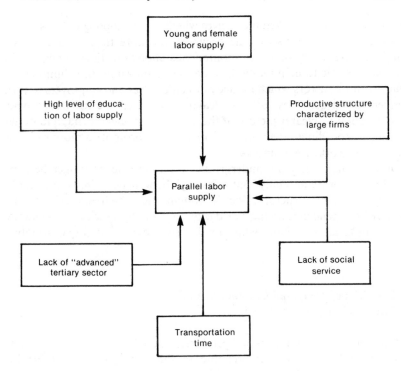

Figure 11-2. Factors Affecting the Market for Parallel Labor

Higher educational levels can be another variable explaining the supply of underground activities. Education enables individuals to adjust more readily to macroeconomic changes (Michael 1972). However, faced with an insufficient number of opportunities for making use of worktime, the effect of higher education is to induce people to shift their preferences to extramarket activities, to forms of self-employment, as well as to forms of temporary work, which represents a kind of transitory "waiting" phase. Therefore, while workers' needs and expectations are undergoing a process of differentiation and rapid change, the productive system seems to remain essentially static. The rising expectations of a school-trained work force are confronted by the limited development of an advanced tertiary sector, while the routinization of industrial work and subordinate work in general frustrates the desire for autonomy and the development of one's specific skills. To the labor supply's need for flexibility in organizing its worktime, the pattern of subordinate employment instead offers rigid schedules and a set of rules which penalize discontinuity in one's career.

A study of the gain from flexibility, both for families and for firms, has considerable impact in determining labor policies. In fact, in the last few years, economists have asked themselves whether, by adopting policies aimed at making existing forms of time organization more flexible, and consequently leaving more room for spontaneous choices in time allocation, it would be possible to help reestablish market equilibrium, thus limiting the impact of those factors which induce both employees and employers to turn to underground activities. Such endeavors would enable us, in the near future, to obtain a clearer picture of these economic phenomena, and in the long run, to coordinate them in such a way as to promote a more rational allocation of work, time, and skills.

On the other hand, the underground economy can no longer be considered a temporary anomaly, but a lasting phenomenon almost inevitably tied to a productive structure, like the Italian one, which is heavily conditioned by its dependence on the world economy and by a series of regulatory and technological restrictions which tend to reduce the flexibility of its labor factor.

The Parallel Economy and Capital Formation: the Case of Housing Construction

The parallel economy goes beyond production activities; in Italy it also concerns capital formation. Data relating to the underground building industry, compared to the official building industry, are shocking.

The number of houses completed in the period 1971-1979, according to ISTAT, is less than half the number of new connections for home electrical consumption effected by the national electric company, ENEL, which provides electricity for a great number of Italians (in certain areas there are municipal electric companies, whose data are obviously accessible to ENEL). In the period 1971 to 1979, 1,480,000 houses were completed, while ENEL effected 3,111,000 new connections for houses; the difference between officially registered new houses and new houses electrically linked up amounted to 1,631,000 (table 11-2).

We cannot explain this enormous gap by arguing that a large number of new connections are affected in preexisting houses: (a) very few houses in Italy are without electricity because of the country's high population density; (b) a substantial exodus from rural areas has reduced the need to bring electricity to scattered houses in isolated areas; (c) according to the 1971 census, only 153,000 houses were without electricity (1.1 percent of the total number). Even if all of these had been linked up in the period 1971-1979, we would still have to explain a gap between new houses, according to ISTAT, and new electrical connections amounting to 1,480,000 units, that is, more than double the official total. We have, therefore, an enormous underground building industry: a phenomenon which, at first sight, would

Table 11-2

Comparison of the Number of Officially Registered New Houses (ISTAT) and the Net Increase in the Number of Domestic Consumers (ENEL), 1972-1979

Region	ISTAT	ENEL	Difference (number)	Difference (percentage)
Northern Italy				
Piedmonte	152,000	263,000	111,000	73
Valle d'Aosta	7,000	20,000	13,000	186
Lombardia	308,000	471,000	163,000	53
Trentino-Alto Adige	40,000	95,000	55,000	138
Veneto	172,000	258,000	86,000	50
Friuli Venezia Giulia	56,000	184,000	128,000	229
Liguria	50,000	124,000	74,000	148
Emilia-Romagna	187,000	228,000	41,000	22
Total	972,000	1,643,000	671,000	69
Central Italy				
Toscana	103,000	169,000	66,000	64
Umbria	15,000	35,000	20,000	133
Marche	47,000	72,000	25,000	53
Lazio	127,000	266,000	139,000	109
Total	292,000	542,000	250,000	86
Southern Italy and Islands				
Abruzzi	24,000	83,000	59,000	246
Molise	4,000	17,000	13,000	325
Campania	29,000	196,000	167,000	576
Puglia	71,000	183,000	112,000	158
Basilicata	4,000	21,000	17,000	425
Calabria	10,000	109,000	99,000	990
Sicilia	54,000	232,000	178,000	330
Sardegna	20,000	85,000	65,000	325
Total	216,000	926,000	710,000	329
Italy	1,480,000	3,111,000	1,631,000	110

seem to be surprising, since there is nothing as visible and as physically ascertainable as a house. It should be pointed out that ISTAT surveys refer to the number of "finished houses," from the point of view of the local authorities in charge of the building industry. As ISTAT itself tells us, "data on the building industry reported in the tables are based on administrative deeds concerning buildings that have been projected, begun, and completed, and which the communes transmit every month." In some cases, ISTAT informs us, the communes do not transmit any data at all, especially in southern Italy, despite ISTAT's requests. These cases are not "oversights;" they are due to the communes' actual lack of data and represent a deficiency in the administrative sectors that issue building permits.

And even when the communes transmit data, they convey only official figures, and as ISTAT tells us, give no information on illegal building activities—obviously, since these illicit buildings officially do not exist for the authorities. Either because of their inability to effect controls, or more likely, because of their complaisant attitude, the authorities allow illegal buildings to be built and to remain in an "underground" condition.

Last, ISTAT points out that there is a temporary discrepancy between data on buildings that have been projected and begun and those concerning buildings that have been completed, since the latter should be deduced from the number of "liveability permits" issued—often these permits are issued several years after the building has been completed and actually lived in.

But we are not simply dealing with a "temporary discrepancy." If it were only that, there would be a systematic gap averaging several years between figures on construction in progress and construction completed. The average for 1972-1976, for example, shows that completed buildings total about 5 million cubic metres, while those underway are more than 6 million. And it is even more remarkable that houses begun between 1972 and 1973 were more than 1.5 million cubic metres, while finished houses totaled an average of 1 million a year from 1975 to 1976.

As we can see, there are two types of phenomena in the underground building industry: buildings that are illegal from the start and buildings that are illegal, because, even though they have been granted a building permit, they have not been issued a liveability permit. This presumably occurs because they do not conform to the building regulations, even if they are comfortably inhabited (because they lack parking space, for example), or because they do not conform to the detailed provisions specified by many communes regarding height, outside wall color, or the size and dimension of the building for which the permits have been issued. Only a part of the underground building industry can be correctly termed "clandestine," that is, truly illegal; the remaining part reflects the "cost of transactions" that a citizen must bear in order to persuade the commune to grant him a liveability permit anyway, thereby accepting the minor changes he has effected; or by making him pay a small penalty. People directly inhabiting an apartment do not need the liveability permit to make use of certain public utilities. In fact they can have the apartment linked up to electricity, telephone, and drinking water without having to produce such a permit, but simply by applying for these connections and paying the respective contributions and fees. Moreover, the owner can rent buildings without a liveability permit, and only in case of a dispute does the lack of a permit become significant. Practically, therefore, only in case of sale, does the problem of regularizing buildings in the underground construction industry come up. But the dynamics of real property in Italy is very limited, because of high sales taxes. Therefore, there is very little incentive to force underground constructions to come to the surface.

A large part of the underground building industry, however, cannot be considered clandestine from a fiscal point of view, either totally or partially. It can be presumed that houses built without a building permit evade the "urbanization contribution" fixed by the new law on urban planning passed in 1977. But its evasion is probably not a sufficient motive to justify illegal activity: usually illegality is determined by the need to build without having to wait for a permit. A permit is difficult to obtain since it may entail a variation in the town plan, or the commune's adoption of the plan, requiring both a considerable amount of time and costly entreaties; or it may even be determined by the builder's need to build in places or in ways that he knows from the very start are forbidden, but thinks that the local authorities will certainly not have the building demolished, once it has been completed, since this type of punishment is held to be an intolerable "social waste" in the light of the present housing shortage.

Many houses that have been built in a clandestine fashion, since they do not conform to urban planning regulations, pay income taxes correctly. In fact, since nonluxury newly built or rebuilt houses are entitled to an exemption from ILOR (local income tax) for a period of twenty-five years, the owners have an incentive to obtain legal documents as soon as possible, so as to benefit from the exemption. This can be done either by producing the liveability permit, or by proving that the new premises are liveable, which is deduced from its being connected to electricity, water, and so forth, or by an inspection, stating its requirements, of course. It is easy to see how a new apartment can be included among those which are entitled to the tax exemption, from a fiscal point of view, while, at the same time, remaining illegal. Furthermore, a taxpayer is supposed to state the amount of his real property for income tax purposes, and this also includes clandestine property.

Only if the general land office were truly up to date, and provided reliable data, and transmitted them to those in charge of assessing the national income would the parallel building economy cease to exist. But it is not foreseeable that this will take place in the near future, nor for quite a number of years, and perhaps it may never take place.

The capital formation in the "parallel" building industry concerns not only housing, but also certainly concerns the construction of buildings for industrial and commercial purposes. In fact, permits are even harder to obtain for these buildings than they are for housing construction, since fire prevention and sanitary authority permits are required, and the builders may be in urgent need to begin the production process.

It is very likely that the process of capital formation has been consistently undervalued.

Notes

1. Despite the fact that domestic technology has freed housewives from a certain number of tedious chores, domestic organization in urban

life has become more and more complicated; as several surveys on time budgets show, the number of hours per week devoted to housework has not decreased at all in the last twenty years, but has increased. (A. Szalai, *The Use of Time* (Paris: La Hague Mouton, 1973); K.E. Walker, "Homemaking still takes time," *Journal of Home Economics,* October 1968.)

The possibility of gaining access to certain services often requires an increase, instead of a decrease in family activity, in terms of both time and resources. (L. Balbo 1976)

2. An econometric study estimating the effects various programs of alternative schedules have on the potential supply of female labor has shown that, other things being equal, part-time work programs have more impact than other types of contracts in northern regions. This means that the labor supply is willing to devote less time to the market. This can be explained by the higher marginal value of extramarket time, due to the fact that family production (in these areas) requires a greater time input. (Colombino 1978)

3. This takes place when nonparticipation in the labor market does not bring about participation in family production (or does so only partially, or inefficiently). (Colombino 1978)

4. However, the industrial area suffered from severe earthquake damage, and the damaged firms were exempted from paying social security contributions, but in order to qualify for these exemptions they had to undergo several inspections. This fact probably explains the scarce amount of irregular industrial work found in this commune in Friuli.

5. Sectoral percentage distribution of second jobs: Agriculture, 24.6 percent; Industry, 37.0 percent; Other activities, 38.4 percent. (CENSIS 1980).

6. The segmentation phenomenon seems to be even more marked in the parallel market (irregular labor and second-job market) than in the surface labor market. In fact, the demand for second jobs does not seem to compete with the demand for marginal labor. The demand for second jobs coming from business firms requires professional skills possessed by already qualified workers and not easily found among unemployed or irregular workers. (Gallino 1980).

References

Balbo, L. *Stato di Famiglia.* Etas Libri, Milan, 1976.

Becathini, G. "The Development of Light Industry in Tuscany: An Interpretation." *Economic Notes,* no. 2/3, Siena, 1978.

Becker, G. "A Theory of the Allocation of Time." *The Economic Journal,* September 1965.

Benham, L. "Benefits of Women's Education within Marriage." In *Econo-*

mics of the Family, Edited by T.S.W. Shultz. Chicago: University of Chicago Press, 1974.

Bulgarelli, A. and Ricolfi, L. "Le tendenze dell'occupazione in Italia: meno lavoro, meno lavoro stabile, più lavoro precario." *Monthly Review,* no. 3, 1978.

CENSIS *L'occupazione occulta.* Fondazione Censis, Rome, 1976.

Colombino, U.; Del Boca, D.; and Negri, N. (edited by G. Martinotti) *Qualità della vita e strategie di comportamento familiare: A survey on 1000 families in Turin.* Milan: F. Angeli, (forthcoming).

Colombino, U. *Il potenziale aggiunto di lavoro in Italia.* Giappichelli, 1978.

Contini, B. *Lo sviluppo di un'economia prallela,* Ed. di Comunità, Firenze, 1979.

Contini, B. and Del Boca, D. "Linee di tendenza e problemi congiunturali del mercato del lavoro in Italia." Economia Istruzione formazione professionale, no. 1, 1978.

Deaglio, M. "L'occupazione invisibile: il caso di un comune del Piemonte." *Biblioteca della Libertà,* no. 4, 1974.

Del Boca, D. and Turvani, M. *Famiglia e mercato del lavoro.* Il Mulino, Bologna, 1979.

Feige, E.L. "How Big Is the Irregular Economy?" *Challenge,* November-December 1979.

Fua, G. *Occupazione e capacità produttive: la realtà italiana.* Il Mulino, Bologna, 1976.

Gallino, L. (a cura di) *Lavorare due volte.* Stampatori, Turin, 1980.

Gutmann, P. "The Subterranean Economy." *Financial Analysts Journal,* November-December 1977.

ISPOL *Rapporto sulla manodopera.* Rome, 1980.

Lizzeri, C. *Mezzogiorno in controluce.* Enel, Naples, 1979.

Michael, R.T. *The Effect of Education on Efficiency in Consumption,* New York: N.B.E.R., 1972.

Mincer, J. and Polachek, S. "Family Investment in Human Capital." *Journal of Political Economy* 82, no. 2, 1974.

Paci, M. *Famiglia e mercato del lavoro, in un'economia periferica,* Milan: F. Angeli, 1980.

Schultz, T.S.W. *Economics of the family.* N.B.E.R., Chicago: University of Chicago Press, 1974.

Saba, A. *L'Industria Sommersa.* Padua: Marsilio, 1980.

Tanzi, V. "Economia sotterranea degli Stati Uniti: Stime e implicazioni." *Moneta e Credito,* Sept. 1980, pp. 303-329.

12 The Second Economy of Italy

Bruno Contini

The most important recent development in the Italian economy—and a source of serious worries—has been a large semiunderground labor market that may include as much as 20 percent of the total working force. Only a couple of decades ago the picture was very different.

The peak of the Italian postwar economic boom—a typical history of export-led development—was achieved in 1962, at which time it was commonly believed that Italy was near full employment. Industrial wages had gained at a slower pace than average productivity since the postwar reconstruction years, investment was high, and the productive system expanded rapidly in the exporting sectors (although considerably less so in sectors aimed at filling internal demand).

Since 1964 Italy has experienced prolonged stagnation, substantially uninterrupted even during periods of mild recovery like the years 1966-1969, 1972-1973, and 1977-1978 (table 12-1). Investments did not recover their 1963 level until 1968; employment in nonagricultural activities fell.

During the years 1964-1970 Italy set a remarkable record for exporting nearly all its internal resources: manpower in the form of migrant labor to the European Economic Community (EEC) countries and Switzerland, goods and services through a continuous surplus in the trade balance, and capital at an average of more than $2 billion per year. In 1971 the trade surplus turned into a deficit that took frightening dimensions after the oil crisis, but has returned near balance since 1977.

Beginning in 1962, wages moved faster than in the previous decade, a natural consequence of the progressive opening of the EEC labor market. The ensuing decline in profits forced Italian manufacturing industries to search for new cost-containment strategies. The decade 1963-1972 was indeed characterized by a massive labor-saving effort of the industrial structure, attained in two ways: first, increasing labor productivity by concentrating the presence of male workers "in prime age" in the industrial labor force—achieved via a substantial reduction of women's participation, a progressive lowering of the retirement age, and hiring practices that excluded the younger labor force; and second, decentralizing the production of labor-intensive items that are not amenable to assembly-line production—

Reprinted with permission of the author from the *Journal of Contemporary Studies*, 4, no. 3, Summer 1981. © 1981 by the Institute for Contemporary Studies.

Table 12-1

Investments and Employment in Organization of Economic Cooperation and Development (OECD) Countries

	Gross Investment Yearly Average 1965-1975 (1963 = 100)	Total Employment 1974 (1963 = 100)
France	186	109
West Germany	150	101
Italy	115	97
Netherlands	173	108
United Kingdom	141	100
United States	133[a]	124
Japan	273	115

Source: OECD, *Main Economic Indicators* (1965-1976).

[a]Not including investments financed by the federal government.

moving toward craft shops, small-scale manufacturing units, and more extensive utilization of work-at-home, all aimed at recovering full labor flexibility.

Throughout the years of the boom, wide and stable wage differentials among major classes of the labor force (male versus female, skilled versus unskilled) were a distinguishing feature of Italy's labor market. In the mid-1960s these differentials began to decrease under the unions' pressure toward egalitarianism, while there were no corresponding gains in average productivity. On the contrary, in those years productivity differentials were moving ever farther apart. The slowdown in economic activity initiated with six months of very tight money in 1963-1964 struck a mortal blow to the construction industry at a time when demand for low-cost housing, services, and social infrastructures was still rapidly expanding in urban industrialized areas, where the boom had attracted large migratory flows from the South through the last decade. Widespread discontent and grievances among the more disadvantaged began to explode. Absenteeism and disaffection rose rapidly, especially among women workers who found it more and more difficult to divide themselves between house and work. Occasionally absenteeism found ambiguous justification in the unions on the grounds that it was a sort of indirect compensation against poor living conditions and lack of adequate social services.[1]

All in all, unit labor costs of the secondary components of the labor force (women, the young, and the aged of both sexes) turned upward and began to move ahead of the costs of "primary" workers, thus harming employment chances for the weakest fringes of the labor force.[2]

The Irregular Economy

Toward the end of the 1960s the situation was ripe for the revenge of the market: money wages in the official labor market could not be compressed (real wages were still lower than in all of the other neighboring countries) and therefore a parallel market for "irregular" labor services began to develop. *Irregular* is here used as a catchall name for all jobs outside the social security system (payroll taxes in Italy add 50-60 percent to the basic pay, in itself a powerful incentive to tax evasion),[3]which are by their nature precarious, unprotected, and beyond any form of organized social control. The supply of the irregular labor force grew rapidly and so did the demand for their services. Low-paid categories of workers more and more seemed to prefer precarious forms of employment that yielded money wages below the official market rates, but allowed a high degree of flexibility in the allocation of their time, to forced inactivity. Firms that had the option of utilizing irregular labor, either directly or by subcontracting to small-scale manufacturers, were eager to take full advantage of it.

From the demand side, the incentive to hire irregular workers to avoid payroll taxation is undoubtedly a major one. But no less important incentives include keeping the unions off limits, paying by piece-rate, and regaining unlimited flexibility of labor utilization in terms of working hours and layoffs.

Labor mobility had been indeed a major target of union unrest since the late 1960s, and for good reasons. Extraordinary financial incentives had been granted in those years to several large industries (both in the private and in the semipublic sectors) to establish new production facilities; especially in the less industrialized South, unions were eager to see new jobs created in areas that had been depopulated by massive emigration in the 1950s and early 1960s. Many of those ventures, especially in basic chemicals and fertilizers where excess capacity was a well-known world phenomenon by the early 1970s, were doomed since their inception, but were nevertheless carried out. Politics and managerial incompetence explain these events. A few years later, when the size of these losses was revealed to the public, many plants were ready to close. At that point, however, the unions fiercely opposed the layoffs on the grounds that workers were not to pay for colossal errors that nobody was ready to admit, let alone pay for.

From the supply side, too, incentives to conceal the employment status are powerful. Income tax evasion is the obvious one, but the flexibility of working time—especially for the women, but also for young and aged of both sexes—is probably at least as important in understanding the seemingly everlasting supply of irregular labor.

Estimating its Size

The starting point for estimating, however crudely, the size and growth of the underground labor market is the phenomenon of rapid decline in the labor force participation rate: in the late 1950s the official overall participation rate (here defined as the ratio of labor force to total population) was nearly 45 percent, comparable to that of most industrialized countries; by the mid-1970s it had fallen to less than 35 percent, way below the trend of all its neighbors, let alone of those countries—such as the United States and France— where female participation rates have risen remarkably in the last decade. It is now widely accepted in Italy that official data on participation rates strongly underestimate labor supply: in several field studies of local communities, observed participation has been found to be 10-20 percentage points higher than official figures. This difference accounts mainly for women and the young and aged of both sexes, who hold various kinds of irregular jobs and will not reveal their true status.

In 1959 the official participation rate was 44 percent (the highest in the postwar period); two ad hoc surveys on the nonworking population estimated it as 42 percent in 1971 (against an official 36.2 percent) and as 41.4 percent in 1977 (against 33.7 percent).[4] Assuming that the official data are correct until 1959, and that the ad hoc estimates of 1971 and 1977 are also correct, the mid-years may be interpolated to obtain an independent estimate of the overall participation rate and hence of the total labor force. The difference between the officially reported labor force and this alternative calculation provides an estimate of the irregular labor force. According to this procedure, the irregular labor force reaches a minimum of 1.6 million in 1962 (at the peak of the "miracle"), more than doubles to 3.8 million in 1972, and fluctuates from there on around a trend which was still moving upward at the end of the 1970s, although at a slower pace. In 1977 the irregular working force amounted to over 17 percent of the total working population. This is undoubtedly a conservative estimate. It may include discouraged working-age unemployed (who should be left out of the count), but it excludes all those who were already irregular workers in the 1950s and have been since (as they were presumably not counted as labor force even in those days). In addition, it fails to account for the estimated 1.5 million people who hold multiple jobs.

Calculating the size of the underground economy as a percentage of GNP is very difficult. Only indirect inferences are possible. Depending on which source one is willing to accept (17 percent of total labor force according to my own estimates, 20 percent according to independent estimates summarized in table 12-3) and accounting for second jobs that may be excluded from either of these counts,[5] one obtains a figure that varies between 14 and 20 percent of the recorded gross national product for 1977. This is undoubtedly a very high figure, although substantially lower than some journalistic accounts, which have placed it above 30 percent of GNP.[6]

Where the Irregular Workers Hide

Decentralization of production and subcontracting to small-scale business appear to be the distinguishing features of the Italian manufacturing industry in the 1970s. Not all branches of production have experienced it in the same degree; capital-intensive industries, where economies of scale play a major role, have remained relatively untouched. Table 12-2 gives a breakdown by industry and geographical location of 1.6 million workers-at-home in manufacturing estimated in a series of local surveys in 1972.

Table 12-2 reflects a conservative estimate of irregular work activities in manufacturing: at the very least it fails to account for all those who are on regular payroll at minimum contractual wage but receive substantial money in excess of the official pay, plus all the overtime earnings off the books. It would be surprising if the majority of irregulars were to be found in manufacturing. After all, the few estimates of underground work activities in most countries of the West indicate that many take place in service and construction sectors (with building maintenance often accounting for a large share).

Table 12-2
Work-at-Home in Manufacturing (1972-1973)

Workers-at-Home	Product	Region
480,000	Hosiery	Emilia, Veneto, Tuscany, Marche, Puglia
150,000	Textiles	Piedmont, Tuscany
150,000	Shoes	Veneto, Tuscany
155,000	Toys	Liguria, Tuscany
100,000	Auto accessories	Piedmont, Lombardy
90,000	Garments	Tuscany, Emilia, Lombardy, Puglia, Lazio
80,000	Leather products	Veneto, Tuscany, Lazio, Lombardy
68,000	Gloves	Campania
30,000	Cosmetic products and wigs	Sicily, Calabria
40,000	Plastic products	Piedmont, Lombardy, Tuscany
25,000	Tiles	Veneto, Umbria, Abruzzo, Sicily
20,000	Electrical motors	Lombardy
15,000	Bicycles	Lombardy, Marche
15,000	Glass	Tuscany
12,000	Furniture	Tuscany
170,000	Miscellaneous	Veneto, Lombardy, Lazio
1,600,000	Total	(Manufacturing only)

Source: S. Brusco, "Prime note per uno studio del lavoro a domicilio," *Inchiesta,* April-June, 1973.

It is not easy to categorize the nearly 4 million irregular workers at the end of the 1970s by activity sector. Independent estimates, such as those reported in table 12-2 are available from various sources, and have been gathered in table 12-3.

This total includes many multiple-job holders. It is known, for instance, that most unrecorded building activity takes place with workers who hold two or more jobs or who are officially unemployed, rather than with people engaged only in the irregular or underground market (as with the vast majority of workers-at-home for the manufacturing sector, mainly women and old persons of both sexes).

Many irregular jobs in the private-service sector (trade and other services) can be attributed to multiple-job holders whose primary activity is often in the public sector—where working hours have traditionally been exceptionally low. A normal working schedule often runs from 8 a.m. to 2 p.m., for less than 30 effective hours a week, which is a peculiar compensation for pay levels that have always been lower than comparable private-sector jobs.

However, it is mainly small and very small businesses that directly utilize irregular work. Indirect recourse to the irregular labor market touches everybody: large firms subcontract to small ones, and these in turn to even smaller ones, all the way down to the sweat-shops and work-at-home A peculiar, but significant, hint of the increasing extent of the underground economy in Northern Italy emerged from a recent survey on labor mobility (see table 12-4).[7]

In the early 1970s, the probability of leaving Fiat and changing jobs was negligible for younger workers and less than 10 percent for older workers. Between 1973 and 1977 this probability increase substantially for all age groups reaching an astounding 45 percent for the younger ones. In addition, 50 percent of the young and practically all workers over thirty who left Fiat joined unidentified firms (according to a regional Chamber of Commerce

Table 12-3

Estimates of Nonagricultural "Irregular" Working Activities in the Mid-1970s

Manufacturing[a]	1.6 million
Construction	0.6 million
Retail and wholesale trade	1.4 million
Services (other)	1.0 million
Total	4.6 million

Source: Various sources reported in B. Contini, *Lo sviluppo di una economica parallela,* Milan (1979).

[a]See table 12-2.

Table 12-4
(Annual) Probability of Leaving a Job with Fiat for Another Job in Another Firm
(percent)

| | Observation Periods | | | |
| | 1969-1972 | | 1973-1977 | |
Age Group	Move to Other "Identifiable" Firm	Move to an "Unidentifiable" Firm	Move to Other "Identifiable" Firm	Move to an "Unidentifiable" Firm
Less than 30	—	—	22.2	22.3
30-50	7.5	—	0.1	16.3
50 and over	8.7	—	—	25.0

Source: B. Contini and V. Colombino, "Labor Mobility in Northern Italy," *Economia, Istruzione e Formazione Professionale,* vol. 6 (1979).
Note: Those surveyed were male blue-collar workers who began working for Fiat before 1969.

survey). This could only happen with minuscule businesses, possibly recently born. It seems reasonable to suppose that most workers leaving Fiat in those years might indeed have preferred an irregular job of their choice, rather than uncertain tenure with a company that was considering layoffs after years of employment expansion.

If this is a reliable account of the major developments of Italy's economy since the mid-1960s, one would expect to find important differences in behavior—and substantially better performance—of small business vis-à-vis the larger ones, since the former have had almost free access to the semiunderground job market. Several available indicators on small- and medium-size business indeed point in this direction.

Table 12-5 shows that small firms, much more than larger ones, have added to their stock of fixed capital in the period 1968-1974 across all branches of manufacturing. Likewise they have decreased the number of workers, while larger firms have substantially increased employment. Indeed, employment figures refer to "official employment," providing a hint on the extensive substitution of officially employed workers with irregular workers by smaller entrepreneurs. Union power prevents the same from happening in larger establishments.

Another indicator of the performance of small as opposed to large firms is provided by the gross (before-tax) profit shares on value added (table 12-6); these, too, look much better for businesses with fifty to ninety-nine employees.

Trouble Ahead

It is clear that the underground economy acts in the short run as a safety valve for the economy at large. There is no scientific evidence on the subject,

Table 12-5

Investments and Employment in Manufacturing, by Company Size (1968-1974)

	Investments 1968-1974 Divided by 1968 Book Value of Plant and Equipment		Employment (Percentage of Variation 1974-1968)	
Branches	Small Firms	Large Firms	Small Firms	Large Firms
Steel mills and foundaries	100	59	− 3.0	29.8
Building materials	90	36	− 6.5	12.8
Engineering and metalworking	100	45	− 9.0	12.1
Machinery and equipment	86	41	− 0.4	13.9
Food and beverages	117	108	− 10.1	20.5
Textiles	55	101	− 10.0	20.2
Lumber and lumber products	110	46	− 6.2	10.1
Publishing	39	22	− 6.0	23.3
Rubber and plastic products	104	34	− 2.2	19.9
Garments	43	38	− 9.6	15.9

Source: Mediocredito Centrale, *Surveys on Italy's Manufacturing Sectors (1968 and 1974)*.

Notes: "Small Firms" 10-50 employees; "Large Firms" 50-1500 employees. "Investments" expressed in 1968 lire.

but chances are that in spite of short-run advantages there will be serious long-run drawbacks in relying on the underground economy as the main source of job creation and foreign exchange, as has sometimes been suggested. In the first place, there must be lasting political repercussions from cementing the cleavage between more and less privileged segments of the

Table 12-6

Gross Profit Shares (on Value Added) in Manufacturing, by Size of Firm (Average 1973-1975)

(percentage)

Branches	All Firms	Small Firms (50-99 employees)
Steel mills and foundaries	15.9	32.2
Building materials	21.5	22.4
Machinery and metalworking	12.5	22.5
Food and beverages	14.3	20.2
Textiles	10.5	18.9
Lumber and lumber products	13.6	14.2
Publishing	6.6	17.0
Pulp and paper	16.8	30.1
Rubber	10.8	24.9
Plastic products	18.9	25.9
Garments	7.3	13.9
Chemicals	22.0	30.9
Footwear	14.7	17.3

Source: ISTAT, "Indagine sul valore aggiunto delle imprese industriali" (1973, 1974, 1975).

Note: Gross profit = Value added − (wage bill + interest payments on total outstanding liabilities).

population. Second, manufacturing that has expanded in these years is bound to lose competitiveness against many countries of the developing world with much lower labor costs. Finally, the composition of investments already appears to be severely affected: capital expenditures in higher technology sectors have substantially decreased in the 1970s, crowded out by investments where low and intermediate technologies prevailed and the advantages offered by the irregular labor market were easier to reap. In the long run this seems myopic. It will widen the technological gap between Italy and the rest of the industrialized world, and consolidate its peripheral position.

The Italian experience in the 1970s therefore was not a happy one. The renewed dualistic structure of the economy has taken hold in concurrence with a major crisis of industrial investment that has yet to end, despite great ferment in the small business sector. As a consequence the industrial structure inherited from the years of the Italian economic boom, largely based on the export potential of labor-intensive commodities produced with mature technologies, appears strongly consolidated. In the early 1960s its development was made possible by the presence of explicit excess supply of labor, while nowadays it feeds upon a not-so-hidden reserve of manpower operating on the fringes of society—with all the attendant dangers to a social order that is already notoriously fragile.

Policy Responses

It is doubtful—at this point—that the government can do much to quickly reverse the trend towards progressive marginalization of the industrial structure. However, several things can and should be done to slow it down and, eventually, bring it to a halt.

First, payroll taxes should be lowered to be in line with those of other European countries; as of now, this is done only selectively. This will take away a major incentive to resort to irregular work. Second, the resulting cut in tax revenues will have to be compensated by more incisive action against direct tax evasion among the middle- and upper-income groups without any adjustment of tax rates necessary. This is in itself a huge task requiring support from all political parties in order to withstand the pressure of those who will have to bear its cost. Third, selective industrial policies in favor of the promising winner sectors should be implemented and pursued with determination. Financial and tax incentives to research and development should also be adopted.

Concurrently a credible plan of manpower redeployment should be worked out in collaboration with unions, employers associations, and local governments. It is now necessary to face the problem of forthcoming layoffs from ailing industrial sectors that should no longer be bailed out. The task is very hard, time is short, and unfortunately the possibility of genuine reform depends crucially on much stronger political consensus than the present coalition government seems able to inspire. The situation for Italy is, consequently, very serious.

Notes

1. Absenteeism rates among female workers were 4.4 times higher in Italy than in the United States in the period 1972-1976 (and about 3 times higher for men). See F. Padoa-Schioppa, "Assenteismo e turnover nell occupazione femminile," *Queste Istituzioni* (1979).

2. Some data on the expulsion of women from the industrial labor force: in 1959 female workers in manufacturing were 1,823,000 (33.3 percent of employment); in 1969 there were 170,000 fewer female workers than in 1959. (down to 27.2 percent of total employment in manufacturing).

3. Payroll taxes are the major source of financing the social security system. Revenue from direct taxation is lower in Italy than in most Western countries, in spite of the marked progressiveness of income taxation, due to the wide areas of income tax evasion in the middle- and high-income brackets.

4. ISTAT, *Indagine speciale sulle non-forze di lavoro,* Rome (1971 and 1977).

5. About 1.5 million jobs (not persons) are missing from my estimate; 0.8 million from the data of table 12-3.

6. It should be pointed out that—to my knowledge—there has been as yet no attempt to estimate the size of hidden GNP in Italy using the monetary approach suggested by Peter Gutmann ("The Subterranean Economy," *Financial Analysis Journal,* 1977) and Edgar Feige ("How Big Is the Irregular Economy?" *Challenge,* Nov.-Dec. 1979) for the United States. This would obviously help clarify the issue, although, I suspect, the underlying methodology is more appropriate for countries in which most or all of the irregular activities are paid in cash. This does not happen in Italy because disclosure of information on banking accounts is precluded by law, so the incentive to revert to cash transactions is not nearly as high as in other countries where the underground economy is rapidly growing.

7. Bruno Contini and V. Colombino, "Labor Mobility in Northern Italy," *Economia, Istruzione e Formazione Professionale,* vol. 6 (1979).

13 The Hidden Economy in Norway

Arne Jon Isachsen,
Jan Tore Klovland
and *Steinar Strøm*

Introduction and Summary

In traditional economic analysis it is common to distinguish between the public and the private sector. However, over the last few years another dichotomy has gained increased attention, that between the registered (or formal, or open) sector of the economy and the unregistered (or informal, or underground, or hidden) one.

A growing tax burden is seen as a main driving force behind the escalation of unregistered economic activity. Also, within the economic profession one should not disregard the existence of a bandwagon effect; once a new and highly controversial topic in terms of methods or research as well as political implications is launched, it is not surprising that the interest of a growing number of economists is aroused.

One problem with the study of the hidden economy is an operational definition of it. Tanzi's (1980, p. 428) definition of the hidden economy is "gross national product that because of unreporting and/or underreporting is not measured by official statistics."[1]

However, the various methods that have been employed to estimate the hidden economy most likely capture different things.[2] Estimates based on the development of the composition of the money stock will not include barter transactions. Analysis performed by the Internal Revenue Service focuses on unreported income that implies tax evasion, whereas the GNP concept of income most likely is broader. However, the lack of a general and operational definition of the hidden economy should not keep researchers from trying to measure parts of it, bearing in mind that different methods most likely capture different unregistered activities.

The present paper is an attempt to measure the hidden economy in Norway in terms of a micro and a macro approach.[3] The micro approach, based on a survey study conducted in September 1980, is rather novel. The focus of that approach is limited to the labor market, that is, questions relate solely to unreported income from work. The macro study is more traditional, focusing on the development of the stock of currency.

We gratefully acknowledge financial support from the Norwegian Taxpayers' Union. We wish to thank Jens Olav Sporastøl for econometric assistance and helpful comments.

At the outset it is pertinent to warn against placing too much confidence in the results. As will become evident, this study abounds with uncertainties, as are other studies of the hidden economy that we are aware of.[4]

The main conclusions of the survey approach can be summarized as follows:

> Over the last 12 months 18 percent of the population over the age of 15 acknowledged *income* from unreported work, whereas 26 percent stated that they had *paid* for unregistered services. Taken together 37.5 percent of the population had been active in the black labor market over the previous 12 months, as buyers and/or sellers.

> Hours worked by males and females decline with age. On the demand side the pattern differs between the sexes. The demand for irregular labor services reaches a maximum for males 25-54 years of age. For females there are two maxima; 25-39 years of age, and 55 years and over.

> *Demand* for hidden labor services increases with years of schooling. *Supply* of hidden labor services first increases and then decreases with years of schooling.

> Based on market prices and on information on the supply of unregistered labor services, the size of the hidden labor market is estimated to be 5.5 billion kroner.[5] This amounts to 2.3 percent of 1979 GNP.

> Buyers of unregistered labor services are generally quite pleased both with the quality of work and the ease with which such work is supplied.

> There is a general feeling that the hidden labor market will increase over time and become more acceptable to society.

> There has been a tendency for the participation rate of younger people to increase relative to other age groups over the last decade.

A final finding in the survey study is that about 80 percent of hidden labor services is paid in cash. This gives some justification to the underlying assumption of the macro approach, namely that transactions in the unregistered sector of the economy are settled in currency. The results of the macro approach are easily summarized:

> In estimating the demand for currency, it is proper to include a tax variable.

> The size of the hidden economy has increased to 14.5 billion kroner in 1978, or 6.3 percent of GNP in that year. It should be emphasized that this measure covers more irregular activities than the income from irregular work.

A Microeconomic Analysis
of the Hidden Labor Market

The Method

At the survey conducted by Markeds-og Mediainstituttet, a private polling organization, in September 1980, the interviewer, in concluding the regular interview, asked the respondent to accept a questionnaire on the hidden labor market, to be filled in and mailed within a week. Of 1,198 persons interviewed, 958 agreed (80 percent) and 877 complied by mailing the questionnaire within the next two weeks. This means that of the total sample 73 percent complied with the request. Among those who did not want to receive the questionnaire (240 persons) there was an overrepresentation of people 65 years of age and over.

Compared to the population of the country, in our final sample of 877 persons there was an overrepresentation of men and of the age group 25-39 years. For some of the results reported we have corrected for this bias in our sample by proper weighting. For the most interesting variables the 95 percent confidence interval was calculated.[6]

Before reporting the main results of the survey, one further comment on the method is in order. A few months before our investigation the newspaper Verdens Gang (VG) reported the results of an interview survey performed by another polling organization (Scan-Fact) on the hidden economy. In this survey, which covered 1,002 persons, the interviewer asked the respondents and noted the answers; one question was whether the respondent over the last 12 months had participated in the hidden labor market. The results of the two surveys are compared in table 13-1.[7]

Table 13-1 indicates that in a pure interview survey people are less willing to acknowledge participation in the unregistered labor market than in a

Table 13-1
Participation Rates in the Hidden Labor Market over the Last 12 Months
(percentage of sample)

	Isachsen, Strøm	Verdens Gang
1. Worked in the hidden market	20	16
2. Paid for work in the hidden market	29	16
3. Worked and paid	9	6
4. = 1 + 2 − 3 Participated in the hidden labor market	40	26

Note: Both surveys were conducted in 1980. In the VG survey the data are not weighted according to sex and age, so for proper comparison, our results are given in unweighted form.

combined interview/postal survey. The reason for this may be that to acknowledge openly one's unregistered economic transactions is more difficult than filling in a questionnaire. Provided one is reasonably certain of preserving anonymity, one may feel less uneasy about putting a few Xs in the proper boxes of the questionnaire.

At any rate it seems safe to assume that both methods will underestimate the size of the hidden labor market. One way to get a grasp of the degree of underreporting would be to have the correct data on hidden economic activities on a subset of the sample, and compare that a priori knowledge with what emerges from the questionnaire. Needless to say, such an approach is quite demanding and was deemed infeasible at the present stage of the project.

The disparity revealed in table 13-1 reminds us of the uncertainties involved in interpreting the results of the survey method when applied to such a sensitive topic as the hidden economy.

The Main Findings

Table 13-2 reveals that the likelihood of a man working in the hidden sector is 27.9 percent or about three times as high as that of a woman, 8.9 percent. However, on average women in the unregistered labor market work twice as many hours over the year as do men.

From lines 1 and 4 it is easy to calculate that whereas women accounted for 42 percent of total unregistered hours of work, they received only 36 percent of the total hidden labor income.

The longer hours of work for women in the unregistered sector may reflect that child care on a regular basis is an important source of income for some housewives. To some extent this could also explain women's relatively lower hourly wage rate.

Comparing lines 5 and 6 reveals that people are more willing to acknowledge payment for unregistered work (on average 4,575 kroner) than income from such work (on average 3,735 kroner). However, as a considerable part of hidden labor services is rendered to the family or household as such (child care, maintenance work on the house, and the like), it may be that in stating payment for hidden labor services one responds on behalf of the household rather than the individual. That would imply an upward bias in line 6 of table 13-2.

The demand for irregular services reaches a maximum for males 25-39 years of age. For females there are two maxima, 25-39 years of age, and 55 years and over. Figure 13-1 reveals that young people more frequently offer their services in the hidden labor market than do older people.

In a pure interview survey conducted in 1971 the participants were asked if they had ever worked in the irregular labor market—21 percent answered

Table 13-2
Participation Rates, Hours of Work, and Payments in the Hidden Labor Market

	Total[a]	Men	Women
1. Worked unregistered last 12 months (174 persons)	18.2% (15.8-20.6)	27.9% (23.8-32.0)	8.9% (6.2-11.6)
2. Paid for unregistered work last 12 months (255 persons)	26.4% (23.3-29.5)	31.7% (27.6-35.8)	22.0% (17.3-26.7)
3. Worked unregistered and/or paid for unregistered work last 12 months (353 persons)	37.5% (34.2-40.9)	47.5% (42.8-52.2)	28.0% (23.1-32.9)
4. Hours worked unregistered, on average, over last 12 months for those who acknowledged such work[b] (167 persons)	110 hours	88 hours	179 hours
5. Unregistered labor income received, on average, over last 12 months, for those who acknowledged such income (167 persons)	3,735 kr.	3,311 kr.	5,128 kr.
6. Amount paid for unregistered work, on average, over the last 12 months, for those who acknowledged such payments[c]	4,575 kr.	4,003 kr.	5,606 kr.

[a]In lines 1-3, the percent figures are weighted as explained in note 6. The 99 percent confidence interval is given in parentheses under the figures. In lines 4-6 the percent is unweighted and is that of the sample.

[b]Seven persons admitted to having worked unregistered, but did not indicate hours of work.

[c]Three persons admitted to having paid for unregistered work, but did not indicate the amount.

yes in 1971, 39 percent answered yes in 1981. Although some of this growth in the participation rate can be explained by the difference in method, this rate of growth accords with the popular view of an expanding black sector due to the large increases in the tax burden over the last decade. A result which supports this view is that the participation rate has increased significantly faster for younger people than for other age groups. The working population has been steadily filled up with people with new tax experiences.

The demand for hidden labor services seems to increase with education. On the supply side, people with 10 to 12 years of schooling most frequently participate in the hidden labor market. One may venture that 10 to 12 years of schooling includes vocationally trained people, who are in a good position to sell their services individually and on a personal basis.

In order to obtain estimates on the size of the hidden labor market in Norway, several calculations were made, of which four are reported in table 13-3.

As we have seen from table 13-2, figures on payments are higher than those on income received. Thus, the figures of line 2 in table 13-3 exceed

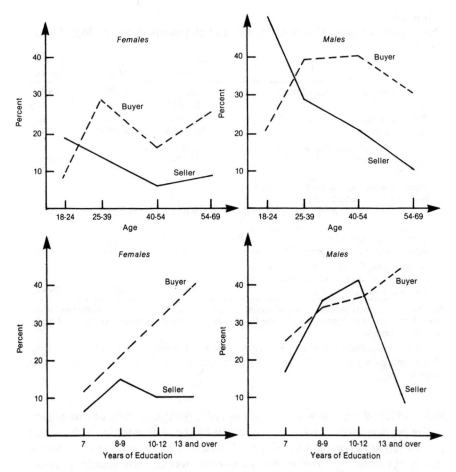

Figure 13-1. Education, Age, and the Hidden Labor Market; Participation
Rates

those of line 1. However, from the first two lines the size of the hidden labor
market by any standard is well below the size implied by the estimates given
by Feige (1979) and Gutmann (1977), within the 95 percent confidence interval at most 2.0 percent of GNP.

On average the price charged for unregistered work was low, less than
40 percent of the price in the regular market. In line 3 the figures on received
unregistered income are based on the market price of such work. This yields
an estimated size of the hidden labor market of 5.5 billion kroner, or 2.3
percent of GNP, with the upper bound of the 95 percent confidence interval
of 3.3 percent.

Table 13-3
Estimates of the Size of the Hidden Labor Market

	Billion Kroner	Percentage of GNP in 1979
1. Received income from unregistered work (167 persons)	2.0 (1.4-2.6)	0.85% (0.6-1.1)
2. Paid for unregistered work (252 persons)	3.5 (2.3-4.7)	1.5% (1.0-2.0)
3. Line 1, estimated at market prices (167 persons)	5.5 (3.3-7.7)	2.3% (1.4-3.3)
4. Received income from unregistered work, at market prices and by use of upper bound on hours and hourly wage. For those who did not acknowledge working unregistered, but stated that it is normal for people in the same profession to do so, their estimates of normal hours in the hidden labor market are employed (167 + 115 = 282 persons)	13.3 (10.0-16.6)	5.7% (4.3-7.1)

Note: The sample has been weighted by sex and age. The 95 percent confidence interval is given in parentheses.

This finding invites two comments. First, hidden labor services may to a considerable extent be offered to friends and relatives at a low price. Second, some of these services may be outside one's own profession which makes it reasonable to charge below-market prices.

In the questionnaire people were asked to evaluate normal unregistered hours of labor for those in the same profession. For those who acknowledged that unregistered labor was common within their profession, but denied participation in this market (115 persons), we employed the figures given as normal for the profession (line 4). Also, we employed the upper-bound values on hours worked as well as on market price for the services rendered.[8] These manipulations were performed to counter the downward bias in the data that arise from people's willingness to acknowledge participation in the hidden labor market as well as the tendency to downplay the extent of unregistered economic activities. The resulting estimate of the hidden labor market was 13.3 billion kroner, or 5.7 percent of GNP. Obviously these manipulations are highly arbitrary. Rather than to arrive at an accurate estimate the purpose of this exercise is to illustrate how varying the assumptions impinges upon the results. The message is simply that no single estimate can be considered the "correct" one.

Let the third line in table 13-3 be deemed a reasonable estimate of the size of the hidden labor market in Norway. Compared to estimates of the hidden economy in the United States, the figure of 2.3 percent of GNP that emerges in the present study is quite modest. In Tanzi (1980, p. 452) seven estimates of the size of the underground economy in 1976 are given, ranging from a high of 21.7 percent of GNP to a low of 3.4 percent. For the hidden sector in Norway to exceed the lower bound of the United States as a percent of GNP, manipulations of the data like those reported in line 4 of table 13-3 are necessary. It should be remembered, however, that we are measuring only one part of the hidden economy whereas Tanzi and others measure the income from all black activities. Our estimates are more in line with the estimate given by Dilnot and Morris (1981). Based on data from an expenditure survey in England, 1977, they estimated the size at 2.3 percent, by coincidence exactly the same figure as given in line 3.

A major purpose of the survey was to collect data which would make it possible to test different hypotheses with respect to the causes of tax evasion and irregular labor. The basic reference in the theory of tax evasion is Allingham and Sandmo (1972). In that paper tax evasion is considered as a decision problem under uncertainty. One important implication of the theory is that undeclared income becomes smaller when the penalty rate and/or the probability of detection is increased. The impact on undeclared income from an increase in a proportional tax is ambiguous due to a positive substitution effect (higher marginal tax) and a negative income effect (higher average tax). When the Allingham-Sandmo approach is extended to allow for a variable labor supply, all the reactions became ambiguous. The reason is that an increase, say, in the penalty rate has an ambiguous impact on the total supply of labor. Ambiguity accumulates since the effect of an increase in total income (declared plus undeclared) on the undeclared part also is uncertain.

In Isachsen and Strøm (1980) the individual supply of labor is divided into two parts, hours worked in the black market and hours worked in the regular labor market. When the utility function has a form that implies inelastic total labor supply, the ambiguity stemming from changes in the probability of detection and/or the penalty rate disappears. It is tempting to conclude, but is not proved, that when the total labor supply is *almost* inelastic unambiguity is still present. When the utility function has a more general form the number of restrictions a priori is rather small.

In the survey the respondents were asked to estimate their marginal tax rate, the penalty rate, and the probability of detection. Since they also provided information on their gross and net incomes we could compare the "true" marginal tax rate with what they considered it to be. Their answers on the penalty rate question could be compared with the actual rules and the estimate of the probability of detection could be compared with qualified guesses made by ourselves. The major result of these comparisons was that the overestimation of the marginal tax rate decreased with income. On the other hand people in lower income brackets also overestimated the probability of detection and the penalty rate. The *net* result of these three misunderstandings could therefore be that the low-income people chose the optimal tax evasion level.

In the estimation of the individual supply of labor in the two markets the following relationship was assumed (see Isachsen and Strøm (1980)).

$$\ln N_B = \alpha 0 + \alpha 1 \, W_R(1-t) + \alpha 2 W_B + \alpha 3 W_B(1-\tau) + \alpha 4 P + \alpha 5 z + u$$

where

N_B is the number of hours worked per year in the black market,
W_R the hourly wage rate in the regular market,
t the marginal tax rate, $0 \le t \le 1$,
W_B the hourly wage rate in the black market,
τ the penalty rate, $\tau \ge 0$,
p the probability of detection measured in percentages,
z a vector of socioeconomic variables whose content is suppressed here,
u normally distributed error term.

The answers given in the survey were used as observations of the variables. In some cases they are probably not in accordance with the "true values." Our interpretation of the answers could be wrong. The respondents might suppress the true answers. On the other hand what matters for individual behavior is how the individuals *think* the world is, and not how it really is.

The results are given below. The figures in parentheses are significance levels.

Males

$$\ln N_B = 2.06 - 0.016 \, W_R(1-t) - 0.0009 \, W_B + 0.1 \, W_B(1-\tau) - 0.02p + z$$
$$\quad (0.0) \quad (0.14) \qquad\qquad (0.82) \qquad\quad (0.13) \qquad\quad (0.0)$$

Females

$$\ln N_B = -0.17 + 0.15 \, W_R(1-t) + 0.005 \, W_B + 0.003 \, W_B(1-\tau) - 0.004p + z$$
$$\quad (0.63) \quad (0.19) \qquad\qquad (0.26) \qquad\quad (0.73) \qquad\qquad (0.20)$$

Except for the coefficient associated with W_B all coefficients in the regression equation for males have the "expected" sign, although it should be remembered that the general theory of tax evasion implies no expected signs. The coefficients associated with wage rates and tax rates are not significant at the 5 percent level. At that level only the coefficient associated with the (subjective) probability of detection is significant. The result indicates that if the probability of detection increases by 1 percentage point, say from 0.10 to 0.11 (from 10 percent to 11 percent) the number of hours worked in the black economy will on the average decrease by 2 percent, say from 100 hours per year to 98 hours per year.

In the case of females no coefficients are different from zero at acceptable levels of significance. It thus seems that the reason females work in the black market is not a result of a calculated decision under uncertainty as could be the case for males. A more reasonable explanation in accordance with our findings and with common observation is that females work in the black market due to the lack of regular job opportunities. Another way of putting it is that *schwartzarbeit* are side jobs. Males are in a position to say yes or no to side jobs to complement or to replace some hours otherwise worked in the regular market. This decision might be explained by the somewhat sophisticated theory of tax evasion. Females on the other hand are often not in this position. Their decision of taking jobs in the black market might therefore not be a result of a calculated decision under uncertainty, but the only way of getting a job at all. Of course, the reason we are not able to explain full specialization in the black market can be due to the survey method. Although some people are willing to admit working in the black economy, fewer are willing to admit full specialization. On the other hand it could in fact be true that few are working full time in the hidden economy.

Of the 252 persons who acknowledged paying for unregistered labor services, 242 were satisfied with the work performed, or more than 95 percent. Bearing in mind that the average wage rate in the hidden sector is about 40 percent of market price it is not unreasonable if the expectations as to the quality of work are more modest in the unregistered than in the registered labor market. However, with the overwhelming majority being satisfied with the services rendered in the hidden sector, one can dismiss the often voiced charge that hidden labor is expensive labor due to the poor quality of work.

In the survey one question inquired whether it was easier or more difficult to get the work done when income was unreported. Of the 252 persons who acknowledged paying for unregistered services, almost 60 percent found the services more easily available when no reporting was made and only 4 percent more difficult. For the remaining it was equally easy to buy the services registered or unregistered.

The answers to four questions relating to people's attitudes toward the hidden labor market and its likely development are summarized in table 13-4.

Table 13-4 reveals a tendency toward increasing acceptance of unregistered work as well as expectations of continued growth. When the answers are stratified according to age group a clear picture emerges: age groups under 40 years are significantly more favorable toward unregistered work than are the age groups over 40. This substantiates the impression from table 13-4, that the hidden sector is a growth sector.

For the 252 persons who paid for unregistered work the distribution of the various modes of payment is given in table 13-5.

About 80 percent of the payments for unregistered work are in cash. Feige's (1979) assertion that hidden transactions quite often are paid for by check does not seem reasonable in the hidden labor market, at least in Norway.

A Macroeconomic Approach to the Measurement of the Hidden Economy

The method of estimating the size of the hidden economy adopted here is based on the demand for currency.

The basic premise of the currency method is that higher tax rates will promote more tax evasion, which, in turn, will increase the demand for currency. The hypothesis is that unregistered economic transactions will be paid for by means of currency in order to minimize the probability of detection by tax authorities.

In a study of the determinants of the currency ratio in the United States, Cagan (1958) provided an interesting empirical analysis of the role of income tax evasion. Comparing the ratio of currency to the broad ($M2$) money stock in June 1945 with the "normal" ratio, assumed to be the one prevailing in June 1940, he found that by 1945 a large amount of "excess" currency had developed. The increase in the demand for currency relative

Table 13-4
Attitudes toward the Hidden Labor Market

	Percentage answering in the affirmative
1. If possible accept unregistered labor income	64
2. Hidden labor services are generally accepted	76
3. Hidden labor services will be accepted increasingly in the future	67
4. The size of the hidden labor market will increase	66

Table 13-5
Modes of Payment for Hidden Labor Services

	Percentage of Number of Transactions	Percentage of Total Payments
Cash	81.6	79.1
Check	5.1	6.1
Bankgiro	2.7	3.1
Postgiro	0.8	6.5
Work	5.5	2.8
Other	3.1	2.1
Not answered	1.2	0.3
	100.0	100.0

to bank deposits could not be attributed to changes in the fundamental determinants of the currency ratio, such as interest rates or real income, since changes in these variables were small and, moreover, tended to offset each other. Cagan discussed at length factors which could explain the excess wartime demand for currency, like tax evasion, black markets, travel, the size of the armed forces and change of residence. He found that, except for tax evasion, none of these variables could account for anything more than a minor part of the increase in currency holdings. On the assumption that the amount of currency held against a dollar of unreported income equaled the amount of money (currency and deposits) held against a dollar of regular income, Cagan (1958, pp. 12-13) concluded that "high income tax rates account for 60-70 percent of the wartime increase in currency." This conclusion was based on an independent estimate of the amount of tax evasion during the war from national accounts and tax returns data. But he went on to argue (p. 13) that "unreported income produces an abnormal demand for currency to hoard," that is, the income velocity of money used in the hidden economy is lower than in the regular sector. In this case Cagan (1958, p. 13) found it "plausible to attribute three-fourths or even all of the wartime increase in the demand for currency to income tax evasion."

In a widely cited article, Gutmann (1977) used essentially the method developed by Cagan (1958), to derive an estimate of the size of the hidden economy in the United States in 1976. For several reasons outlined below the calculations made by Gutmann are much harder to accept at face value than the conclusions drawn by Cagan for the earlier period.

There are four assumptions underlying Gutmann's analysis:[9]

1. The hidden economy uses currency as the exclusive medium of exchange.

2. A bench-mark period can be identified, in which there was no extra-ordinary demand for currency to be attributed to tax evasion motives.

3. The ratio of currency to deposits prevailing during the benchmark period would have remained unchanged except for changes induced by the growth of the hidden economy.

4. The income velocity of money (currency) in the hidden economy equals the income velocity of money (currency and deposits) in the official economy.

Assumptions *1* and *2* are common to both Cagan and Gutmann, except that Gutmann used 1937-1941 as the base period. The first alternative considered by Cagan corresponds to assumption *4*, but as noted above, he also made another estimate with a lower velocity in the unregistered sector. Whereas assumption *3* was carefully analyzed by Cagan, and found to be valid as a first approximation, it is not examined at all by Gutmann. This is somewhat awkward in view of the fact that Cagan's extrapolations only applied to 5 years, whereas Gutmann's extended over a 35-year period. Now we know from a number of empirical studies of the determinants of the currency ratio that it moves systematically with transactions volume and interest rates, so the neglect of factors other than tax rates casts severe doubt on the usefulness of the calculations made by Gutmann (1977).[10]

In order to alleviate this obvious shortcoming of the currency method it seems a priori to be more fruitful to try to separate secular and cyclical changes in the currency ratio from changes due to tax evasion within a multiple regression analysis. This line of approach was also pursued by Cagan (1958) and later by Macesich (1962) on Canadian data. In both studies it was found that the demand for currency relative to deposits increased with the percentage of personal income taxed.

A recent study by Tanzi (1980) using this method, was explicitly designed to measure the extraordinary demand for currency attributable to tax evasion. He estimated the ratio of currency to demand deposits in the United States over the 1929-1976 period as a function of income measures, the share of wages and salaries in personal income as well as three alternative measures of the tax level. These were (T_1) the ratio of personal income taxes to personal income net of transfers, (T_2) the top-bracket statutory tax rate, and (T_3) the weighted average tax rate on interest income. All of these tax variables exerted a significantly positive influence on the currency ratio. This applies in particular to T_3, which, according to Tanzi, is also most likely to capture changes in the level of income taxes over the period. On this basis he then proceeded to calculate the size of the underground economy, using assumptions *1, 2* and *4* outlined earlier.

The usefulness of the currency method hinges crucially on each one of these four assumptions. Obviously, one can say of each of these assumptions that it is rather unlikely to hold in any exact way.

Feige (1979) has challenged assumption 4 on the ground that the hidden sector is more integrated and consists of a larger proportion of services than the regular economy, which would imply a higher turnover of cash balances in the hidden economy. However, as noted above, Cagan (1958) refers to the plausible hypothesis that unreported income generates a stronger inclination to currency hoarding than does regular income. This argument would in isolation work in the opposite direction, producing a lower velocity in the hidden economy. In addition, it may also be somewhat questionable to equate the turnover of *currency* in the hidden economy with the turnover of *money* (currency and demand deposits) in the regular sector.

Thus it seems difficult to avoid the conclusion that the currency method is a very indirect one, requiring a number of conditions to be fulfilled in order to provide reliable estimates. A crucial aspect is the extent to which payment practices and financial innovations have shifted the relative demand between currency and bank deposits as well as among the various categories of deposits. In this light a natural extension of this approach is to estimate the demand for currency separately to alleviate the problem of substitution among several types of deposits caused by innovations in financial markets.[11]

The Determinants of Currency Demand

Following the approach taken by Baumol (1952) and Tobin (1956) and the subsequent elaborations upon this basic model[12] the transactions demand for money can be specified as

$$m_y = m_y(y, i, b), \partial m_y/\partial y > 0, \partial m_y/\partial i < 0, \partial m_y \partial b < 0 \qquad (13.1)$$

where m_y is the real value of money demanded for transaction purposes, y is the volume of transactions, i is a vector of yields on substitute assets like noncheckable bank deposits, bonds and commodities, and b denotes real costs of transferring money to or from deposit accounts.

However, such an approach to currency demand neglects some special factors which influence the transactions demand for cash, and which have a long tradition in studies of currency demand. Mitchell (1913, pp. 490-494) and Hawtrey (1928, pp. 94-97) have pointed to two factors which affect the relative use of currency over the business cycle.[13] First, in retail transactions relatively more currency is used per transactions volume than in other transactions. Second, an increase in the relative income of wage earners enhances currency demand, since wages are more likely to be paid in cash than are other incomes. However, in recent years wages are often transferred directly to the employee's bank account so the second factor has become less important. A positive correlation between currency demand and the share of wages in factor incomes might still be observed,[14] but it might also be attributable in part to the increased volume of retail transactions that follow as wage earners spend their incomes. For this reason, and partly also because of data availability, we will focus only on the first effect in the empirical section which follows.

We doubt that the demand for currency can be explained by pure transaction motives alone. There still seems to be a significant demand for hoarding currency which is only partly explainable by tax evasion. The newspapers abound with stories about people who lose large amounts of currency in fires or in robberies. The motives for hoarding cash far beyond ordinary transaction needs seem to be rather obscure; we can only conjecture that these include general economic and political uncertainty, distrust in banks, tax evasion, and old people's desire to conceal wealth.[15] These factors may vary greatly in importance over time and their empirical counterparts may be hard to obtain.

To proceed with the analysis of the role of tax evasion motives in currency demand, we simply assume that the extent of tax evasion is directly related to some measure of tax rates T, and that the greater the scale of tax evasion the greater the demand for currency.

In the empirical analysis the long-run demand for currency was initially specified as

$$\ln(C^*/P) = \alpha 0 + \alpha 1 \ln y + \alpha 2 i_D + \alpha 3 \pi^+ \alpha 4 (CON/Y) +$$
$$\alpha 5 T, \alpha 1, \alpha 4, \alpha 5 \geq 0, \alpha 2, \alpha 3 \geq 0 \qquad (13.2)$$

where

C	= currency held by the public
P	= implicit price deflator of gross domestic product (GDP)
Y	= real GDP
i_D	= rate of return on time deposits
π	$= 100 \cdot (\ln P_t - \ln P_{t-1} 0) =$ the rate of inflation
CON/Y	= private consumption expenditure as a percentage of GDP
T	= gross taxes excluding import tariffs, as a percentage of gross domestic product.[16]

In 13.2 gross domestic product is used as the transactions variable. The yields on bank deposits and real capital are the opportunity costs of holding currency and the fraction of private consumption in GDP represents the Mitchell-Hawtrey effect.

The short-run adjustment of currency and deposits to long-run levels is assumed to follow the conventional stock adjustment hypothesis. Here, it is specified in nominal terms where θ is the speed of adjustment parameter.

$$\ln C - \ln C - 1 = \theta(\ln C^* - \ln C - 1) \quad 0 \le \theta \le 1 \qquad (13.3)$$

From 13.2 and 13.3 we derive the estimating equation

$$\ln(C/P) = a0 + a1\ln y + a2i_D + a3\pi + a4(CON/Y) +$$
$$a5T + a6\ln(C-1/P) \qquad (13.4)$$

where

$$a0 = \theta\alpha0, \; a1 = \theta\alpha1, \; a2 = \theta\alpha2, \; a3 = \theta\alpha3$$
$$a4 = \theta\alpha4, \; a5 = \theta\alpha5, \; a6 = (1-\theta).$$

Based on data from the period 1952-1978 the following results were obtained (t-ratios in parentheses below the coefficients):

$$\ln(C/P) = -1.58 + 0.377 \ln y - 0.007 \, i_D$$
$$\quad\quad\quad (4.29) \quad\; (3.47) \quad\quad\; (0.71)$$
$$\quad + 0.00021\pi + 0.00093 \; (CON/Y) + 0.0010T$$
$$\quad\quad (0.14) \quad\quad (2.60) \quad\quad (0.33)$$
$$+ 0.445 \ln(C-1/P)$$
$$\quad\quad (3.65) \qquad\qquad\qquad\qquad\qquad\qquad (13.5)$$

with[17] $R^2 = 0.982$
$$SEE = 0.0144$$
$$\varrho = 0.819$$
$$(7.08)$$

Equation 13.5 implies a long-run income elasticity of 0.85. The influence of the time deposit rate, the Mitchell-Hawtrey transactions variable and the tax measure is in the hypothesized direction, but only the Mitchell-Hawtrey effect is significantly different from zero.

To improve the results we employed a fourth-degree Almon-lag polynomial of the tax variable with no endpoint constraint. The estimated equation, reads:

$$\ln(C/P) = -1.25 + 0.309 \ln y - 0.024 i_D$$
$$\quad\quad\quad (3.65) \quad\; (3.41) \quad\quad\; (2.54)$$
$$\quad + 0.0000\pi + 0.00049 \; (CON/Y)$$
$$\quad\quad (0.03) \quad\quad (1.44)$$
$$\quad + 0.0069T + 0.534\ln \; (C-1/P)$$
$$\quad\quad (2.70) \quad\quad (4.73) \qquad\qquad\qquad\qquad (13.6)$$

where $R^2 = 0.933$
$$SEE = 0.129$$
$$\varrho = 0.379$$
$$= (2.13)$$

The coefficient on the tax variable refers to the sum of lag coefficients. The effect of the tax variable becomes stronger and is significantly different from zero, with a t-value of 2.70.

The shape of the lag distribution of coefficients was somewhat humped, with the peak occurring at 4 lags.

These results look fairly reasonable from the point of view that the full effect of higher tax rates on tax evasion, and, by assumption, also on currency demand, is likely to be spread out in time. Engagement in the activities of the hidden sector is surely a process that may require some time of adjustment for familiarizing with market opportunities.

Although the specification of the model of currency demand no doubt still may be improved upon, the results are deemed reasonably satisfactory, so that they can provide a basis for further analysis of the role of tax-induced currency holdings.

Measuring the Size of the Hidden Economy

We now proceed to estimate the size of the hidden sector based on the effect of taxes on the demand for currency. We first present the methods of calculation and the results, then the various sources of uncertainty underlying these estimates.

First, we rewrite the demand for currency equation, 13.2, as

$$\ln C = \ln P + \alpha \cdot Z + \alpha 5 T \qquad (13.7)$$

where Z is the vector of all explanatory variables except the tax variable T, and α is the corresponding vector of coefficients. Given the estimates of α and $\alpha 5$, denoted by $\widehat{\alpha}$ and $\widehat{\alpha 5}$ respectively, the predicted value of currency holdings from 13.7 in any year t is

$$\widehat{C}_t = \exp(\ln P_t + \widehat{\alpha} Z_t + \widehat{\alpha 5} T_t). \qquad (13.8)$$

However, if the tax rate had remained at the same level, say T_0, as in some base year we would predict currency holdings being equal to

$$\widehat{C0}_t = \exp(\ln P_t + \widehat{\alpha} Z_t + \widehat{\alpha 5} T0). \qquad (13.9)$$

The change in currency demand motivated by the change in taxation between the base year and year t is then computed as

$$CU_t = \widehat{C}_t - \widehat{C0}_t. \qquad (13\text{-}10)$$

Thus, CU_t is a measure of the increase in the amount of currency needed to fuel the unregistered economy in excess of the amount already in use in this sector in the base year. Only if there were no hidden activities in the base year will CU_t be a total measure of all currency circulating in the hidden economy.

From regression equation 13.6 $\alpha5$ was estimated as

$$\widehat{\alpha5} = a5/(1-a6) = .0069/(1-.534) = .0149 \qquad (13.11)$$

According to this estimate a one percentage point increase in T (for example, from 50 to 51 percent) will in the longrun create an additional currency demand of about 1.5 percent in Norway. In 1978 these figures would imply an increase in the currency circulation of 232 million Norwegian kroner.

Based on equation 13.6, the holding of currency attributable to increased taxation (CU) between 1952 and 1978 was then estimated to be 2,904 million kroner, or 19 percent of outstanding currency in 1978.

To convert the estimate of the tax-induced currency holdings into an estimate of the size of the hidden economy, we need an estimate of the amount of annual income supported by a krone of currency, or, which amounts to the same thing, the income velocity of currency. The economics literature abounds with references to this variable, but measuring it with precision seems to be extremely difficult. Any attempt to do so must accordingly be regarded as highly tentative and uncertain.

As a first approach we adopt the procedure followed by Tanzi (1980), who assumed that the income velocity of currency in the hidden economy equals the observed income velocity of $M1$ money (currency and demand deposits) in the regular sector. Thus, the velocity is estimated as

$$V1 = GDP/(M1\text{-}CU) \qquad (13.12)$$

where GDP is observed gross domestic product; $M1$ includes currency, demand deposits and postal giro deposits held by the public;[18] and CU is the estimate of tax-induced currency holdings derived above. Income generated in the hidden economy is then estimated as

$$YU1 = CU \cdot V1. \qquad (13.13)$$

With $V1$ being calculated as 6.7 for Norway this implies an estimate of income in the hidden sector of 19,457 million kroner in Norway, equalling 9.2 percent of observed GDP.

However, the bank giro system makes it possible to transfer money directly from a time deposit account, provided such transfers do not exceed

10,000 kroner per month, no costs are incurred. It is thus reasonable to enlarge the definition of transaction balances to include a fraction of time deposits. With no data available we had to rely on guesses from people in the banking community, implying that 10 percent of total time deposits should be considered as transaction balances. Allowing for this adjustment, the income velocity of currency is reduced from 6.7 to 5.0, and the size of the hidden economy to 14,520 kroner or 6.3 percent of GNP in 1978.

There are two basic sources of uncertainty underlying the estimates presented here. These are the estimates of currency holdings attributable to tax evasion (CU) and the velocity of currency in the hidden economy (V).

Estimates of CU

Estimates of CU used here stem from one particular equation; obviously, other model specifications and other estimation periods will imply different values of CU. Moreover, since the nature of the problem necessarily requires the use of a proxy variable for the extent of tax evasion in the estimation of currency demand, there is also the question of how well this variable reflects the incentives for tax evasion. The relationship between tax rates and tax evasion is presumably far more intricate than was hypothesized in this empirical analysis. Crucial factors that are likely to impinge on this relationship are the mix between direct and indirect taxation, threshold effects and the state of general tax morality, which may itself be a complicated function of current and past tax rates as well as other socioeconomic variables. In addition there are two special assumptions underlying the estimate of CU as developed here, both of which tend to bias the calculated values of CU downward. First, the assumption that there was no tax evasion at the beginning of the estimation period (1952), is certainly not true. Second, as our survey study revealed, some of the income earned in the hidden economy is paid by check, giro, or labor. Neither of these factors has been taken into account here.

Estimates of V

It is evident that there are many sources of error in estimating the income velocity of currency in the hidden economy. As a first approximation the income velocity of money in the regular sector of the economy may serve as the best available estimate, since direct measures of currency velocity are hard to obtain. By their nature, transactions in the hidden economy often involve larger amounts and notes of higher denominations than elsewhere in the economy. Since these notes are held to evade taxes, and thus cannot be spent too openly on purchases of real or financial assets, they are conceivably also hoarded to a larger extent than usual. Accordingly, a krone of currency may support less income in the hidden economy than in the regular economy. On the other hand, the hidden economy is likely to be more integrated than the regular economy because of the larger service component of the former, and therefore requires fewer intermediate transactions to produce a given value of output. On balance, then, the direction in which the observed income velocity in the regular economy should be adjusted is not clear. However, our feeling is that the income velocity in the hidden sector is probably less than that of the regular one.

Concluding Remarks

Whereas the micro approach yielded a "best" estimate of the income from working in hidden sector of 2.3 percent of GNP in 1979, the result of the macro approach was 6.3 percent of GNP in 1978.

The considerable disparity of these results may be attributable partly to the fact that the two methods measure different things, and partly to the inherent uncertainties involved in the use of each of the methods.

Compared to reported results on estimating the hidden sector in other countries, the size of the Norwegian hidden economy seems modest. The findings of the survey, that people generally have a favorable attitude toward unregistered work, and that such work is expected to become more common in the future (an expectation that is particularly strong in the younger age groups), may be more disturbing from a political point of view, than is the present extent of unregistered economic activities.

Notes

1. Feige's (1979, p. 6) definition is: "those economic activities that go unreported or are unmeasured by the society's current techniques for monitoring economic activity," whereas Macafee (1980) offers a third definition.

2. For a brief survey of methods of estimations, see Tanzi (1980, pp. 430-433).

3. The presentation that follows is a condensed version of Klovland (1980) and of Isachsen and Strøm (forthcoming).

4. Among other studies we would like to mention Dilnot and Morris (1981), Feige (1979, 1980), Gutmann (1977), and Tanzi (1980).

5. As of March 4, 1981, 5.38 Norwegian kroner equaled 1 U.S. dollar.

6. Stratification or weighting according to sex and age is done as follows:

For each *stratum in the population* let the estimated value of the variable a_k be

$$\widehat{a}_k = N_k \cdot \overline{X}_k$$

where

N_k = number of persons in the population in *stratum k*.
$\overline{X}_k$ = average value of the variable in our *sample* in stratum k.

For the *total population* the estimate of the variable a is

$$\widehat{a} = \sum_k \widehat{a}_k$$

The variance of this estimate is calculated as

$$\text{Var } \widehat{a} = s_a^2 = \Sigma_k N_K \frac{N_K - n_k}{K-1} S_k^2$$

where
n^k = number of persons in the sample in *stratum k*
N_k = number of persons in the *population* in stratum k
s_k^2 = empirical variance in stratum k for the variable a that is estimated.

The 95 percent confidence interval for an estimated variable a is thus given by $\widehat{a} \pm 1.96 \sqrt{\text{var } \widehat{a}}$.

7. Although the questions in the two surveys were not identically worded, the difference was so moderate as to be ignored.

8. If a respondent marked that he or she worked betwen 100 and 199 hours over the last 12 months, the figure 150 hours was employed in lines 1-3 in table 13-3, and 199 hours in line 4.

9. These assumptions were outlined and discussed by Feige (1979). For additional discussion of the Gutmann (1977) article, see Garcia (1978), Laurent (1979) and Bowsher (1980).

10. See, for example, Cagan (1965).

11. For some unsuccessful attempts to discover a hidden sector in the Norwegian economy based on estimation of various currency/deposit ratios, see Klovland (1980).

12. See Barro and Fischer (1976) for a survey of the recent literature.

13. The Mitchell-Hawtrey theory of currency demand is briefly outlined and critically examined in Cagan (1965, pp. 143-147).

14. As for example, it appears from the empirical study by Tanzi (1980).

15. Old people may have a number of irrational as well as rational economic motives for hoarding currency. One motive for conceiling financial wealth is to maintain a more direct control over it in case of removal to old age homes, serious illness, or the like. Evasion of estate taxes may also create an additional motive.

16. Also experimented with an average marginal income tax rate based on data about personal income tax and social security premiums paid by employees. Data and sources are given in Klovland (1980).

17. $\bar{R}^2$ is the coefficient of determination adjusted for degrees of freedom. SEE is the standard error of estimate and ϱ is the estimate of the first order autocorrelation coefficient.

18. Demand deposits include ordinary checking accounts as well as wage accounts at commercial banks, savings banks, and the Post Office savings bank. Postal giro deposits are also included.

References

Allingham, Michael G. and Agnar Sandmo (1972). "Income Tax Evasion: A Theoretical Analysis," *Journal of Public Economics* 1 (November).

Barro, R.J. and Fischer, Stanley (1976). "Recent Developments in Monetary Theory." *Journal of Monetary Economics* 2:133-167.

Baumol, W.J. (1952). "The Transactions Demand for Cash: An Inventory-theoretic Approach." *Quarterly Journal of Economics* 66:545-556.

Bowsher, N.N. (1980). "The Demand for Currency: Is the Underground Economy Undermining Monetary Policy?" *Federal Reserve Bank of St. Louis Review* 62 (January):11-17.

Cagan, Phillip (1958). *The Demand for Currency Relative to Total Money Supply.* National Bureau of Economic Research, Occasional Paper 62.

Cagan, Phillip (1965). *Determinants and Effects of Changes in the Stock of Money 1875-1960.* New York: National Bureau of Economic Research.

Dilnot, Andrew, and C.N. Morris (1981). "What Do We Know about the Black Economy?" *Fiscal Studies* (March). Reprinted as chapter 10, this volume.

Feige, E.L. (1979). "How Big Is the Irregular Economy?" *Challenge* (November—December), 5-13.

Feige, E.L. (1980). Den dolda sektorns tillväxt—70-talets ekonomiska problem i nytt ljus, *Ekonomisk Debatt* 8:570-589.

Garcia, Gillian (1978). "The Currency Ratio and the Subterranean Economy," *Financial Analysts Journal* (November/December), pp. 64-66, 69.

Gutmann, P.T. (1977). "The Subterranean Economy." *Financial Analysts Journal* (November-December):64-66 and 69.

Hawtrey, R.G. (1928). *Trade and Credit*. London: Longmans, Green and Co.

Isachsen, A.J. and Strøm, Steinar (forthcoming). *Den skjulte økonomi*. (Universitetsforlaget, Oslo).

Isachsen, A.J. and Strøm, Steinar (1980). "The Hidden Economy: The Labour Market and Tax Evasion." *Scandinavian Journal of Economics* 82:304-311.

Klovland, J.T. (1980). "In Search of the Hidden Economy: Tax Evasion and the Demand for Currency in Norway and Sweden." Discussion paper 18/80, Norwegian School of Economics and Business Administration, Bergen.

Laurent, R.D. (1979). "Currency and the Subterranean Economy." *Federal Reserve Bank of Chicago Economic Perspectives* (March-April): 3-6.

Macafee, Kerrick (1980). "A Glimpse of the Hidden Economy in the National Accounts." *Economic Trends* (February):81-87. Reprinted as chapter 9, this volume.

Macesich, George (1962). "Demand for Currency and Taxation in Canada." *Southern Economic Journal* 29:33-38.

Mitchell, W.C. (1913). *Business Cycles*. Berkeley: University of California Press.

Tanzi, Vito (1980). "The Underground Economy in the United States: Estimates and Implications." *Banca Nazionale del lavoro Quarterly Review* 135:427-453. Reprinted as chapter 4, this volume.

Tobin, James (1956). "The Interest Elasticity of the Transactions Demand for Cash." *Review of Economics and Statistics* 38:241-247.

14 The Underground Economy in a High Tax Country: The Case of Sweden

Ingemar Hansson

During the last decade the potential importance of the underground economy has been a matter of increasing interest in Sweden. Most Swedes apparently believe that the underground economy is growing.[1] The mass media reports on the underground economy and politicians discuss lower taxes and increased controls as remedies for tax evasion. However, few serious studies have been undertaken on the underground economy in Sweden. Scholars as well as private and governmental institutions are just about to start to devote effort and money to such studies.

Causes of the Underground Economy

Taxes

High taxes, especially the very high taxes on marginal earnings are almost unanimously recognized as the major cause of the underground economy in Sweden. Higher direct and indirect taxes and lower transfers absorb 75 percent of a marginal gross earning for the median male income earner.[2] For a 50 percent higher income, total taxes on marginal earnings amount to 85 percent, while the corresponding figure is 66 percent for a 50 percent lower income. This means that small as well as large underreporting of income involves tax savings exceeding 65 percent of the underreported income for most income earners. This obviously provides strong incentives for tax evasion. The median male income earner, whose net earnings equal 25 percent of his gross earnings on the margin, may offer half the price and still earn twice as much from a marginal hour of work in the untaxed underground economy as compared to the taxed ordinary economy. This certainly leaves wide scope for mutually beneficial agreements between sellers and buyers of goods and services at the expense of the tax authorities.

Thanks are due to Åke Tengblad and Peder Kjellegård at the National Central Bureau of Statistics for their cooperation. The financial support of the Bank of Sweden Tercentenary Foundation is gratefully acknowledged.

233

System of Controls

The size of the underground economy tends, however, to be mitigated by the relatively efficient tax control system in Sweden as compared to other countries. Employers are obliged to report each employee's income to the tax authorities and most employers conform to this rule. Each firm is obliged to keep records of income and expenditures which are available for the tax authorities upon demand. Local tax committees review tax returns and may, for example, compare reported income and the standard of living for people known in the neighborhood. More generally, the traditional relatively high degree of social coherence, relatively efficient bookkeeping, and relatively limited corruption among governmental officials in Sweden tend to restrict the size of the underground economy. These factors may even be interpreted as necessary conditions for the joint appearance of 65 percent to 68 percent taxation of marginal earnings and a reasonably large remaining tax base.

Economists, politicians, and the mass media reveal, however, a growing concern about the long-run effects of the current tax levels on the size of the underground economy. The high taxes are claimed to produce a growing tolerance between individuals to underreporting of income, thereby opening the way for still more tax evasion agreements within small groups. As an example, self-employed carpenters may now ask whether a job is to be done "with or without a receipt," running only a slight risk of being criticized by the customer.

Tax evasion through, for example, excessive compensation for work expenses and changes from employed to self-employed status are thought to become increasingly common. This widespread perception of a growing underground economy appears to be reasonable in view of the tax increases during the last decades. The taxation of marginal earnings for the median male income earner rose from 48 percent in 1952 to 75 percent in 1980. As is discussed later, the empirical data do not, however, support this perception.

Regulations

The underground economy also often avoids governmental regulations and negotiated agreements with labor unions on job safety, environmental standards, and wages. This cause of underground activities tends, however, to be overshadowed by the tax effects. An exception is provided by the rule that prohibits unannounced immigrants from engaging in ordinary employment until all legal arrangements are completed, which may take up to two years. This rule is recognized as a factor stimulating the underground economy.

Estimation of the Underground Economy

Monetary Methods

Gutmann (1977) estimates the size of the monetary underground economy by assuming that this economy uses currency as its sole medium of exchange, while the ordinary monetary economy uses currency and demand deposits in a constant proportion over time. Assuming that the underground economy is negligible at some starting point of time, time series on currency and demand deposits may be used to estimate the size of the monetary underground economy as a share of the monetary ordinary economy. An increase in the amount of currency relative to the amount of demand deposits is interpreted as an increase in the share of the underground economy.

Applying this method to Swedish data on currency and *total deposits* in banks, the Swedish business magazine *Veckans Affärer* (1978, 22) estimated that the monetary underground economy amounted to 10 percent of the observed economy in the middle of the 1970s.

A closer examination does, however, raise serious doubts on this estimate. Unfortunately, the estimate has been cited extensively both in Swedish and international literature.[3] Applying Gutmann's method to the data for 1952 produces the unreasonable estimate that the monetary underground economy exceeded the ordinary economy in that year. After 1952, the share of the monetary underground economy is estimated to have declined to 40 percent in the middle of the 1970s rather than 10 percent, as stated by *Veckans Affärer*.

Estimates based on time series for currency and demand deposits instead of currency and total deposits, in closer accordance with Gutmann's method, produce similar results.[4] A reasonable conclusion is that the relative amount of currency and deposits measured in different ways have been influenced by changes in the method of payments, such as the change from cash to check payments of most wages and the development of new methods of payments, to such an extent that these time series provide no reliable basis for an estimate of the underground economy using Gutmann's method.

Total Expenditures and Reported Income

Sweden's official statistics provide a basis for a more reliable estimate of the size of the underground economy defined as the amount of income that should be, but is not reported to the tax authorities. Total consumption expenditures are then estimated on the basis of consumer interviews including a sample of households that keep complete records of all expenditures during two weeks.[5] After cross-checking and adjustment, using information from other nontax sources of data, this survey provides an estimate of total private consumption.[6] Net savings are estimated from financial statistics and data on net investment in the household sector.[7] The sum of private consumption and net savings gives an estimate of the total use of income. In addition total disposable income is calculated from income reported to the tax authorities. The difference between the total use of income and the disposable income provides an estimate of the amount of income that should be but is not reported to the tax authorities.[8] This estimate of the size of the underground economy in relation to gross national product (GNP) is shown in figure 14-1 for the period for which data are available, 1970-1980.

Figure 14-1 reveals two interesting features:

1. The estimated share of the underground economy is surprisingly low, on average 3.8 percent, compared to estimates for other countries.[9] A possible explanation is that people underestimate their consumption in the Family Expenditure Survey due to, for example, forgetting minor expenditures, underreporting purchases of goods and services from the underground economy, and postponing purchases until after the survey period. Cross-checking with other nontax data sources indicated such underestimates mainly for alcoholic beverages, tobacco, sweets, and some types of communication. Overestimates were, on the other hand, indicated for furniture, cars, and clothing. On balance, information from other data sources resulted in a 7 percent upward adjustment of total private consumption as

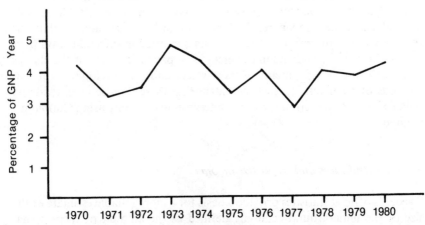

Figure 14-1. Income that Should Be but Is Not Reported to the Tax Authorities as Share of GNP

compared to the Family Expenditure Survey. The estimates in figure 14-1 include this adjustment. The upward adjustment indicates, however, a remaining underestimate for the subgroups of consumption where no other nontax data are available, in turn indicating an underestimate of the underground economy.

From figure 14-1 a lower bound for the underground economy is estimated to be 3 percent of GNP. Allowing for a remaining 3 percent underestimation of total consumption in the calculation of the upper bound, this estimate suggests an underground economy amounting to 3 percent to 7 percent of GNP. As with most earlier estimates, this estimate does not include barter.

2. Figure 14-1 also shows that the share of the underground economy is estimated to have been roughly constant during the 1970s in spite of the tax increases. This may be due to the tightening of tax controls during the 1970s, including an extension of the firms' obligation to keep records of income and expenditures, an increase in the number of tax inspectors, and an extended use of citizens' numbers and computers to check reported income with other sources of information. The data still, however, contrast with the common perception of a growing underground economy in Sweden.

Distribution among Sectors

Interview Studies

SIFO (1980a) asked members of an organization of small firms (SHIO-Family firms): "Does your firm experience large, some, or no competition from people working in the underground economy?" Among firms giving definite answers, 48 percent experienced large or some competition (14-34 percent). More interesting were the proportions of firms experiencing large or some competition—75 percent in construction, 55 percent in services, 47 percent in small-scale production and repair services, 39 percent in trade, and 22 percent in industry. Similarly, SIFO (1980b) asked a sample of citizens: "Have you done a job in the underground economy without receipt this year, or have you not?" An affirmative answer was given by 14 percent. The corresponding figures were 26 percent for people working in construction, 13 percent for people working in trade or manufacturing, and 11 percent for people working in health and social care.

These studies revealed an uneven distribution of the underground economy, with a high proportion being in sectors with relatively small firms. The later study also revealed that the proportion admitting work in the underground economy decreased with age (from 30 percent for ages 18-24 to 6 percent for ages 50-64) and with social class (13 percent for unskilled workers, 20 percent and 22 percent for two different groups of skilled workers, 12 percent for lower middle class, 13 percent for upper middle class, and 9 percent for upper class).

SIFO also asked: "Have you paid somebody to get a job done in the underground economy without receipt this year, or have you not?" This question received an affirmative answer from 19 percent. The proportion again decreased with age (from 31 percent for ages 25-29 to 6 percent for ages 65-70) but now increased with social class (from 22 percent for unskilled workers to 33 percent for upper class). The considerably higher figures for young people may be interpreted as an indicator of a long-run growth of the underground economy. The result may also, however, be interpreted as a life-cycle effect.

Among the 19 percent admitting payments to get a job done in the underground economy, 81 percent stated that the job amounted to less than $220, 17 percent admitted payments in the range of $220-$2,200, and the remaining 2 percent admitted payments in excess of $2,200. Calculated on the two interval means and $4,400, this results in an admitted payment of $69 on average for the entire sample, corresponding to 0.6 percent of GNP in 1979. This figure probably underestimates the size of income that should be but is not reported to the tax authorities, for several reasons. People probably tend to underestimate payments to the underground economy in an answer to an unknown interviewer. In many cases the purchaser does not know if the seller reports the revenue from a good or a service to the tax authorities. Even if a person knows that, say, a certain restaurant pays no taxes, many people would not include a meal at this restaurant as "payments to somebody to get a job done in the underground economy without receipt." Furthermore, people with large purchases from the underground economy probably tend to refuse to answer the question or take part in the interview. Despite these systematic errors, the very low figure, 0.6 percent of GNP, provides some additional weak support for the earlier estimate of a relatively modest underground economy in Sweden.

Underground Economy in Construction

Myrsten (1980) estimated the size of the underground economy in different subsectors of construction such as painting and decorating, carpentry, plumbing, and electric work as the difference between the estimated total hours of work and reported hours of work in the ordinary economy. After adjustment for sickness and unemployment, normal full-time work was estimated to include 1,500 hours of work in 1974. Since average reported work in the ordinary economy amounted to 1,250 hours for employees in painting and decorating, this gave 250 hours of work in the underground economy within normal hours of work. Myrsten assumed that the average employee, in addition, worked 100 hours in the underground economy on overtime. The average employee was thus estimated to have worked 350 hours in the underground economy per year. For self-employed painters, average reported income corresponded to 1,000 hours of work per year. The work in the underground economy was estimated to be 600 hours within normal hours of work plus 400 hours of work on overtime. Applying this method to different groups of subcontractors in construction, Myrsten estimated that the hours of work in the underground economy amounted to, on average, 15 percent of the hours of work in the corresponding sectors in the ordinary economy. As was pointed out by Myrsten, this may be an overestimate, due to the use of the difference between estimated total and actual hours of work to activities other than work in the underground economy. The estimate may, however, also be on the low side since work on the underground economy is also done by nonprofessionals and senior citizens.

Kjell Olsson of the Associated General Contractors and Housebuilders of Sweden applied the same method with data from three construction firms to estimate that the hours of work in the underground economy amounted to 10 percent of the hours of work in the corresponding sector in the ordinary economy.

If the price per hour of work in the underground economy is 60 percent of the price in the ordinary economy, these estimates suggest that value added in the underground economy amounts to 6-9 percent of value added in the ordinary economy for the construction sector. This estimate, combined with SIFO's result that on average 14 percent admitted work in the underground economy while the corresponding figure was 26 percent for people working in the construction sector, indicates that the total underground economy amounts to 3-5 percent of GNP. This result provides some further support for the estimated 3-7 percent range for the underground economy.

Implications of the Underground Economy

Effects on Tax Revenue

To evaluate the effect of the underground economy on tax revenue, suppose that all income is reported to the tax authorities after a certain time. This is likely to increase the price and decrease the quantity of goods and services that are produced in the underground economy. Assuming that the percentage changes of price and quantity are of the same magnitude, the increase in the tax base approximately equals the current underground economy. The tax base is thus estimated to increase by 3-7 percent of GNP. Applying a marginal tax rate slightly below that for the median male income earner, say 70 percent, this means that tax revenue would increase by 2.1 percent to 4.9 percent of GNP if all income is reported to the tax authorities. Such an increase in tax revenue could be used to decrease the average tax rate on income generated in the ordinary economy from the current level (around 54 percent)[10] to 49-52 percent according to this rough estimate.

This result may be interesting from an equity point of view. From an efficiency point of view the existence of an underground economy requires a somewhat higher tax rate in the ordinary economy with associated extra efficiency losses arising from additional misallocation of labor and capital as between the ordinary economy and untaxed activities such as household production and leisure.

Resource Allocation and the Underground Economy

The underground economy is often restricted to using a specific set of technologies, typically small-scale, and a specific type of organization, typically person-to-person contacts involving high transaction costs. The ordinary economy may typically apply a larger set of technologies and less costly methods of organization. Moreover, the consumer's choice among goods and services produced by the two sectors is tilted in favor of goods produced in the underground economy. The existence of an underground economy thus produces an inefficient distribution of resources between the ordinary and the underground economy, where less efficient methods of production and organization survive in the latter due to the strong tax effect. In a long-run equilibrium with equal net returns from marginal hours of work in the underground and in the ordinary economy, the value of the marginal product of labor in the underground economy is only 25 percent of the value of the marginal product of labor in the taxed ordinary economy for the median male income earner, when the value of the marginal product is measured in terms of utility, including disutility in the form of moral costs for tax evasion.[11]

The underground economy may also, however, increase welfare by allowing for mutual beneficial exchanges that would not otherwise arise due to the taxation of exchanges in the ordinary economy. The welfare effect of the entire underground economy thus depends on whether this economy mainly attracts labor and capital from the ordinary economy or from other untaxed sectors such as household production and leisure. On the margin, a reallocation of resources from the ordinary economy produces a considerable efficiency loss, while the net utility of a marginal reallocation from another untaxed sector tends to be zero. A marginal increase in the size of the underground economy thus tends to involve welfare losses.

Distributional Effects

The high taxation of marginal earnings in Sweden is intended to yield a more even distribution of after-tax income. By underreporting income, people with high actual income may avoid taxes and receive income-related transfers. The existence of an underground economy thus hampers the intended redistributional effects from taxes and transfers.

A Broader Perspective

The existence of an underground economy also involves indirect costs arising from a lower tendency to comply with other types of laws and regulations. More generally, the underground economy may contribute to a lower degree of social coherence with obscure but potentially very important effects on society.

Summary

The high taxes on marginal earnings are considered to be the major cause of the underground economy in Sweden. Measured as income that should be but is not reported to the tax authorities the underground economy is estimated to amount to 3-7 percent of GNP. This share is estimated to have been roughly constant during the 1970s in contrast to the common perception of growing tax evasion in Sweden. The existence of an underground economy involves several types of misallocation of resources among the ordinary economy, the underground economy, and the household sector. The large tax differential between the ordinary and the underground economy provides a misallocation through a strong bias in favor of the underground economy. The underground economy has potentially important effects on income distribution and the performance of the society in a wider perspective, but such effects are very difficult to verify and assess.

Notes

1. See, for example, Du Rietz (1980), Myrdal (1978), and Myrsten (1980).
2. Cf. Hansson (1980a).
3. Delorozoy (1980) and Isachsen and Strøm (1980).
4. Cf. Hansson (1980b).

5. The *Family Expenditure Survey*, National Central Bureau of Statistics.

6. NR-PM 1980:26, National Central Bureau of Statistics.

7. *Statistical Reports* N 1980:17, National Central Bureau of Statistics.

8. Due to lack of data, interest income, dividends, operating surpluses in farming, pensions, and some other transfers are estimated from sources other than income reported to the tax authorities. Public pensions and some transfers are reported directly to the tax authorities, suggesting zero under-reporting for these sources. The share of underreporting for interest income, dividends, operating surpluses in farming and private pensions, amounting to 7 percent of total income, is assumed to be the same as the share of underreporting for wages and operating surpluses outside farming.

9. See, for example, Delorozoy (1980), Feige (1979), Internal Revenue Service (1979), and Tanzi (1980).

10. *Revenue Statistics* 1965-1978, OECD, Paris 1979.

11. For a further analysis of resource allocation between taxed and un-taxed sectors see Stuart (1981).

References

Delorozoy, R. "Le Travail Clandestin." Assemblée Permanente des Chambres de Commerce et d'Industrie, Paris, 1980.

Du Rietz, G. "Marginalskatter, moms och arbetsgivaravgifter bakom växande svart sektor." SSAF-tidningen 32, 1980.

Feige, E.L. "How Big Is the Irregular Economy?" *Challenge*, November-December 1979.

Gutmann, P.M., "The Subterranean Economy." *Financial Analysts Journal*, November-December 1977.

Hansson, Ingemar. "Beräkning av totala marginaleffekter." Department of Economics, University of Lund 1980a. Mimeographed.

Hansson, I. "Sveriges svarta sektor," *Ekonomisk Debatt* 8, 1980b.

Internal Revenue Service. *Estimates of Income Unreported on Individual Income Tax Returns*. Publication 1104, Washington, D.C.: Government Printing Office, September 1979.

Isachsen, A.J., and Strøm, Steiner. "Den skjulte økonomi og det svarte arbeidsmarked." University of Oslo. Mimeographed.

Myrdal, Gunnar. "Dägs för ett battre skattesystem." *Ekonomisk Debatt* 7, 1978.

Myrsten, K. "Det illegala bygghantverket." Brottsutvecklingen, Brotts-forebyggande Radet, Rapport 1980:3.

Stuart, Charles E. "Swedish Tax Rates, Labor Supply, and Tax Revenues." *Journal of Political Economy*, 89 (October 1981).

Tanzi, Vito. "Underground Economy and Tax Evasion in the United States: Estimates and Implications." *Banca Nazionale del Lavoro Quarterly Review*, December 1980. Reprinted as chapter 4 of this volume.

15 The Second Economy of the USSR

Gregory Grossman

The standard Western image of the Soviet "command economy" is one of a state-owned, hierarchically organized, centrally planned and managed, price-controlled, and otherwise regimented system, rigidly geared to the goals and priorities of the Soviet leadership, and operating in compliance with a a myriad of state-imposed laws, regulations, and directives. However valid this image might be—and, while greatly oversimplified, it is not entirely incorrect—there is another, very significant side to Soviet economic reality, where production and exchange often take place for direct private gain and just as often violate state law in some nontrivial respect. This is the so-called "second economy," also referred to by Western observers as "counter-economy," "unofficial economy," "parallel market," and "private enterprise."[1] It comprehends a vast and varied set of activities that is attracting ever greater attention from Western scholars. Closely tied to it is widespread corruption of officialdom. Both exist on a large scale in the Soviet Union and in Eastern Europe, and, of course, have many analogies in non-Communist countries, both developed and underdeveloped.

Second Economy Defined

As some scholars define it, the *second economy* comprises all production and exchange activity that fulfills at least one of the two following tests: (a) being directly for private gain; (b) being in some significant respect in knowing contravention of existing law. So defined, the second economy includes much of the perfectly *legal* private activity which is possible in the USSR. To explain this paradox, it is important to note that legal private activity, though formally sanctioned and ideologically tolerated, is nevertheless ideologically alien to the Soviet system. Its operating principles are sharply different from those of the "first" economy. Furthermore, in many cases one cannot practically draw a line between legal and illegal private activity, since the former often serves as a front for the latter and both support one another. In light of this last consideration, and since this chapter will deal primarily with the illegal and "semilegal" aspects of the second economy, it may be useful at the outset to describe precisely that private economic activity in the USSR that is legal.

Reprinted from *Problems of Communism*, vol. 26, September-October 1977, pp. 25-40.

By far the most extensive and best studied part of Soviet legal private economic activity is the "private plot"—if smaller, the "garden plot"—in agriculture.[2] The private plot can be cultivated by a peasant household that belongs to a collective farm, by a household with primary employment at a state farm, or, as is often the case, even by one with primary employment outside of agriculture altogether. It has been estimated that in 1974 private agriculture accounted for almost one-third of all manhours expended in agriculture and almost one-tenth of all manhours expended in the whole economy.[3] The land making up the private plots invariably belongs to the state, and the cultivator pays no rent as such. For *kolkhozniki*, or members of collective farms, the plot has lately averaged about three-tenths of a hectare (three-fourths of an acre), on which not only field crops are grown, but some fowl, smaller livestock, and a strictly limited number of large livestock are usually kept as well. Urban "garden plots" tend to be even smaller. Still, the approximately 50 million such tiny farms, whose area represents only about 3 percent of the national total of cultivated land, have a gross output which is more than one-fourth of the gross output of Soviet agriculture. Their contribution to production is especially significant in potatoes, vegetables, fruit, and animal products. Their logical adjuncts are the so-called collective-farm markets, marketplaces where producers sell directly to final consumers and where demand-and-supply relations reign almost supreme.[4]

Although in principle the private plot and the kolkhoz market are legal, they are quite frequently associated with illegalities. For example, limitations on plot area and on livestock holdings may be surreptitiously exceeded; various inputs—particularly fodder, but also fertilizer, water, implements, means of transport, and the like—may be illegally obtained from the socialized sector; and produce may be marketed with the help of middlemen. The collective-farm markets invite violations of the law as well, most notably the disposal of stolen goods.

Considerable private activity is to be found in the housing sector of the Soviet economy also. By law, the private ownership of housing is allowed only for the owner's occupancy, with some exceptions. And although owner occupancy of houses is not a productive activity in the common sense of the phrase, it is worthy of note that even sixty years after the Russian Revolution, approximately one-half of the Soviet total population and about one-quarter of the urban population still resides in privately owned housing.[5] What is more, as late as 1975 some 30 percent of all new housing space (measured in square meters) was completed by nonstate entities: housing cooperatives, collective farms, and individuals, with the last accounting for the greatest share.[6] Again, while in principle such construction may be legal, there is little doubt that much of it involves the acquisition of materials on the black market, illegal hiring of construction help, unauthorized use of state-owned vehicles, bribery of officials, and other violations of the law.

To complete our list, the law also permits private activity in certain professions, such as those of physician, dentist, teacher, and tutor; in the provision of certain household and repair and personal services, in rural areas only; in a very few (and quite unimportant) crafts and trades; in the prospecting and extraction of some valuable metals, such as gold, by so-called *starateli* (prospectors); in the hunting of some fur-bearing wild animals; and in some other rather exceptional instances.[7] Private prospectors and hunters must surrender the fruits of their efforts exclusively to the state at posted prices. Finally, the sale of used personal objects to other persons is permitted. This, however, opens a loophole for illegal trading.

Other forms of private activity in production or exchange are proscribed. The employment of one individual by another is prohibited, except in the case of household help (which, incidentally, is rather hard to find these days). Any purchase and resale with intent to profit—so-called "speculation"—is illegal regardless of difference in time or place of purchase and sale. Private possession of foreign currency or of monetary metals is illegal also, such prohibition being common to all countries practicing stringent foreign exchange control. Except for authorized persons, moreover, all transactions with foreigners are against the law. As already mentioned, the plying of nearly all crafts and trades for private gain is prohibited. And needless to say, the law forbids turning socialist property to private lucrative use; theft from the state and cooperatives, as well as from private persons; bribe-taking by official persons; and bribe-giving, in money or *natura*.[8]

Within the state sector itself, the violation of the innumerable laws, rules, regulations, norms, directives, and plans pertaining to the everyday activity of managers, technicians, workers, clerks, functionaries, administrators, and everyone else, is punishable either by law or by administrative sanction. Nevertheless, despite far-reaching and rigorous prohibitions—and in some measure precisely because of them—and despite the often severe penalties threatening transgressors, the breaking of economic laws and regulations and the passing of bribes are commonplace everyday phenomena in which virtually the whole population of the USSR is continuously enmeshed, and in which some individuals are involved on a large and at times gigantic scale.

How can this be determined? Readers not conversant with the topic may wonder where one obtains information on "economic crime" in the USSR. (This Soviet term embraces theft from the state and from cooperatives, bribery, and the whole range of illegal activities involving production and exchange.) Generally speaking, the accumulation of data is no problem whatever in regard to sheer volume. The Soviet press is replete with articles on the theme, mostly in the form of case descriptions of theft, bribery, illegal production and trade, and the like, going into remarkable detail, and often with seeming candor. Similar descriptive information can be found in Soviet juridical literature and in books on such subjects as public order, auditing, "people's control," and party activity. How accurate and representative information filtered through Soviet censorship is, however, another question. Such information contains obvious lucanae. For example, Soviet printed sources rarely mention cases of failure of law enforcement. (Naturally, the most successful illegal activities, those that go undetected, are not publicized at all.) They pass by in silence such crucial problems as corruption of the party *apparat*, of high government officials, and of police and other law-enforcement authorities;[9] and they fail to mention, to this author's knowledge, the startling phenomenon of the sale, for high capital sums, of governmental and party posts. Faith in the rectitude of the pillars of the political regime must not be undermined by the press, even though the truth must surely be known by a substantial part of the public. Furthermore, the print media are typically silent about any shenanigans in the vast defense sector and in the armed forces. They may deliberately distort the facts of individual cases. They rarely print generalizing analyses about the second economy or corruption;[10] and, if the authorities dispose of quantitative estimates of the overall extent and incidence of second economy activities or some parts thereof, as they probably do, such never appear in the press. Nonetheless, a researcher can learn a lot from simply reading the newspapers.

Other major sources of data available to the scholar include accounts by foreign correspondents in the USSR,[11] the scholar's own personal contacts and observations in that country, and—of major importance lately—the written and oral testimony of recent emigrants.[12] Of considerable help, too, are similar sources in or from the Communist countries of Eastern Europe, since both the underlying causes of the second economy and its symptoms and manifestations are essentially the same there as in the USSR, even though general conditions, the extent of permitted private activity, and official policies may vary from country to country.

Clearly, then, there are sufficient sources of raw data on the subject to allow the researcher to assert that illegalities exist in all sectors of the Soviet economy. Given this conclusion, it is necessary to examine the forms which these illegal manifestations of the second economy normally assume.

Forms of Economic Illegality

The enormous variety and occasional complexity of illegal and semilegal activities in production and distribution are ensured by the pervasiveness of controls and the massive number of prohibitions in the state and household sectors of the economy, and appear to be limited only by human ingenuity, though, naturally, the most ingenious schemes, being presumably also the more successful ones, tend to escape identification by Soviet authorities and detached observer alike. A series of classifications and typologies for these activities could be developed. One is perforce provided by Soviet law in terms of its different articles and the acts that they proscribe.[13] Another, a typology of markets, is offered by Katsenelinboigen, to whose work we have already referred.[14] But no such classification will be made here in any formal sense. Rather, we will only provide a concise summary of the chief forms of relevant activity.

Doubtless the most common economic crime in the USSR is stealing from the state, under which we subsume stealing from all official organizations, including collective farms. All sources agree that it is practiced by virtually everyone, takes all possible forms, and varies in scale from the trivial to the regal. All also agree that the public takes it for granted,[15] attaches almost no approbrium to it—and, on the contrary, disapproves of those who do not engage in it—and sharply distinguishes between stealing from the state and stealing from private individuals. The latter is generally condemned. With some liberty, one might perhaps assert that the right to steal on the job, within certain conventional limits, is an implicit but integral part of the conditions of employment in the Soviet Union. It not only furnishes significant additional income in kind and in money to much of the public, conversely representing a major item of expense for the state,[16] but also provides an important, often indispensable, basis for the second economy. The peasant steals fodder from the kolkhoz to maintain his animals, the worker steals materials and tools with which to ply his trade "on the side," the physician steals medicines, the driver steals gasoline and the use of the official car to operate an unofficial taxi; and to all of them income from private activity on the side may be more important than the wage or salary they earn in their official jobs.

An important variant of stealing on the job is the diversion and black-market sale by truck drivers of freight in their custody. This is precisely the source of the apparently considerable amount of building material that enters illegal channels and makes possible much private, kolkhoz, and at times even state enterprise construction. A more lordly way of stealing, if one is highly placed, is to use the resources of one's own firm or organization to personal advantage. The Soviet press is full of examples: have the firm build you a summer house (*dacha*) at little or no cost to yourself,[17] or have it remodel your apartment in town or provide a company car for your wife. Such illegal perquisites—in addition to the legal ones that important officials and managers enjoy—seem often to be taken for granted.

Theft from the state does not take place only on the job, however. By all indications, a great deal of it is perpetrated by what might fairly be called professional criminals—the ordinary worker pilfering tools or materials at the factory does not think of himself in these terms—and even by well-organized gangs of criminals capable of pulling off daring and large-scale feats. There is little doubt that the merchandise so stolen in large measure enters the black market as well and partly feeds illegal production in the second economy.

There are also less crude forms of stealing from the state. A very common one consists of the diversion of finished goods, supplies, or materials by enterprise managers themselves. The goods might be recorded in the books as legitimately spoiled or lost in transit, for the books must of course show everything to be in order. But the diverted goods in fact are disposed of on the black market, or, in the case of intermediate materials and parts, used to manufacture items that can then be profitably sold. The proceeds are appropriated, though they may have to be shared with those within and outside the firm who are privy to what has happened.

The aim of those who divert goods is not always private peculation, however; it may be to promote the success of one's firm in terms of official indicators, which, to be sure, could indirectly benefit the operators of the diversion. The diverted goods may be used to barter against needed supplies when these are not available through legitimate channels, to improve the well-being and raise the morale of the firm's rank and file, and so on.[18] An important point that follows from this is that Soviet production statistics may not only be overstated by managers eager to show plan fulfillment in order to earn their bonuses, but may also occasionally be understated, particularly in the light and food-processing industries, where diversion of goods is relatively simple. There is no way, though, for the outside observer to estimate the extent of such understatement by industries and commodities or overall.

Generally speaking, in an economy with pervasive goods shortages such as exist in the Soviet Union, physical or administrative control over goods often confers both the power and the opportunity for economic gain to the individual, be he or she ever so humble in the formal hierarchy. It is clear that many take advantage of this fact. Thus, when goods in high demand arrive in state-owned retail stores, it is common for salespeople to lay them aside for favored customers from which they can expect good tips, if not to preempt the goods themselves for profitable resale. The salesperson usually has to split any gains with his or her supervisor, who most likely again splits his share with the next higher supervisor, and so on up the chain of command.[19] Nevertheless, over time the additional net income gained may easily exceed—sometimes severalfold—the salesperson's salary and legal bonuses, which, perhaps for this very reason, are very modest to begin with. The individual, in fact, may have little choice but to fall in with the system of extralegal gain.

Functionaries in the administrative bureaucracy who handle the allocation of producer goods—and they are very many—and those who are in charge of waiting lists for automobiles, other major consumer durables, and housing also have considerable opportunity for graft and apparently take advantage of it, though how commonly we are unable to say.[20]

Finally, as has already been mentioned, there is widespread speculation in goods which are hard to come by. Given the invariable maldistribution by the state of goods over time and space, and chronic shortages of many items in the USSR, the opportunities for black-market trading for profit are nearly unlimited. The objects of speculation run the gamut from food, through foreign-made clothes purchased from visitors from abroad or in foreign currency (*valuta*) stores, to precious metals and foreign currency. The speculators may be relatively innocent individuals who pick up a few things on a visit to Moscow for resale to friends at home, or highly professional large-scale operators.[21]

In addition to illicit trade there is illicit production.[22] Although the private practice of nearly all crafts and trades is forbidden, it is far from suppressed. A large number of household repair and building services, typically provided by people moonlighting outside, or even during, working hours; automotive repair; the sewing and tailoring of garments;[23] the moving of furniture and other transport services—these and many others are regular illegal or semilegal features of Soviet life. On a larger scale are the operations of seemingly well-organized migratory gangs of builders who contract themselves out, chiefly to collective farms, for specific jobs at preagreed and relatively very high prices. Both individual moonlighters and gangs of workers are referred to as *shabashniki* (literally: free-time workers).

Last, there are the underground entrepreneurs in the full sense of the word: that is, individuals who promote and organize production on a substantial scale, employ the labor of others, obtain materials and machinery on the black market, and distribute their output widely. They invest their own capital, for underground firms are privately bought and sold at capitalized values that presumably reflect their expected profitability discounted for risk. The products involved are often consumer goods (garments, footwear, household articles, knickknacks, and the like) but can be producer goods as well. Large-scale private operations such as these commonly take place behind the protective facade of a state-owned factory or a collective farm—naturally, with appropriate payoffs to those who provide the cover—in what might be called crypto-private manner.[24] Another variant of crypto-private (or pseudo-socialist) operation is the following: the enterprise is in fact state-owned and produces the output called for by its plan, but is operated virtually as a private firm by the manager, who pays a fixed sum or a proportion of enterprise revenue to the state and pockets the rest. Naturally, this is most practicable in smaller establishments, especially those producing services with a low material component, so that the output cannot be easily controlled as a function of material input.[25]

Widespread Corruption

Illegal activities such as those just summarized are hardly the sole cause of corruption of Soviet officialdom and authorities, but they are surely a major contributing factor. Given the plethora of administrative superiors, controllers, inspectors, auditors, law enforcers, party authorities, expediters, and just plain snoopers that beset every economic activity, legal or illegal, in the Soviet Union, anything done out of line requires the buying off of some and often very many people.

It should be noted first of all that law enforcement officials in the USSR are apparently frequently bribed. Those involved include the regular police (the militia), the special economic police (OBKhSS: Department for Combating the Theft of Socialist Property), and at times personnel in prosecutors' offices.[26] One source even reports the case of an official who actively promoted underground enterprise within his jurisdiction in order to expand his graft base.[27]

No doubt most bribe-taking and bribe-giving is rather petty, consisting of generous tips dispensed to salespeople for goods in short supply (such tips may not even be thought of as bribes by either side)[28] or of baksheesh extracted from the public by many a clerk wielding an official rubber stamp. But some bribes are far from petty and can add up to substantial sums over the year.

Compounding the picture presented here is the Russian tradition of *prinosheniye* (literally, "bringing to"), the regular bringing of valuable gifts to one's superiors or others in proximate authority, as satirized, for instance, nearly a century and a half ago by Gogol in his immortal comedy *The Inspector General*. Thus, *prinosheniye* is not bribery in relation to a particular act or event, but a general and regular way of ingratiating oneself with authority, and one which is expected by both parties. *Prinosheniye* is given by individuals to their superiors;[29] but of course on a large scale it is dispensed by enterprises, collective farms, and, needless to say, underground entrepreneurs to their various "protectors." The major beneficiaries are highly placed authorities, ranging up to the ministerial level; local government chiefs; and, not least, local, provincial, and possibly higher party secretaries and first secretaries. Rural officials of various kinds apparently regularly take in large amounts of choice food from collective and state farms in their jurisdictions. Nor are higher-ups adverse to simply demanding tribute when their whim so dictates.[30]

The next logical step in the development of corruption would seem to be the capitalization of expected future streams of graft, and hence the purchase and sale of lucrative official positions. This step, too, seems to have been taken in the USSR. Zemtsov reports the widespread purchase and sale around 1970 of high party and high government positions in Azerbaydzhan for sums ranging from 10,000 rubles for lesser posts to 250,000 rubles for that of Minister of Trade.[31] If one assumes his information is correct, some interesting questions and inferences suggest themselves. Who receives such capital sums? Are they appropriated by one person in each case, or are they split among cliques of individuals? How do the buyers of positions raise such huge amounts? What return do they expect? How secure are they in their acquired "property rights"? Indeed, to what extent has an aura of property rights arisen around certain positions? At the very least one can deduce that the purchase and sale of positions for large sums of money signifies the profound institutionalization in the Soviet Union of a whole structure of bribery and graft, from the bottom to the top of the pyramid of power; that considerable stability of the structure of power is expected by all concerned; and that very probably there is a close organic connection between political-administrative authority, on the one hand, and a highly developed world of illegal economic activity, on the other. In sum, the concept of *kleptocracy,* developed by sociologists with reference to corrupt regimes and bureaucracies in underdeveloped countries, does not seem inapplicable to at least certain portions and regional segments of the Soviet party government hierarchy.[32]

Soviet Particularities

Certain aspects of the second economy and corruption in the USSR appear to play a particularly important role in shaping the special characteristics of the Soviet *kleptocracy.* Before one tries to estimate the size and ultimate significance of the second economy itself, therefore, some comments about the particularities of the Soviet case seem in order.

Quite apart from the significance of the private plot in furthering illegal private economic activity in the USSR, the collective farm itself plays an important role in this regard. The following are some of the reasons. Formally, it is relatively easy to set up subsidiary enterprises at collective farms. While official policy intends such enterprises either to produce materials or services for the farm's own use or to process its agricultural products, they seem readily turned into fronts for illegal private operations. In fact, some enterprises exist on paper only and serve exclusively front purposes. Furthermore, the farm often can provide illegal undertakings with premises, transport, and labor—all of which are hard to obtain in the city. Finally, the collective farm is subject to less stringent controls than are state-owned enterprises and organizations with regard to conversion of bank money (that is, deposit balances in the State Bank) into cash. This point is crucial for underground operations, which derive revenue from the state sector, because state-owned entities, which may find ways of paying for services rendered with bank money, as a rule dispose of very little currency. Bank money must be converted into currency, however, to pay individuals for their productive contributions, to purchase materials on the black market, to grease the palms of officials where necessary, and to retain a profit for the enterpreneur himself. The collective farm accomplishes this conversion.

Also important to the success of illegal economic activity is the role of persons in direct charge of small means of transport, such as truck drivers, taxi drivers, and, lately, owners of private automobiles. The reasons are of course obvious. A good deal of the demand for private automobiles—at high official prices, and even at much higher black-market prices[33]—is generated by the desire to provide transport to the second economy, which at once generates the need for nonofficial vehicles and provides the purchasing power necessary to acquire them.

A further aspect of the Soviet case which one can hardly fail to make note of is that alcohol suffuses and penetrates much of the second economy. Vodka—both the illegal "home brew" (*samogon*) and the state-produced variety, the latter especially since 1972 when restrictions on conditions and hours of sale were tightened[34]—is a major object of black-market trading. It seems likely that a disproportionate fraction of the moderate amounts earned in the second economy or from bribe-taking is spent on alcohol (high incomes so earned are more likely to be spent on tangible valuables or to be hoarded), thus, incidentally, swelling the coffers of the state treasury. Furthermore, vodka itself occasionally serves as the means of payment of illegal wages or petty bribes. It also functions as a standard of value, in that the price of the *shabashnik's* services is sometimes specified beforehand as so many half-liter bottles of standard vodka, even though the ultimate payment may be the current ruble equivalent thereof.[35]

Last among the special characteristics to be referred to here is that the Soviet second economy has a geographic and regional pattern. Since a significant component of supply on the black market consists of foreign goods smuggled into the country by merchant-marine crews, port cities such as Leningrad, Riga, and Odessa are obviously major funnels that feed the second economy. The Odessa black market enjoys high renown. In fact, illegal private activity and corruption seem especially highly developed in the southern regions of the country, in Transcaucasia, and in Central Asia. Some aspects of venality and illegality in Azerbaydzhan have already been cited. However, Georgia has a reputation second to none in this respect.

The Georgian unofficial economy seems to have at least two distinct, if not unrelated, parts. The first rests on the fact that for climatic reasons Georgia has a monopoly on citrus fruit production in the USSR and shares with only a few other regions considerable advantage in growing out-of-season fruit and flowers. The state attempts to obtain these goods for distribution throughout the country (one wonders if it could handle the latter task) at prices that are a fraction of what the products bring growers in the open markets of the Soviet Union's northern population centers. Naturally, Georgian peasants prefer the open markets. In effect, for some time now there has been an undeclared war going on between state authorities and the peasants, a contest in which the peasants have shown enormous determination and remarkable ingenuity in overcoming the formidable obstacles which the state has placed in the way of their pocketing the large economic rent offered by the open market.

The second part of the Georgian unofficial economy consists of private activity in industry, trade, and other areas. In form this activity may now differ greatly from what takes place in other regions, but in Georgia it seems to have been carried out on an unparalleled scale and with unrivaled scope and daring. Eyewitnesses report significant control by the largest underground entrepreneurs over major party appointments within the republic.[36] Or at least such was the situation until the issuance of the now well-known resolution of the Central Committee of the Communist Party of the Soviet Union, dated February 22, 1972, regarding the work of the Communist Party Committee of Tbilisi, which triggered a massive purge in the Georgian party leadership and in the republic as a whole, aimed at rooting out corruption, illegal private economic activity, and other economic crimes and violations. Even today, however, it does not seem that the purification has fully achieved its aims.[37]

Because of the greater density of economic crimes in the southern republics, any attempt on the part of central authorities to enforce the law inevitably carries with it significant implications for the general pattern of relations between Moscow and the periphery and between the Slavic majority of the USSR and the respective minority nationalities. These relations are already complicated enough.

Large and Growing?

How large is the Soviet second economy? So far as its *lawful* component alone is concerned, one can refer to estimates for 1968 prepared by the U.S. Central Intelligence Agency,[38] which show that 10 percent of Soviet gross national product (GNP) (in the sense of value added) originated in the legal private sector, and that of this, 76 percent originated in agriculture, 22 percent in housing construction (completions), and 2 percent in services. Viewed in another way, legal private activity contributed 31 percent of value added in Soviet agricultural production and marketing, 32 percent of value added in housing completions, and 5 percent of value added in services. Before 1968, however, the share of the legal private sector had been declining steadily—in 1950 it had been 22 percent of GNP—though owing not so much to an absolute diminution of the private sector as to the rapid expansion of the socialist sector. Today the legal private sector is probably rather less than 10 percent of Soviet GNP.

Now, 10 percent of GNP may not be much, but considering the country, it is noteworthy. What is more, the legal private sector produces almost nothing aside from consumer goods (including housing services) and new residential construction. Since household consumption in 1968 claimed only about one-half of GNP (at factor cost), the contribution of private value added to household consumption must have been at least 15 percent, and, in regard to household food consumption, perhaps around 25 percent.[39] It is probably similar today.

To turn from the legal to the *illegal* private sector (for the moment excluding from consideration illegal activities on socialist account), not even an educated guess of size can be attempted by an outside observer. Perhaps estimates are compiled by one or another institute in the USSR; but even without these one can assert with considerable confidence that illegal private economic activities are a major and extremely widespread phenomenon that for a very large part of the population is, in one form or another, a regular, almost daily, experience. This holds especially if one includes consideration of such common practices as the paying and taking of large tips (really black-market surcharges), petty bribes, and gifts (*prinosheniye*) that are in fact bribes. Moreover, whatever its opinion of large underground operations or more exotic dealings, the public seems to accept petty illegalities as a normal and even inevitable part of making one's way in a refractory and shortage-ridden environment. Little condemnation is leveled at those who benefit from the illegalities (so many do, after all!), and less yet at those who pass money to them.[40]

Eyewitnesses have frequently been of the opinion that both illegal economic activities and corruption have been markedly on the increase during the Krushchev and Brezhnev administrations,[41] though it is not always clear whether they mean in terms of absolute growth of the phenomena or of their relative growth in relation to the "first" economy, which, of course, has been growing at a good rate itself. Thus, while absolute levels cannot be estimated by the outside observer, a significant increase of the illegal economy over the last twenty years can plausibly be assumed. The diminution of terror after Stalin's death; the spread of cynicism in regard to the official economic system and party rule, reported by many observers; the boost in consumer expectations created by successes of the economy in many fields, not least in the achievement of a sharp improvement in per capita consumption, and by greatly expanded foreign contracts—all of these trends should have been expected to contribute both to mounting demand for consumer goods and services on the black market and to greater responsiveness of black-market supply. In addition, growth of the second economy and of corruption tends to feed on itself. People learn what they can get away with, success elicits imitation, and many are caught in a web from which they cannot escape even if they so desire. Events like the highly publicized introduction of the death penalty for graver economic crimes in 1961-1962, or the aforementioned crackdown on corruption in Georgia in 1972, do not seem to have seriously retarded the historical trend toward expansion of both phenomena, at least not insofar as an outsider can judge. In contrast, major crop failures or years when the economy seems to grind down across the board, as happened in 1969 and 1977, may—we don't really know—give an added boost to the illegal economy over the short term.

Other factors favoring the long-term trend of expansion can be mentioned. The considerable rise in private-car ownership which has taken place since 1970 appears to have given a strong push to the second economy activities and corruption connected with nearly every aspect of the acquisition, operation, maintenance, and repair of automobiles.[42] A similar effect on the second economy generally can be attributed to the opening of the Soviet Union to foreign travel in both directions at the end of the 1950s and to the rapid expansion of the Soviet merchant marine (and of Aeroflot operations, perhaps), with the consequent inflow and resale of smuggled foreign goods and currency. Last, the impact of a sharp increase in the liquidity of the Soviet household sector should be noted. Taking total savings deposit balances at the end of the year as a percent, first, of produced national income (current prices, Soviet concept) and, second, of total sales in state and cooperative stores during the year, we obtain for 1958, 6.8 and 12.9 percent; for 1965, 9.6 and 17.9 percent; for 1970, 16.1 and 30.0 percent; and for 1975, 25.0 and 36.4 percent.[43] The only other major liquid asset held by the Soviet public is currency, which might perhaps be assumed, by way of first approximation, to have grown in the aggregate proportionately with savings deposits. It is difficult to dismiss the possibility that the extraordinary rise evidenced above of the Soviet public's liquidity in relation to two major relevant aggregates in the first economy has tended to favor the development of the second economy—and perhaps, conversely, has in itself been conditioned by the second economy.[44]

Significance of the Second Economy

Does it matter that the illegal economy and corruption are large and growing phenomena in the USSR? Cannot the same be said of many non-Communist countries as well, developed and underdeveloped? Has the United States not passed through a period of extraordinary revelations of corruption recently?[45] The answer to these questions is twofold. It is true that the illegalities of non-Communist countries are bad enough, and in certain underdeveloped countries are extremely serious, though expert opinion holds varied views on the subject. But in Soviet society economic illegalities raise some peculiar and difficult problems for the system's directors.

The prevalence of illegal production and trade and of bribe-taking for private gain and enrichment—together with other negative features of the system—controvert such philosophical bases of Soviet society as the solidarity of the various population groups with one another and with the party and its leadership, the moral transformation of Soviet man since the revolution, and inevitable progress toward a society of full communism. It erodes the authority of the Communist Party and the legitimacy of the Soviet dictatorship. It raises questions, as had the Chinese earlier, concerning the USSR's moral right to lead the Communist world and to stand as a beacon to the world's revolutionary forces and as a model to the less developed world. It aggravates cynicism and lawlessness inside the Soviet Union, and even within the party itself.

Furthermore, the prevalence of economic illegalities and corruption casts doubt on the ability of the Soviet system to provide minimal material benefits to its population or to administer its own socialist economy according to its own principles and rules. In a sense, as shown earlier, it elevates the power of money in society to rival that of the dictatorship itself, rendering the regime's implements of rule less effective and less certain. And it redistributes income between social groups and regions and seriously complicates the conduct of regional and nationality policy.

Yet the regime's attitude toward economic crimes may well be ambivalent, and the subject of what to do about them controversial within the leadership, since economic crimes in the USSR have their positive as well as negative features in terms of economic performance indicators as defined by the authorities themselves. Hence, violations such as those within the state and collective-farm sectors and the illegal and semilegal provision of household services by private individuals seem to encounter a relatively more tolerant attitude from the authorities than do "speculation," the use of socialist firms for private gain, or foreign currency violations. In any case, the ability of the authorities to effectively enforce the law on all counts seems to be severely limited—more so on some counts than on others. By the same token, their ability to allot lucrative positions within the hierarchy and to threaten citizens with individual prosecution (since nearly everyone is guilty) may add significantly to their control of subordinate hierarchies and thus strengthen the regime as a whole. But would Lenin recognize his party and his state in these conditions?

To turn to the more strictly economic implications of the second economy, a few selected observations can be made, though it should be added that much in this area remains unresearched and poorly understood. As stressed throughout this chapter, the Soviet economy is in fact significantly different in its mode of functioning and in some of its dimensions than one would gather from a study of its legal and official portion alone. Much of our quantitative data calls for revision, although even considerable effort may not produce satisfactory results in this regard, owing to the nature of the subject matter involved.

As is frequently asserted, the illegal side of the Soviet second economy adds considerably to the consumer's well-being, both by enhancing the flow of goods and services available to him, qualitatively as much as quantitatively, and by providing him with extra income (the two are really opposite sides of the same coin in national accounting terms). And while in the aggregate the addition provided is not a net one, for at least some of the resources now going into the illegal—as well as legal—channels of the second economy are doubtless diverted from the socialist sector, it is still highly likely that much of the effort, energy, and enterprise invested in the functioning of the second economy would find little application in working for the state. Furthermore, the state would not necessarily devote the relevant resources fully to the cause of personal consumption; hence, the gain from the second economy in this regard is correspondingly larger.

There is, however, a serious complication in such reasoning. The state depends heavily on monetary incentives—promotions, bonuses, premiums, prizes, piece-rate pay—to elicit performance from its workers and employees. Paradoxically, the effectiveness of such incentives is simultaneously strengthened and weakened by the presence of the second economy. It is weakened insofar as the pursuit of illicit gain on the job, gain which can be much larger than that provided by legal incentives, deflects people's attention and efforts from approved activities. But at the same time the existence of a parallel, second-economy market greatly enhances the attraction of money, including money legitimately earned on the job, and accordingly validates with the public the worth of official monetary incentives.

A further word on the last point. There has been some discussion of late among sovietological economists as to whether repressed inflation exists in the household sector of the Soviet-type economy.[46] Based on the analysis presented here, it would seem that the very presence of a large second economy, and particularly of a black market, in a sense does away with repressed inflation, despite fairly rigid control of official retail prices. In the second economy, prices tend to be high enough to eliminate any overall "monetary overhang" (that is, excess of purchasing power over the total supply of goods and services at effective prices) and to forestall a repressed inflationary situation in relation to the controlled and noncontrolled sectors taken together. However, there still remains disequilibrium of relative prices, both between controlled and noncontrolled prices and among the controlled prices themselves. This condition inevitably creates many problems for the authorities, inconvenience for consumers, and invitation to private gain.

Thus, a fundamental characteristic of the present-day Soviet economy is, broadly speaking, a two-tiered (or many-tiered) structure of prices and personal incomes, a structure common in countries with widespread black markets for goods and labor. On the lower tier are controlled wholesale as well as retail prices; on the upper tier, corresponding free prices, relevant in the legal collective-farm market and in the black market, the latter of which covers a much wider range of goods and services than the former.[47] The situation is similar with respect to labor incomes, which can be much higher in the second economy than in the first,[48] to say nothing of the financial gains of underground traders and entrepreneurs or of the graft-swollen incomes of officialdom.

The two-tiered structure of prices and incomes that exists in the USSR and the productive contribution of the second economy lead one to question the accuracy of some Western quantitative notions about the Soviet economy. Consider international comparisons either of individual prices or of general price levels, retail and wholesale, of the sort that are frequently undertaken for various purposes and which result in statements of the following kind: "American prices (at a given time, for a given category of goods) are x times higher than Soviet prices," or "The purchasing power of the ruble is y times that of the dollar." Even after all necessary adjustments for differences in quality, servicing, and conditions of sale, the stated ratio may be quite inaccurate if only official (or list) prices in the two countries have been consulted. In the USSR the acquisition cost of a good to the buyer often may be substantially higher than the official price, owing to black market differentials, bribes, bribe-like gifts, and the like. In the United States, on the other hand, the average actual acquisition cost is likely to be below list, thanks to sales, giveaway, discounts, under-the-counter rebates, and so forth. Thus, ratio x may be typically overstated, and sometimes probably greatly overstated, while ratio y may be typically understated.

Also in need of possibly appreciable correction are our notions of levels of personal money income in the Soviet Union. Sovietological economists generally obtain these notions from published data on individual wages and salaries, average wages and salaries for various categories of labor, and consumer budget surveys. But surely all such data—and most privately communicated figures as well—refer only to legal incomes. Therefore, they may fall significantly short of true total incomes, which include illegal or semilegal earnings and thefts on the job. Even *legal* incomes from private activity are probably seriously underreported, owing to the heavy special tax rates applying to them.

Accordingly, serious doubt is thrown, for instance, on the recent attempts in the West to reconstruct and interpret the size distribution of personal incomes in the USSR. Quite apart from the very scanty data base available for such exercises, and despite the truly ingenious methods used to circumvent this handicap, the attempts can hardly give us an accurate picture of income distribution unless unreported personal earnings are insignificant —which we doubt—or are distributed in relation to legal incomes so as not to affect the chief measures of inequality—which remains to be demonstrated.

Two specific examples may be adduced in illustration. First, the Soviets publish data on average wages/salaries and *kolkhoznik* incomes by republic and by region of the RSFSR, which might be taken as indicators of relative material well-being in different parts of the country. Yet, because of the unequal significance of illegal incomes regionally, such statistics may distort the picture. And second, two occupations on which there is a fair amount of information regarding official rates of remuneration are those of physicians and of retail-trade employees. The rates are relatively low, those of physicians being especially low in international terms. But physicians collect large tips and conduct a certain amount of private practice which earns them substantial fees; and retail-trade employees collect large tips also, and are reputed to be heavily involved in speculation. Under these circumstances, what is the significance of official data?

Mention has already been made in passing of the fact that production data for some individual commodities, especially consumer goods, may require significant upward revision to account for unreported, mostly illegal, production. Similarly, some output data call for downward adjustment, owing to the deliberate overreporting characteristic of the Soviet economy.

As for data on the national income or product as a whole and its major components, the exclusion of illegal activities in the Soviet instance follows standard world practice. Nevertheless, a strong case can be made for the inclusion of illegal activities in the data of those countries (at least for the most relevant sectors of the economy) where illegalities are so widespread and significant as to appreciably affect some portions of the national accounts, as in the USSR. If this were done, possibly with some adjustment for the two-tiered nature of prices and incomes, it might require notable revisions in our breakdown of Soviet national income by sector of origin, and of the national product by end use. It might even alter our estimates of Soviet rates of growth, overall and by sector and end product. But the recomputation suggested will be very difficult to do with any accuracy in the foreseeable future.

Finally, one might ask about relationships between the second economy (and corruption) and prospects for institutional change in the Soviet economy. An adequate response, in this author's view, must take three factors into consideration.

1. Soviet authorities may find it necessary to increase rates of remuneration and incentive pay in a selective manner, in order to compete with the pecuniary attraction of illicit side incomes on the job. Even so, in many cases it will probably be rather futile for them to try to compete.

2. They may expand the scope of *legal* private activities, that is, may legalize some activity that is now proscribed (thus recognizing an inability to eradicate it), forcing down its prices, and diminishing both the burden of law enforcement and the extent of corruption. In this case, they would be following the example of several East European countries, where the scope of legal private activity is considerably wider than in the USSR (but where much economic illegality nonetheless persists). In fact, the draft of the new Soviet constitution made public on June 4, 1977, contains some open-ended wording that may be interpreted to indicate a trend in this direction. It provides for lawful "individual labor activity" based exclusively on the individual labor of citizens and members of their families in the areas of crafts and trades, agriculture, services to the public, and *"other forms of labor activity."*[49]

3. As for the likelihood of another try at economic reform (decentralization, liberalization, and the like) in the state sector, it must be borne in mind that the second economy, grafted onto the present institutional setup in the USSR, is a kind of spontaneous surrogate economic reform that imparts a necessary modicum of flexibility, adaptability, and responsiveness to a formal setup that is too often paralyzing in its rigidity, slowness, and inefficiency. It represents a de facto decentralization, with overtones of the market. It keeps the wheels of production turning. At the same time, the second economy in the state sector is a source of considerable illicit income, in high places as well as low. There must be very many persons of power and influence who have a strong vested interest in the present situation and who may well resist and sabotage any important steps toward formal liberalization of the economy or, especially, toward the elimination of the now ubiquitous administrative management of scarcity. Such considerations need not be decisive in determining prospects for economic reform, but they may well be more than minor.

In any case, it seems clear that the Soviet second economy and the phenomena associated with it are here to stay for some time, and with them the social institutions and public mentality that have helped make them what they are today.

Notes

1. The terms "second economy" and "parallel market" seem to have been coined by K.S. Karol, in "Conversations in Russia," *New Statesman* (Jan. 1, 1971), pp. 8-10. In the article Karol also speaks of the "third economy," the network of restricted and well-stocked shops in the USSR available only to the privileged.

2. See, especially, the definitive work by Karl-Eugen Wädekin, *The Private Sector in Soviet Agriculture* (Berkeley: University of California Press, 1973).

3. Murray Feshbach and Stephen Rapawy, "Soviet Population and Manpower Trends and Policies," in U.S. Congress, Joint Economic Committee, *Soviet Economy in a New Perspective* (Washington, D.C.: Government Printing Office, 1976), table 13, p. 138.

4. On the *kolkhoz* market, see Wädekin, *The Private Sector,* chapter 6.

5. See Henry W. Morton, "What Have the Soviet Leaders Done about the Housing Crisis?" in *Soviet Politics and Society in the 1970s,* ed. Henry W. Morton and Rudolf L. Tökés (New York: Free Press, 1974), p. 175. Information on the private housing sector in the USSR and Eastern Europe, in its illegal as well as legal aspects, is conveniently brought together in Laszlo Revesz, *Mieter und Wohnung im Ostblock* [Tenants and Housing in the Eastern Bloc], (Bern: Schweitzerisches Ost-Institut, 1963). See also note 17.

6. The exact amount built by private individuals cannot be ascertained because housing built by collective farms as such is lumped in with it in available statistics. It is not unlikely that some private construction escapes identification in official statistics.

7. An up-to-date review of which private activity is legal and which is not, together with a lively commentary, can be found in Valeriy Chalidze, *Ugolovnaya Rossiya* [Criminal Russia] (New York: Khronika Publishers, 1977), pp. 246-90. I am indebted to Professor V.G. Treml for bringing this source to my attention.

8. On the law pertaining to bribery, see ibid., pp. 230-245; and to the theft of socialist property, ibid., pp. 291-303. Chalidze points out the curious fact that the granting of sexual favors by a woman to an official is not now regarded in Soviet law as a bribe, though at one time it was; see ibid., p. 238.

9. Nonetheless, allusions to the corruption of law-enforcement authorities occasionally sneak through. See the hint in an article on an anti-speculator raid at a provincial collective-farm market that all the speculators had been forewarned by someone inside the police force; *Pravda* (Moscow, May 13, 1977).

10. A notable exception is the concise but informative article by A. Kirpichnikov, "A Criminological Study of Bribery," *Sotsialisticheskaya zakonnost* (Moscow), no. 12 (1975), pp. 41-43.

It is important to note in connection with Soviet press coverage that the periodical *Soviet Analyst* (London) frequently prints and comments upon information on economic crime in the USSR, culled mostly from the Soviet press, and that the Central Research Service of Radio Liberty (Munich) maintains a file on what it calls the unofficial economy, with material from both Soviet and non-Soviet sources. I would like to express my thanks to Keith Bush of Radio Liberty for sharing parts of the Radio Liberty file with me.

11. Of these, the most informative is in Hedrick Smith's best-selling book, *The Russians* (New York: Quadrangle, 1976), chapter 3, entitled

"Corruption: Living Na Levo." *Na levo* literally means "to (or on) the left," and is the idiomatic Russian expression for doing things illegally or not quite legally. Other useful recent accounts by journalists in English are Robert J. Kaiser, *Russia: The People and The Power* (New York: Atheneum, 1976); and James N. Wallace, "How Private Enterprise Helps the Russians Survive," *U.S. News and World Report* (Washington, D.C., Dec. 22, 1975), pp. 52-54. The accounts of foreign correspondents are themselves in large measure based on material in the Soviet press, as well as on personal contacts and observations.

12. The only published summary of the results of interviews with emigrants seems to be Zev Katz, "Insights from Emigrés and Sociological Studies on the Soviet Economy," U.S. Congress, Joint Economic Committee, *Soviet Economic Prospects for the Seventies* (Washington, D.C.: Government Printing Office, 1973), pp. 87-94.

On the other hand, recollections published by the emigrants themselves are getting to be quite numerous. Notable among these is A(ron) Katsenelinboigen, "Coloured Markets in the Soviet Union," *Soviet Studies* (Glasgow, January 1977), pp. 62-85, an attempt at a typology of legal, semilegal (or gray), and illegal markets, with much interesting incidental information. Of particular interest, too, is the book by Il'ya Zemstov, *Partiya ili Mafiya: Razvorovannaya respublika* [A Party or a Mafia: The Plundered Republic] (Paris: Les Editeurs Réunis, 1976). Azerbaydzhan is the republic in question, and Zemtsov claims to have had access to secret information on internal conditions, partly on the basis of which he paints an especially dark picture of venality, corruption, crime, and hopelessness. An informative concise account, also in Russian, is L. Shpiller, "Soviet Everyday Life," Novyy Zhurnal (New York, June 1977), pp. 180-200. A more general essay is Dimitri K. Simes, "The Soviet Parallel Market," *Survey* (London, Summer 1975), pp. 42-52. Also in English is Yuri Brokhin, "Hustling on Gorkey Street: Sex and Crime in Russia Today" (New York: Dial Press, 1975). As the title indicates, this book leans heavily in the direction of sensationalism, which tends to diminish its value for serious research, although much of its supposedly factual material is in line with what is now generally known.

13. Chalidze, *Ugolovnaya Rossiya.*

14. See note 12.

15. "Nobody can subsist on his wage or salary; everyone has to steal and moonlight in order to live," is the standard view.

16. This applies on a *ceteris paribus* premise. Of course, if no one stole from the state, the state could afford to pay higher wages and salaries and would probably have to do so to some extent. In other words, the state compensates for its loss through theft by paying lower wages, at least on the average if not in every case. This in turn provides implicit justification for the individual to steal from the state, and the circle closes.

17. The whole *dacha* business—renting, owning, building, maintaining—is shot through with illegalities, as vividly described by Christopher S. Wren in *The New York Times* (Aug. 17, 1977), p. 2.

18. The "informal" side of Soviet enterprise operation is by now long and well known to Western observers. See Joseph S. Berliner, "The Informal Organization of the Soviet Firm," *Quarterly Journal of Economics* (August 1952), pp. 342-365; also his *Factory and Manager in the USSR* (Cambridge: Harvard University Press, 1957).

19. See Katsenelinboigen, "Coloured Markets," p. 76; and Smith, *The Russians*, p. 87.

20. Mention of corruption of such functionaries is fairly frequent in the press. For a vivid account of parasitism in the textile trade, see K. Andreyev, "A Moth in the Yarn," *Sotsialisticheskaya industriya* (Moscow, Feb. 4, 5, and 6, 1976). Regarding housing, see Shpiller, "Soviet Everyday Life," pp. 184-185.

21. A Moscow resident once told the present author: "In this city you can get anything for money, though sometimes it takes a lot."

22. Not all of the activities enumerated in this paragraph are equally illegal, or equally illegal in all localities and under all conditions.

23. Those who can afford to do so shun ready-made garments of Soviet manufacture, for reasons evident to any visitor to a Soviet department store, and either seek out foreign-made clothes or have clothes made to order by what must be a large number of tailors and seamstresses, who work either privately at home or, if in state-owned tailor shops (*atel'ye*), usually with the benefit of a tip or bribe. A striking story of a whole village in the Caucasus privately knitting warm woolen outerwear and marketing it by mail-order catalog is in an article by V. Pankratov and V. Prokhorov in *Pravda* (Aug. 13, 1976).

24. Such crypto-private operation is revealingly described in detail in "The 'Black' Millions," *Radio Liberty Research* (Munich), RL 179/77 (July 27, 1977). Interestingly, crypto-private activities described in the report go back to 1952, that is, to Stalin's time.

25. See, for instance, the case of the hairdresser cited by Katz, "Insights from Emigrés," p. 91.

26. See Zemtsov, *Partiya ili Mafiya*, pp. 26 and 80; "The 'Black' Millions," *Radio Liberty Research*, p. 3; Smith, *The Russians*, p. 87.

27. "The 'Black' Millions," *Radio Liberty Research*, p. 7.

28. Where the gift ends and the bribe begins is a question that is occasionally debated in the pages of Soviet newspapers. See, for example, "Gift or Bribe," *Literaturnaya gazeta* (Moscow), Aug. 27, 1975, p. 12. Excerpts from this and similar articles are to be found in German translation in *Osteuropa* (Aachen), October 1976, pp. A548 ff. See also an article by V. Kotenko in *Pravda* (June 28, 1976).

An important area of large tipping and gift-giving is that of medical care. In effect, the nominally free services of surgeons, physicians, nurses, and other medical personnel, command black-market fees. There is also an active black market in medicines. See David K. Shipler, "Soviet Medicine Mixes Inconsistency with Diversity," *The New York Times*, June 26, 1977, p. 1; and Shpiller, "Soviet Everyday Life," passim.

29. Even research institute directors benefit from *prinosheniye* (author's private information).

30. See Shpiller, "Soviet Everyday Life," p. 183; Zemstov, *Partiya ili Mafiya*, and Smith, *The Russians*, p. 99.

On corruption in the USSR generally, see Steven J. Staats, "Corruption in the Soviet System," *Problems of Communism*, January-February 1972, pp. 40-47; and John M. Kramer, "Political Corruption in the USSR," *Western Political Quarterly*, June 1977, pp. 213-224. Both authors interpret "corruption" broadly, to include violation of regulations by factory managers. There is of course a large descriptive and analytical literature on corruption, written mostly by political scientists and pertaining to both developed and underdeveloped countries. Some of it appears to be relevant to Soviet and East European experience. See, for example, Arnold J. Heidenheimer, ed., *Political Corruption: Readings in Comparative Analysis* (New York: Holt, Rinehart and Winston, 1970); and James C. Scott, *Comparative Political Corruption* (Englewood Cliffs, N.J.: Prentice-Hall, 1972).

31. Zemstov, *Partiya ili Mafiya*, pp. 26-35. The average legal wage or salary in the USSR in that year, by comparison, was 122 rubles per month. Similar sales of posts seem to have taken place in Georgia, at least prior to the 1972 republic purge (Smith, *The Russians*, p. 97). Whether the sale of positions for capital sums took place or is taking place outside of Transcaucasia, we do not know.

32. On *kleptocracy*, see the contributions by S. Andreski and S. Rajaratnam in Heidenheimer, *Political Corruption*.

33. The official retail prices of new cars, high as they are, typically are not the full cost to the buyer, who has to grease many palms before his treasured object is duly acquired, registered, and garaged, and before he receives a driver's license. To maintain and repair his car the owner will have to turn to the second economy for labor, spare parts, and supplies. He will partly recoup if he obtains his gasoline on the black market as well; stolen from the state, it sells for a fraction of the official retail price. See Smith, *The Russians*, p. 82; "New Assault on the Rights of Soviet Workers," *Radio Liberty Research*, RL 188/75, May 2, 1975, pp. 2-3; "Pocket Gasoline," *Sotsialisticheskaya industriya*, March 11, 1977; and "Kings of the Gasoline Pump," *Pravda*, Aug. 18, 1977.

34. For the 1972 measures, see *Pravda*, June 16, 1972. In his carefully researched paper, "Production and Consumption of Alcoholic Beverages in

the USSR: A Statistical Study," *Journal of Studies on Alcohol* (New Brunswick, N.J.), March 1975, pp. 285-320, Vladimir G. Treml estimates *samogon* to have accounted for 25 to 30 percent of all alcohol consumed in the USSR around 1970, with this share gradually declining with urbanization. He also estimates per capita consumption of distilled spirits in the USSR (despite a large Moslem population) to be the highest in the world, and to have been rising at about 5 percent a year between 1957 and 1972.

35. These statements on the uses of vodka are based on private information in the hands of the author. At present the official price of a half-liter bottle is 3.62 rubles, or about four times the average gross legal hourly wage.

36. See Ia.A. Chianurov, "Georgia and Her Party Leaders," *Radio Liberty* dispatch, Nov. 27, 1972, p. 3. For brief descriptions of the vigorous underground economic life of Georgia, see Kaiser, *Russia*, pp. 110 ff.; and Smith, *The Russians*, pp. 95 ff.

37. The original CC CPSU resolution was followed up four years later (*Pravda*, June 27, 1976) by a second one which, though appearing to stress positive changes, clearly indicated that the situation was still far from satisfactory. For additional information, see *The New York Times* (Jan. 31 and May 11, 1976); *Christian Science Monitor* (Boston, July 8, 1976); and Elizabeth C. Sheetz, "Criticism of the Administration Organs in Georgia," *Radio Liberty Research*, RL 60/77, March 14, 1977.

38. U.S. Central Intelligence Agency, Office of Economic Research (Barbara Severin and David Carey), "Trends in Official Policy Toward Private Activity in the USSR" (March 1970), processed, pp. 3 ff. and appendix. GNP in this study presumably encompasses only the legal sectors of the Soviet economy.

39. For comparison, see the 1970 breakdown of GNP at factor cost in terms of value added by sector of origin and end use, in Rush V. Greenslade, "The Real Gross National Product in the USSR, 1959-75," in *Soviet Economy in a New Perspective*. A compendium of papers submitted to the Joint Economic Committee of Congress, October 14, 1976, pp. 284-285. Greenslade estimates total GNP (legal sectors only) at 340,219 billion rubles (BR), total household consumption at 164,731 BR, food consumption at 81,982 BR, and value added in agriculture at 69,405 BR.

40. On the public's attitude, see especially Simes, "The Soviet Parallel Market," also Smith, *The Russians*, p. 87.

See Shpiller, "Soviet Everyday Life," pp. 108 ff., who relates the rapid growth of corruption and illegal private activity to the public's "disorientation" after Khruschev's de-Stalinization campaign began in 1956; and compare Katz, "Insights from Emigrés," p. 90, who imputes it to the Brezhnev era. The introduction of the death penalty by Khruschev in 1961/62 for some economic crimes would seem to point in the direction of Shpiller's view.

42. See "The Dawn of the Automobile Era Gives a Boost to the Black Market" *Radio Liberty Research*, RL 132/75 (March 27, 1975); Yu. Kaz'min in *Pravda* (Dec. 23, 1974), p. 4; Yu. Shpakov in ibid. (March 16, 1976), p. 3; and D. Epifanov in ibid. (Feb. 9, 1977), p. 3.

43. This information is available in official Soviet statistical yearbooks.

44. The anonymous author of "The 'Black' Millions" reports that in 1970 he was told by a supposedly well-informed friend that some 28 billion rubles had been diverted from normal circulation and were being hoarded "in mattresses," presumably by those who acquired them illegally. An outsider is at a loss as to how to evaluate such information. The problem of "laundering" illicit cash is a major one in the USSR. One way is to purchase lottery tickets or lottery bonds that have already won but have not yet been cashed in; the black-market price (the transaction is illegal) appears to run 1.5 to 2 times the winnings, that is, one clean ruble equals 1.5 to 2 dirty ones; see "The 'Black' Millions," *Radio Liberty Research*, p. 3; and V. Maksimov in *Sotsialisticheskaya industriya*, March 25, 1977, p. 4.

45. The extraordinary revelations, such as those of the Lockheed case, are too well known to require listing here, but a few aggregate estimates may be noted. In 1975, "crimes against business"—only one kind of "economic crime"—supposedly amounted to between $23 billion and $40 billion in the United States, and such crimes are believed to be growing rapidly in both number and scope; see *The New York Times* (Sept. 18, 1976), and *U.S. News and World Report* (Feb. 21, 1977), pp. 47-48. The larger figure includes $7 billion of bribes to corporate purchasing agents (*Dun's Review* (New York, March 1977), pp. 76 ff., and letters to the editor in the May and June issues), a mirror image in the American buyers' market of bribes to materials allocators in the Soviet sellers' market. Improprieties at a steel mill construction project in Indiana, the *Wall Street Journal* (June 8, 1976), p. 1, are highly reminiscent of illegalities in the Soviet economy. The American press typically identifies the corruption losses of businesses with losses to the economy. This practice is questionable, however, for many of the crimes involved, as in the Soviet Union, are primarily redistributional and do not necessarily diminish real national wealth or income.

46. Little of this discussion has yet appeared in print; but see Richard Portes, "The Control of Inflation: Lessons from East European Experience," *Economica* (London, May 1977), pp. 109-130. Portes questions the view that repressed inflation is chronic in "centrally planned economies," but gives only passing attention to the black markets.

47. Changes in collective farm market prices (on which there are official data) may not, therefore, be a sufficiently accurate indicator of changes in the aggregate demand-supply balance, as is sometimes assumed. Ideally, reference should also be made to a sample of black-market prices, but these

are very hard for the outside observer to come by. Black-market prices likely to be quoted for their sensational implications (for instance, gold at 12 rubles per gram, as cited in *Sotsialisticheskaya industriya* (Feb. 25, 1977), p. 4) need not be representative in their movements.

48. Our very casual inquiries indicate that (*grosso modo*) in Moscow in the early 1970s the remuneration of *shabashniki* was about three times that for similar labor in the "first" economy, on an hourly basis. While no accuracy is claimed for this figure, it is roughly confirmed, as of 1977, in an article by V. Lipatov in *Pravda* (Aug. 9, 1977), which speaks of daily earnings of up to 30 and 40 "unrighteous" rubles by plumbers servicing private apartments.

49. See Article 17 of the Draft Constitution, *Pravda* (June 4, 1977). Emphasis added.

Part IV
The Underground Economy in
Selected Other Countries

16

Canada's Irregular Economy

Rolf Mirus and
Roger S. Smith

In recent years there has been increasing interest in the size of irregular or underground economic activity. Its existence in Canada has been acknowledged by Revenue Canada (Gourlay 1980) and its implications are by now so well known that they need only briefly be sketched. If, indeed, a sizable and perhaps growing part (whether 5 or 20 percent) of economic activity escapes present measurement methods, then such crucial statistics as the growth rate of real gross national product (GNP), the unemployment rate, and the inflation rate convey potentially seriously biased information to policymakers. Also, since it is very likely that income earned in the irregular economy escapes taxation, there is the issue of fairness of the tax system. A higher tax rate must be applied to regular income in order to raise the revenue needed by government. This concern for fairness is of particular importance in a tax system such as the Canadian, which relies on self-assessment.[1]

In comparison to the United States, where the Internal Revenue Service (IRS) (1979) has undertaken a detailed study of the phenomenon, the evidence to date on Canada's irregular economy is lacking.[2] This chapter is an attempt to quantify the extent of such irregular economic activity in Canada by applying methodological approaches that have been used for the United States. The resulting range of estimates provides a basis for discussion and a gauge of how serious the concern should be in the Canadian context. In addition, information on Canadian results provides a bench-mark for the U.S. estimates and helps identify weaknesses of the methodologies that may further stimulate research on the subject.

To be sure, there is little comfort to be derived from the estimates of the phenomenon in the United States. All studies that have been undertaken in the last four years point to a sizable problem. Gutmann (1977) estimated the irregular economy as 10 percent of the *total* economy for 1976. Feige (1979) found it to be 19.1 percent in 1976, rising to 26.6 percent in 1978. As a result of the publicity attendant on Gutmann's estimates, the Internal Revenue Service (1979) made an effort to arrive at an estimate of income unreported on individual income tax returns. For 1976 the IRS estimates of the sum of

Reprinted with permission from *Canadian Public Policy—Analyse de Politiques* 7-3 (summer 1981):444-453. The authors are indebted to Jim Mahaffey for his research assistance, and to two anonymous referees for helpful suggestions.

unreported legally earned and illegal income ranged from $100 billion to $135 billion, or 5.6-7.4 percent of total economic activity,[3] and do not include income derived from skimming of expense accounts and activities such as barter.[4] Tanzi (1980) concentrated on taxation-induced irregular activity, finding that this part of the irregular economy amounted to 3.3-4.8 percent of total economic activity for 1976. While differing drastically in method, these studies all point to significant and possibly increasing irregular economic activity in the United States.

The Canadian economy is less complex than that of the United States, thus possibly leaving less room for irregular activity. On the other hand, it is characterized by a nominally more progressive income tax in the middle and upper-middle income ranges, and more generous social benefits that might favor irregular activity. Therefore, an a priori judgment for Canada cannot easily be made.

Methodologies

The attempt to measure what is by its nature intended to be unmeasurable creates serious methodological problems. It seems safe to assume that much of the underground economy is cash-based. Illegal activities in particular, such as drug trafficking, prostitution, fencing, and gambling, tend to be on a cash basis. With respect to legal activities, unreported income may derive not only from tips, from work by household and farm help, from independent contracting, but also from barter and covert rental and lending activities.

It is somewhat less cogent to argue that the medium of exchange for this segment of the irregular economy is strictly currency. For example, a check received for irregular activity could be endorsed and used as payment to third parties. The assumption that the underground economy is cash-based when, in fact, checks are occasionally used as well, tends to impart a conservative bias into estimates based on methodologies discussed below.[5] Similarly, failure of the methodologies to impute a value for barter biases the estimate downward.

Gutmann (1977) assumes that (a) currency is used as the medium of exchange in the irregular economy; (b) an appropriate bench-mark period, when such activity was negligible, can be identified; (c) the ratio of currency to demand deposits would have remained constant were it not for growth in the irregular economy; and (d) income produced by a dollar of currency in the irregular economy is the same as that produced by a dollar of currency or demand deposits in the regular economy. By comparing the actual to the base-year currency/demand deposit ratio, Gutmann arrives at his estimates of currency use for irregular economic activity.

The assumption that currency alone is used for irregular transactions results, as we have mentioned, in a conservative estimate. And while the choice of an appropriate bench-mark confers an element of arbitrariness to the effort, it is the last two assumptions that are most subject to question. As Garcia (1978), Garcia and Pak (1979a, 1979b), and Porter, Simpson, and Mauskopf (1979) have shown, the variations in the currency/demand deposit ratio of the United States can be attributed to a decline in demand deposits of firms as new financial techniques, such as repurchase agreements, resulted in fewer demand deposits.[6] So, when an increasing currency ratio is observed, it might well be due to missing demand deposits rather than increased currency holdings, particularly since the currency/GNP ratio has remained relatively stable. One could also question whether the velocity of irregular currency holdings is as large as the income velocity of money in the regular economy. For both reasons, the Gutmann results for the United States may have an upward bias.

In the Canadian context there is also reason to acknowledge a possible decrease in the demand deposit component. In the mid-1970s, the chartered banks began to encourage corporations with a number of regional accounts to centralize them and to invest closing balances overnight. This resulted in a structural shift of the demand for demand deposits and biases upward estimates of the irregular economy based on the methodologies used here. On the other hand, the historically larger currency ratio in Canada—due to proportionately fewer demand deposits, not higher currency per capita— left less room than in the United States for economizing on deposit holdings. In addition, the increased use of credit cards and checks might have been expected to reduce the ratio of currency to GNP. The fact that this did not happen may well be due to growth in the irregular economy, especially if one considers how much credit cards have reduced one's own need to carry cash.

Feige (1979) also relies heavily on currency and demand deposit data, but he believes that information concerning the *volume of transactions* supported by currency and demand deposits will lead to more accurate estimates of the irregular economy. Accordingly, he assumes that in the absence of irregular activity the ratio of the total value of transaction with currency and demand deposits to measured GNP would have remained constant. Since Feige focuses on transactions, his results are independent of the currency/demand deposit ratio, so that he escapes the criticisms directed at Gutmann's approach. On the other hand, Feige's results are sensitive to the way in which the volume of transaction is estimated: he relies on estimates of the number of transactions a unit of currency can physically sustain before wearing out.

Despite the apparent validity of various objections, critics have conceded "that a great part of the increase in currency may be due to illegal activities" (Laurent 1979, p. 6). Similarly, another observer concludes, "The great stock of currency outstanding and its persistent expansion in the face of higher costs of holding currency and the widespread use of currency substitutes (for example, credit cards) certainly supports suspicions of increasing irregular transactions. . . ." and "the persistent expansion in currency outstanding at a time of strong incentives to avoid reporting could indicate that unreported activities have been expanding faster than economic activity generally" (Bowsher 1980, p. 15).

The historical rise in the personal income tax burden may well be a major factor contributing to the rise of the irregular economy, as individuals show themselves more and more disinclined to report taxable income. Tax evasion may therefore be a significant part of the phenomenon under study.

Tanzi's measurement of the irregular economy is based on the idea that, indeed, if currency is used for the vast majority of irregular activities, it should be possible to identify a statistically significant relationship between currency holdings and the personal tax burden. Explaining the ratio of currency to broadly defined money with such variables as the tax burden, the share of wages and salaries in personal income, real per capita income and the interest rate on time deposits, Tanzi estimates what currency holdings would have been with historically low taxation levels. The extra currency holdings attributable to tax evasion are then identified and multiplied by normal $M2$-velocity to obtain his results without having to assume that there was no irregular economy in the base year chosen.[7]

While the Gutmann methodology in particular has been subjected to criticism, evidence from the United Kingdom (Illersix, 1979) and the results of the IRS (1979) study prove consistent with the order of magnitude of the hidden economy estimated for the United States. Moreover, since better methodologies have not yet been developed, reliance here is on the existing ones when studying the phenomenon in Canada.

Canadian Estimates

Occasional evidence of the problem in Canada has surfaced in reports such as the case of false invoice selling in Montreal, and the illegal jewelry trade.[8] Also, infomation circulars of Revenue Canada on "Prosecutions" show an increase in "tax on which convicted" from $2.3 million in 1974 to $7.0 million in 1979, a doubling in real terms, as well as a tripling of cases involved. This suggests that possibly greater awareness of the problem has prompted greater enforcement efforts. Another indication is found in the increase in $50, $100, and $1,000 notes in circulation. Between 1969 and 1979 when GNP grew by 226 percent in current prices, these notes increased by 291, 288, and 641 percent respectively.[9]

To use Gutmann's approach requires the choice of a base year for the currency/demand deposit ratio against which recent developments of this ratio can be contrasted.[10] There is little question that the estimate of the irregular economy will vary with the base period chosen. In Canada, this ratio rose from .33 for 1937-1939 to .53 in 1944, reflecting a sharp war-time increase in the accumulation of currency relative to demand deposits. With controls and rationing off, the ratio diminished gradually to .40 in the late 1950s. After a bulge in 1959-1961 it increased, if unevenly, to over .56 in 1980. For comparability with Gutmann's results, the 1976 currency/demand deposit ratio is contrasted to that of the 1937-1939 base period. This results in an estimate of $2.68 billion in currency attributable to irregular economic activity. The irregular economy can therefore be credited with $31.3 billion, or 14 percent of total economic activity for 1976.[11]

There is also a significant growth trend in the share of the irregular economy which is consistent with the results for the United States. Whatever the imperfections in the methodology, the estimates, if anything, are slightly higher for the Canadian case, possibly reflecting the more generous unemployment insurance provisions and the somewhat higher average level of income and profits taxes in Canada (Perry 1980). Since, however, it is likely that the growth in the estimated size of the irregular economy is related to the effects of inflation on the tax burden, as well as such factors as decline in taxpayer morality, it becomes difficult to engage in U.S.-Canadian comparisons on this score. On the one hand, Canada's tax system is now somewhat indexed against the effects of inflation; on the other, Canadian marginal income tax rates would on average be higher than in the United States.

In order to apply Feige's methodology in the Canadian context, one needs to know the value of total transactions supported by currency and demand deposits. Then a base year GNP must be chosen to determine the ratio of total transactions to GNP that is used as the reference point for later years. Dividing the estimated value of total transactions by this (critically important) ratio gives the estimates of total economic activity. Subtraction of measured GNP leaves an estimate of irregular income.

Data on annual demand deposit transactions are reported by Statistics Canada.[12] To estimate transactions in currency is more problematic. While data on the number of the various notes outstanding exist, one needs to estimate how frequently they turn over on average. With no concrete information available on the lifetime transactions of Canadian notes, we used the more conservative of Feige's two assumptions that a bank note can change hands 125 times before wearing out.[13]

From information on worn-out notes returned to the Bank of Canada for replacement, the normal life of the various notes could be ascertained.[14] For example, $20 bills have an average life of three years. Hence, it is assumed that each supports 125/3 transactions per year. If there are 20 million such bills, then 20 million times $20 times 125/3, or $16.7 billion, is the value of transactions supported by the stock of $20 bills.

Before adding the values of transactions for demand deposits and bills, it is necessary to make an adjustment for strictly financial transactions. Such an adjustment is difficult because the ratio of demand deposit transactions to demand deposits is not available for individual metropolitan areas across Canada, as it is in the United States. And even if it were, determining the share of transactions which are strictly financial in nature is a difficult task. Consequently, it was decided to exclude Calgary, Montreal, and Toronto on the basis of their relatively high level of demand deposit transactions due to financial activity.[15]

With 1939 as the base period, the Feige approach leads to the conclusion that in 1976 21.9 percent of total economic activity in Canada was of the irregular variety (19.1 percent in 1978). No doubt this will strike many as shockingly large, just as Feige's estimates for the irregular economy appeared too high to many observers.

It has already been mentioned that the existence and growth of an irregular economy may well be the result of a disinclination to report taxable income in the face of an increasing real tax rate or a decline in real income growth. Tanzi's approach is designed to shed light on the particular contribution of a rising tax burden to irregular economic activity. Not only has the growth of real disposable income, on a per capita or a per worker basis, slowed down in Canada in recent years; the personal income tax burden would appear to have increased historically since its post-World War II drop (figure 16-1).

Following Tanzi's method, a relationship was specified between the currency/demand deposit ratio and such explanatory variables as the ratio of personal income taxes to personal income net of transfers (T), the share of wages and salaries in personal income (W) and real per capita income from the national accounts (Y).[16]

Since the intent is to determine the order of magnitude of tax-induced currency holdings, rather than a detailed investigation of the currency/demand deposit ratio per se, we rely on ordinary least-squares versions of our estimated regression equations for the period 1936-1977 to predict what the ratio would have been had the tax burden remained at its historical low for the period.[17]

From the currency/demand deposit ratios thus calculated one arrives at currency holdings of $0.9 and $1.4 billion for 1976 that are attributable to a rise in the tax burden since 1936. Multiplying these extra currency holdings by the GNP velocity of M1 for that year gives $9.6 and $14.9 billion as the estimates of the irregular economy. This amounts to 4.8-7.2 percent of total economic activity, or 5.0-7.8 percent of measured GNP. Given the dif-

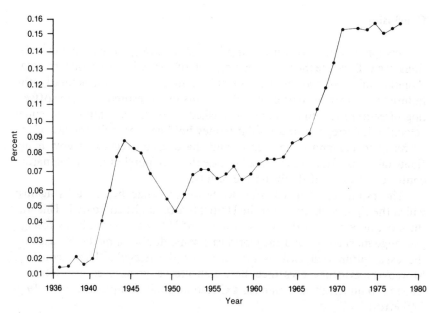

Figure 16-1. The Personal Income Tax Burden in Historical Perspective: Personal Income Taxes (Federal, Provincial, Local) as a Percentage of Personal Income Net of Transfers

ferences in specification, these estimates cannot be compared directly to Tanzi's 3.4-5.1 percent, yet there is similarity. It is noteworthy, perhaps, to observe that the lower estimates from this approach may be the consequence of correcting for the bias in Gutmann's method: the variable Y may have adjusted the currency/demand deposit ratio for shifts in the demand for deposits.[18]

Table 16-1 summarizes the results based on the three approaches to estimating irregular economic activity.

Table 16-1
Estimates of Canada's Irregular Economy for 1976

| Method | Estimate | | Base Year |
	Dollar Amount (billions)	As Percentage of Total Economic Activity	
Gutmann	31.3	14	1937-1939
Feige	53.7	21.9	1939
Tanzi	9.6-14.9	4.8-7.2	1936

Conclusion

To reemphasize the critical assumptions that have gone into the calculations, we will restate them. The assumption of a strictly cash-based irregular economy might be too restrictive, resulting in low estimates. Similarly, the failure to account for barter activities results in low estimates. In the offsetting direction the estimates may be pushed up by the assumption of equal velocities for irregular and regular money holdings. As well, the use of the currency to demand deposit ratio and the decision regarding how many financial transactions to exclude because they are purely financial in nature confer an element of doubt on the results.

The estimates adduced provide, however, some benchmarks against which the figures obtained for the United States can be compared. This was the more necessary, as the widespread use of U.S. currency in black foreign exchange markets around the world cast some doubt on methods based on the assumption that cash is the basis for the irregular U.S. economy. Moreover, evidence presented here indicates a great need for Revenue Canada to undertake and publish a Canadian study comparable to the 1979 IRS effort.

The results, while varying with the approach, indicate an irregular economy of from 5 to 20 percent of *total* economic activity for 1976. In 1981, 5 percent would be around $16 billion, and 20 percent around $80 billion. Even the smallest of these estimates pertaining to only the tax-induced portion of irregular activity is cause for concern.

If there is so much production ignored by our statistical measures, a substantial element of bias may be contained in the reported unemployment rates, price indexes, and GNP, imparting an inflationary bias to economic policy on these statistics.

Personal tax rates in many countries have increased sharply since 1950, and concern has grown about the increasing burden of financing government. Higher marginal tax rates have meant increased incentives to underreport taxable income, with one result being growth in the irregular economy. If, in fact, the connection between marginal tax rates and the irregular economy is a strong one, broadening the tax base and lowering tax rates may be important steps in control of the irregular economy.

Attention has also focused on the many special tax provisions, or tax expenditures, that create inequities in the tax system. Knowledge that others are not paying their share, due either to "perceived" inequities in tax law or awareness of underreporting provides further reason to participate in the irregular economy.

For an income tax system that relies heavily on self-assessment, the size (and growth) of the irregular economy is worrisome. Governments would be well advised to keep attuned to taxpayer attitudes. Do taxpayers believe that the existing income tax system is a fair one? If not, any step that makes the system appear less fair—such as the elimination of indexing—may contribute to increased irregular economic activity. The danger is that taxpayer attitudes may make a self-assessment system obsolete. The result would be sharply increased administrative and enforcement costs. Stiffer penalties for those who evade taxes may also be needed. The relatively light penalties for those who knowingly "steal" from the government by evading taxes has long been a source of debate. A large and growing irregular economy may also lead to a need to place greater reliance on indirect taxes.

Whatever the reasons for the irregular economy's existence, be it a general decline in taxpayer morality, a loss of faith in the fairness of the tax system, or the like, the rough evidence presented in this paper suggests cause for doing much further detailed analysis of the irregular economy in Canada.

Notes

1. As early as 1974 the Minister of National Revenue was observing "There are indications that the average wage earner feels cheated: that the government is overtaxing *him* rather than socking it to the rich and powerful. Somehow, he feels *others* must be ripping off the system, and he is being made to pay the price." The Honourable Robert Stanbury, "It's Self-Assessment Time", *Taxes—The Tax Magazine* (March, 1974):162.

2. Sherbaniuk (1977, p. 27) reported that he "had been given to understand that Revenue Canada has underway a project to measure the tax "gaps" on the basis of controlled statistical samples." Revenue Canada has yet to make the results of any such studies known to the public, although the Director General for compliance policy has acknowledged the problem (Gourlay 1980).

3. Evidence for the United Kingdom is of the same order of magnitude: "Earnings which evade tax might be as much as £10 billion a year" (Illersic 1979, p. 693). This figure is equivalent to approximately 7.5 percent of GNP or 7 percent of *total* economic activity.

4. Smith (1980) has put the figure as high as $300 billion.

5. We are grateful to an anonymous referee for this point.

6. Other structural changes include telephone and automatic transfer between demand and savings deposits and NOW (negotiated order of withdrawal) accounts.

7. Only those of Tanzi's results that are based on the historically low taxation level have been reported. Those based on zero taxation appear unreasonably large to us.

8. The *Montreal Gazette* (February 15, 1977) reported on a scheme where 48 companies were found to be selling false invoices "More than 275

concerns are known to have bought fictitious invoices from the 48 vendors, which trade under 65 different company names. The practice involved at least $50 million in false transactions on which income taxes of about $25 million would normally have been paid, according to a government source" (Sherbaniuk 1977). The *Financial Times of Canada* (June 9, 1980) reported that the illegal jewelry trade may exceed the $340 million in legitimate retail sales. The primary cause is seen to be the incentive to smuggling caused by high Canadian excise taxes.

9. These data were provided by the Bank of Canada.

10. Data on currency and demand deposits are from the Bank of Canada's *Statistical Survey, Annual Supplements* (various issues) and the Bank of Canada *Review*.

11. In 1976 the currency ratio was large relative to both 1975 and 1977. Using the 1978 currency ratio gives $32.9 billion, or 12.4 percent as the share of irregular in *total* 1978 economic activity. With 1950-1952 as the base period, somewhat lower estimates of 8.4 percent and 6.5 percent respectively, result for 1976 and 1978.

12. Demand deposit transaction data are from various issues of the *Canada Yearbook* and from Statistics Canada, *Cheques Cashed in Clearing Centres* (various issues).

13. The alternative assumption, based on improved quality of the paper used for bank notes, is 225. This is the estimate that leads to the large figures for the U.S. irregular economy reported earlier.

14. These ranged from slightly over one year for $1, $2, and $5 notes to over nine years for $100 notes, and eighteen years for $1,000 notes.

15. While this may strike readers as arbitrary, if no adjustment is made for financial centers, the irregular economy would be estimated as $200 billion for 1978, as a result of a continually increasing ratio of transactions to GNP.

16. Tanzi used the ratio of currency to $M2$. For consistency with Gutmann's and Feige's approaches, we use the currency/demand deposit ratio. Also, there are difficulties of getting a good proxy variable for the interest rate on Canadian savings deposits. Data for T, W, and Y are taken from the Statistics Canada *Cansim* file.

17. The equations used are (t-value in parentheses)

(a) $\ln (C/DD) = .064 \ln T - 1.335 \ln W + .283 \ln Y$
$\qquad\qquad\quad (2.6) \qquad\quad (-7.0) \qquad\quad (11.2)$
$\quad R^2 = .76 \ DW = 1.36$

(b) $\ln (C/DD) = -.213 + .105 \ln T - 1.199 \ln W + .196 \ln Y$
$\qquad\qquad\qquad\qquad\quad (2.2) \qquad\quad (-5.2) \qquad\quad (2.2)$
$\quad R^2 = .76 \ DW = 1.35$

The availability of recent tax data to construct T limits the period of observation. Use of these equations as outlined requires the assumption that the other regression coefficients remain unchanged.

18. It is evident from existing empirical work that a satisfactory explanation of the movements of the currency/demand deposit ratio requires further research.

References

Bank of Canada (1972). "The Note Issue." *Review*, June.

Bowsher, Norman N. (1980). "The Demand for Currency: Is the Underground Economy Undermining Monetary Policy?" *Federal Reserve Bank of St. Louis Review* 62 (January), no. 1, pp. 11-17.

Feige, Edgar L. (1979). "How Big Is the Irregular Economy?" *Challenge*, November-December, pp. 5-13.

Financial Times of Canada (1980). June 9, p. 22.

Garcia, Gillian (1978). "The Currency Ratio and the Subterranean Economy." *Financial Analysts Journal*, November-December, pp. 64-66.

Garcia, Gillian and Pak, Simon (1979a). "Some Clues in the Case of the Missing Money." *American Economic Review* 69 (May):330-334.

Garcia, Gillian and Pak, Simon (1979b). "The Ratio of Currency to Demand Deposits in the United States." *The Journal of Finance* 34 (June):703-715.

Gourlay, James L. (1980). "Tax Abuse—A View from Revenue Canada." *Canadian Taxation* (Summer 1980):82-87.

Gutmann, Peter M. (1977). "The Subterranean Economy." *Financial Analysts Journal*, November-December, pp. 26-28.

Gutmann, Peter M. (1978). "Professor Gutmann Replies." *Financial Analysts Journal*, November-December, pp. 67-69.

Gutmann, Peter M. (1979). "Statistical Illusions, Mistaken Policies." *Challenge*, November-December, pp. 14-17.

Illersic, A.R. (1979). "Tax Evasion in the United Kingdom." *Canadian Tax Journal* 27 (November-December):693-699.

Internal Revenue Service. (1979). *Estimates of Income Unreported on Individual Income Tax Returns*. Publication 1104, Washington, D.C.: Government Printing Office (September):9-79.

Laurent, Robert D. (1979). "Currency and the Subterranean Economy." *Economic Perspectives*. Federal Reserve Bank of Chicago, March-April, pp. 3-6.

Perry, David B. (1980). "Fiscal Figures: International Tax Comparisons." *Canadian Tax Journal* 28 (January-February):89-93.

Porter, R. D.; Simpson, T.D.; and Mauskopf, E. (1979). "Financial Innovation and Monetary Aggregates." *Brookings Papers on Economic Activity* 1, pp. 213-229.

Sherbaniuk, D.J. (1977). "Report of the Director of the Thirty-First Annual Meeting of the Canadian Tax Foundation." Toronto: Canadian Tax Foundation, April 12.

Smith, Lee (1980). "The $50 Billion That the IRS Isn't Collecting." *Fortune*, March 10.

Stanbury, R. (1974). "It's Self-Assessment Time." *Taxes—The Tax Magazine* 53 (March):159-168.

Tanzi, Vito (1980). "Underground Economy and Tax Evasion in the United States: Estimates and Implications." *Banca Nazionale del Lavoro Quarterly Review*. 135 (December), pp. 427-453. Reprinted as chapter 4 of this volume.

17 Illegal Trade Transactions and the Underground Economy of Colombia

Roberto Junguito and
Carlos Caballero

Colombia, a country traditionally known as a coffee commodity oriented economy, has recently acquired a reputation as the foremost world exporter of drugs. Figures published in U.S. newspapers and popular magazine articles talk of tens of billions of dollars of drug exports, without much supporting evidence. This chapter analyzes the illegal trade transactions of Colombia and their repercussion on the domestic economy, mainly through the capital market. It sets more realistic limits to the possible range of the drug trade and presents estimates of the illegal flows of more traditional exports and imports. It also discusses the subtle ways through which the illegal foreign exchange proceeds are transformed to local currency in a foreign exchange controlled economy.

International Trade and the Black Foreign-Exchange Market

Analyses of export patterns in countries of the same level of development as Colombia suggest that exports should represent around 23 percent of gross domestic product (GDP)[1] However, according to the registered statistics, the proportion in Colombia has only been around 17 percent. Such disparity between the international patterns and the Colombian performance, together with the more casual information of underground trade flows, has led us to formulate a quantitative hypothesis as to the volume of illegal exports. Such exports take the form of traditional agricultural commodities and manufactured goods, as well as of drugs such as marihuana and cocaine.

Illegal Exports of Traditional Products

What are the objective conditions for the presence of vast unregistered traditional export in Colombia? The incentive to export illegally arises from differentials between international and domestic prices in the various product categories. In the case of coffee this difference is the result of internally controlled prices for the producer at levels far below the international prices and of the presence of a complex combination of taxes and fiscal charges to absorb such differential.[2] The price differential in the case of other agricultural and industrial products is due not to the export taxes but to the system of prior authorization to export and domestic price controls which provoke such differentials. Therefore, Colombia's policies have provided incentives to export illegally.

Table 17-1 summarizes the estimates of the volume and value of illegal exports of the more traditional agricultural and manufactured products. Column 1 presents the Banco de la República estimates of illegal coffee exports, and columns 2 and 3 the authors' estimates.[3] For the period 1956-1965 the volume figures correspond to statistics taken from reports of the U.S. Embassy in Bogotá, while the 1966-1975 data was calculated as the difference between total production estimates by the U.S. Department of Agriculture and those of the National Coffee Federation records, which explicitly exclude contraband; the 1976 and 1977 figures are the Federation's own estimates.[4]

Although the sources of information differ in magnitudes, it is obvious that incentives to export illegally arise in those periods when the national-international price differential increases, and during the periods when the international coffee agreement on quotas has not been operating and as a consequence, when there has not been a strict control of the geographical origin of the coffee in the market. For this reason periods like 1975-1978 could have been more propitious for coffee contraband since the agreement on quotas was suspended in 1973 and since from 1970 on the price differential increased substantially.[5,6]

The case of sugar contraband is again the result of increasing international prices coupled with controlled domestic prices and export prohibitions and licenses. It has been calculated that illegal sugar exports increased from 1968 on and continued until 1976.[7] In the following two years the narrowing of the price differential discouraged illegal exports; indeed, in 1978, the international price (US $.07 per pound) was below that established for domestic consumption.[8]

The illegal exporting of live cattle to Venezuela seems also to have been significant and to have shown an increase. This can be seen in table 17-1, which shows both Banco de la República estimates of the value of illegal exports and its estimate of the number of head of cattle exported in this manner.[9]

Cement has been another illegally exported product. An analysis of published figures indicates that illegal exports were especially high in 1976. The cement case is similar to that of sugar in the sense that both are products subject to export licenses and to domestic price controls.

Table 17-1
Volume and Value of Illegal Exports of Traditional Products
(millions of current U.S. dollars)

	Coffee			Cattle		Other Items		Total	
	Value		Volume	Volume					
Year	Central Bank (1)	Authors' Estimates (2)	(Thousands of 60-kilo bags) (3)	(Thousands of heads) (4)	Value (5)	Authors' Estimates (6)	Central Bank (7)	Authors' Estimates (8)	Central Bank (9)
1956	54.6	52.6	100	90.0	6.0	15.0	15.0	73.6	70.6
1957	18.8	26.5	300	100.0	7.2	52.8	52.8	86.5	78.8
1958	11.4	16.1	250	187.0	14.4	40.6	40.7	71.1	66.5
1959	14.0	11.5	200	167.0	14.4	40.6	40.6	66.5	69.0
1960	10.0	10.9	200	164.0	14.4	30.6	30.6	55.9	55.0
1961	10.0	8.5	150	106.0	8.5	16.5	16.5	33.5	35.0
1962	10.0	2.3	50	125.0	8.5	16.5	16.5	27.3	35.0
1963	10.0	5.0	100	121.0	9.0	6.0	6.0	20.0	25.0
1964	10.0	22.2	350	121.0	13.0	13.0	13.0	47.2	35.0
1965	28.0	22.2	360	67.0	8.0	4.0	4.0	34.2	40.0
1966	29.5	5.4	100	67.0	8.0	5.0	5.0	18.4	42.5
1967	15.0	7.8	150	204.0	25.0	21.4	3.0	54.2	43.0
1968	10.1	7.2	150	208.0	22.7	14.6	7.6	44.5	40.4
1969	9.9	7.7	150	215.0	22.8	17.2	10.2	47.7	42.9
1970	5.8	6.2	100	270.0	32.5	18.1	21.1	56.8	59.4
1971	4.4	11.0	200	233.0	34.0	31.2	24.3	76.2	62.7
1972	4.2	20.1	300	173.0	29.4	19.2	35.1	91.6	68.7
1973	3.5	30.4	500	170.0	43.5	59.1	43.1	133.0	90.1
1974	3.3	39.4	500	175.0	53.4	90.7	65.4	183.5	122.1
1975	31.0	54.6	700	181.0	58.0	120.8	106.8	233.4	195.9
1976	184.0	145.7	1000	210.0	61.0	181.0	158.0	387.7	403.0
1977	135.0	131.6	500	70.0	20.0	186.6	199.0	338.2	254.0

Sources and Methods:

Col. 1: Banco de la República.

Col. 2: Col. 3 × Average export price of Colombian coffee.

Col. 3: 1956-1965: U.S. Embassy; 1966-1975: Test estimates; 1976-1977: Federation of Coffee Growers.

Col. 4 and Col. 5: Banco de la República.

Col. 6: 1956-1966: Banco de la República, as appears in col. 7; 1967-1977: Banco de la República Col. 7 + sugar and cement illegal exports.

Col. 7: Banco de la República.

Col. 8: Col. 2 + Col. 5 + Col. 6.

Col. 9: Col. 1 + Col. 5 + Col. 7.

In addition to the traditional products mentioned, it is estimated that Colombia annually exports some other manufactured goods whose composition changes from year to year depending on the economic circumstances. Most of these goods are traded through unregistered border transactions. The estimate of their value by Banco de la República, using records of arrivals of tourists to Colombia in the border areas, gives a figure around US $100 million per year. The column "others" summarizes the heterogeneous grouping, while the last columns show the Banco de la República and the authors' estimates of the total flow of illegal exports of the main traditional products; that is, excluding marihuana and cocaine.

Illegal Exports of Marihuana and Cocaine

Since the mid-1970s both the Colombian and foreign press—and Colombians in general—have been speculating on the size of both the production and exports of marihuana as well as the processing and sale of cocaine.[10] However, little academic analysis has been done on this subject. In this section we will review the estimates of production and inflow of foreign exchange from these two activities.

Marihuana. There is no reliable measure of the number of hectares planted with marihuana in Colombia. It is known that in some regions the plant grows wild and that its cultivation, begun in small plots of land towards the end of the 1960s, has been increasing. It is also known that the main productive region is the Guajira and parts of the Sierra Nevada de Santa Marta,[11] although the area cultivated in the eastern plains of the country could also be increasing.

The most publicized estimate of marihuana cultivated hectarage is that given in a report by Procuraduriá General de la Nación just after the Turbay Ayala administration took office.[12] This report, quoted repeatedly by both national and foreign publications, concludes that on the Atlantic coast there are 70,000 hectares planted with marihuana. Other sources, including the U.S. Embassy, have calculated the number of hectares to be around 30,000.[13]

In order to have an idea of the magnitudes implicit in the above figures it is useful to compare them with other agricultural products' acreages. An area of 70,000 hectares in marihuana would be greater than that dedicated individually to sesame, banana, cacao, barley, soya, tobacco, and wheat, and less than that planted with coffee, cotton, rice, sugar cane, and corn.

According to reliable U.S. Embassy information, productivity per hectare in the cultivation of marihuana could be on the order of 1,000 pounds per year (discounting drying and pressing), or a bit less than half a ton. This estimate differs from that of other sources which place productivity between 1.5 and 2 tons per hectare.[14] Once again, in comparing marihuana productivity with that of other products, it is found that productivity per hectare would lie between that of the traditional variety of coffee and that of tobacco (1.5 tons/hectare-year). Thus, if it is assumed that the cultivated surface of 40,000 hectares and an average productivity of one-half ton per hectare, annual production would amount to 20,000 tons, a figure very different from the 100,000 tons cited in foreign articles.

In conclusion, the marihuana-cultivated area could oscillate within a range of 30,000 and 70,000 hectares. It is more likely that the real size is close to 40,000 hectares. On the other hand, the volume produced would range theoretically between 20,000 and 60,000 tons—again, the lower level seems the more likely estimate.

Choosing the correct prices is crucial in determining the total income generated by the production and trade of marihuana. Prices at different stages in the selling process must be analyzed to determine the distribution of margins and to avoid the common error in all foreign publications of overestimating the value of the foreign exchange that flows to Colombia. There are great differences between the price received by the producer; those realized by the intermediary, who organizes the exporting (by plane or ship) and the wholesale and retail prices in the United States, as is the norm in all commodity exports.

The many available sources of information in 1978 indicates that a ton of marihuana in a Colombian port was being priced at one million pesos. The Procuraduría's report for the same year fixed the price at $960,000 per ton. Such a price would indicate, at the then going exchange rate of $40 per dollar, that a pound in a Colombian port had been selling at US $12.50, a figure which coincides with that provided by the U.S. Embassy in Colombia.[15] Out of that total, the producer would get a price that varied between US $4 and US $5, an estimate used by official U.S. bodies. As to U.S. mainland prices, the U.S. Embassy estimated a wholesale price of US $100 per pound; since one pound of marihuana makes 250 marihuana cigarettes, sold at US $2 each, the most likely retail price was then about US $500 per pound.

Table 17-2 estimates the proportion of the gross income appropriated by each of the various agents engaged in the marihuana production and distribution process. Two alternatives for area cultivated are shown: one of 70,000 hectares and the other of 40,000 hectares. Also included in the estimates is a 20 percent probability of confiscation—that is, for every 100 pounds produced in Colombia, only 80 pounds reach the United States.[16] According to U.S. Embassy information, one out of every ten shipments of marihuana is detained, and more marihuana has been confiscated in Colombia than in the United States.[17] Table 17-2 shows that Colombia's share

Table 17-2
The Marihuana Economy: Gross Incomes Appropriated by Different Agents

Agent	Price per U.S. pound[a] (US$)	Alternative 1	Percentage	Alternative 2	Percentage
Producer	4.00	280	1.0	160	1.0
Salaries[b]		32		23	
Inputs		42		24	
Profits and rents from land		206		113	
Intermediaries to Colombian ports	12.50	476	1.7	272	1.7
U.S. wholesaler	100.00	4.900	17.5	2.800	17.5
U.S. retailer	500.0	22.400	79.8	12.800	79.8
Total income		28.056	100.0	16.032	100.0
Colombia's share		756	2.7	432	2.7

Method:
Alternative 1: 70,000 hectares of cultivation with a production of 70,000 million U.S. pound per year.
Alternative 2: 40,000 hectares of cultivation with a production of 40,000 million U.S. pound per year.
[a]454 grams.
[b]Assuming one man-year per two hectares and a daily wage of $100.

of the total income from the production and sale of marihuana is only 2.7 percent, and that the remaining 97.3 percent is appropriated by intermediaries, mainly in the United States. This 2.7 percent share would represent a figure between US $432 million and US $756 million, depending on the size of the cultivated area. A figure closer to US $500 million would probably be accurate if the cultivated area and productivity estimates (obtained previously) are taken into account.

It is interesting to note that, according to table 17-2, the contribution of this subsector of Colombian agriculture to the gross agricultural product would amount to US $130 million or 3.2 percent of domestic agricultural production in 1976.[18] Similarly, if it is assumed that the activity of the intermediaries to Colombian ports constitutes value added from the commercial sector, its participation in the gross commercial product (net of costs; input, transport, and the like) amounted to 10 percent of the sector's output in 1976.[19] Consequently, marihuana's share in GDP could be estimated, in 1976 prices, to amount to 2.7 percent.

Cocaine. It is well known that Colombia's role in the cocaine business is processing and distribution, not production. Recently it has been said that Colombians are involved in the distribution of the drug in the United States.[20]

To calculate the quantities of raw materials entering and final output leaving Colombia annually, it is necessary to consider estimated consumption in the United States and to use the available figures on the share of exports from Colombia in the total American market. According to the U.S. Embassy in Colombia, between 15 and 20 tons of cocaine are consumed annually in the United States; of this total, around 70 percent to 90 percent comes from Colombia. Thus, if it is assumed that the 1978 U.S. market was 17 tons, an estimate of the amount processed in Colombia would have been 14 tons, or 80 percent of cocaine consumption in the United States. These 14 tons enter the country as "base," namely, after having been transformed from "leaves" into "paste" and then into "base." Introducing cocaine into Colombia in the form of "paste" increases its volume and the probability of seizure, so a preferred option is to introduce it after having processed it one stage further. Thus, the last processing stage takes place in Colombia, when the cocaine is turned into "powder."

Press reports give very different price quotations. For example, an article reproduced in *El Tiempo* mentioned US $4,000 as the price of one kilo of 90 percent pure cocaine sold in Bogotá and US $40,000 when sold in New York. A month later *El Espectador* reported that a kilo sold for approximately US $13,000 to US $15,000 in Bogotá and had a wholesale price of approximately US $50,000 to US $55,000 in New York.[21]

In 1978, after discussions with U.S. authorities, we developed the following price estimates for cocaine, according to its stage of purity (prices are in U.S. dollars per kilo): paste, $4,000-$5,000; base, $8,000-$10,000; powder, $20,000; U.S. wholesale, $50,000; U.S. retail, $500,000.

The estimate of the foreign exchange inflow into Colombia originating from the illegal export of cocaine "powder" is relatively simple to determine if it is assumed that the 14 processed and exported tons are bought at "base" price and then sold at a price corresponding to one stage higher in purity (powder), given a nill probability of seizure. If a buying price of US $9,000 per kilo and a selling price of US $20,000 are chosen, the inflow of dollars in 1978 could have not been greater than US $154 million.

The figure of US $154 million certainly is different from the sensationalist reports which affirm that "cocaine is as vital to the Colombian economy as is coffee." Moreover, the differences in prices depending on stage of processing is so pronounced that while US $154 million remain in Colombia, wholesale dealers in the United States get US $420 million (three times as much) and the retail dealers get more than US $5,000 million (thirty times as much).

The value added in Colombia would be slightly below that of the net inflow of foreign exchange since it has to subtract a cost of other inputs of US $1,000 per kilo, or a total of US $14 million. Value added would then be US $140 million. At 1978 prices this would represent 4.2 percent of the gross manufacturing product of Colombia and 0.9 percent of GDP.

A series constructed from the *El Tiempo* archives show that confiscations in the last eight years amounted to 2.5 tons. The customs information for the thirty-four months between January 1976 and October 1978 shows a total seizure of half a ton. Again the confiscations seem low, considering that 14 tons are processed every year. The year showing the largest amount of confiscations was 1977 when apparently half a ton was seized.

Export Underinvoicing and Overinvoicing

In addition to illegal exports, historically Colombia has registered cases of both under- and overinvoicing of exports. The former seek to keep accrued foreign exchange outside the economy; the latter seek to obtain benefits in the form of qualifying for an export subsidy or of "legalizing" the conversion of illegally generated foreign exchange into pesos; the alternatives are to leave it outside the country as "Colombian assets abroad," or sell it on the black exchange market at very unfavorable rates.

Conditions favorable to "underinvoicing" arise when the country goes through a balance of payments crisis—with strict controls on the possession or taking out of foreign exchange—and when, as a consequence, there are substantial differences between the black market and the official exchange rates.[22] As can be seen from table 17-3, a typical period for such underinvoicing was between 1967 and 1970, because not only was there a system of foreign exchange control, but also, as a result, there were substantial differences between the black and official exchanges rates.[23]

There is evidence, at least for 1970, that underinvoicing of exports was taking place. A recent study compared the figures of various countries' importation of goods coming from Colombia with Colombian exports statistics, finding that, for the whole group of OECD countries, Colombia was "underinvoicing" its exports by 14 percent, while those sent to the United States and Canada were underinvoiced by 9 percent.[24] This phenomenon was identified not only in Colombia, but also in all those countries showing a marked difference between the black and official exchange rates.[25]

On the other hand, conditions favorable to overinvoicing arise when it becomes profitable to deliver a greater volume of dollars to the Banco de la República than the real value of the exports, for this higher volume of foreign exchange permits the generation of more pesos (owing to exchange rate and the government tax-exempt export subsidy, CAT). Thus it becomes better to bring the foreign exchange to the country than to acquire it in the black foreign exchange market. As table 17-3 illustrates, this incentive has appeared since 1971. Between 1971 and 1974 the CAT was 15 percent of the value exported while the differential between the official and black exchange rate was below this percentage. Consequently, it was profitable to overinvoice. In the 1975-1978 period it was still profitable to overinvoice, even though the CAT had been reduced for some export goods, because the black exchange rate was below the official exchange rate. In the last few years the incentive to overinvoice exports of both goods and services has arisen from the necessity of, and wish to, convert into pesos the international reserves generated by illegal commerce as well as that external capital which aims to enter the country due to the relative profitability of the Colombian capital market.[26]

It is relatively easy to demonstrate overinvoicing in more recent years. On the one hand, in 1972/73 there were verified cases of overinvoicing in emerald exports, whose total value was estimated at close to US $90 million.[27] This overinvoicing is made evident when trends of export "registrations" in those years are analyzed. Emerald exports were US $5.9 million in 1971, US $43.8 million in 1972 and US $49.0 million in 1973, coming down again in 1974 to US $6.3 million.[28] A similar analysis could be used for identifying atypical export registration of the other goods during those years.

However, it is the overinvoicing of services, especially tourism, which has acquired the biggest proportions. Banco de la República analyses of the entry of tourists into Colombia and the normal spending they do in the

Table 17-3
Official and Black U.S. Dollar Exchange Rates
(pesos per dollar)

Year	Quarter	Official Dollar Rate	Black Dollar Rate	Black Rate to Official Rate
1967	1	13.5	18.0	33.3%
	2	14.5	17.3	19.3
	3	15.3	17.5	14.4
	4	15.8	17.8	12.7
	average	14.7	17.7	20.4
1968	1	16.0	17.3	8.1
	2	16.3	17.3	6.1
	3	16.6	17.1	3.0
	4	16.9	17.2	1.8
	average	16.4	17.2	4.9
1969	1	17.0	17.8	4.7
	2	17.2	19.0	10.5
	3	17.6	19.2	9.1
	4	17.7	19.4	9.6
	average	17.4	18.9	8.6
1970	1	18.0	20.0	11.1
	2	18.3	20.9	14.2
	3	18.6	21.6	16.1
	4	19.0	23.2	22.1
	average	18.5	21.4	15.7
1971	average	20.0	21.8	9.0
1972	average	21.9	23.0	5.0
1973	average	23.6	24.9	5.5
1974	1	25.3	26.7	5.5
	2	25.6	27.8	8.6
	3	26.1	27.0	3.4
	4	27.9	28.5	2.1
	average	26.1	27.5	5.4
1975	1	28.5	28.7	-2.7
	2	30.6	30.1	-1.6
	3	31.7	31.2	-1.6
	4	32.6	32.1	-1.5
	average	30.9	30.5	-1.3
1976	1	33.6	33.1	-1.5
	2	34.5	34.1	-1.2
	3	35.2	34.8	-1.1
	4	36.0	35.4	-1.7
	average	34.7	34.3	-1.2

Table 17-3 *(continued)*

Year	Quarter	Official Dollar Rate	Black Dollar Rate	Black Rate to Official Rate
1977	1	36.1	35.1	−2.8%
	2	36.5	34.9	−4.4
	3	36.7	33.7	−8.1
	4	37.5	34.5	−8.0
	average	36.8	34.8	−5.4
1978	1	38.2	35.7	−6.5
	2	38.7	36.2	−6.5
	3	39.6	37.4	−5.6
	4	40.0	37.4	−6.5
	average	39.2	36.7	−6.4

Source: The official exchange rate was taken from various publications of *Revista del Banco de la República*. The black market exchange rate of 1967-1970 was taken from Roberto Junguito and Juan C. Jaramillo, "Determinantes Económicos del Comportamiento Bursátil Colombiano," *Primer Simposio del Mercado de Capitales,* Banco de la República. The 1971-1973 figures were taken from F. Hung and A. Villamizar, "Indice del Poder Adquisitivo de Bolívar en Colombia," *Revista del Banco de la República,* Dec. 1977. The 1974-1978 figures were taken from unpublished data from Banco de la República.

country—especially in the border areas—make possible the spotting of potential differences between what is "registered" as tourism and what can effectively be attributed to it.

Table 17-4 shows estimates of potential overinvoicing of services and tourism. Columns 1, 2 and 3 indicate, as could be expected, that toward the end of the 1960s and the beginning of the 1970s tourism registrations were nil despite the entry of tourists at the borders. So one could conclude that during those years tourists did not "sell" foreign exchange on the official market. This was the period of the underinvoicing of exports and tourism entries.

Since then, and particularly in the period 1976-1978, the opposite situation obtained. The income registered under tourism surpassed the normal spending done on the borders in quantities almost double the amount calculated as total entries under tourism (a figure which itself seems high). The conclusion is that overinvoicing of tourism has been one of the ways through which it has been possible to convert into pesos at least part of the "surplus" of foreign exchange that results from the difference between the illegal export produce and external inflows of capital, and the foreign exchange needs for illegal imports.

It is also possible that in the last few years other sources of overinvoicing took place, through other items of the exchange balance and even through registration of minor exports. This could be so since one of the

Table 17-4
Services and Tourism Exports
(millions of dollars)

| Year | Registered Exports | | Real Apparent Exports | | Overinvoicing | |
	Tourism (travel)	Services	Tourism (travel)	Services	Tourism (travel)	Services
1967	0	171.3	46.0	156.0	− 46.0	− 15.3
1968	0	123.4	45.0	185.0	− 45.0	− 61.6
1969	0	125.0	45.0	218.0	− 45.0	− 93.0
1970	0	129.4	50.0	246.0	− 50.0	− 116.6
1971	0	130.0	61.0	244.0	− 61.0	− 114.0
1972	0	147.1	59.0	248.0	− 59.0	− 100.0
1973	0	232.6	72.0	338.0	− 72.0	− 105.4
1974	48.1	213.0	105.0	500.0	− 57.0	− 287.0
1975	108.8	391.5	141.0	540.0	− 32.0	− 148.5
1976	254.2	772.9	175.0	692.0	79.2	80.9
1977	436.6	841.2	241.0	755.0	195.6	86.2

Source and Method:

Columns 1 and 2: Banco de la República, Balanza Cambiaria, 1967-1977. Mimeographed.

Columns 3 and 4: Banco de la República, Balanza de Pagos de Colombia. The 1967-1971 figures were taken from the Annual Report of the Manager to the Board of Directors, 1970-1971, Second Part. 1972-1977, mimeographed. The group of services includes freight and insurance, other transport, travel, foreign capital credits, and government services not included in "other losses" and "other services."

Column 5 = Column 3 − Column 1.

Column 6 = Column 4 − Column 2.

most surprising, and apparently satisfactory, results of the last few years has been the fact that minor exports have not suffered much deterioration even after the implementation of a discouraging real effective exchange rate policy.[29] Such a result is contradictory to the conclusions of a goodly number of econometric studies done in Colombia which confirm not only the close link between the behavior of minor exports and the real effective rate of exchange but also the fact that changes in the effective rate lead to adjustments in export activity in less than a year.[30] Even though recent explanations have been given on the causes of the success of exports despite the behavior of the effective rate of exchange doubts remain as to the reasons for the high relative export registrations in those years.[31]

Illegal Imports

Illegal imports are the consequence of differences between domestic and international prices caused by tariffs, other import duties, and domestic sales taxes, and by import prohibitions and controls.[32]

Import contraband has existed for many years. Unregistered imports that are part of the other economy are mostly cigarettes, liquor, household appliances, cosmetics, toys, crystal, canned goods, fabrics, and clothing. These goods are sold on the streets, in the institutionalized market shops and in the "San Andresitos" or contraband zones in the different cities of Colombia. In addition to this institutionalized contraband it has also been common practice to illegally import motor vehicles.

Unfortunately, although the types of illegally imported goods have been identified and the location of the main distribution centers is known, neither Banco de la República or any other official entity has followed closely the volume and value trends of contraband goods. Consequently, the figures available on "illegal imports" and "unregistered imports" are only approximations.

Table 17-5 summarizes the different estimates. These reflect largely the value of border commerce and may consequently underestimate the total value of illegal imports. Also shown is the value of imported ships not

Table 17-5
Value of Illegal and Unregistered Imports 1957-1977
(millions of dollars)

Year	Illegal Imports	Imports Not Registered Flota Mercante	Total	Illegal Imports to Total Imports (percentage)
1957	20	5	25	4
1958	20	6	26	5
1959	20	2	22	5
1960	20	3	23	4
1961	20	3	23	4
1962	51	0	51	10
1963	40	0	40	8
1964	50	7	57	9
1965	30	7	37	7
1966	25	19	44	4
1967	29	4	33	6
1968	43	0	43	10
1969	47	0	47	10
1970	56	0	56	10
1071	57	27	86	9
1972	56	36	92	8
1973	64	0	64	9
1974	80	0	80	8
1975	80	0	80	6
1976	88	32	120	5
1977	164	0	164	9

Source: 1957-1971: Carlos Díaz-Alejandro, *Foreign Trade Regimes and Economic Development in Colombia* (New York: Colombia University Press, 1976): Tables 3-5; 1972-1977: Banco de la Republica.

registered by the Flota Mercante Grancolombiana (a Colombian official merchant line that has sought to escape import duties). As the last column shows, illegal imports as a proportion of total registered imports fluctuated between 5 percent and 10 percent between 1957 and 1977. They were proportionally higher in periods of greater foreign exchange restrictions (the 1960s) than in "bonanza" periods in which the freedom to import was greater (the late 1950s and the late 1970s).

It should be noted that since 1972 a process of liberalizing imports has taken place, characterized by the formal elimination of forbidden imports lists, by the transfer of imports under "previous" license to the category of free imports, and by tariff reductions.[33] Given this, the decrease in the percentage in the last column seems logical and the Banco de la República figure for illegal imports in 1977, of US $164 million, is surprising. When these imports reached only between US $80 million and US $100 million, the difference would correspond to foreign exchange inflows not compensated by outflows by way of imports, so that the category of errors and omissions in the balance of payments would be higher.[34]

There are no estimates available on the composition of illegal imports. However, one way of appreciating their relative importance is through the frequency of confiscation of the products imported. An analysis made by Dirección General de Aduanas (Customs Administration) on confiscations between 1976 and 1978 indicates that the products confiscated most frequently were vehicles and household appliances. In second place were cigarettes, followed by liquor. The products confiscated least frequently were cosmetics, toys, perfumes, canned goods, and costume jewelry.[35]

Over- and Underinvoicing of Imports

Import overinvoicing, or the registration of import costs higher than the real ones, has the main aim of taking out foreign exchange from the country of destination of those imports. This can be stimulated by a situation where, for example, strict controls exist on the remittance of foreign exchange (profits and royalties) by foreign investors. This way of taking out foreign exchange illegally could be more profitable to the firms than keeping these funds frozen in local currency in the country or buying the foreign exchange on the black market.

A series of comparative studies of international and domestic prices of raw materials imported by foreign firms makes it possible to identify various cases of overinvoicing in Colombia during the 1960s. The most outstanding case was that of the pharmaceutical industry, where overinvoicing of up to 120 percent was detected.[36]

Analyses of overinvoicing in the importation of goods and capital equipment have been done for other countries. This type of operation takes place when the additional income obtained from selling foreign currency on the black market is higher than the additional cost of tariffs and taxes incurred by overinvoicing.[37] It is likely that this type of overinvoicing was widespread in Colombia during the 1960s,[38] possibly making an inefficient use of resources as it favored capital-intensive techniques and activities and encouraged underutilization of capital so evident then in Colombia.[39,40]

To sum up, the overinvoicing of imports is a mechanism that induces the taking out of foreign exchange. Moreover, there is some additional evidence presented by the price studies of the National Planning Department of Colombia to confirm that this phenomenon was relatively common in Colombia in the 1960s; besides, export statistics of goods manufactured in the principal developed countries and sent, between 1964 and 1969, to Colombia were consistently lower than the Colombian import registrations of those goods.[41]

Finally, it is necessary to analyze import underinvoicing, which in the present Colombian situation seems to be even more relevant. The underinvoicing of imports is usually a means of profiting from avoiding the payment of customs duties and sales taxes on the product imported, over and above the additional cost of foreign exchange required to obtain funds on the black market to pay for the imports. There is also an incentive to underinvoice imports when imports are strictly controlled by licenses and, consequently, there is a premium between the domestic and the international price.[42]

In the Colombian circumstances of the late 1970s, there were two clear incentives to underinvoice: on the one hand, the importer saved on tariffs and sales taxes; on the other, since 1976 he was in the privileged position of acquiring foreign exchange on the black market at prices lower than the official ones, as shown in table 17-3. To identify the amount of underinvoicing, compare the corresponding data on exports to Colombia and imports registered in Colombia for the same goods. In the absence of this information the experiences of other countries should be considered. Studies of the case of Turkey indicate that the degree of underinvoicing has reached, on average, 15 percent of registered imports.[43] Moreover, the case of Turkey is a good example since the average tariffs of 30 percent are similar to the Colombian ones and that country has a 5 percent "stamp duty" equivalent to the Promotion of Exports Fund (PROEXPO) surcharge on imports in Colombia. Besides, Turkey does not have the incentive of a black exchange rate lower than the official one.

The Black Foreign Exchange Balance

We will now summarize our previous findings and try to construct what could be called a "black foreign exchange balance."

Table 17-6 shows an estimate of the black international reserves generated by the difference between illegal exports and illegal imports. An analysis of the way in which such reserves have presumably been absorbed and converted into pesos by the official foreign exchange market is also presented, leaving in the last column an estimate of the dollars which have not been monetized in Colombia and have thus remained as "Colombian assets abroad" or, if the expression is preferred, as "flight of capital."

Thus, column 3 estimates the annual amount of total illegal exports, as the sum of illegal exports of traditional products (column 1) and the value of inflows brought to Colombia as a result of exports of marihuana and cocaine (column 2). The latter estimate was prepared under the assumption that such activities had a gradual and linear growth from 1970 to the levels calculated previously for 1978. In order to obtain the gross accumulation of what could be called "black reserves," the sum of illegal imports (column 4) was subtracted from total illegal exports as calculated in column 3.

Columns 6-12 analyze the use, or destination, of the black reserves, part of which become official and thus form part of the country's international reserves. One way of legalizing reserves is through the overinvoicing of tourist activities (column 6), a phenomenon which started in 1976. Another device used has been to overinvoice other services. In this respect column 7 estimates the deviation of such receipts in the balance of payments over and above this category's trend in the previous decade.

Reserves can also be made legal by overinvoicing exports and underinvoicing imports. Columns 8 and 9 estimate the possible volume of foreign exchange which comes in by these mechanisms. According to the previous analysis, export overinvoicing should have taken place during 1970-1977, given that the official exchange rate plus the government tax-exempt subsidies was higher than the black exchange rate during that period. A 6 percent overinvoicing rate on exports (excluding coffee) was adopted as estimate for the following reasons: first, because coffee can not be overinvoiced as there are stringent controls and overinvoicing would imply the payment of the advalorem export tax that applies to coffee; and second, because such a percentage is conservative, considering the level of underinvoicing that took place with Colombian exports during the 1960s. It is worth noting that the estimate of import underinvoicing in column 6 was applied to total imports, but only from 1975 to 1978, given that the black exchange rate was below the official one during these years. The underinvoicing percentage of 6 percent was also used, as it was the one detected in the 1960s. Finally, column 10, "Others," was added to the sources of "officializing" reserves. This column corresponds to credits to the Colombian balance of payments which could not be canceled with corresponding payments and which form part of the "errors and omissions" category of the balance.[44]

Table 17-6
Use of Reserves Generated by Illegal Commerce
(millions of dollars)

| | Generation of Reserves | | | | | | Use of Reserves | | | | | |
Year	Illegal Traditional Exports (1)	Marihuana and Cocaine Exports (2)	Total Exports (3)	Total Imports (4)	Accumulation of Reserves (5)	Tourism (6)	Other Services and Transport (7)	Export Over invoicing (8)	Import Under invoicing (9)	Others (10)	Total (11)	Capital Flight (12)
1970	56.8	1.0	57.8	56.0	1.8	−50	—	17.9	—	—	−32.1	38.9
1971	76.2	20.0	96.2	86.0	10.0	−11.0	—	24.4	—	—	−36.6	46.6
1972	91.6	30.0	121.6	92.0	29.6	−59.0	—	28.4	—	—	−30.6	60.2
1973	133.0	50.0	183.0	64.0	119.0	−72.0	—	40.3	—	—	−31.7	150.7
1974	183.5	100.0	283.5	80.0	203.5	−57.0	—	46.7	—	—	−10.3	213.8
1975	233.4	200.0	433.4	80.0	353.4	−32.0	100.0	46.7	79.0	69.0	262.7	90.7
1976	387.7	300.0	687.7	120.0	567.7	79.2	100.0	44.0	104.2	137.8	465.2	102.5
1977	338.2	500.0	838.2	164.0	674.2	195.6	140.0	47.7	106.2	−12.6	476.9	197.3

Source and Method:

Col. 1: Table 17-1, Col. 8.
Col. 2: Calculated according to text analysis.
Col. 3: Col. 1 + Col. 2.
Col. 4: Table 17-5, Col. 3.
Col. 5: Col. 3 − Col. 4.
Col. 6: Table 17-4, Col. 5.
Col. 7: Calculated according to text and table 17-4, Col. 2.
Col. 8: (.06) × (Minor Exports).
Col. 9: (.06) × (Total Imports)
Col. 10: Blance of "errors and omissions," Balance of Payments except Tourism (Col. 6).
Col. 11: Col. 6 + Col. 7 + Col. 8 + Col. 9.
Col. 12: Col. 5 − Col. 11.

Thus, table 17-6 shows that the accumulation of black reserves fluctuated between US $350 million and US $760 million between 1975 and 1978. Of this total, the great majority of the reserves were made official through the previously mentioned mechanisms. Only between US $90 million and US $280 millions annually remained as "Colombian assets abroad" or "flight of capital," as can be seen from column 12.

Consequently, even by the conservative criteria used to estimate flows it is found that illegal exports have acquired truly alarming proportions in Colombia, amounting to over US $280 million in 1974 and to US $838 million in 1977. It can be calculated that illegal exports as a proportion of exports registered in the balance of payments were on the order of 23-41 percent in the late 1970s. Furthermore, our findings indicate that the share of exports in the gross domestic product of Colombia is higher than that shown in the official statistics, as the latter do not consider either the foreign exchange that remains as "Colombian assets abroad" or the resources legalized in imports and service transactions. Thus, the evidence supports our hypothesis on the underinvoicing of exports.

Illegal Revenues and Parallel Capital Markets

Colombia has been registering savings ratios (measured as a proportion of GDP) less than those that could be expected according to international norms and standards. This phenomenon, along with low levels of taxation, has also lead to the hypothesis of the existence of a wide and growing parallel capital market.

In this section we will summarize the information on the size of the black capital market. We also consider the possible relation that this market's growth in the last few years might have had to the growth of what previously were called black international reserves which have been made official and converted into pesos.

Financial Development in the 1970s

To interpret the reasons behind the surge of a black capital market, a brief account of the financial development in the 1970s becomes useful. As some authors have shown,[45] the decade started with a financial sector with few intermediaries besides commercial bank lending supported by subsidized rediscount resources from the Central Bank submitted by various specific purpose "revolving funds."[46]

An important innovation occurred in 1972 through the establishment of long-term indexed credit facilitated by a new mortgage corporation (Corporaciones de Ahorro y Vivienda). Its resources were obtained from an also-indexed liquid savings deposit plan that provided an all-inclusive mechanism to finance Lauchlin Currie's designed development plan geared toward construction and urbanization.[47]

The major financial reform took place in 1974/75 under a new administration whose main priority was the stabilization policy. Its design was undoubtedly inspired by Ronald McKinnon's financial liberalization scheme.[48] The principal changes involved an overall rise in both passive and active interest rates especially on ordinary savings and time deposits, as well as the fixing of a maximum ceiling on the indexing component of the UPAC system. There was also an attempt to reduce, by making more costly, the Central Bank credit and the rediscount facilities. Also, a large step was undertaken to eliminate forced investments of insurance companies and commercial banks.[49]

The 1975-1979 coffee boom and its ensuing inflationary pressures induced, during the rest of the decade, a slowing down of the devaluation rate and the adoption of a severe and growing contractionist monetary policy with important impact on the development and structure of the financial sector. As the principal tool, a 100 percent marginal reserve requirement on current deposits was set up in 1977, as well as a rise in average reserve ratios on all other deposits. Moreover, the government, through the Central Bank, began to compete with the financial sector in the savings mobilization effort by first issuing the so-called exchange certificate (certificado de cambio), a short-term paper intended to delay the monetization of foreign exchange report earnings[50] and, later on, through the sale of 15-, 30-, 60-, and 90-day liquid and high interest rate yielding certificates of participation (certificados de participación).[51] Besides, on the foreign borrowing side, a whole set of quantitative restrictions were imposed on private borrowing, at the same time that the government strategy was to reduce its outstanding foreign debt.[52] Thus, despite liberalization efforts a severe credit restriction was then characteristic of the official capital market in the late 1970s.

Interest Rate Differentials

Table 17-7 summarizes the situation and evolution of the nominal rates of interest since 1971 and compares the going rates in the non-banking market, the institutional domestic market, and the interest rates of international markets.

Columns 1 and 2 refer to the profitability of investing abroad in terms of pesos. Column 1 corresponds to the sum of the New York prime rate and the official devaluation rate of the currency, or, in other words, it represents the profitability of permitted or official investments. However,

Table 17-7
Interest Rates for Investments Abroad, in the Domestic Institutional Market, and in the Nonbanking Market
(rate of interest)

	Investments Abroad		CAT	Institutional Investments		Nonbanking Market	
Year	Authorized (1)	Nonauthorized (2)	(3)	Time Deposits (4)	UPAC (5)	Assets (6)	Liabilities (7)
1971	13.8	7.6	15.0	13.6	—	21.0	18.0
1972	14.8	10.8	17.0	13.6	19.3	21.0	18.0
1973	15.9	16.4	20.0	13.6	26.2	24.0	21.0
1974	21.4	21.2	23.0	26.2	26.2	26.5	23.5
1975	18.8	13.8	23.0	25.6	24.5	28.6	25.5
1976	19.3	19.3	25.0	25.6	22.7	29.0	26.0
1977	12.3	8.3	26.0	25.6	22.7	30.0	27.0

Source:

(1) New York prime rate + percent change official rate of exchange (table 17-3).

(2) New York prime rate + percent change in black rate of exchange (table 17-3).

(3) Discount rate implicit in CAT: Mauricio Carrizosa, "Inflación, Tasas de Interés y Financiación del Sector Cafetero," *Financiamiento Externo,* 1977. Banco de la República y Asociación Bancaria, table 1, p. 340.

(4), (5). Effective rate of interest of UPAC accounts and certificates of time deposits, Fernando Gaviria, "El Mercado Extrabancario y las Tasas de Interés en Colombia," *Revista del Banco de la República,* June 1978, p. 804, table 4.

(6) 1971/72: Sources cited in the text; 1974, 1975, 1977, and 1978 special tabulations from industrial survey of FEDESARROLLO; 1973 and 1976 were interpolated linearly.

(7) Col. 6 − 3 percent.

the real opportunity cost for resources generated by illegal exports, or for those who wish to invest abroad in the form of flight of capital, is given by the sum of the prime rate and the devaluation in the black foreign exchange market. This is the rate of interest shown in column 2. Columns 3-5 show the nominal rates of interest of the three main official papers issued by the Colombian institutional market: the Government tax-exempt subsidy (CAT), time deposit certificates and UPAC accounts. Columns 6 and 7 show, respectively, the interest rates paid by the users of the nonbanking market, and the corresponding active rates, namely those obtained by savers who channel their resources in that market.

As can be seen, the nonbanking market rates are higher in all years than the corresponding ones in the international market and the institutional Colombian market. The incentive to put resources into the parallel capital market is thus apparent.

Two main aspects should be emphasized with respect to the results in table 17-7. The first is the comparison between international and national rates of both official and extrabanking markets. The result observed is that the international market was less profitable than the national one and that it was only toward 1973-1974 that the former became competitive. Furthermore, from 1976 onward the differences in favour of the domestic capital market became more marked, as the slow rate of devaluation of the official exchange rate and the virtual stagnation of the black rate meant that the national market was two or three times more profitable.

The fact that the national capital market was more profitable than the international one provoked distortions and pressures in the former. On the one hand, importers found it less costly to go into debt abroad; to prevent it the government imposed severe quantitative restrictions.[53] On the other hand, savers, especially those with available foreign exchange coming from illegal exports found it much more profitable to legalize their foreign exchange, converting it into pesos and investing in Colombia rather than keeping their assets abroad in the form of "flight of capital." The years in which there was the greatest incentive to invest in Colombia (1976-1977) were precisely those in which there was the most legalization of black reserves according to the analysis. Likewise, the year of the greatest "flight of capital" (1974) was not only the one in which a reform government took office, but also the one in which it was more profitable to invest abroad. In summary, the situation and actual circumstances of the rates explain and justify the efforts to legalize the black reserves.

Another point is the difference between the interest rates in the Colombian parallel and institutional markets, as shown in table 17-7. Although the black market rates have been higher, by 4 or 5 points, than the institutional ones, they have not been significantly greater. Indeed, during the 1974 financial reform these differences were temporarily eliminated. This development indicates that, on the lenders' side the preference for the parallel markets has been primarily due to the fact that resources channeled to them evade taxes and, only secondarily to the differential itself between the nominal rates of interest. The users of funds, on the other hand, had to resort to the black market, given the severe restrictions on credit established by the monetary authorities.

Size of the Black Capital Market

It is difficult to determine the size of the parallel capital market. An approximate measure is given by the use of nonbanking funds borrowed by firms, both corporations and limited liability companies, as it is assumed these firms are the main users of this type of credit. Therefore, it is possible to arrive at an estimate of the size of the black capital market by using data from a recent study of the nonbanking capital market in Colombia.[53] (See note 53, this chapter.)

In order to make an estimate of the utilization of nonbanking resources, one must start with the fact that the limited liability firms under official control comprise only 5 percent of all enterprises; therefore it is necessary to adjust the registered figures on the consolidated liabilities of limited societies by multiplying them by 20.[54]

Table 17-8 estimates the use of funds by the nonbanking market between 1971 and 1976. The table differentiates the type of organization and, for each type, analyzes both short-and long-term liabilities. The overall result is that the use of nonbanking credit increased from $8,768.9 million in 1971 to $30,894.7 million in 1976; it more than tripled in six years.

It should be noted that of the growth of the parallel capital market during 1976 ($9,402.6 million) and during 1977 (more than $15,000 million), a substantial part was presumably due to the legalization of foreign exchange obtained in illegal international trade operations. If one takes into account that in 1976 US$465.2 million was legalized, and in 1977 US$476.9 million, a rough estimate could be made that close to half of the increase in the black capital market funds could be attributed to these inflows.[55]

Summary

The natural deficiencies in the information required for this study imply that the latter lies on the borderline between science fiction and economics. Consequently, it is clearly necessary to improve the data as much as possible in order to give greater reliability to the findings.

Table 17-8
Liabilities of Corporations and Limited Liability Societies with the Nonbanking Capital Market
(millions of pesos)

Year	Corporations			Limited			Total		
	Short-term	Long-term	Total	Short-term	Long-term	Total	Short-term	Long-term	Total
1971	2.220.1	5.104.9	7.325.0	0.332	1.112	1.444	2.552.0	6.216.9	8.768.9
1972	3.031.5	6.669.6	9.701.1	1.070	1.428	2.498	4.101.5	8.097.6	12.199.1
1973	1.984.3	6.714.9	8.669.2	2.150	2.610	4.760	4.134.3	9.324.9	13.459.2
1974	4.376.0	9.163.4	13.539.4	1.520	5.310	6.830	5.896.0	14.473.4	20.369.4
1975	3.419.9	9.318.2	12.738.1	3.114	5.640	8.754	6.533.9	14.958.2	21.492.1
1976	3.924.6	14.554.1	18.478.7	3.308	9.108	12.416	7.232.6	23.662.1	30.894.7

Source: Fernando Gaviria, op. cit. table 16, p. 804.

The authors wish to analyze the findings more thoroughly before making policy recommendations or interpretations of the findings within the framework of the economic history of the 1970s. However, one fact that stands out is that the government, concerned at the beginning of 1975 with a possible fall in the country's international reserves and, later, with interest rate policies and credit restrictions, opened the door to the legalization of inflows of foreign exchange from illegal exports of traditional products and drugs. This phenomenon not only caused undesired inflationary pressures, but may also have possibly contributed to a concentration of income through the consolidation of a capital market operating outside the law. The main benefits of the policy were the contribution of illegal trade to the accumulation of today's nearly US$5 billion in international reserves, and the increase in the growth rate of the Colombian economy with a consequent lowering of unemployment.

This study's proper limits would be overstepped if value judgments and recommendations were made in regard to the "other economy" flourishing in Colombia. The government, politicians, and businessmen should analyze the facts and come to their own conclusions.

Notes

1. See, Hollis Chenery and Moises Syrquin *Patterns of Development 1950-1970,* World Bank, 1975, table 10.

2. For greater detail on the fiscal charges of the coffee trade, see FEDESARROLLO, *La Economiá Cafetera Colombiana,* part 5, "Instrumentos de Política Cafetera," 1978.

3. Banco de la República is Colombia's central bank.

4. For 1975, 1976, and 1977 there are differences between the United States import records, according to the U.S. Department of Agriculture, and Colombian export figures of 228,000, 299,000 and 200,000 bags of 60 kilos, respectively.

5. See FEDESARROLLO, *La Economía Cafetera Colombiana,* part 4, "La Política Internacional del Café," 1978.

6. The following figures illustrate the evolution of the differential: the domestic price per 125 kilos of "pergamino" (equivalent to 100 kilos of green coffee) was $1,304 pesos in 1970; $1,500 in 1972; $2,207 in 1974; $2,728 in 1975; $5,532 in 1976 and $7,175 in 1977. The price per pound of green coffee exported in the same years were: .44; .60; .60; 1.01; and 2.02 dollars per pound (respectively). The figures imply a relationship between the international price and the domestic one during these years of 1.4; 1.3; 1.6; 1.5; 1.4; and 2.3.

7. FEDESARROLLO estimates of the annual volumes of sugar contraband in *Las Economías Azucareras y Panelera en Colombia* were a result of different methodologies, some statistical and some based on figures of transportation of sugar to the Atlantic coast zone in comparison with the consumption levels of that region. It is calculated that contraband fluctuated between 40 and 60 thousand tons annually, reaching annual figures of unregistered exports of US$7.0 million between 1968 and 1973; US$24.0 million in 1974; US$16.5 million in 1975 and US$11.0 million in 1976.

8. Nevertheless, the 1980/81 situation with international prices around US$.30 per pound is promoting new illegal trade flows.

9. It is estimated that contraband in the form of cattle illegally exported to Venezuela amounts to approximately 200,000 head annually (10 percent of annual slaughtering (or disappearances)).

10. For example, see "Big Expansion in Colombian Cannabis Sowings," in the *Latin American Commodities Report,* October 1978, vol. 2, no. 41, p. 163; and "Explosivo Artículo en E.U. sobre Colombia," *El Espectador,* Oct. 22, 1978, p. 11A.

11. On the Atlantic coast of Colombia.

12. 70,000 Hectáreas de Marihuana en la Costa," *El Tiempo,* Aug. 13, 1978, pp. 1A and 8A.

13. "La Magnitud del Negocio," *Alternativa,* no. 135, Oct. 10-17, 1977, p. 5; and "El Café y la Marihuana: Dos Economías y Dos Culturas," Sunday Magazine, *El Espectador,* Feb. 12, 1978, p. 1.

14. "Big Expansion in Cannabis Sowings," p. 163. The publication *Alternativa* No. 135 estimated productivity at 10 tons per hectare and a cultivated surface of 30,000 hectares, which would imply an annual production of 300,000 tons.

15. Even though the already cited edition of *Latin American Commodities Report* estimates the price at port between US$20 and US$25 per pound of 500 grams.

16. According to information published in *El Tiempo*, June 1, 1977, 17 percent of the drug sold in Colombia and 10 percent of that sold in the United States is confiscated.

17. In a nine-month period in 1978, 2 million pounds were confiscated in the United States and 3 million in Colombia.

18. Figures based on "Colombian National Accounts," supplement of *Revista Banco de la República*, May 1978, p. 21.

19. Assuming US$287 million of aggregate value at $35 per dollar and comparing with the global figure of the commercial sector of the National Accounts for 1976.

20. "Mafia Teme a los Colombianos," *El Tiempo*, Sept. 26, 1978, pp. 1A and 6A. This was also the information given to the authors by the U.S. authorities.

21. "Mafia Teme a los Colombianos," and "Explosivo Artículo en E.U. sobre Colombia."

22. For an excellent analysis of periods of control and the efforts to liberalize trade see Carlos Díaz-Alejandro, *Foreign Trade Regimes and Economic Development in Colombia* (New York: Columbia University Press, 1976), especially chapters 1, 5, and 7. The topic of foreign exchange scarcity and abundance has been developed by Ricardo Villaveces and Alfredo Fuentes in "La Actual Liberación de Importaciones y su Perspectiva Histórica," *Coyuntura Económica*, vol 6, no. 2, 1976.

23. According to table 17-3, there was a 20 percent difference between the black and official rates in Colombia during that period.

24. See Jagdish Bhagwati, Anne Kruger, and C. Wibulswasy, "Capital Flight from L.D.C.'s: A Statistical Analysis," in *Illegal Transactions in International Trade*, ed. Jagdish Bhagivati (North Holland, 1974), table 1, p. 151.

25. Ibid. It was found that nine out of eighteen countries had exchange rate differentials which gave incentive to underinvoicing.

26. According to an article by J.C. Jaramillo and Fernando Montes, "El Comportamiento del Endeudamiento Privado Externo para la Financiación de las Importaciones: 1971-1977," *Revista del Banco de la República*, May 1978, the cost of the external debt was lower than the cost of the domestic debt by 8.9 percent, 1.6 percent, 11.1 percent and 12.2 percent in 1974-1977. Such differences reflected the greater profitability of investing in Colombia than abroad for those who could invest in either pesos or in dollars.

27. See end-of-year press statements of the then Director of the Promotion of Exports Fund, PROEXPO, at the end of 1974.

28. Banco de la Republica, *Registros de Importación y Exportación*, various years.

29. The concept of a real effective exchange rate to the exporter represents a true index of the incentive to export, as it includes not only the behavior of the official exchange rate and of international prices with relation to domestic inflation (or real rate of exchange) but also the implicit incentives given by the government tax exempt export subsidies, credit subsidy of PROEXPO and Plan Vallejo (tax-free import of inputs to produce export goods, etc.). The real rate has registered a substantial fall since 1971 when the index (1967 = 100) reached a top figure of 114.1. Around 1976 this index returned to 100 and in 1977 it was 83.0. The real effective rate has also diminished. It reached 100 in 1967 and 113 in 1971, then fell to 90 in 1976 and 77 in 1977. See *Coyuntura Económica*, FEDESARROLLO, "Comercio Exterior," May 1977 and April 1978.

30. See Jose D. Tegeiro and Anthony R. Elson, "El Crecimiento de las Exportaciones Menores y el Sistema de Fomento de la Exportación en Colombia," FEDESARROLLO, July 1975; Sheahan and Clark, "La Res-

puesta de las Exportaciones Colombianas a las Variaciones de las Tasa Efectiva de Cambio,'' FEDESARROLLO, 1972; and Díaz, *Foreign Trade Regimes.*

31. One of the explanations has to do with international monetary adjustments which require that the exchange rate be "weighted" according to sales in various markets and the currency (yen, marks, whatever) received in these transactions. If this explains why the real rate did not vary substantially until 1975, it also shows the reason for the big deterioration that took place in the last three years. See *Coyuntura Económica,* FEDESARROLLO, May 1978.

32. A FEDERACAFE-FENALCO study, "Un Análisis del Contrabando en Colombia" (November 1978) found a surcharge of 64 percent on "officially" imported cigarettes, of 46 percent on transistor radios and of 100 percent on television sets and stereo equipment.

33. An analysis of the liberalization process of imports between 1972 and 1974 is found in Garay et al. "Análisis de la Estructura de Control a las Importaciones en Colombia," FEDESARROLLO, 1974. With regard to the liberalization process carried on under the Lopez administration, Villaveces and Fuentes, "La Actual Liberalizacion de Importaciones y su Perspectiva Historica."

34. FEDERACAFE-FENALCO study, "Un Análisis del Contrabando en Colombia," places the value of illegal imports at US$1 billion, a figure that seems too high and without solid foundation.

35. The following analysis shows the number of months in which the customs administration mentions the confiscation of any particular good (34 months between January 1976 and October 1978): vehicles, 34; household appliances, 34; cigarettes, 31; liquor, 26; cosmetics, 22; toys, 18; watches, 17; automobile spare parts, 17; perfumes, 14; polyester fabrics, 7; canned goods, 4; costume jewelry, 3.

36. See National Planning Department, Section of Industrial and Agricultural Studies documents on the transfer of technology during 1969 and 1970. See also the first study of this kind by Constantino Vaitsos, "Transfer of Technology and the Preservation of Monopoly Rents," Harvard University (unpublished paper), 1970.

37. The case of Pakistan is described in the article by Gordon Winston, "Over-Invoicing, Underutilization and Distorted Industrial Growth," in *Illegal Transactions in International Trade.*

38. As table 17-3 shows, the differential between the black and the official exchange rates was substantial between 1967 and 1970. Before the exchange control law of 1967 there were also differences between the "free" market rate and that applicable to such imports. In addition, capital goods have traditionally had low tariffs and low sales taxes.

39. Winston, "Over-Invoicing."

40. See Francisco Thoumi, *La Utilización de Capacidad Instalada en la Industria Colombiana*, World Bank, 1974, and the industrial surveys of FEDESARROLLO published semiannually in *Coyuntura Económica*.

41. See Díaz, *Foreign Trade Regimes*. The degree of overinvoicing after discounting 10 percent for the CIF and FOB difference was above 6 percent. This method of analyzing overinvoicing by comparing the figures of different countries was analyzed in the economic literature of the 1950s. See Oskar Morgenstern," On the Accuracy of Economic Observations," in Bhagwati, *Illegal Transactions*.

42. Jagdish Bhagwati, "On the Under-Invoicing of Imports," in *Illegal Transactions*.

43. Ibid. This was found by comparing the imports of Turkey with the exports of the main supplier countries (France, Italy, Germany, the United States, and others).

44. According to the Colombian balance of payments, the "errors and omissions" account shows a credit balance of US$37 million in 1975; US$217 million in 1976 and US$183 million in 1977. Of such balances the officialization of reserves from tourism explains part of the leftover. The rest appears in the "others" column in table 17-6.

45. The survey is based on the following papers: J.C. Jaramillo, "El Proceso de Cambio hacia un Mercado Financiero Liberalizado en Colombia"; Zuleta and Valencia *Sector Financiero Colombiano: Un Análisis del Desarrollo de la Intermediación Financiera*; C.J. Fajardo and N. Rodriguez, "Tres Décadas del Sistema Financiero Colombiano," in *Sistema Financiero y Políticas Antiinflacionarias 1974-1980*, Asociación Bancaria, 1980; and A. Figueroa, et al., "El Sector Financiero, Sus Perspectivas, Necesidades de Crecimiento y Cambios Institucionales," in *El Sector Financiero en los Aˉos Ochentas*, Asociación Bancaria, 1979.

46. Among them, Fondo Financiero Industrial, Fondo de Inversiones Privadas, Fondo de Promoción de Exportaciones, Fondo de Desarrollo Urbano, and Fondo Financiero Agropecuario. See M. Carrizosa, "Los Fondos Financieros del Banco de la República," in *El Sector Financiero en los Años Ochentas*.

47. Currie's traditional vision appears in his classical work *Accelerating Development: The Necessity and the Means* (New York: McGraw-Hill, 1966). Currie, as foreign advisor to the government in 1972, was the designer of the development plan. República de Colombia, *Las Cuatro Estrategias*, Departamento Nacional de Planeación, 1972.

48. Ronald McKinnon was an advisor to the government in the second half of 1978 just at the time when the financial reform was being formulated. Entire meetings of the "new economic team" were dedicated to study and discuss McKinnon's book.

49. The ceiling figure for indexing was fixed at 20 percent. Ordinary

savings deposit rates were increased from 8.5 percent to 12 percent, and time deposits, up to then nonexistent, to 24 percent. The government was also allowed to issue a treasury bill (Pagaré Semestral de Emergencia Económica (PAS). Initially, also, average reserve requirments were lowered, being fixed at a higher level for current deposits than for time deposits as part of the financial deepening target.

50. The "certificado de cambio" or exchange certificate also implied a de facto revaluation and a differential exchange rate for the most competitive exports (coffee, agricultural products, and service items), given that the exporter was given the option of obtaining their peso proceeds immediately at a discount at the Central Bank or a lesser one at the Stock Exchange or at its par value after a given period (sixty to ninety days).

51. The "título de participación" or participation certificate earned a highly competitive interest rate and immediate liquidity with a low discount.

52. Quantitative restrictions had to be imposed given the differential or gap between domestic interest rates, over and above 30 percent per year and the international interest rates in the order of 10 percent plus a devaluation rate around 5 percent. Such a differential would induce short-term foreign capital inflows and monetary expansion. The rate differential, nevertheless, provoked an undesired delay in the payment of imports and unknown amounts of illegal capital inflows registered as services and exports. See G. Perry, et al., "Endeudamiento Externo de Colombia en la Década de los Setentas," CIEPLAN, Santiago de Chile, March 1981, chapter 3.

53. This subject has been well documented in J.C. Jaramillo and Fernando Montes, "El Comportamiento del Endeudamiento Privado Externo para la Financiación de las Importaciones: 1971-1977." See also Pablo Salazar, "El Financiamiento del Sector Externo," in *Financiamiento Externo*, 1977.

54. This adjustment coefficient was taken from a detailed study on the limited societies supervised by the Superintendency with comparison to the total. The study was done in 1972 by the International Finance Corporation and was cited by Fernando Gaviria, "El Mercado Extrabarcario y las Tasas de Interés en Colombia," *Revista del Banco de la República*, June 1978, p. 779. Presumably, the societies outside the Superintendency's control are active agents in the "black" capital market and at the same time do not declare the use of resources they receive in order to evade taxes.

55. The US$465.2 million legalized in 1976 is equivalent to a gross inflow of $16,300 million, and would be equivalent to an increase of $13,800 million in the aggregate national value, and, therefore, a potential nondeclared savings of close to $5,500 million. A similar analysis could be done for 1977.

18 The Underground Economy in Australia

Mark Tucker

The problems posed by the underground economy have been with society since time immemorial. With its various labels—underground, black, subterranean, hidden, unrecorded—the level of such activity is causing increasing concern to governments worldwide.

The underground economy cannot easily be defined. However, for the purpose of this chapter it is defined as the sum of those legal and illegal transactions involving cash, checks, or the bartering of goods or labor which either go unreported to the appropriate authorities or are not detected by conventional statistics. One estimate is that it amounts to nearly $11 billion in Australia, or 10 percent of gross domestic product (GDP).

The underground economy can operate under many disguises, from housewife activity, tradesman activity, through the controversial areas of tax evasion, hidden company perks and bribes to the hard-core world of drugs, prostitution, and gambling. The underground economy accounts for a significant proportion of current marketplace activity and covers a wide range of people. Clearly, it can affect various aspects of our lives such as work incentives, attitudes toward crime, law, security, and a person's moral fibre.

While there is general agreement on the existence of the underground economy, this is certainly not the case when it comes to estimating its size. Methods for measuring it have been suggested overseas but, to our knowledge, no such studies have been undertaken for the Australian economy.

In this article, a benchmark level of underground activity in Australia is established. The article discusses:

the world-wide phenomenon of the underground economy;

some factors encouraging it;

problems created by its existence;

two methods used in estimating the size of the Australian underground economy; and

the conclusions that can be drawn from the calculations.

Reprinted from "The Commercial Bank of Australia Limited," *Economic Review*, September 1980.

Worldwide Underground Economies

Governments worldwide are today losing billions of dollars in revenue through uncollected taxes. The English have their "hidden economy", the Germans their *Schwarzarbeit*, the French their *travail noir*, Argentinians their *morocho*. The Soviet Union calls it the "unofficial economy," while the Italians have their *lavoro nero*. In the United States it is called the "subterranean economy" after the pioneering work of Professor P.M. Gutmann, who estimated that it produced extra, unreported gross national product (GNP) of $176 billion in the United States in 1976, or about 10 percent of the official GNP of $1,693 billion.[1]

Factors Encouraging the Underground Economy

The growth of the underground economy can be attributed to a number of factors operating in the legal economy. These factors include:

the growth of government regulations, prohibitions and reporting requirements which encourage firms and individuals to avoid the associated costs and problems of legal employment;

the imposition of taxes which encourage activities to go "underground" to avoid payments that seem disproportionately high when compared with the income earned;

the rising inflation rate, which has pushed individuals into higher tax brackets, and provided an incentive to seek alternative sources of income that are not detected by the taxman;

the growth of certain illegal activities such as drugs, gambling, and prostitution, which are transacted in cash and reflect the type of society we live in;

the knowledge that loopholes exist in our present laws which encourage people to try to "buck the system";

the ever-increasing level of transfer payments in the form of unemployment benefits, pensions, medical care and so on, which are often a disincentive to work in the legal economy;

the growing sense of cynicism and disillusionment by many individuals, which has encouraged them to bypass conventional procedures. This is particularly true of those who are unemployed and unable to find suitable legal employment (those who believe they have prospects of legitimate employment would not enter this category);

the increased leisure time resulting from the reduction of working hours since World War II, which is frequently used to earn extra untaxed income in a second job (moonlighting);

the opportunity for young skilled people to earn extra untaxed income by using their skills outside their main place of employment.

Problems Posed by the Underground Economy

Many of the policies introduced to correct perceived adverse economic trends subsequently prove to be ineffective, at least partly because of the growth of the underground economy and the consequent distortion in the recording of statistics relating to macroeconomic variables such as employment, growth, and inflation.

Employment

Employment statistics cover individuals in the labor force. However, those who are employed only in the underground economy are excluded from the statistics, thus understating employment levels. At the same time, unemployment statistics could be overstated by including those people who work in the underground economy and have no intention of working in the legal economy, yet register as unemployed so as to receive benefits. Hence, an element of "disguised employment" distorts these statistics. This causes policymakers aiming for full employment to plan from a base of incorrect assumptions.

Official employment statistics also conceal "disguised unemployment." This refers to people who work in a family business or other capacity at less than their full potential, because they are unable to find more suitable employment; those who would like to work but are precluded from registering for unemployment benefits because of an employed spouse; and (mostly young) people who elect to continue their education rather than register as unemployed.

Any such disguised unemployment does not neutralize, and may be more than offset by, the disguised employment in the underground economy. In any case, both situations distort employment statistics.

Growth and Inflation

If the underground economy is growing faster than the legal economy, economic resources will shift from the latter to the former. Further, as the rate of economic growth is measured only in the legal economy, actual economic performance is understated.

At the same time, inflation in the total economy is overstated. Workers in the underground economy do not pay tax and so are prepared to accept lower wage rates than those in the legal economy. Suppliers of other inputs are also avoiding government-induced costs, so are prepared to accept lower prices for goods and services produced.

Both the level and rate of price increase in the underground economy are therefore lower than in the legal economy, with the result that the officially recorded inflation rate overstates the true position.

Savings and Consumption

Economic data concerning savings and consumption are understated, because part of the income from which savings and consumption are drawn is underground income, which is excluded from official calculations.

Productivity

An additional problem is that those who are employed in both the underground and the legal economies may cause lower productivity, by being tired on the job, or by being prone to frequent absenteeism. They will also be more prone to accidents and dangerous procedures.

Thus the operations of the underground economy have major implications for the legal economy in terms of monetary and fiscal policy, income distribution, and productivity. The array of statistics compiled is misleading, and results in biased conclusions and possibly incorrect policy prescriptions.

Estimating the Size of the Underground Economy

Increasing attention is being directed toward methods of measurement, especially in the United States, using monetary data. Many of these methods are based on the belief that an increasing amount of cash held by individuals indicates a flourishing underground economy dominated by cash transactions. The increased circulation of high denomination notes is cited as further evidence.

In Australia, the amount of notes in circulation was about $285 per capita in June 1979, compared with $54 in June 1949—an increase of 428 percent. During the same period, inflation increased by 494 percent.

Since World War II, the value of higher denomination notes in circulation in Australia rose even more sharply as shown in table 18-1. The value

Table 18-1
Notes in Circulation

| June | Value of Total Notes in Circulation | | Value of Notes $20 (£10) and above | Ratio B/A |
	$ Per Capita	Total $ Million (A)	$ Million (B)	(percentage)
1949	54	425.7	108.6	25.5
1959	79	790.1	277.7	35.1
1969	90	1,107.5	447.3	40.3
1979	285	4,107.4	3,184.1	77.5

of notes $20 (£10) and above accounted for 25.5 percent of the value of notes in circulation in 1949, and for 77.5 percent in June 1979, representing an increase of 2,832 percent.

It is difficult to assess the significance of these changes in the amount and type of cash in circulation, as any interpretation of such movements is complicated by the awareness of a declining need for cash in a credit card society and the opportunities for holding interest-earning assets instead of cash. On the other hand, if more cash is held and in a higher denomination, there are obvious legitimate reasons, such as the declining value of money. The conclusion therefore is that this may not be a reliable method of assessing the extent of the underground economy.

An article by Tanzi published in the *IMF Survey* of 4 February 1980 summarized a number of other methods, which may be of interest to readers (see references).

The Gutmann Approach

Peter Gutmann was the first to use monetary statistics as an indirect measure of the underground economy in the United States. In any economic transaction, only currency or checks are used as the final medium of exchange. Gutmann's basic premise was that all underground activities avoid the use of checks and rely on currency for transactions.

Therefore he concludes that, if the holding and use of currency is increasing faster than the use of checking accounts, then underground activities, financed by cash, are growing.

Adapting Gutmann's approach (outlined in an article published in the November-December 1977 issue of *Financial Analysts Journal*), the underground economy in Australia during 1978/79 is estimated at about 10.7 percent of officially estimated gross domestic product—a similar figure to Gutmann's estimate for the United States. In arriving at the Australian figure, it was assumed that the "normal" ratio of currency to current deposits in checking accounts was 30 percent; that is, for every $1,000 in current deposits, $300 was held in currency. The ratio fluctuated around this level throughout the late 1950s and the 1960s, as shown in figure 18-1 and in table 18-2.

If this ratio had been maintained to 1978/79, the Reserve Bank's volume of money measure ($M1$) required to produce the officially estimated GDP of $101.2 billion should have been $11.2 billion, made up of $2.6 billion in currency and $8.6 billion in current deposits. In fact, $M1$ for 1978/79 was $12.4 billion (annual average).

According to the Gutmann approach, the difference of $1.2 billion is attributable to currency held in the illegal or underground economy. Using the same velocity factor of a dollar of $M1$ as in the legal economy, this $1.2 billion would produce a further $10.7 billion of GDP. Hence the "total" GDP for 1978/79 would in reality be $111.9 billion, and not $101.2 billion as reported by the Australian Bureau of Statistics.

However, there are several problems with this approach. For statistical reasons, it is nearly impossible to determine a base period when the ratio of currency to current deposits can be assumed to be "normal"—that is, implying no underground economy existed. At best, it can only be assumed that

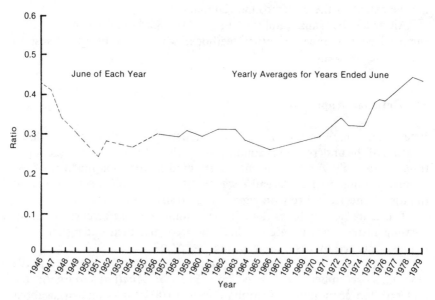

Source: Reserve Bank of Australia.

Figure 18-1. Ratio of Currency to Current Deposits Based on Volume of Money Statistics

Table 18-2
Underground Components of *M*1 and GDP: Ratio of Currency to Current Deposits, 1978-1979

	Base Period (1960s) (percentage)	1978-1979 (percentage)	Average M1 ($000M)	Percentge of "total" GDP	GDP ($000M)
Currency					
Illegal	0	13.9	1.2	9.6	10.7 illegal
Legal	30.0	30.0	2.6	90.4	101.2 official
Current Deposits	100.0	100.0	8.6		estimate by ABS
Total			12.4	100.0	111.9 "total"

the underground economy in a chosen base period was relatively unimportant. The choice of a different base period from that assumed above would naturally yield different results.

Another major problem centers around the underlying reason for the increase in the ratio of currency to current deposits, as depicted in figure 18-1. Critics of Gutmann's approach argue that the ratio increase in the United States was due more to the low growth in current deposits than to the fast growth in currency.

In Australia's case, however, it appears that the ratio increase can be attributed to faster growth in currency during the past ten years. During the 1950s and the 1960s, both currency and current deposits, on a per capita basis, grew at a slower rate than inflation. But during the 1970s, this situation changed. While growth in current deposits per capita continued to be below the inflation rate, currency per capita increased at a faster rate.

Under an environment of rising inflation, one would have thought that the public would prefer to hold income-earning financial assets rather than cash. Therefore, the Australian result in the 1970s certainly lends support to the belief that the increased usage of cash was due to the growing underground economy.

While a discussion of the other approaches adopted in the United States is beyond the scope of this chapter, it should be pointed out that the estimates from the various methods (including Gutmann's) have differed quite significantly. However, it is not certain to what extent these variations are the result of the differences in methods employed, or to what extent they are the result of the different concepts of what constitutes the underground economy.

Conclusion

Despite the associated difficulties, the underground economy in Australia during 1978/79 can be estimated at more than $10 billion, or 10 percent of the measured GDP, by using the Gutmann approach. However, we do not wish to argue whether this is a correct assessment or not. The more important fact is that there is a significant underground economy in Australia which has serious adverse implications for economic management. Clearly, a more detailed analysis is required.

The underground economy cannot be eliminated completely, but it can be reduced. Government reassessment of present regulations, taxes, and wasteful expenditures would create a climate where the average honest worker is not subsidizing, by taxation, the dishonest workers in the illegal, underground economy.

More important, the government statistician needs to look at the problem. His department must devise ways to estimate the degree of underground activity in the Australian economy, and the national accounts—especially the statistical discrepancy—must then be adjusted accordingly.

Note

1. Peter M. Gutmann, "The Subterranean Economy," *Financial Analysts Journal* (November-December 1977), pp. 26-27, 34.

References

Bowsher, Norman N. "The Demand for Currency: Is the Underground Economy Undermining Monetary Policy?" Federal Reserve Bank of St. Louis, *Review* 62, no. 1 (January 1980), pp. 11-17.

Feige, Edgar L. "How Big Is the Irregular Economy?" *Challenge, The Magazine of Economic Affairs* 22, no. 5 (November-December 1979), pp. 5-13.

Gutmann, Peter M. "The Subterranean Economy," *Financial Analysts Journal* (November-December 1977), pp. 26-27, 34.

Gutmann, Peter M. "Are the Unemployed, Unemployed?" *Financial Analysts Journal* (September-October 1978), pp. 26-29.

Macafee, Kerrick. "A Glimpse of the Hidden Economy in the National Accounts," *Economic Trends*, Central Statistical Office (U.K.) (February 1980), pp. 81-87. Reprinted as chapter 9, this volume.

Tanzi, Vito. "Underground Economy Built on Illicit Pursuits is Growing Concern of Economic Policymakers," *IMF Survey*, 4 February 1980, pp. 34-37.

The Bulletin, 20 November 1979, cover story.

19 Estimate of Tax Evasion in Israel

A good many statements on the extent of tax evasion have been made in public.[1] This is a delicate subject and there is in fact no way of arriving at a sound evaluation. The reliability of the existing total national income estimate has been questioned. We had no way of examining this proposition and it does not appear to us to be provable given the state of available statistical information today. Another possibility is that within the national income total there are income components not caught by the tax system. In order to examine this possibility we tried to locate all incomes covered in principle by the tax assessment process and to calculate the difference between them and the national income estimated from the expenditure side. It should be stressed that all parts of the estimate are conservative and the resulting gap may very well be a minimum estimate.

Table 19-1 presents the estimates, whose details appear in the appendix to this chapter (see table 19A-1 and the accompanying explanation). In table 19-1, which covers 1968-1974, compensation of employees, interest, rent, and corporate profits have been deducted from national income. The difference appears in line 3, and comes to about 20 percent of national income (line 6). Assessed noncorporate profits can be subtracted only up to 1972,[2] and it is a reasonable assumption that the gap that then remains (line 5) consists mainly of income which the tax authorities failed to reach. The gap comes to I£ 500 million in 1968, rising to I£ 2,000 million in 1972, or I£ 4,000 at today's prices. In 1968 the gap came to 4.5 percent of national income, and 8 percent in 1972 (line 7).[3]

The method used does not enable us to distinguish accurately between erosion in compensation of employees and other types of erosion and evasion, and there may be some double counting; it is however unlikely to exceed 10 percent of the gap shown. In this connection we must stress two points. First, the gap for 1968-1972 gives some indication of the proportion of national income not caught by the tax authorities in subsequent years. Second, although in this country, as elsewhere, some gap is only to be expected—what gives cause for concern and requires explaining is the fact that over the years it has grown in relative terms. Part of the explanation lies in the renewed inflation which began in 1970-1971. In years of rapid inflation, the assessing procedures do not manage to keep up with the growth of incomes

Reprinted from *Proposals for the Reform of Direct Taxes, Report of the Commission on Tax Reform* (Haim Ben-Shahar, Chairman, Jerusalem, March 12, 1975), pp. 3-5 to 3-16.

Table 19-1
National Income and the Assessment Gap: 1968-1974
(current prices)

	1968	1969	1970	1971	1972	1973	1974
I£ milliard							
1. National income[a]	11.6	13.5	16.1	20.2	25.6	35.0	46.9
2. *less* Compensation of employees, rent, interest, corporate profits (assessment)	− 9.2	−10.7	−13.1	−16.1	−20.3	−27.9	−38.0
3. Residual, including noncorporate profits (1 *less* 2)	2.4	2.8	3.0	4.1	5.3	7.1	8.9
4. *Less* Noncorporate profits (assessment)	− 1.9	− 2.2	− 2.3	− 2.7	− 3.3	—	—
5. Unexplained gap (3 *less* 4)	0.5	0.6	0.7	1.4	2.0	—	—
Percentage of national income							
6. Gross residual (3/1)	21.1	20.7	18.6	20.2	20.9	20.2	18.9
7. Unexplained gap (5/1)	4.6	4.6	4.2	6.7	7.8	—	—
Marginal tax rate (percent) at monthly income[b]							
8. I£ 1,500	19	—	28	28	27	27	28
9. I£ 3,000	34	—	46	54	55	47	55
10. I£ 5,500	56	—	69	70	69	68	73
Consumers Price Index (percent increase over preceding year)	2.1	2.5	6.1	12.0	12.9	20.0	35.0

Source: Table 19A-1. and Research Department of State Revenue Administration. Consumers Price Index, Central Bureau of Statistics, *Statistical Abstract of Israel 1974*, no. 25, p. 248.
[a]Expenditure-side estimate, converted to fiscal years.
[b]At January 1975 prices.

(see the rate of price increase shown in line 11 of table 19-1).[4] Moreover, the rapid increase in marginal rates (lines 8 through 10) were an incentive not only to avoidance but also to evasion. Our recommendation to link the tax schedule and reduce marginal rates is intended, among other things, to do away with this incentive.

The 1972 unexplained gap of I£ 2,000 million represents an amount of I£ 700 million in tax revenue that should have accrued for that year but which does not, according to existing files and the collection records, appear to have been collected.[5] This should be taken as an indicator of tax evasion.

For 1974, the residual (including noncorporate profits) is close to I£ 9,000 million. Assume that at least I£ 1,000 million of this is a "normal" gap on which tax cannot be levied; a tax revenue of about I£ 3,600 million should accrue on the remaining I£ 8,000 million. Assuming that taxpayers and tax authorities behaved in 1974 as they did in 1972, only half of the potential revenue was realized. In 1974 actual receipts from noncorporate profits, as advances during the year and on account of previous years, will come to only I£ 1,700 million. This kind of computation should be made for each tax year, in order to estimate both the potential revenue and the cumulated collection lag. Implementation of the Reform Act in 1975 and the efforts of the tax authorities to deepen collection are likely to result in actual collection being closer to the potential. In any case, a computation of this type is required since it can set a challenge, and perhaps also serve as a yardstick of performance, to the Income Tax Commission. Lastly the estimate of tax revenue under the reform proposals assumes that increased effectiveness of collection will eventually lead to a considerable reduction in tax evasion.

The Measurement of National Income

In most countries income tax authorities are the principal source of data on business incomes, corporate or noncorporate. Tax evasion naturally gives such data a downward bias. One way of determining the extent of the bias is to compute the net national product from the expenditure side and to subtract compensation of employees from it.[6] In principle the following equality holds: total income from property and entrepreneurship *equals* net product *less* various imputations (such as dwelling services or the food consumption of the armed forces) *less* compensation of employees. The computation appears in lines 1 through 4 of table 19A-1; income from property and entrepreneurship appears as a residual in line 5 and is converted to fiscal years in line 6. Before looking into the composition of this residual and the volume of evasion, note that the figure may be biased for several reasons:

sales of goods or services not reported to the tax authorities and which are also not recorded on the expenditure side of the national accounts will automatically not appear at all (for example, a visit to a doctor or a repair workshop). In practice it is at present impossible to assess the magnitude of such errors. But although some parts of the estimate may be too low,[7] it does not seem to us that the total product (estimated as the sum of private and public consumption, investment, and the import surplus) as derived from various sources can possibly leave room for evasion of an order of I£ 1,000 million.[8]

Another source of bias arises in the wage erosion items (table 19-1). It can be assumed that today most of these items (such as professional literature, convalescent pay, training fund, travel allowances) appear in the statistics on both sides of the national product account.

However, one or the other items may be covered in the expenditure estimate but not in compensation of employees. In this case, the income from property and entrepreneurship is overstated (residual line 5 or 6 in the table). For example, part of the costs of keeping a car may be included in the residual because of the method of computation. This source of bias does not seem serious for previous years (until, say, 1972), both because there was then less tax avoidance on this count (in real terms) and because the relative price of keeping cars was lower than it is today.[9]

We must now identify the components of the residual: corporate profits (line 7), interest (line 8), and assessed noncorporate profits (line 11). The sum of these three items is smaller than the alternative estimate obtained as a residual in line 6.

Line 11 is the difference between the two in 1968-1972, and conceptually it should consist of that part of national income not caught by the tax authorities.

In principle, the discrepancy could arise in any one of the items in the table—compensation of employees, corporate profits, interest, and noncorporate profits. However, interest is a fairly small item, while the data on compensation of employees and profits of corporations (which are legally obliged to keep books) are comparatively reliable, so that it is plausible to ascribe most of the gap—particularly in the more recent period—to underreporting by the self-employed.[10]

The gap for 1973 and 1974 cannot be estimated since assessments for self-employed are not available after 1972. Lines 10 and 11 are therefore combined in a single residual (line 9) for 1973/74. Note that this combined residual has been fairly steady at around 20 percent of national income throughout the period.[11]

Last, it is worth noting that in constructing the estimate, considerable caution was exercised. Thus for example we used the upper limit of the estimate of the measured gap between assessed and declared corporate profits.[12] Similarly, our depreciation adjustment may be too small.[13] In other words, the 1972 gap and the global residual in 1973/74 could be underestimated.

It would be desirable to look into this matter at the branch level and on the basis of assessments for 1968-1974. A partial clue to one source of the considerable increase in profits (and perhaps part of the concealed profits of past years) can be obtained from the industrial origin of product figures as they appear in the *Statistical Abstract*. For purposes of illustration we used the data on construction and public works, in which growth was particularly rapid between 1968 and 1973. As can be seen in table 19A-2, total factor incomes in this branch grew 4.5 times (compared with the national average of 2.8) in the period. The returns to capital component (including self-employed labor returns) grew by a factor of almost 7, in effect twice as fast as compensation of employees in each of the years 1969-1972.[14] As can be seen, the assessment estimates for construction do not show such a rapid growth rate when the estimated increase in the number of self-employed is taken into account.

Between 1968 and 1972 the average assessment for general contracting rose from I£ 15,000 to I£ 42,000 and for subcontracting from I£ 13,200 to I£ 23,400. If it is assumed that the number of files increased at the same rate as the number of self-employed, then assessed profits rose by a factor of 3.6 and 2.3 for general contracting and subcontracting respectively, compared with 5 for the total income from property and entrepreneurship of the branch as estimated from the product figures.

Notes

1. See, for example, the Nadel Report.

2. This is the latest year for which an estimate can be made at all for the self-employed and even then it is based on final assessments for no more than *one-third* of the assessees.

3. Had the percentage gap stayed constant since 1972 the absolute gap would in 1975 be close to I£ 5,000 million.

4. An example (the assessment lag in construction) appears in the appendix to this chapter (table 19A-2).

5. About I£ 1,500 million at today's prices.

6. Compensation of employees may also be understated.

7. For example, the valuation of dwelling services.

8. The Central Bureau of Statistics (CBS) puts the margin of error of the product estimate at no more than 1 or 2 percent.

9. We estimate the upper limit of the possible error in this item as no more than I£ 200 million in 1972, and probably no more than I£ 400 million in 1974.

10. In principle, income from property and entrepreneurship also includes the nonwage income of employees, who may, of course, also underreport this part of their income.

11. The low 1974 figure may be due to an upward bias in the corporate profit figures.

12. Estimated at 10-15 percent by the State Revenue Administration.

13. The difference between total depreciation and book-value depreciation was estimated by the CBS at I£ 875 million in 1972 (see *Statistical Abstract of Israel 1974*, no. 25, p. 171, "depreciation adjustment"). Only about one-third of this amount is taken into account in our calculations (see note to line 7 of table 19A-1).

14. The data on other branches, not presented here, show similar rates of growth for each of the two components.

Appendix 19A

Table 19A-1
National Income, 1968-1974
(I£ million at current prices)

	1968	1969	1970	1971	1972	1973	1974
Calendar years							
1. National income from the expenditure side	11,221	12,911	15,192	18,945	23,813	30,976	43,255
2. *less* Compensation of employees	-6,669	-7,480	-9,005	-10,952	-13,206	-17,234	-23,283
3. *less* Public sector property income	-236	-286	-346	-430	-509	-630	-790
4. *less* Imputed rent and commodities	-872	-985	-1,291	-1,661	-2,376	-3,195	-4,315
5. Private income from property and entrepreneurship (1 through 4)	3,444	4,160	4,550	5,902	7,722	10,307	14,876
Fiscal years							
6. Private income from property and entrepreneurship (line 5)[a]	3,625	4,260	4,890	6,355	8,370	11,445	16,380
7. *less* Corporate profits (assessment)[b]	-865	-1,110	-1,470	-1,800	-2,425	-3,675	-6,715
8. *less* Interest	-300	-355	-415	-475	-600	-690	-800
9. Residual (6 through 8)	2,460	2,795	3,000	4,080	5,345	7,080	8,865
10. *less* Noncorporate profits (assessment)	-1,930	-2,170	-2,335	-2,730	-3,340	—	—
11. Unexplained gap (9 *less* 10)	530	625	670	1,350	2,005	—	—
12. National income (line 1)[a]	11,643	13,481	16,130	20,162	25,605	35,046	46,935
Percentage of national income							
13. Residual including noncorporate profits (9/12)	21.1	20.7	18.6	20.2	20.9	20.2	18.9
14. Unexplained gap (11/12)	4.6	4.6	4.2	6.7	7.8	—	—

Source: Lines 1 through 5, national accounts data of the CBS for 1974, adjusted by Ministry of Finance estimates. Line 7, fiscal year data of the State Revenue Administration Line 8, Estimated from deduction-at-source data of the Research Department of the State Revenue Administration *plus* an estimate of tax-exempt interest (I£ 80 million in 1972). Line 10, assessments of noncorporate profits for 1972/1973, from data of the Research Department of the State Revenue Administration.

[a]Prorated by quarters.

[b]Adjusted from source data by adding an estimate of the gap (15 percent) between balance-sheet profits and final assessment and deducting a depreciation adjustment (10 percent of profits) and factor payments to the rest of the world (about I£ 100 million annually according to the CBS).

Table 19A-2

The Product of Construction and Public Works, 1968-1973

(current prices)

	1968	1969	1970	1971	1972	1973[b]
Net Product[a]						
I£ million						
Compensation of employees	640	757	932	1,171	1,456	1,886
Income from property and entrepreneurship	411	710	1,015	1,435	2,066	2,798
Total	1,051	1,467	1,947	2,606	3,522	4,684
Percent increase over preceding year						
Compensation of employees	—	18.3	23.1	25.6	24.3	29.5
Income from property and entrepreneurship	—	72.7	43.0	41.4	44.0	35.4
Estimated average assessment (I£ thousand)						
General contractors	15.1			36.5	41.9	
Subcontractors	13.2			20.3	23.4	
Number of self-employed (thousands)	13			13	17	

Source: Product data, CBS, *Statistical Abstract of Israel 1974,* no. 25, pp. 171-172, tables vi/9 and vi/10. Number of self-employed, ibid., pp. 322-325, tables xii/12 and xii/13. Assessment data, Research Department of the State Revenue Administration.

[a]Includes public utilities, not more than 10 percent of the total value added.

[b]Based on data for 9 months.

Index

Absenteeism, women and, 200, 208
Alimony, income from, 100
Allingham, Michael G., 216
Annuities: reportable income from, 96*t*; unreported income from, 95*t*
Argentina, 112
Audits, tax, 131
Australia, underground economy in, 14, 315-322; employment and, 317; estimating size, 318-321; inflation and, 317-318, 321; productivity and, 318
Azerbaydzhan, USSR, 252-253, 254

Bahamas, U.S. dollars in, 111
Banco de la República, Colombia, 286, 288
Bank of England, 155
Barter, U.S., 8, 121-122
Baumol, W.J., 222
Belgium: clandestine workers, 31, 39; income/expenditure discrepancy, 7, 9
Berndt, Louise, 59-60
Black foreign-exchange market, Colombia, 285-302
Black market: Colombia, 285-302; income taxes and, 78; USSR, 254-255, 256-257, 260; World War II, 48
"Black Market for Dollars in Brazil, The," 112
Bookmaking, unreported income from, 71, 99*t*
Brazil, 112
Brezhnev administration, 256
Bribery, unreported income from, 71
Bureau of the Census, 123, 133
Bureau of Economic Analysis (BEA), 6, 49-51, 57, 72, 98, 119-124, 133
Bureau of Labor Statistics, 137

Caballero, Carlos, 285-308
Cagan, Phillip, 13, 48, 74-75, 219-220, 221, 222
Calgary, Canada, 278
Canada, underground economy in, 18, 273-284; currency/demand deposit ratio, 276, 277-278; moonlighting, 31; tax system, 276, 277
Capital gains, unreported income from, 95*t*
Carter, Jimmy, 137
Census of Manufacturers, 123, 130, 133
Census of Retailers, 130, 133
Central Committee of the Communist Party of the Soviet Union, 255
Central Intelligence Agency, USSR, 255
Central Statistical Office, United Kingdom, 164
Centre for Social Investment Studies (CENSIS), 31, 188
CERES, 12
Child labor, clandestine, 32
Clandestine workers, characteristics of, 33-34
Cocaine: illegal exportation of, from Colombia, 291-292
Colombia, underground economy in, 285-308; black foreign-exchange market, 285-302; cocaine, illegal exportation of, 291-292; coffee, illegal exportation of, 286; exports, illegal, 286-292; illegal imports, 296-299; interest-rate differentials and, 303-306; marihuana, illegal exportation of, 288-291; under- and overinvoicing, 292-296
Commission of the European Communities, 33, 34
"Commodity-flow" technique, 49-50

333

List of Contributors

Bruno S. Frey, University of Zurich

Werner W. Pommerehne, University of Zurich

Raffaele De Grazia, International Labor Organization

Barry Molefsky, U.S. Library of Congress

Berdj Kenadjian, U.S. Internal Revenue Service

Robert Parker, National Income and Wealth Division, Bureau of Economic Analysis, U.S. Department of Commerce

John Gorman, National Income and Wealth Division, Bureau of Economic Analysis, U.S. Department of Commerce

Peter Reuter, The RAND Corporation

Kerrick Macafee, Central Statistical Office, United Kingdom

Andrew Dilnot, The Institute for Fiscal Studies, London

C.N. Morris, The Institute for Fiscal Studies, London

Daniela Del Boca, University of Turin

Francesco Forte, University of Turin

Bruno Contini, University of Turin

Arne Jon Isachsen, University of Oslo

Jan Tore Klovland, University of Oslo

Steinar Strøm, University of Oslo

Ingemar Hansson, University of Lund

Gregory Grossman, University of California

Rolf Mirus, University of Alberta

Roger S. Smith, University of Alberta

Roberto Junguito, Fedesarrollo, Bogota

Carlos Caballero, Fedesarrollo, Bogota

Mark Tucker, Caulfield Institute of Technology, Melbourne

About the Editor

Vito Tanzi, director of the Fiscal Affairs Department of the International Monetary Fund, received the Ph.D. from Harvard University. Before joining the International Monetary Fund he was professor and chairman of the Department of Economics at American University. He has published three books and many articles dealing with various areas of economics, in such journals as the *American Economic Review, The Journal of Political Economy, The Review of Economics and Statistics, The Economic Journal,* and many others. His major interests are public finance, monetary theory, and macroeconomics. He is a leading expert on fiscal problems of developing countries.